How to Write an Essay

Enid A. Goldberg

New York University

Scott, Foresman and Company

Glenview, Illinois

Dallas, Tex.   Oakland, N.J.   Palo Alto, Cal.   Tucker, Ga.   London, England

This book is for

Elizabeth & Daniel

An *Instructor's Manual* for *How to Write an Essay* is available. It may be obtained through a Scott, Foresman representative or by writing to English Editor, College Division, Scott, Foresman and Co., 1900 East Lake Avenue, Glenview, Illinois 60025.

Library of Congress Cataloging in Publication Data

Goldberg, Enid, A
    How to write an essay.

    Includes index.
    1. English language—Rhetoric. 2. Exposition (Rhetoric). 3. College readers. I. Title.
PE1471.G6   808'.042   80-20921
ISBN 0-673-15181-6

1 2 3 4 5 6 7 - VHJ - 86 85 84 83 82 81 80

Acknowledgments

From "Lessons of the Street" by Bruce Jay Friedman. Copyright © 1971 by Bruce Jay Friedman. Originally appeared in *Harper's* Magazine, September 1971. Reprinted by permission of Candida Donadio & Associates, Inc.

Specified excerpt from "Removal" (pp. 1-2) in *One Man's Meat* by E. B. White. Copyright 1938 by E. B. White. Reprinted by permission of Harper & Row, Publishers, Inc.

From "The Libido for the Ugly" from *A Mencken Chrestomothy* by H. L. Mencken. Copyright 1927 by Alfred A. Knopf, Inc., and renewed 1955 by H. L. Mencken. Reprinted by permission of Alfred A. Knopf, Inc.

From "Eyes Left! Eyes Right!" by James Austin, from *Saturday Review* (August 9, 1975). Copyright © 1975 by Saturday Review. Reprinted by permission.

From *The Naked Ape* by Desmond Morris. Copyright © 1967 by Desmond Morris. Reprinted by permission of McGraw-Hill Book Company, the author, and Jonathan Cape Ltd.

Eliot Porter. *The Place No One Knew.* San Francisco: Sierra Club, 1963, 1966, p. 11.

From "On Writing Good" by Ronald Berman, From *The New York Times* (January 29, 1978). © 1978 by The New York Times Company. Reprinted by permission.

From "Pulitzer Prize-Winning Poet Anne Sexton Found Dead," *The Washington Star*, October 6, 1974. Reprinted by permission of The Associated Press.

From *The Death Notebooks* by Anne Sexton, Published by Houghton Mifflin Company. Copyright © 1974 by Anne Sexton. Reprinted by permission.

From "The Jesus Papers" from *The Book of Folly* by Anne Sexton, published by Houghton Mifflin Company. Copyright © 1972 by Anne Sexton. Reprinted by permission.

From *To Bedlam and Part Way Back* by Anne Sexton, published by Houghton Mifflin Company. Copyright © 1960 by Anne Sexton. Reprinted by permission.

From Samuel Clemens, *Life on the Mississippi*, 1883.

From pp. 3-6 from *Black Boy* by Richard Wright. Copyright 1937, 1942, 1944, 1945 by Richard Wright. Reprinted by permission of Harper & Row, Publishers, Inc.

"Pencils Down" from *Fits & Starts: The Premature Memoirs of Andrew Ward* by Andrew Ward. Copyright © 1977 by Andrew Ward. Originally appeared in *The Atlantic*. By permission of Little, Brown and Company in association with the Atlantic Monthly Press.

From "The Elephant's Child" excerpted from the book *Talking Woman* by Shana Alexander. Copyright © 1976 by Shana Alexander. Reprinted by permission of DELACORTE PRESS.

From *The Death of the Moth and Other Essays* by Virginia Woolf, copyright 1942 by Harcourt Brace Jovanovich, Inc.; renewed 1970 by Marjorie T. Parsons, Executrix. Reprinted by permission of Harcourt Brace Jovanovich, Inc., The Author's Literary Estate, and The Hogarth Press Ltd.

"Knoxville: Summer 1915" from *A Death in the Family* by James Agee. Copyright © 1957 by The James Agee Trust. Used by permission of Grosset and Dunlap, Inc.

Reprinted by permission from *The Way to Rainy Mountain*, by N. Scott Momaday, © 1969 by the University of New Mexico Press. First published in *The Reporter*, January 26, 1967.

From "Baking Off" condensed by permission of Alfred A. Knopf, Inc. from *Crazy Salad: Some Things About Women*, by Nora Ephron. Copyright © 1973 by Nora Ephron.

"Slang Origins" from *Without Feathers*, by Woody Allen. Copyright © 1975 by Woody Allen. Reprinted by permission of Random House, Inc. and Rollins and Joffe.

From pp. 25-31 in *You Learn by Living* by Eleanor Roosevelt. Copyright © 1960 by Eleanor Roosevelt. Reprinted by permission of Harper & Row, Publishers, Inc.

"Music of This Sphere" from *Lives of a Cell* by Lewis Thomas. Copyright © 1971, 1972, 1973 by the Massachusetts Medical Society. Copyright © 1974 by Lewis Thomas. Reprinted by permission of Viking Penguin Inc.

"The American Tradition of Winning" by George Plimpton, from *Mainliner* Magazine (1976). Copyright © 1976 by East/West Network, Inc. Reprinted by permission of East/West Network, Inc.

Preface

How to Write an Essay is designed to provide the basis for a complete course in college composition. It is a very practical text, written in response to the needs of instructors who feel that most rhetoric texts are too theoretical for their students. This book is aimed directly at students who need practical and straightforward instruction in writing.

In this text, students will find an accessibly informal style, clear and pertinent examples, helpful exercises and assignments, and an easy-to-use organization. In addition, both student and professional examples of essays have been included to provide both the best illustrations of the modes discussed and samples of good student prose which can be held up as an attainable goal.

How to Write an Essay is divided into four parts: The Writing Process, Methods of Organization, Readings, and Handbook. Part One emphasizes a step-by-step approach to the writing process beginning with the prewriting stage — how to generate ideas and focus on a thesis — and continuing with addressing a specific audience, writing paragraphs, composing the essay as a whole, and improving style by developing an awareness of diction and syntax.

Part Two considers the basic strategies of essay writing: narration, description, example, definition, comparison/contrast, classification, process, and cause and effect. In addition, there is a chapter on persuasion and another describing how to prepare a research paper. Students will be made aware of how various patterns of organizations can be combined, and are given an ample and interesting array of essay topics and exercises through which to practice the principles explained and illustrated in the text.

Each chapter in Part Two is organized to present (1) a clear definition of the essay pattern under consideration, (2) practical advice on developing that type of essay, (3) warnings against common problems that may arise, (4) a sample student essay, and (5) questions for discussion, exercises, and essay topics. Each chapter ends with a box summarizing the principles presented in that chapter.

The patterns discussion in Part Two are further exemplified by the readings in Part Three. Four professional essays are provided for each mode. These essays were carefully chosen for their aptness in illustrating the mode; equally important, their subject matter and readability will appeal to students.

Part Four, the handbook section, offers a quick guide to basic writing skills, with self-tests for each subsection, and a trouble-shooting index to help students identify and solve technical problems of writing.

How to Write an Essay needs no supplementation as the basis for a complete course on expository writing. It contains everything an instructor or a student needs to develop a good grasp of the principles and the practicalities of essay writing.

The Instructor's Manual which accompanies *How to Write an Essay* includes a rationale for the exercises and questions included in the apparatus, and provides a course outline and methodological hints for setting up and teaching a course based on this text. The syllabus shows how this book can be used as a basis for a one- or two-semester course.

In the making of this book, many thanks are due to program directors, faculty members, and students whose insights, intelligence, and hard work provided much of the inspiration. Those at New York University to whom I owe special thanks are Professors Maurice Baudin, Harry Edwards, Joseph Byrnes, Robert Raymo, James Tuttleton, John Maynard, and Paul Magnuson; and my students, especially Peter Lehrer, Andrew Nitze, Florence Eiseman, Steven Ordorica, and Fred Loney. I would like to thank Sandra Kurtinitis and her student Theresa Clark O'Roark for providing a sample student research paper.

Of help in honing and polishing the finished product were reviewers Francis Hubbard, California State University; Tina Blue, University of Kansas; Donald Nemanich, West Virginia Northern Community College; Catherine Moore, North Carolina State University; Richard Harp, University of Nevada – Las Vegas; Judith S. Van Alstyne, Broward Community College; May L. Ryburn, College of Du Page; William Pixton, Oklahoma State University; and Robert Rudolph, University of Toledo.

Once the ideas in this book reached the composing process, another milieu was necessary for their development. For ensuring this development I owe thanks to many at Scott, Foresman — to Harriett Prentiss, Anita Portugal, Ed Stokien — and particularly to Stan Stoga, whose patience, insightful editorial advice, faith, and friendship not only assisted these ideas in becoming a complete book, but also made the entire experience an enjoyable one.

E. A. G.

Contents

Part One

The Writing Process

1

Planning the Essay

Learning to write effectively is not an easy task. As with all skills, writing is a trial-and-error process that requires the application of principles, patience, and practice. There are two basic principles that underlie the successful essay: the writer must have something significant and interesting to say; and he or she must use certain tools, such as style, organization, logic, and mechanics, to help *communicate* these significant and interesting ideas.

Having Something to Say

Essays are about ideas, and everyone has ideas. Writing an essay is a way of conveying your thoughts to an audience. Students frequently ask how they can tell if an idea they have is important enough to write about. The answer is that if an idea interests the writer — if he or she likes it, hates it, is amused by it, is angered by it, or feels strongly about it in any way — then the subject is likely to be significant and interesting to a reader as well. The reader may not always agree with the writer's viewpoint, but if the writer is excited about his or her subject, some of this enthusiasm will be conveyed to the reader.

Before you begin to write your essay, you must have a specific *purpose* as well as a subject in mind. One purpose may be to share an experience with your readers, another may be to instruct or inform them about your subject, and a third may be to persuade them to adopt, or at least to sympathize with, a certain point of view.

If your purpose is to share an experience . . .

One reason for writing an essay is to relate an incident you have experienced, much as you might in a letter or diary. For example, John Steinbeck, in *Travels with Charley,* explains to the reader his motivations for deciding to drive across the country with only a poodle for company:

> " When the virus of restlessness begins to take possession of a wayward man, and the road away from Here seems broad and straight and sweet, the victim must first find in himself good and sufficient reason for going. This to the practical bum is not difficult. He has a built-in garden of reasons to choose from. Next he must plan his trip in time and space, choose a direction and a destination. And last he must implement the journey. How to go, what to take, how long to stay. This part of the process is invariable and immortal. I set it down only so that newcomers to bumdom, like teen-agers in new-hatched sin, will not think they invented it. "

Here, Steinbeck establishes for the reader that his purpose is to share the adventures he has experienced. Making such a statement creates a bond of confidence between the writer and the audience. The reader is invited to share for a while the experiences of another person's life.

If your purpose is to instruct or inform . . .

Another reason for writing an essay is to inform your reader about a topic, or to demonstrate your knowledge in a particular area. You might wish to describe how an event unfolded or how a machine works; you might wish to illustrate by examples how this country overemphasizes sports; or you might wish to define a political philosophy or analyze the causes and effects of a major historical event. You could choose to show the differences between an alligator and a crocodile by means of comparison and contrast, or to explain the properties of a nova to budding astronomers by means of classification and division. In all these cases, your purpose is to enlighten your readers, who may know little or nothing about your subject.

Jacob Bronowski, for example, states at the outset of his essay, "The Reach of Imagination," that his purpose is to inform:

> " For three thousand years, poets have been enchanted and moved and perplexed by the power of their imagination. In a short and summary essay I can hope at most to lift one small corner of that mystery; and yet it is a critical corner. I shall ask, What goes on in the mind when we imagine? You will hear from me that one answer to this question is fairly specific: which is to say, that we can describe the working of the imagination. And when we describe it as I shall do, it becomes plain that imagination is a specifically *human* gift. To imagine is the characteristic act, not of the poet's mind, or the painter's, or the scientist's, but of the mind of man. "

In the same informative fashion, the remainder of Bronowski's essay proceeds with an extended definition of the human imagination, and with examples of the imagination in action.

If your purpose is to persuade . . .

A third reason for writing an essay is to convince your readers to accept your opinion on a particular subject or to persuade them to take specific action. Newspaper editorials, reports to student committees, recommendations for new job procedures — all are intended to persuade readers to accept certain ideas.

Jessica Mitford, in *Kind and Usual Punishment: The Prison Business,* attempts to convince her readers of the injustices of the American penal system and to persuade them that abolition of the prison system is necessary. She writes, in conclusion,

" When people come upon the celebrated statement of Eugene V. Debs — "While there is a soul in prison, I am not free" — they are prone to regard it as an affirmation of extraordinary human compassion. This it is. But it also may be viewed as a profound social insight. And not only because the prison system, inherently unjust and inhumane, is the ultimate expression of injustice and inhumanity in the society at large. Those of us on the outside do not like to think of wardens and guards as our surrogates. Yet they are, and they are intimately locked in a deadly embrace with their human captives behind the prison walls. By extension so are we.

A terrible double meaning is thus imparted to the original question of human ethics: Am I my brother's keeper? "

The purpose you have in writing your essay should be made apparent. It can be contained in a thesis statement, a clear and concise declaration of your subject matter, or it may be implied in your essay. The implied thesis of *Travels with Charley* is that human nature is the same everywhere; of *Passages,* that there are certain predictable crises in adult life; and of *Kind and Usual Punishment,* that the prison system is cruel and should be abolished. (The process of narrowing your subject and establishing a thesis is discussed at greater length in Chapter 2.)

Assessing your audience

In determining the subject and purpose of your essay, it is helpful to have in mind a picture of your audience — the readers to whom you are conveying your ideas. In general, the essays you prepare in your composition course will be read by your instructor and, occasionally, by the other members of your class. At times, however, you might wish to aim your writing at a more specific audience.

When writing for your composition class or your instructor, assume that you are writing for a general audience. This audience is reasonably intelligent and well informed, but it is not necessarily united around a highly developed interest in a given subject. The entire audience would not necessarily have a strong background in engineering, for instance, although one or two of its members might be studying in this field. Likewise, this audience probably would not share a love of politics, though several members might aspire to law school or be active in campus government. In short, although the group as a whole might exhibit a general interest in most subjects, its members are diverse in their levels of knowledge and presumably motivated to learn more about unfamiliar subjects. This group will be your audience for most of the essays you will be expected to write this term. Unless you are instructed to gear your essays to another more specifically defined group, you should direct your essays to this general readership.

On occasion, as previously suggested, your instructor might suggest that you write for a group with more-than-average interest in and knowledge about a certain area. You might, for example, be asked to direct an essay on bridge-building to a group of civil engineering students. For these readers, you could use technical terminology, and you could take for granted their basic knowledge of the field without being afraid of confusing them. Or you might be asked to write an essay defending a candidate to an opposing political group. This kind of audience would require that you be very careful about how you present your material so as not to antagonize, and lose, your readers.

When you are writing to a specific audience, you should try to determine the background of its members. Are these people knowledgeable about your subject or not? Are they old or young? Hostile or friendly? Concerned or indifferent? You should have a reasonably clear audience profile so that you know what kind of information to present and how to convey it. For example, if you are explaining to a prekindergarten class how a snake sheds its skin, you might have to determine whether or not the class knows what a snake is. Your older and more knowledgeable readers, however, expect you to treat them as intelligent and well-informed people. If you are writing a report about a new marketing plan for the sales representatives of a company that manufactures silicone, you do not have to tell them what silicone is or how it is made.

If your readers are hostile to your position on an issue, you should employ strategies different from those you use when you and your readers are in basic agreement. For example, if you are writing a piece in support of a candidate for student office who opposes the honor system, and your appeal is to the students who framed the honor code in the first place, you will have to explain to your readers, without misrepresenting your candidate, why they should still vote for him. In planning your essay, consider first the problems and counterattacks you expect to meet. In other words, try to determine what your audience's objections will be and refute them immediately. Ignoring or belittling the views of your readers will never persuade them to support your ideas. Indicate respect for their views while arguing logically for your own.

In summary, "having something to say" means not only choosing a topic, but having a purpose, focusing on a point, and identifying your audience. Once you are sure you have something to say, you need to know how to say it effectively.

Knowing How to Say It

In order to convey your ideas to the reader, you must be able to plan and write your essays with structural accuracy, stylistic smoothness, and logic. Towards this end, an important decision to be made is the selection of a rhetorical mode. Rhetorical modes are patterns of organization, different ways of arranging ideas into a coherent essay. There are nine basic modes: narration, description, example, definition, comparison and contrast, classification and division, cause and effect, process analysis, and persuasive argument.

In the process of learning to write essays according to these patterns, you will discover different and effective ways of expressing your ideas. In the "real" world, your subject and your audience will often determine or suggest which pattern to use, and you should know the fundamentals of each mode and how these basics can be applied to the purpose you wish to fulfill. Although this text shows you how to practice each mode individually, keep in mind that most essays are written in a combination of patterns. Description, definition, and example, for instance, may often be used in essays organized primarily as argument or process analysis. Moreover, some rhetorical modes can be merged with others: for instance, cause and effect may operate through a narrative.

A mastery of all these essay forms will provide you with a working set of tools that you will be able to use in other courses and throughout your professional life. And you can learn to use these tools in much the same way that other skills are developed. In carpentry you must first know how to use a saw, hammer, chisel and plane before you can build a solid piece of furniture. In writing you must first know how to use each of the writing tools separately before you can use them together to create a solid piece of composition.

Assignment: *For Comprehension and Practice*

Questions for Discussion

1. What are the purposes you may have for writing an essay that relates an experience? For one that informs or instructs? For one intended to persuade?
2. Why is it important to assess your audience carefully when writing an essay on a political issue?
3. Why is it important to determine the age of your audience if you are writing an essay that describes how an automobile engine works?
4. Why is it necessary to know who your audience is before you can focus your essay?

Exercises

1. Choose one of the following topics:
   a. my best friend

b. a memorable political contest

c. our football (soccer, tennis, baseball) team

d. the cheerleaders at our school

e. a science-fiction film I have seen

f. my favorite food

Now, write a topic sentence that presents the subject in each of the following ways: in an informal and personal manner; in an informative and instructive manner; in a persuasive manner.

2. Consider each of the following topics and write a paragraph identifying the kind of audience to whom you would expect it to appeal:

a. how to construct a model airplane

b. how a pogo stick works

c. the distinction between conservatism and liberalism

d. an anecdote about Bert and Ernie of "Sesame Street"

e. why "Sesame Street" appeals to preschoolers

f. a comparison of two Victorian novels

g. why a snake sheds its skin

h. how a suspension bridge is constructed

i. what marsupials are

(Be sure to consider the age, background knowledge, and interests of your audience.)

3. For each of the following audiences, think of an appealing or useful essay topic. Then write a thesis statement for an essay on this topic, taking the particular audience into account:

a. a preschool playgroup

b. your school orchestra

c. a conservation club

d. a convention of book salesmen

e. auto mechanics

f. the American Medical Association

g. gourmet cooks

h. cross-country skiers

i. varsity basketball players

j. parakeet owners

Essay Topics

1. Write an essay explaining what a political party is, directing your essay to a college political-science class.

2. Write on the same topic, but direct it to a fifth-grade class learning about politics.

3. Write an essay supporting the governmental control of water pollution. Direct the essay to a group of officials from a textile company known to be dumping polluted water into a major river, thereby killing most of the fish and making the recreational use of the river impossible.

4. Write a letter to a friend describing a trip you took to a tourist attraction that you had heard a lot about.

5. Describe the same trip in a letter to your seven-year-old cousin.

6. Write an essay to the members of a driver's education course on how to change a flat tire.

Your essay should be approximately 500 words long. Start with a clear purpose and be sure to keep in mind your prospective audience.

2

Getting Started

Many beginning essay writers have difficulty getting started. "I have a lot of ideas, but I don't know how to begin to express them" is a common complaint of expository writing students. The task of channeling the ideas, methods, techniques, and mechanics of essay writing into a 500-word, finished product seems at best elusive, and at worst impossible. Where do you start? With your subject.

Choosing Your Subject

Choosing a subject is one of the most crucial decisions you will make in the essay-writing process. Composition topics range widely. Students have written successful and interesting essays about everything from hang-gliding to getting sick at an autopsy arranged by the Pre-Med Society.

If your subject excites you, then it should be possible to make it exciting to others. The student who wrote about hang-gliding began with a description of the hang-glider in flight:

" There I was — finally — up above the trees, floating as if I were on water, but really airborne. I had dreamed since early childhood of having my own wings and flying, and that ridiculous wish had unbelievably come true at last.

The air felt cool and pleasant on my perspiring face. It was quiet in the sky. I had not thought about what it would sound like in flight, but the quietness was noticeable and startled me. The people and things below me looked very small — make-believe, almost — and the colors beneath were very beautiful. "

This student's exhilaration is contagious and probably very appealing to anyone who has ever wondered how it feels to be a bird.

Instead of selecting a subject you personally find uninteresting — one that doesn't concern you one way or the other — choose a topic you genuinely care about, either positively or negatively. If you dislike horticulture, for example, you will be able to write a more imaginative, impassioned, and thus interesting essay on "Why I Hate Planting Flowers" than you will on the subject of "How to Plant Nasturtiums."

The student who attended the autopsy had a negative reaction to her subject — it made her physically ill — yet her essay has a high interest level and demands close attention from the reader. She describes the dissection of the corpse, scalpel cut by scalpel cut, and also considers her own reactions to the scene. She writes:

" The medic led us into the operating room. It was cold and not very brightly lit, although there was a glare in the center of the room. The glare shone down on a table where a body — a human corpse — was covered by a grayish sheet. I started to shiver. The door to the room closed. My eyes were glued to the sheet. The pathologist began to talk. I couldn't understand what he was saying because I couldn't concentrate on anything but that sheet. He spoke in a high, rapid wordlessness. Then my eyes bulged as he lifted the sheet and a scalpel simultaneously. He placed the scalpel on the skin of the corpse's arm and moved it. I expected the blood to gush, but it didn't. He moved it a second time and this time I saw red, but it was not the corpse; it was behind my eyes. I stumbled towards the closed door, half expecting it to be locked. It opened. I went out and threw up. "

You might begin looking for topics among the unique experiences you have had. Hang-gliding and attending an autopsy certainly fit into this category. When faced with a wide-open assignment, or when asked to choose a topic of your own, do some brainstorming to see what you've done that nobody else has.

If an interesting or unique topic does not immediately present itself, hunt for a fresh approach to a mundane one. If you have to talk about a familiar subject, do so with an unusual approach. If, for example, you are assigned an essay about what you did last summer, and all you really did was take a typing course, talk about the day your instructor's tie got ripped in the typewriter carriage-return mechanism, not about the order in which you learned the keys.

If you are asked to prepare a composition on what you did on an ordinary school day, do not give a predictable minute-by-minute breakdown of a "typical" day, beginning with the ringing of your alarm clock at 6:45, and including such items as brushing your teeth, setting your books in order, doing your homework, and watching television. The other members of your class will be less than fascinated, since most of their daily experience probably revolves around a similar routine, varying only, perhaps, in the selection of TV fare or the flavor of their toothpaste.

A more imaginative approach to this topic would focus on out-of-the-ordinary incidents that make interesting reading. You might describe your daily struggle with your cat for possession of the clothes you had carefully laid out the night before; your rush to pick the inevitable cat hairs off your sweater as you prepare your soccer-team training breakfast of three eggs, bacon, toast, cereal, two juices, milk, a sweet bun, wheat germ, honey, and a vitamin pill; your experiences while working in a fast-food franchise after class; your feelings about being a member of your school's first soccer team; your description of doing homework upside-down in a yoga position.

You can make even a mundane subject interesting by looking at it from your own unique and individualized angle. Approach your subject, even if it seems a hopelessly boring one, with freshness and imagination, and with a series of personal anecdotes and examples that enliven your paper. You can always find a unique view of a subject. Even the description of a routine day can be made interesting by developing it into an essay on the oppressiveness of routine. Even a tiresome subject like "My Pet Cat" can be energized by looking at it from the point of view of your neighbor's dog.

Narrowing Your Subject

Once you have chosen — or have been assigned — a general topic, you should narrow it to a specific subject that can be handled in a short paper. Narrowing your subject means seeing it in a specific, rather than general, light. "Cheerleaders" is a general topic that can be made more specific and personal if you approach it from the point of view of "My Best Girlfriend, the Cheerleader," or "How I Tried to Become the Head Cheerleader and Failed," or "Cheerleaders Vs. Football Players." "Camping" is a general topic that can be made more specific and personal if you talk about "My First — and Last — Ten Days as a Camper," "The Night We Nearly Drowned When We Tried Camping on a Canoe," or "Sitting Around the Campfire: A Place to Fall in Love."

The process of narrowing and focusing your ideas is an important one because too broad a subject often results in a superficial essay: in a short paper, you cannot spend enough time or space on any one aspect of a large subject to say anything of specific interest about it. For example, if your general subject for a 3–5 page paper is "Holiday Seasons," and you state a few trite and familiar generalities about Halloween in the first paragraph, then go on to treat Thanksgiving in the second, and July 4th in the third, your essay would not be focused specifically enough to maintain audience interest. Your readers know that if you have only one or two sentences to devote to each holiday, you will give each occasion only superficial attention. They have heard it all before, so chances are they will put the essay down long before you get to Labor Day.

On the other hand, if you choose to narrow "Holiday Seasons" down to "Thanksgiving," and focus even more specifically on "The Thanksgiving My Brother Tom Came Back from Service in Vietnam," you will certainly generate reader interest; moreover, you will undoubtedly write with more feeling about a reunion with your brother than you would if you tried to describe those Indians and Pilgrims and what they ate 300 years ago.

Make certain, however, that in narrowing your subject you do not focus it so specifically that you have nothing of interest to say about it. Your Thanksgiving reunion dinner pruned down to a mere discussion of the turkey won't encourage your reader to come back for seconds.

Developing Your Thesis

The process of narrowing your subject should lead you to the thesis of your paper. In starting with a general subject and making it more specific, you are really asking yourself, "What point am I going to make about this topic? What will my purpose be in discussing the subject?"

The student who wrote about getting sick at the autopsy had been assigned an essay on her participation in extracurricular activities. The Pre-Med Society had constituted her main interest outside of class, and when asked to write about it, she began thinking of the most interesting aspect of the club in order to narrow the subject. The trip to the morgue stood out above all the society's other activities. Once she began thinking of the autopsy, however, feelings of disgust surfaced and she realized that her main reason for focusing on this event was to explain her decision to switch her major field from pre-med to economics. She wrote:

> By the time I returned to campus, the nausea had worn off, but the disgust hadn't. It never did. The first thing I did the next morning was make an appointment to see my pre-med advisor. I told him I wanted to switch my major — to economics.

Not everyone will change majors as a result of narrowing down a subject, but most people should be able to come up with a good reason for writing when thinking specifically about a topic.

Once you have established your purpose for writing, you should be able to sum it up in a sentence or two called a *thesis statement*. Many essays actually contain this thesis statement. Often, in fact, it is included in the first paragraph so that the reader is informed immediately of the writer's purpose. Consider again the autopsy essay. After deciding that she wanted to discuss her reactions to the autopsy, and the consequences thereof, the student constructed a very clear thesis statement which appeared in the beginning of her essay: "Although I am registered as a pre-med, I learned through an excursion I took with the Pre-Med Society to the city morgue that I am neither suited for nor desire to have a career as a physician."

Depending on the desired effect, the thesis statement may also be placed in the middle or at the end of the essay. One student, writing about his decision to return to college after he had dropped out for a year, first described a job he had had as a toll-collector on the New Jersey Turnpike. Then, in the middle of the essay he inserted his thesis concerning the value of a college education. He concluded with a description of the kind of job he intended to get after he earned his degree.

Another student first described all the pros and all the cons of joining a sorority before finally arriving at her thesis — a statement in support of the independent life — at the end of her essay.

Some essays do not contain an actual thesis statement at all, but rely on implication to inform the reader of the author's purpose. The student who wrote about hang-gliding had a clear point to make in his essay: hang-gliding is a unique and exhilarating experience. He could have formulated a thesis statement to say just that, but he chose instead to *imply* this idea to his readers. He was able to convey the message through his description of the sport.

Your thesis statement sums up what you are trying to say to your reader. It should therefore say no more than you can demonstrate or prove in the paper itself. It would have been meaningless, for example, for the ex-pre-med to say in her thesis statement that her essay would evaluate *every* activity offered by the Pre-Med Society. That would have been too broad a topic, one that could not have been adequately developed in 500 words. Similarly, the hang-glider would have been up in the air had he begun his composition by saying, "This essay will prove that hang-gliding is the culmination of man's desire to fly." A 500-word essay is too short to encapsulate a history of aviation.

Selecting Your Organizational Pattern

Once you have narrowed your subject to a manageable topic and have arrived at a suitable thesis, you should select an organizational pattern that will best convey your ideas.

There are several kinds of patterns, and your selection of one will depend on your reason for writing. If your purpose is to comment on an event that occurred in your past or to relate an incident you know about, you should elect to write a *narrative*. One young woman chose the narrative form to come to grips with the trauma of her parents' divorce. She related the sequence of events leading up to the separation, and then considered the divorce itself, reflecting finally on how the event affected her.

If your purpose is to write about how someone or something looks and acts, how an event has taken place, or how a place appears, you should use *description*. One young man wished to convey the inspiring impression he had received from a visiting clergyman and used character description to do so. Another student used the descriptive mode to recreate a place she had dreamed about and wished very much to find.

If your purpose is to make a point and emphasize it by means of various illustrations, you should use the mode of *exemplification*. Perhaps you wish to illustrate the contention that college students are not interested in pursuing a certain major out of a liking for the subject, but rather out of the desire to get a well-paying job. In this case, you might use as examples certain of your more ambitious classmates.

If your purpose is to explain to your readers a certain word, theory, principle, idea, subject, or object, you would write a *definition* essay. One student who chose to write about nuclear energy centered her paper on a definition of the term *fusion*.

If your purpose is to demonstrate why and how ideas, objects, and systems differ, you should use the technique of *comparison and contrast*. An effective essay in this mode was written by a student who compared the writing in *Newsweek* to that in *Saturday Review* to illustrate that journalistic styles not only vary, but project different points of view as well.

If your purpose is to organize a group of ideas or objects into a system for the purpose of explaining your subject more fully, your choice of organization would be *classification and division*. An imaginative college writer turned an essay on food into a delightful cataloguing of "The Most Delicious Bad Foods I Have Known" by means of this technique.

If your purpose is to show how a machine, a principle, a theory, or an idea works, you should use *process analysis*. One student whose essay focused on "The Best Way to Avoid Meeting the Physical Education Requirement" developed his thesis with an analysis of the process involved in sidestepping a curriculum.

If your purpose is to explain why an event occurred, a theory evolved, or a product or object emerged, you should use the *cause and effect* pattern of organization. One student wrote an essay showing that her decision to become a physician resulted from her father's untimely death by heart attack.

Finally, if your purpose is to convince the reader to share your point of view, you would write a *persuasive argument*. An example of this pattern of organization is an essay recently submitted by a student who reasoned that all college students should hold jobs, regardless of need, to give them the appreciation that comes of earning one's own education.

All of these patterns of organization are discussed individually and more fully in Part II of this book, and models of each type of essay are presented in Part III.

Your thesis statement should suggest an organizational pattern. The student who wrote about hang-gliding wished to suggest implicitly that it was an exhilarating activity. The most logical way for him to *show* the reader his exhilaration was to describe the sensations of a hang-glider in flight. The woman who attended the autopsy wished to communicate the reasons behind her decision to drop out of the pre-med program. A natural choice of organizational pattern for her was cause and effect — a choice, in this case, explicitly communicated in her thesis statement.

There may be times when your subject matter and thesis statement suggest a combination of organizational patterns. It may be your purpose, for instance, to define what a representative student government is, and then to illustrate how it works by providing examples of student government in action at several colleges. You would thus be combining definition and exemplification. Or you might wish to compare and contrast two activities, such as downhill and cross-country skiing, and then describe each for your reader. You would then be combining comparison-contrast and description.

In every case, your thesis statement, whether implied or declared, should suggest the means you have chosen for organizing your essay.

Preparing Your Essay

After you have chosen an organizational pattern suitable to your thesis, you must decide how to arrange your thoughts on the subject. A helpful way of going about this is first to list *all* the ideas you have relating to your subject. Even if this initial list seems somewhat random, you will at least have committed to paper all the relevant thoughts floating through your mind. You can then refer to this list frequently as you order your thoughts, thus making sure that you are not leaving out an important point. For example, if your thesis deals with the poor quality of the dormitory food at your school, you might jot down the following random thoughts:

- The food in Spencer Dorm is often undercooked or overcooked.
- The food is frequently stale and cold and has been sitting around for a while.
- The food is often primarily starch. The meals aren't balanced.
- The quality of dorm life is directly related to the quality of dorm food.
- I can't stand the dorm food.
- It is unfit even for laboratory animals.
- The menu is not varied very much from week to week. Only the names of the dishes change ("Ambrosia Delight" instead of "Paradise Supreme"), not the dishes themselves.
- The university administration should be made aware of the situation.
- The students should organize and complain.
- We're paying high board bills for inferior meals.
- Once we had potatoes, corn, and spaghetti at the same meal.
- Once there was a crust on the fruit salad.
- Once the chicken bled when it was cut into.
- When I visited a friend at another college last week, I ate in the dorm and actually enjoyed the meal.
- Even my sister cooks better than the dorm cook.
- I hope the food situation can be improved.

Next, you might state your thesis — namely, that your fellow students (who comprise your audience) should protest to the university administration about the quality of the food. Your logical choice for an organizational pattern would be persuasion, since you are trying to convince your audience to accept your point of view and to take action.

You have now reached the point at which a preliminary outline can be written. One general format looks like this:

I.   Introduction (State the purpose of your essay.)
   A. Identify your broad subject.
   B. Narrow it down.
   C. Explain why you wish to discuss it.
   D. Include a statement of your thesis — the actual point you are going to make in your composition.
II. Background (State how you arrived at the point you are going to make and include a definition of your terms, if necessary.)
III. Supporting examples (List concrete illustrations, from your own experience, if possible, that provide reasons or support for your point of view.)
   A. Illustration 1 (general and specific)
   B. Illustration 2 (general and specific)
   C. Illustration 3 (general and specific)

etc.

IV. Conclusion (Write a final statement reiterating your original contention, or offer a specific recommendation relating to your thesis statement.)

Now you can fill in the specifics of the subject, including the ideas from your list as they fit into your format. (If any ideas are irrelevant to your composition plan, do not be afraid to discard them.)

    Let us assume that you have narrowed the subject of "Dormitory Life" down to "The Food in Spencer Dorm." You might then arrange your ideas in a more specific outline, as follows:

I.   Introduction (Statement of Purpose)
   A. Broad subject: "Dormitory Life"
   B. Narrowed-down subject: "The Food in Spencer Dorm," or even more specifically, "the quality of dorm life is directly related to the dorm food, which is of poor quality."
   C. Reason for discussing subject: "I would like to see the situation improved."
   D. Thesis statement: "Students living in Spencer Dorm should make the university administration aware of the poor quality of the dorm food in order to try to improve it."
II. Background
   A. How you arrived at your point: "Visiting other schools convinced me that dorm food could be better than it is at Spencer."
   B. Defining or explaining your terms: In this case, the terms should be self-evident, though you might want to describe a meal in detail to show the reader what you mean by "poor food." This could be done at the very beginning of the essay in order to attract the attention of the reader.
III. Supporting examples (Proof of Your Point of View)
   A. General: "The dorm food is often undercooked or overcooked."
      Specific: "Once the chicken was so raw it bled when it was cut into."

B. General: "It is frequently stale." Specific: "Once there was a crust on the fruit salad."

C. General: "The menu is rarely varied from week to week; only the names of the dishes change." Specific: "Monday's 'Ambrosia Delight' became Tuesday's 'Paradise Supreme.'"

D. General: "The meals aren't balanced; they are primarily starch."
Specific: "Once we had potatoes, corn and spaghetti in the same meal."

IV. Conclusion or Final Statement: "Because we're paying high board bills and receiving inferior meals, as illustrated by the above examples, I would like to encourage those members of the student body living in Spencer Dorm to make the situation known to the university administration in the hope of gaining improvement in the fare. Petitions, letters, and meetings might be tools to consider using for this purpose."

In this way you will have selected the most cogent of your ideas to include in your essay, as well as the most logical order in which to arrange them. All that remains is to expand each point in your outline into a complete paragraph.

You may find that some of your original points are too strongly expressed and need toning down. For example, statements such as "I can't stand the dorm food" or "It is unfit even for laboratory animals" are clearly too informal to be included in a college paper and should be moderated to read, "The dorm food is not of the highest quality." Other ideas, as strongly as you feel about them, may not really be relevant to your composition and should be dropped. For example, the fact that your sister cooks better than the dorm cook does nothing to strengthen your argument and should be eliminated from your outline.

When you have finished planning your ideas, you have established a skeleton for your essay. It is now time to flesh out the bones, adding descriptive details and narrative illustrations to make your composition come to life.

The kind of planning you have been asked to do before you write an essay is all part of thinking clearly. You should know your purpose in writing; you should know what your thesis is as well as your broad topic; you should know who your audience is, as well as what type of organizational pattern it would be logical to use. You must plan your essay, and most important of all, you must be able to focus your essay. If you keep all these "shoulds" and "musts" in mind, you will come up with a meaningful, coherent paper with a minimum of difficulty.

Assignment: *For Comprehension and Practice*

Questions for Discussion

1. Why is it more difficult to write about a general topic than a specific one?
2. Would there be any value in presenting ideas in order of their importance to you, and not as they fit into a logical pattern?
3. Does a thesis always differ from a subject? Explain.

Exercises

1. Narrow these broad subjects to specific topics:

    a. summertime   **c.** astronomy

    b. sports   **d.** books

2. Write a hypothetical thesis sentence for each of these topics:

    a. Fighting Pollution on the Great Lakes

    b. Dormitory Life at My College

    c. Getting Involved in the School Newspaper

    d. Dropping My First Economics Course

    e. Professors Are Human

3. List four specific topics that would lend themselves to good thesis statements, and four that would not. Explain your reasons.

4. Which organizational pattern would you use for each of the four "good" topics listed above?

5. Place the following ideas in an organizational pattern (adding any other relevant ideas and eliminating any irrelevant ones):

    a. Psychology should be taught to every college student during the first term of freshman year.

    b. The principles of psychology can be used in every course.

    c. Psychology courses teach an approach to learning any subject.

    d. Psychology teaches you how to deal with your fellow students.

    e. I got a "B" in Psychology and only a "C" in Economics.

    f. Psychology teaches you how to deal with your professors.

    g. Psychology teaches you how to cope with yourself.

    h. Psychology is fascinating: it teaches how man's mind works.

    i. The courses freshmen take now are too specific and career-oriented.

    j. Psychology textbooks are fun to read.

    k. Psychology is a 3-credit course; all other introductory courses are 4-credit courses.

    l. Psychology is a requirement for many other majors.

    m. The psychology professors are all well known in their fields.

Essay Topics

Choose a general topic from those listed below:

    a. Vacations

    b. Cities

    c. Family Life

    d. Careers

Narrow down your chosen topic, develop a specific thesis, determine who your audience will be, outline and title your ideas, and produce an essay. The length of your essay should be approximately 500 words. As you write, be sure that your purpose is clear in your own mind at all times.

3

Composing Paragraphs

The basic unit of your composition is the paragraph. Each paragraph should convey one idea which develops the thesis of your essay. Your first paragraph could introduce your topic; your second, provide background; your third, cite an example; and so on. Each paragraph should be limited to one main idea *only*, and each should be part of the orderly progression of the paper.

Planning Your Paragraphs

Once you have established your thesis statement and an organizational plan similar to the example in Chapter 2, you should construct a series of paragraphs to flesh out the skeleton of your essay. Each point in your organizational plan should lend itself to treatment in a paragraph. Let us see how this process works.

Suppose your general subject is "City Life." Now suppose that you have narrowed the subject to "Coping with Social Life in the City" (which could also serve as your title), and that you have arrived at a thesis, "Dating is nearly impossible for a college student returning to the city on vacation." The organizational pattern you have selected is exemplification, a mode you have decided is best suited to your subject matter and purpose for writing. You have arranged your thoughts in this way:

I. Introduction: Thesis stated: The difficulty of dating in the city
II. Examples cited to illustrate this predicament
   A. Getting around the city is difficult.
   B. Going out at night is expensive.

    C. Going out during the day to less expensive places is a hassle.
III.   Conclusion: Resolution or consequences of this predicament

      Each point in your outline should now be developed into a paragraph of its own, with the statement you make for each point on your outline serving as the topic sentence of each paragraph. The topic sentence should sum up what the paragraph is about. It may be placed at the beginning, middle, or end of the paragraph, and it should be elaborated upon or described in the rest of the paragraph.

      Following the outline above, you might construct paragraph 1 as follows. Your topic sentence would be "Dating is nearly impossible for a college student returning to the city during vacations." This is a statement of the main idea of paragraph 1, as it will be for the essay as a whole. (In this case, the thesis statement for the entire essay is the same as the topic sentence for the paragraph.) In order to catch the reader's eye, you might want to use a short anecdote or another attention-getting device to vividly introduce your thesis:

    " Eight o'clock. I'm supposed to be at Ellen's house picking her up to go to an 8:30 movie, but I'm in a cab and the traffic isn't moving. If I get out to find a phone, I'll never get another cab and we'll be late for the film. If I stay in the cab, she won't know why I'm late, and if the traffic doesn't move soon, the cab ride will be so expensive I won't have enough money left for the movie. It's frustrating but true: dating is nearly impossible for a college student returning to the city during vacations. **"**

      The next paragraph, II.A. on your outline, presents the first example you will use to illustrate your thesis. This paragraph will deal with one reason why dating in the city is nearly impossible for a college student. The topic sentence for that paragraph is your outline statement "Getting around the city is difficult." You would then elaborate on this statement by describing specific examples which show that getting around the city is difficult. You might say:

    " The first reason for this frustration is an obvious one. Just getting around the city is difficult. To get from your home to your date's home to the restaurant or theater and back involves a selection of one of several equally inefficient means of travel. If you aren't lucky enough to live within walking distance of both your date and your destination, you can take a bus, but this is time-consuming, crowded, indirect, and unreliable. It never stops exactly where you want it to and it frequently stops running after 10 p.m. so you might have to wait 30 minutes for a bus after a film. Or, you can go by subway and face delay, dirt, noise and the possibility of being mugged. Another alternative is to borrow the folks' car, but this involves parking it somewhere — often several times in the course of an evening. Garages are extremely expensive, legal parking spaces are difficult to come by, and illegal parking spaces are risky because you don't want to end a perfect evening by finding that your parents' car has been towed away. Cabs are the most efficient means of hopping around the city, but, as I mentioned before, the chances are you won't have enough money left to do anything else. Your last alternative would seem to be to date the girl next door and go out locally, but even dating locally has its drawbacks. . . . **,,**

Each sentence serves to illustrate or elaborate on the idea expressed in the topic sentence.

After completing the previous paragraph, you would then take the next point on your outline, "Going out at night is expensive," and expand it into a paragraph as your second illustration. You could say:

" Another problem is that going out at night either close to your home or far away is expensive. Most good restaurants are beyond the means of the average college student. A dinner for two at a "moderately priced" French restaurant recently cost me more than I spent for books last semester. Theater tickets are now prohibitive, and even films cost as much as $5.00 a person in some cinemas. **,,**

Your next point, "Going out during the day to less expensive places is a hassle," could be expanded into a paragraph in this way:

" There are difficulties even if you do not limit your social life to the evenings. Dating during the day — going to places in the city that are less expensive or free — can be a hassle. A museum might seem a good place to take a date, and a snack in the park might appear to be a reasonable follow-up. My recent trip to the museum, however, resulted in a four-hour wait to see the Chinese exhibit. There were so many other viewers going through at the same time that all I actually got to see was the back of the hat on the woman in front of me. Moreover, that snack in the park wound up being a cold Dutch pretzel and a warm soda. **,,**

Again, you would have used a point in your outline as the topic sentence and basis for your paragraph. As indicated in your outline, you could conclude the essay with a discussion of the consequences of the problem identified in your thesis statement. You also might add a suggestion or two concerning how to remedy the situation. You might write:

" The problems a college student on vacation faces in trying to maintain a social life in the city discourage many students from trying to date, or from coming home at all. The solution? Vacationing college students might get together for parties, or encourage religious institutions to provide opportunities for young adults to socialize, or organize groups of people to attend sporting events or activities. Vacations should be times to be social, not lonely. **,,**

Limiting Each Paragraph

It is important that you limit the material in each of your paragraphs so that your thoughts progress in a unified and coherent way. One rule of thumb is that, by definition, a paragraph must develop one and only one idea. This idea is contained in the topic sentence of the paragraph (often a general statement). It is supported by means of examples or explanatory sentences (expressed in specific terms) and can be repeated in the conclusion (again, a general statement). An outline of the structure of a typical paragraph might look like this:

I.   Topic sentence: the main idea of your paragraph (in general terms)
II. Body
     A.   Definition or explanation of your topic (if necessary)
     B.   Specific support for your paragraph topic (examples or explanation)
III. Concluding statement: the final word on your paragraph topic (again, in general terms)

To illustrate how this structure might underlie a real paragraph, let us analyze paragraph 2 in the sample essay:

I.   Topic sentence: "Getting around the city is difficult." (This is a general statement.)
II. Body
     A.   The topic "Getting around the city. . . ." is defined in the body of the paragraph as "getting from your home to your date's home to the restaurant or theater and back."
     B.   The topic is illustrated by several specific examples. The paragraph cites the difficulty of traveling by bus, by subway, by car, and by taxi.
III. The final word about the topic is "Your last alternative would seem to be to date the girl next door and go out locally. . . ."

Even if you were to read only this paragraph, you would have a general idea of what the essay is about and a very clear idea of one of the major points the essay is making.

If you include too much in a paragraph, the reader will be confused and the purpose of your paragraph — to present one idea — will be muddled. For instance, suppose paragraph 2 had been written this way:

❝ Getting around the city is difficult. The buses, subways, cars and taxis all present problems for the college student on a limited budget trying to establish a social life. I earned a bit of money working in the library this semester, but why blow it all on transportation? Library jobs are hard to come by. I was lucky to get this one. If it hadn't been for the mark I received in history I never would have gotten the job. My history teacher, Professor

Cohen, liked me and wrote me a good recommendation. However, I did decide to switch majors and Professor Cohen's course turned out to be my last history course. **,,**

This paragraph includes too much information. It is rambling and disjointed. Your reader would neither understand the point you were trying to make nor follow your reasoning.

Attaining a Sense of Progression

Your ideas should be arranged so that they logically progress from one paragraph to the next. You can achieve this progression through the use of effective transitions. A paragraph should have one or more transitional sentences, at the beginning or at the end, which connect it to what has gone before, to what will follow, and to the main idea of the essay itself.

If we expand the typical paragraph outline to include transitions, it would look like this:

I.   Transitional sentence(s) linking this paragraph to the preceding one or to the main idea of the essay.
II.   Topic sentence: the main idea of your paragraph.
III. Body
    A.   Definition of topic (if necessary)
    B.   Support for your paragraph topic (examples or explanation)
IV.   Concluding statement: the final word on your paragraph topic.
V.   Transitional sentence connecting the paragraph to what will follow.

In the sample essay we have been composing, the first transitional sentence for paragraph 2 is "The first reason for this frustration is obvious." This sentence refers to the main idea of the essay, the frustration of dating in the city, and it tells the reader that you are going to discuss one of the reasons for the problem.

The concluding transitional sentence (or, in this case, part of a sentence) is ". . . but even dating locally has its drawbacks." Here you indicate where your essay is going next — what your next paragraph will discuss. If you are using effective transitional sentences, your reader knows where you've been and where you're headed, and he or she can follow your train of thought from paragraph to paragraph.

In organizing your paragraphs, be sure that you stick to the topic you are considering. Avoid adding extraneous details or introducing new subjects. When discussing city dating, for instance, don't write about your library job or your aversion to Chinese restaurants, and don't introduce your cousin's problems with country dating. Remember at all times the importance of maintaining focus in your essay.

In conclusion, a paragraph is a miniature essay in itself. It has a structure — a beginning, a middle, and an end. It has a topic sentence, supporting statements, and a conclusion. Most important, it is part of the progression of ideas which form your essay.

In the next chapter, we will look at the larger unit — the whole composition — and we will consider how to proceed from paragraph to essay.

Assignment: *For Comprehension and Practice*

Questions for Discussion

1. Have you related each paragraph to your main idea?
2. What is the function of a topic sentence? What characterizes a good topic sentence? What characterizes a bad one?
3. How can you encompass a transition in the concluding statement of a paragraph?
4. What is the function of the body of your paragraph?

Exercises

1. Provide supportive and concluding sentences for each of the following topic sentences:
    a. The director of admissions has one of the toughest jobs at the university.
    b. Freshman English is both instructive and fun.
    c. Choosing a dog requires a great deal of thought.
    d. Participation in college politics prepares students for an understanding of state and national politics.
2. Organize the following statements into a logical paragraph structure:
    a. Therefore, it is not only fair but essential that students have a voice in this organization.
    b. At present there is no student representation in this body.
    c. It is important that there be student representation in the University Senate.
    d. Faculty members and administrators try to take the students' viewpoint into consideration, but they are not always aware of student opinion.
    e. Only the students themselves can speak with authority about issues that affect them.
3. Write a topic sentence for each of the following subjects:
    a. the student government at my university or college
    b. my college newspaper   **d.** my major subject area
    c. the freshman curriculum   **e.** the college president

Paragraph Topics

Write a practice paragraph on each of the following subjects:

a. a scene in a book
b. a scene in a film
c. a person in your family
d. a pet
e. a traffic jam
f. a fashion trend
g. a specific course

Make sure that each paragraph has a topic sentence, a body of supportive sentences, and a concluding statement.

4

The Essay As a Whole

A student recently complained that there was a big difference between the process of choosing and organizing a topic, and actually writing the essay. He said he rarely had difficulty deciding what to write about, but somehow his mind froze between the planning and the execution of the essay. He could never quite put together all the elements that form an interesting essay.

Not too long ago this same student elected to write about whales — an interesting enough topic and one that he knew something about. His father was a marine biologist, and the student had spent several summers working in an aquarium. He wanted to write an essay that would emphasize the attractive characteristics of whales. He thought that if he evoked in his readers a sympathetic interest in whales, he could show them the need for an organization that concentrated on the preservation of whales.

He focused his ideas into a thesis statement, decided to present his views in a descriptive mode, and outlined his thoughts. He even tried to write out a few paragraphs, but the essay just did not seem to gel. The student worried so much about sticking to his outline and making his point that he never really got around to choosing lively examples and bringing in realistic or amusing details which would support his ideas.

Although it is true that an essay must have a central idea and a unifying structure comprised of several paragraphs, it is *not* true that thesis and structure alone, or just any series of unified paragraphs, necessarily make a good essay. Also needed is a sense of life — a feeling that the writer has been there, has really experienced or knows about the events under consideration, and really cares about the idea he or she is writing about. The writer must convince the reader that his or her essay is worth reading and worth heeding. But this is possible only if the selection of details and examples tells the reader that the writer is interesting, stimulating — and human.

The First Draft

When you have selected a subject, arrived at a thesis, opted for a rhetorical pattern, and organized your thoughts, sit down and write out a first draft of the entire essay as completely as you can. Do not worry if your grammar is not perfect, if you do not spell everything correctly, or if some of your sentences are not as well-constructed as they might be. Just get your thoughts committed to paper. You can always go over the essay and correct it later. Sometimes your first thoughts are your freshest — the ones most likely to appeal to your reader. But even if the details you select the first time around are not just right, you can change them in a later revision. The important thing is that you have made a start: you have something to work with.

Choosing Openers

The task of writing a first draft will be far easier if you come up with a lively and interesting introduction. If you have begun well, the remainder of your essay will proceed smoothly.

Thus your first job when writing out a first draft is to find an opener that will engage the attention of your reader. You may introduce your purpose in the opener. Or you may wish to sharpen your reader's interest in your subject by offering an illustration of the subject, saving your thesis statement for a later paragraph.

Anecdotes • You could start with an anecdote. One student submitted an essay about being visually impaired that begins this way:

" I always used to sit in the back of the room in junior high school because I didn't want anyone to think I was trying to be the teacher's pet. From my position in the center back of algebra class I thought I had a perfect view of the board at the front of the room. It was an unobstructed view because there was a center aisle between the two sections of desks. Only the back row went all the way across the room and I sat in the very middle of it so I could look straight up the aisle to the board. I was a copious note-taker in those days, and I began the year by committing first to my notebook and then to memory everything I saw on the board.

It wasn't until the first algebra test that I realized everything which had appeared on the board had reappeared in my notebook, doubled. When my teacher wrote

$$a(b + c) = ab + ac,$$

I wrote

aa bb cc aa bb aa cc.

I didn't write anything for the "(," "+," ")," or "=" because I couldn't actually see these little signs from my vantage point. My first exam score — a zero — was so out of line with the scores in the rest of the class that my teacher realized something was wrong. She traced the problem to my notebook and I was remanded to an optometrist. **,,**

In beginning this way, the student interests and involves the reader in her subject, which is the eye disorder she grew up with and its symptoms and treatment. An anecdote of this sort is more likely to engage the general reader's attention than a clinical categorization of the same subject. It is a more human way of introducing the subject than stating, "Eye disorders often have the following symptoms. . . ." or "Diagnosis and treatment consist of. . . ."

Scene-Setting • Another type of opener closely related to anecdote is scene-setting. Establishing the mood of an essay through description of a scene can be an effective way of attracting a reader's attention. Scene descriptions can range from the quasi-gothic:

" The door creaked as I entered the hall. I had never been in a college admissions office before and this one sure didn't look like my high school principal's office. The walls were brown stone, and they sweated. They were damp to the touch and so was I. The ceiling was two stories high — at least — and the effect was to make me feel even smaller than my 5′9″. . . . **,,**

to the contemporary:

" Everything was geometric. The door was triangular, the rug a pattern of cut diamonds, the seats hexagonal. One wall was completely adorned with dials and knobs and I wasn't sure whether it was a computer or a mural. I half expected the admissions officer to look like R2D2. **,,**

and in-between:

" I went for my first college interview yesterday. The campus was in the first bloom of magnolias and dogwoods. The river in the distance looked very blue and very pure. I felt very comfortable strolling across the green to the white bungalow labeled "Admissions." The very word had a reassuring ring, as if the building and those within didn't know the meaning of the word "rejections." **,,**

Setting the scene prepares your reader for the mood that you will establish in the rest of your essay. The last example sets a comfortable mood. The middle example is somewhat tense, though witty, in tone. The first is awe-inspiring.

Quotations • Another way of introducing the reader to your subject is to begin with an appropriate quotation that epitomizes your subject. Quotations can be serious or witty as long as they are appropriate to your subject and attract the attention of the reader. The quotation can be taken from a work of literature or from a professional commentary on the subject you are considering in your essay. One student in a composition course opened an essay on why she wanted to become a nun with a quotation from Milton: "They also serve who only stand and wait." Another student who wrote about developing an interest in Freudian psychoanalysis began with a quotation by Freud that had originally stimulated her interest: "Psychoanalysis falls under the head of psychology; not of medical psychology in the old sense, nor of the psychology of morbid processes, but simply of psychology." Both of these quotations sum up the point of view of the essay they introduce, and they tell the reader what to expect.

The quotation might also be included for humorous effect. One student began an essay on hunting with a quotation from Woody Allen: "Why does man kill? He kills for food. And not only food: frequently there must be a beverage." Although in this case the quotation is only marginally related to hunting, it captures the attention of the reader. At the same time it performs another important function of the introduction: it sets the tone for the piece to follow. This essay on hunting was a witty account of how the writer learned that he actually was not fit for hunting at all

Rhetorical Questions • Alternatively, you might open your essay with a rhetorical question, a question you ostensibly ask the reader, but which you really proceed to answer through the essay itself. A typical introductory rhetorical question might be "Are you tired of the same old faces during the student government elections," or "Are you getting your tuition's worth out of the college's curriculum?" Such questions indicate the writer's point of view immediately and suggest a direction for the essay which follows. The first question implies dissatisfaction with the current student government and could be "answered" with a proposal to accept an alternative procedure. The second suggests that the writer believes the course structure at State University to be unsound; this question could be "answered" with a proposal for reevaluation of the curriculum.

Dramatic Statements • Yet another opening device you could employ is the dramatic statement. You might announce, "Administration closes Library at night to save oil!" thus immediately grabbing your reader's attention. You might then go on to show how the national energy crisis is affecting everyone, or to argue that other means of conservation would be more sensible. Such statements have the desired impact, however, only if they are new and true.

Openers to Avoid •   It is useful to keep in mind certain opening devices, but it is also essential to avoid ones which annoy the reader or impart a whining tone to your essay. Do not indulge in apologies or complaints in your introductions. "I am only writing this because I was assigned to" or "No one likes this subject, but here goes anyway" are weak openers because they tell the reader the writer has no conviction that the subject of his or her essay is either correct or meaningful.

If you have a genuine complaint, present the reader with the facts and let your grievance become objectively obvious. Don't begin with "This university has been unfair to me. It won't let me arrange my own major." Start instead with a positive approach: "Other universities have begun to institute an innovative approach to education: they are allowing students to arrange their own major programs. I feel this would be a good direction for State University to follow." It is important not to lose your audience initially, and whining is a sure way to turn off a reader.

Selecting Details

Even after you have composed an opener that is human and engaging, you must still find the specific details that will make the rest of the essay come alive. A student brought in a book not too long ago about the duties of college placement counselors. The book was filled with generalizations and advice about college counseling but failed to provide even one anecdote or story that clarified the ideas and held the reader's interest. As a result, the book was not only boring, but unconvincing as well. Readers are not likely to care about or remember information that is not illustrated in an interesting way. Good writing is writing that people *want* to read, and it is easier to be interested in generalizations when they are exemplified by descriptions with human interest.

Whenever you make a general statement, support it by specific details. For instance, if you are talking about a general idea ("Crime doesn't pay"), back it up with facts ("75 percent of all those committing crimes in this state are caught"). The book about counseling mentioned previously would have been more interesting had the author made a generalization such as "Most students at the local high school eventually found the right college for them" and then backed it up with specific factual information: "Four girls who wanted to study architecture were steered away from schools they thought they wanted by the college placement officer who informed them that these schools had outdated architecture programs. The counselor instead interested them in schools with more modern programs. The girls are now happily enrolled as budding architects" and "One young man insisted that he wanted to go to an Ivy League school because his brother had done so. The counselor knew the student wanted to study accounting, but none of the schools to which he had applied offered an accounting program. The counselor suggested a state college with an excellent program in business and accounting, and the student is currently well on his way to becoming a C.P.A."

Let us illustrate this point even further. Suppose you are writing an essay about marriage as a changing institution. In your first paragraph, you might introduce the topic with an appropriate quotation. You could then discuss the ways in which the institution of marriage has changed over the last three generations and speculate as to where it might be headed. Starting with the oldest generation, you might write:

" People who today are between 60 and 80 years of age have always viewed marriage as an essential and natural part of life. They married young, did not consider any alternate lifestyles, and scorn any members of the younger generation who opt for some form of personal involvement other than wedlock. "

This information is all very clear, but the reader might still feel unsatisfied with its presentation. Missing are the personal details that bring the paragraph to life — details which give shape to the ideas expressed. The essay could have a deeper and longer-lasting effect if the paragraph were written like this:

" My grandparents have always viewed marriage as an essential and natural part of life. They married young. Grandmother was 18; so was grandfather. They were farmers and were ready to assume responsibility at this age. My grandfather's parents had died and he had inherited his father's farm. He needed a partner — someone to run the household and take care of the small animals. He and my grandmother never considered any lifestyle other than marriage. It wouldn't have made any sense. And because it was so natural and worked so well for them, and because they worked so well together, they could never see the value of any form of involvement other than wedlock. My cousin moved into an apartment with his girlfriend and both of them pursue separate careers, seeing each other mainly on weekends. My grandparents, neither of whom are particularly self-righteous or super-moralistic, just can't see that this set-up makes any sense. "

Here the reader would sense that the paragraph is about real people with real ideas. Moreover, the narrative detail is engaging and easy to follow. The reader can grasp the reasons for the writer's position and is likely to remember the ideas more vividly than if they were presented as a dry list of generalizations.

Interesting examples are of paramount importance, but they must at the same time be relevant to your topic. In other words, they must illustrate the main point you are trying to make. The following paragraph, had it been included in the essay just cited, would have strayed far afield from the main point — namely the issue of changing roles in marriage.

" My cousin's girlfriend, by the way, has a great job. She does the public relations for a recording company and she's gotten to meet all sorts of terrific rock stars — Peter Frampton, George Harrison, and others. In fact, just last week she had lunch with an agent who encouraged her to form her own rock group. "

This passage is obviously beside the point and as such would divert the reader's attention from the main theme of the essay.

Arriving at Interesting Conclusions

The details you select in your essay should all be directed to your main point. This point may be made initially and supported by your selection of details, stated implicitly or explicitly somewhere in the body of your essay and substantiated by your illustration, or added later as a climax to the statements you have made throughout your paper. Whether you make your main point at the end of the essay or use your final remarks to reemphasize the main point, the conclusion should be one that is forceful, interesting, and memorable.

Concluding Illustrations • There are certain techniques you can use to achieve such a conclusion. You can, for instance, employ an appropriate illustration. The student writing about eye disorders effectively concluded her essay with this example:

" The artist Vincent Van Gogh was thought to have suffered from an eye disorder, glaucoma, which may account for his painting halos around his stars and lights. Glaucoma victims actually perceive lights this way. Van Gogh's distorted vision resulted in such famous paintings as "Starry Night." But in the case of many other less talented victims of eye disease, such problems can cause severe handicaps, both physical and mental. The best way to avoid such problems is to exercise awareness, early detection, and early treatment. "

Concluding Quotations • You could also end with a quotation. One student who wrote about the college admissions office ended his essay with an apt quotation from a college bulletin which summed up the point of his essay. He wrote:

" The college bulletin states that "This is an environment suited to learning and developing you to your greatest potential, intellectually, physically, socially. This college tries to convey its flavor and appeal to you from the very first moment you enter the admissions office." This certainly was true when I visited it. "

Concluding Questions • Alternatively, you could conclude by suggesting other issues or questions that might have been raised by your handling of a particular topic. You could, for example, conclude the essay about the changing role of marriage over the past three generations in this way:

" What do these changes mean for the future? Will the pattern continually progress to the point where people don't even pair off any more, but live in communal-style groups? Or will the pendulum swing back? Will I, age 80, be asking my grandchildren, hastily rushing into an early marriage, "Why wed? In *my* day such a thing was considered useless." And will they answer, "Oh, Grandpa, you just don't understand these things!"? **,,**

Concluding Dramatic Statements   •   Yet another essay might lead up to a forceful ending. For instance, the hypothetical essay about the closing of the university library at night to conserve fuel might present a plan by which students could inform the university of suggestions for energy conservation. An effective ending, then, might be a dramatic statement urging the university to burn the midnight oil for the sake of the lamp of learning. Such an essay, published in the student newspaper, would likely have an effect on university policy.

Concluding Descriptive Scenes   •   Or you could bring your essay to a slower end by including relevant descriptive passages. One student, after writing about a particularly horrible college interview, ended his essay on a note of ironic tranquility:

" The birds on the quad were sweetly welcoming in the evening. The leaves on the trees were just beginning to turn an inviting golden. The chapel bells were tolling out the alma mater. And I knew that somewhere inside these hallowed stone walls, amid the notes welcoming others to join this serenity, a rejection notice was being prepared for me. **,,**

The details you choose for your introduction, body, and conclusion will help to bring out your personality as a writer. If these details are interesting, they will enable your reader to know you as a person, and not merely as an impersonal source of generalizations.

Revising Your Draft

After you write your first draft, it is time to revise it. You should check your draft carefully and answer the following questions:

1. Have you followed your outline plan?
2. Have you adequately stated, developed, and supported your thesis?
3. Have you included every idea on your outline plan in its own paragraph? If not, are you satisfied with your reasons for eliminating certain points?
4. Have you added any ideas that were not originally on your plan? If so, do they really belong in the essay?
5. Are there any spelling, punctuation, or grammatical mistakes?
6. Are all your sentences clear, concise, and comprehensible? Do they say what you want them to?
7. Is your essay written in the tone you wish it to assume?
8. Is your focus clear?
9. Have you determined who your audience is to be? Is the essay you have written suitable to that audience?

10. Does the essay fulfill the assignment or the purpose for which it was written?

If you can answer all these questions satisfactorily, you are able to proceed in the essay-writing process. If not, you will have to stop and correct or rewrite your essay.

If possible, it is a good idea to allow some time to elapse between writing and checking over your first draft. A delayed second reading will enable you to view your essay with more objectivity than if you corrected it immediately after writing it. You will also benefit by reading your essay aloud to someone else. An objective listener can often find flaws in organization, presentation, or style that the writer has missed.

Some students submit their first drafts, or versions of their first drafts corrected for grammar, punctuation and spelling, as their completed essays. If, however, your aim is to write the best essay you can, it is wise to check your first draft against the list of questions just mentioned; better still, you might present this list to your "objective listener" so that he or she can provide specific and constructive criticism of your writing.

Assignment: *For Comprehension and Practice*

Questions for Discussion

1. Why is it a good idea to avoid worrying about technicalities when writing your first draft?
2. What kinds of essay openers are available to writers? Can you think of others not listed in this chapter?
3. How can you be sure that the supportive details you select will appeal to your readers? Is it necessary to assess your audience before selecting these details? Why?
4. What options do you have in concluding your essay? To what extent does your selection of a concluding technique depend on your purpose?

Exercises

1. Compose three different openers for a hypothetical essay entitled "Coed Dorms Help Eliminate Artificial Barriers Between Men and Women."
2. Select at least three detailed examples which might be used to support such a statement.
3. Invent three different conclusions for the same topic.

Practice in Writing

Choose an essay you have written for a previous assignment. Consider it as a first draft and correct it, revising partially or totally as necessary, and taking into account your instructor's criticisms.

5

Writing with Style:
Effective Words and Sentences

"Write with style," the composition instructor says, and you nod your head, jot the advice in your notebook, and vow never to write flat prose again. That evening, you spread out your books, take pen in hand, and, determined to be spirit-stirring, fill four pages with your best-flowing thoughts in your best-flowing hand. However, even your roommate cannot suppress a yawn while reading the result. Can you accomplish this well-intentioned resolve? Is it possible for you to produce a scintillating essay instead of a dull one? Can you learn to "write with style"? Yes, you can. You can learn techniques which, if practiced, can make your prose less prosaic, and more memorable.

In short, "style" is nothing more than choosing words, phrases, and sentence patterns that present your ideas to your reader in a manner appropriate to your purpose.

Words and Phrases

"The butterflies were rumbling in my stomach," wrote a student. She was trying to make her writing more interesting by inserting a metaphor, but she selected the wrong word, "rumbling," to convey the image she wished to present. Instead of describing exactly what her thoughts and feelings were, she used an inappropriate word that threw her metaphor out of kilter. As Mark Twain said, "The difference between the almost right word and the right word is really a large matter — 'tis the difference between the lightning-bug and the lightning."

The words and phrases you choose should be suitable and appropriate to the idea, message, or image you wish to convey. One student, for example, wrote about "fear" in this way:

> " The youngster and I were alone in the boat and our paddles were gone. Nightfall was coming fast, and I found a feeling of utter despair taking hold of me. However, I could not show my feelings to the little boy. I did not want him to panic, so I kept reassuring him that we would be rescued shortly. I even told him that he should not worry at all, because I could always think of a way to save us. I tried to get him involved in conversation in order to take his mind off the chaotic situation we were in. We joked about the stories we were going to tell the boys at camp. I forced myself to laugh at his jokes, and the louder I laughed, the more frantic were my silent prayers. "

The words and phrases that are particularly effective in conveying the mood this writer wishes to create are "alone," "paddles were gone," "Nightfall was coming fast," "utter despair," "panic," "rescued," "worry," "save us," "chaotic situation," "frantic." The language seems natural and the words have been chosen with care. The reader can easily imagine a frightened but brave young narrator, trying to convince himself and his younger friend that help will come.

Your choice of diction should be precise and exact. You would convey your meaning far more accurately if you described a suspense movie you recently saw as "spooky" and "mysterious" than if you labeled it "far-out" and "groovy." Your diction should also be appropriate to your audience and purpose. If you are writing for a group of peers, you would select words that would convey your meaning and attitude to them in the most effective and natural way possible. You might use words such as "gothic" or "Victorian" to describe the settings in the film if you knew that your readers would understand these terms. If you were writing about the same subject in a letter home to your little brother, however, you would substitute a less sophisticated set of words, such as "scary" and "dark." In yet another letter to your grandmother, you might use words such as "gruesome" and "disturbing."

Avoid vagueness at all costs. Do not, for example, use *this* or *that* to indicate a person, thing, or idea that has not been previously identified. Remember that these words are pronouns — words that replace nouns. Sometimes students use *this* or *that* to refer to the entire preceding paragraph and the reader is left with only a vague idea of what the writer means. If *this* or *that* cannot be replaced by a noun, do not use such a word. Nonspecific words such as *thing* and *one* should also be avoided, if at all possible. Compare the two passages below. Which one is more interesting and memorable?

> " I wish to join the diplomatic corps, even though I heard from someone that there are times when it can be dangerous as well as interesting. This can come about because of situations that one can find oneself in which lead to danger. One could think it would be fun to indulge in such interesting and exciting things, despite their danger. "

" My career goal is to be a diplomat even though the life of a diplomat is often as dangerous as it is glamorous. The father of my best friend was a member of a diplomatic mission in Latin America. Although he often went to elaborate parties and formal receptions, and although his time in Latin America included evenings spent at concerts and plays, he was also shot at on two occasions. Moreover, he once found himself investigating a crime in the jungle and he was bitten by a poisonous snake during the investigation. Such a life appeals to me because of my sense of adventure as well as my desire to serve my country. "

The first passage is dull, repetitious and aimless, whereas the second vividly expresses the writer's ideas through effective diction.

Levels of Specificity

It is also important to remember that words and phrases have different levels of abstraction. If your purpose is to make a general statement, you would use general terms:

Professors are interested in developing students' minds.

This sentence uses nouns which refer to general categories, not individuals. If your intent in using this sentence was to be general, then it would suffice as written. If, on the other hand, you wished to be more concrete and specific, you could say:

A professor at State University believes in developing the minds of his students.

Here you are referring to a specific professor and specific students, though they are still not individuals in the mind of the reader. A still more specific statement would be:

Professor Thomas made a particular attempt to develop the minds of Susan, Lester, and Adam in his history course last semester.

This is the most specific of the three examples given because the reader is provided detailed information about the particular people involved. The more specific you want your statement or example to become, the more *concrete* are the details you would add.

Specific statements are usually included in supportive and illustrative information, whereas introductory statements and generalizations tend to be less concrete and more abstract.

Connotation and Denotation

A word is most effective when it has both the right denotation and the right connotation. The denotation of a word is its factual, explicit meaning. The connotation of a word is its implicit meaning — a meaning suggested by the attitude or feelings of the person using it. A man may be denotatively described as *slender,* for instance; but to call him *scrawny* would significantly change the connotation of that description. In another case, the words *boar* and *swine* both denote a type of pig. However, *boar* connotes an animal that is fierce, majestic, and wild, whereas *swine* connotes an animal that is slovenly and fat. At the same time, the denotative term *pig,* if applied to a human being, would take on a decidedly negative connotation.

Exact connotations as well as denotations can be found in a good collegiate dictionary. Do not rely on a thesaurus because some words listed as synonyms for other words have varying connotations. One enthusiastic freshman attempted to increase the effectiveness of her writing by selecting from a thesaurus uncommon synonyms for common words. In one instance she wrote, "My father's enormity upset my mother." She meant, "My father's recent weight gain upset my mother" but she could have been mistakenly interpreted as saying, "My father's heinous offense upset my mother," The word *enormity,* connoting "heinous offense" made her intended meaning ambiguous.

Metaphors and Similes

You can further increase the power of your words by including occasional metaphors and similes in your writing. A metaphor is an implied comparison made between one object or person and another, as in "That teacher is a monster." A simile is an explicit comparison using the words *as* or *like,* as in "The five minutes I had to wait to find out if I'd passed the exam seemed like a year." Such comparisons suggest to your reader a wider range of feelings and experience than less descriptive phrases might, and are thus an economical form of writing. It might take an entire paragraph of literal prose to convey the same image as contained in a single simile or metaphor.

Idioms

Writing, particularly informal or personalized writing, can be made more lively and colorful by the inclusion of idioms — established, though often not grammatically logical, expressions. Idioms such as "track down," "easy does it," "in good stead," and so on, are heard and remembered as we grow up. Although they are impossible to figure out grammatically, they are easily understood, and as such, can be used to impart a "natural" tone to prose.

Jargon

Many organizations and professions use a number of terms that may be familiar to the people associated with them but are unintelligible to outsiders. This specialized language is called *jargon*. In general, unless the audience to which you are addressing your essay is familiar with a particular kind of jargon, it is best to avoid such language — particularly since jargon often substitutes for clear and creative thinking.

The following sentences each contain jargon. Each would be difficult to understand unless the reader were familiar with the vocabulary of the activity or subject.

A linguist would understand what the words "guttural," "fricative," "glottal stop," and "yogh" referred to.

"A plié followed by an entrechat and a rond de jamb" would be understood by a ballet dancer.

A chef would understand a recommendation for the use of one type of wire whisk for whipping, a different one for beating, and yet a third type for blending.

Wordiness

One of the most common writing faults is wordiness, particularly when it is used to cover up a lack of substance.

Avoid excess words. Constructions such as "the fact that" or "thus, it can be seen that" rarely add meaning to a sentence and almost always reduce its impact. Conciseness contributes greatly to effective writing. Why say, "My career objectives center on my desire to be successful in the business world — in particular, in the field of accounting" when you might simply state, "I hope to become an accountant"?

One cause of wordiness is the overuse of the passive voice, which almost always requires the addition of extraneous words and phrases to make the meaning of the sentence clear. Note the following passive construction, for instance:

The skiing had been done and the cocoa had been finished before Susan was asked by Alex for a lift back to the dorm.

Here is the same idea expressed in the active voice:

Alex had finished his skiing and his cocoa before he decided to ask Susan for a lift back to the dorm.

Here is another pair of examples:

Passive: **The mother had been asked by her son Bill whether dinner had been cooked by his grandmother yet.**

Active: **Bill asked his mother whether his grandmother had cooked dinner yet.**

In both cases, the passive construction is wordier and more confusing than the active.

At times, of course, the passive voice will be unavoidable; but an overall effort to emphasize the active voice will ensure conciseness and notably improve your writing style.

In general, as you write your first draft and, later, your revision, be sure to pay particular attention to refining your diction. Does every word mean precisely what you intend it to mean? Do your words elicit concrete and vivid images and connote appropriate and enlightening associations? Are there original and colorful words you could substitute for stale and worn-out ones? Have you used words such as *this* or *thing,* or abstract generalizations that weaken the impression you are trying to make? These questions may at times be difficult to answer, but the effort pays off. Style brings language to life, and the roots of style are the writer's very words.

Sentences

The style of your essay is also dependent on its sentences. The kinds of sentences you use and the order in which they are placed determine the rhythm and flow of your writing, the smoothness, beauty, and effectiveness of your prose.

Kinds of Sentences

There are three basic types of sentences you can employ in prose writing: the balanced sentence, the cumulative sentence, and the periodic sentence.

The *balanced sentence* is composed of two or more parts, all of which have parallel structures. (Each part is a complete clause with a subject and a predicate. See *Handbook* for further details.) The ideas in each of the parts are equal in importance as well as similar in structure; when separate ideas of this nature are put together, they are said to be coordinated. Examples of balanced sentences are as follows:

1. No one in my dorm is planning a career in medicine: about half the students are pre-law; the rest are hoping to teach.
2. Either I go to history lecture and satisfy the intellectual side of my nature, or I go to the coffee shop and satisfy the hedonistic side.

At times, a subject or a predicate may be only implied, but the sentence can still be considered balanced, as in the following examples:

1. Either I choose the lecture hall and satisfy my mind or the cafeteria and satisfy my stomach.
2. My roommate really wanted to be a pre-med student but switched to pre-law when he flunked physical chemistry.

A set of ideas

I set out to go fishing. The day was warm. I took my fishing tackle out of the closet.

can be coordinated as follows:

The day was warm so I took my fishing tackle out of the closet and set out to go fishing.

Be sure the parts of your balanced sentence are parallel in construction (see *Handbook*). Lack of parallelism results in confusion or awkwardness.

Parallel Construction: The wind was blowing hard and the trees were whipping against the windows.

Non-parallel construction: The wind was blowing hard and the windows were being whipped by the trees.

The second sentence does not contain parallel constructions. It shifts from the active to the passive voice and consequently sounds awkward.

The *cumulative sentence* consists of one basic thought, expressed in an independent clause at the beginning of the sentence and followed by a series of words and phrases which expand on or modify the basic idea. Unlike the balanced sentence, which is symmetrical in both form and content, the cumulative sentence is one-sided. Its main idea is set forth first, and everything that follows elaborates upon this main idea and is subordinated to it. An example of a cumulative sentence is as follows:

I wondered whether my mother would let me go, the day being at its height, and my destination being two bus rides and a short walk away.

The reverse of the cumulative sentence is the *periodic sentence*. In this case, the main independent clause containing the basic idea of the sentence appears at the *end* of the sentence. What precedes this clause is a series of subordinated, supportive ideas which elaborate on or describe the final main clause, as in the following sentence:

Because the hour was late and I didn't have time for breakfast or even a shower, and because no one was even concerned about my whereabouts, I began the trip with a bad feeling.

Each type of sentence, the balanced, the cumulative, and the periodic, has a different structure and develops differently — in much the same way different paragraphs develop differently, depending on their pattern of organization.

In other words, each type of sentence is suitable to a specific way of expressing ideas and should be selected accordingly.

The use of a variety of sentences in your prose — a combination of all three types noted above — results in forceful, energetic, and sophisticated writing. The placement or order of your sentences accounts for the rhythm of your writing, so it is important to vary your sentence structure. Below are two passages, one with a similar sentence pattern repeated throughout, the other utilizing a variety of sentence patterns:

I like the music of John Denver. His songs have personal meanings. He sings about his wife, Annie. He sings about his children. He sings about the place he lives. He sings about love and life. The tunes he composes are quite beautiful. The lyrics are poetic. He makes me feel what he sings about. His songs are effective.

I like the music of John Denver because his songs have personal meanings. He sings about his wife, Annie; his children, the place he lives; love; life. The tunes he composes are quite beautiful; the lyrics are poetic. Because he makes me feel what he sings about, his songs are effective.

The first passage sounds staccato and dull. There is no attempt to alternate sentence patterns. The second passage, with its combination of balanced, cumulative, and periodic sentences, is more interesting and sophisticated than the first passage, though both concern the same subject and contain essentially the same information.

The rhythm of your prose is an important part of your style; it keeps the reader interested in and continually receptive to the new ideas and thoughts contained in your writing.

Assignment: *For Comprehension and Practice*

Questions for Discussion

1. What function do similes and metaphors serve?
2. Ambiguity in writing can be either a negative or a positive trait. Explain.
3. Do you think there can be a valid reason for including a fragment or a run-on sentence in a composition? Why or why not?

Exercises

1. Identify the denotation and connotation of the following words:
   a. home   **b.** steed

      c. lily   **g.** electric eel
      d. moonlight   **h.** shark
      e. medieval   **i.** tiger
      f. toadstool   **j.** snowstorm

2. Make each of the following words more interesting by using a simile or metaphor to describe it:

      a. cow   **c.** table
      b. rain   **d.** baby

(Try to avoid being trite.)

3. Combine the following groups of simple sentences so as to coordinate some ideas and subordinate some ideas to others. Consider the use of periodic, cumulative, and balanced forms, and make your sentences as concise as possible.

      a. *The Mill on the Floss* is my favorite book. George Eliot wrote *The Mill on the Floss.* George Eliot was a Victorian author whose real name was Mary Anne Evans.

      b. The river is turbulent today. I can see the river from my living room window. My living rom window faces east.

      c. Young children are often picky eaters. All they ever want to eat is hamburgers. They also like French fries. They usually detest vegetables. One frequent exception, though, is carrots.

      d. Choosing a major is an important aspect of a college career. Your major subject often indirectly dictates your entire future. Therefore, it is important to select your major with some care.

      e. The debating society is a good opportunity to develop your thinking processes. It is also fun. Moreover, you can improve your speech patterns through debating.

4. Rewrite the following awkward sentences in the active voice instead of the passive voice. Aim for clarification of ideas and simplification of wording.

      a. Shakespearean scenes are often tried out with by aspiring actors interested in joining the dramatic society.

      b. The forum was left quickly by everyone during the fire drill.

      c. The hay was stacked in ricks by the farmer, the cows were milked by him, and the dog was bathed by him — all before sunset.

      d. Paris was loved by and thought of as home by Ernest Hemingway during the 1920's.

      e. The registration forms were asked to be filled out by the students by the registrar.

5. In the following paragraph, find and correct the run-on sentences and the sentence fragments:

It was dawn when I awoke with a start and found the door to my dorm room had been forced open. No one seemed to be in my room though the closet was a mess no one was in the hallway although there were footprints on the mat outside the door and the door to the bathroom was ajar. I crossed the hall and pushed the bathroom door. It opened. A man in a blue raincoat. The intruder jumped when he saw me he tried to run past me but I tripped him. Although he stood up again, and although the exit wasn't too far away. He turned and ran the wrong way — right into the arms of the night watchman. Later he was found to have taken my blue silk scarf and my jade necklace. Plus my typewriter, which he had secreted away under the stairs.

Editing for Style

Edit an essay already written for a previous assignment, paying particular attention to words and sentences.

Part Two

Methods of Organization

6

Narration

"On a particularly forlorn corner of Columbus Avenue, John double-parked, dug a finger in my ribs, and pointed to what he described as a group of junkies "on the set." I turned to look and he said, "Don't just wheel around that way. If they see two of us staring, it's all over. Pretend you're talking to me and use the car mirror." Feeling very Paul Newman, I did so and saw a group of stooped-over people not having very much to do with one another. "A junkie 'hanging' that way means either one, he's had his shot; two, he's steering people to a connection: or three, he's actually holding something. Watch, and you'll see some shit go down." After a moment or so, one of the men ambled over to another. "Closer," said John, "closer, closer —" The two men exchanged a Harlem "take five" slap of hands and John said, "That was it."

"That was it?"

"That was it," he repeated.

"I don't really think I saw anything."

"Of course you didn't," said John. "Neither would a radio car, circling the corner for hours. It takes a trained junk dick to see a hit like that."

Feeling as though I'd slowed the march of justice, I asked John if, under normal circumstances, he would have made an arrest in a case like that. He said no — the department doesn't have enough personnel to bother with one-bag transactions. "What you're after is your half-load and full-load twenty-five bags of heroin collar. When you get one, you immediately turn the man into a confidential informer. 'You give us X number of collars and we'll write a letter to the D.A. to get you a suspended sentence.' The trick, though, is always to work up, getting a half-load man to lead you to a one-key man.

"And then one day," he said, swallowing hard, "you make that fifteen-key collar." (Bruce Jay Friedman, "Lessons of the Street")"

In this passage, you can see some of the features and characteristics of an effective narrative. Friedman takes an event and makes it come alive by the use of vivid and logically arranged details, a brisk pace, well-blended dialogue, and a striking conclusion. Along the way, Friedman also makes a *point* about John and, by extension, about other narcotics detectives in general — namely, that they are trained to spot things that other people overlook and that they do not bother small-time pushers. At the same time, the author lets us see that he is an untrained observer of such scenes. Not only is this narrative entertaining and lively, but it also says something significant about its subject — and even about its author. And Friedman accomplishes all this in slightly more than 300 words.

What Is a Narrative Essay?

A narrative tells of an event or a series of closely related occurrences. Narratives can be either personal, written from the point of view of the author, or objective, written from the perspective of an observer who does not participate in the action.

Narratives are chiefly intended to inform the reader about the significance of an event or series of events. The presentation of information in narrative form readily allows the reader to grasp the point the writer is making. Narratives are also meant to entertain. For example, Friedman informs his audience about the activities of narcotics detectives by writing a story about one of them. He could have conveyed the same information by giving a few disembodied "facts" about his subject: "John is a hard-boiled detective who can spot a drug deal with uncanny accuracy and who wants to arrest only big-time pushers. From him, I learned to observe things I hadn't noticed before." But the essay as written is clearly more effective: the "facts" of the story are made vivid and memorable by means of the narrative mode, in which real people speak real dialogue in real situations. Friedman's purpose is evident, too: he tells his story because he found the event interesting, and also because he has something significant to say about his subject.

Although it helps to have a subject that is naturally exciting, many writers are able to use apparently insignificant or minor events to make a point. In "Removal," E. B. White, one of our finest prose stylists, tells about his attempts to sell an old gilded mirror that had become a familiar fixture in the house from which he was moving:

❝ So I walked out the door hatless and in my shirtsleeves and went, round the corner to a junk shop on Second Avenue — a place which displayed a thoroughly miserable assortment of bruised and castoff miscellany. The proprietor stood in the doorway.

"Do you want . . ." I began. But at that instant an El train joined us and I had to start again and shout.

"Do you want to buy a gold mirror?"

The man shook his head.

"It's *gold!*" I yelled. *"A beautiful thing!"*

Two kibitzers stopped, to attend the deal, and the El train went off down the block, chuckling.

"Nuh," said the proprietor coldly. "Nuh."

"I'm giving it away," I teased.

"I'm nut taking it," said the proprietor, who, for all I know, may have been trying to simplify his own life.

A few minutes later, after a quick trip back to the house, I slipped the mirror guiltily in a doorway, a bastard child with not even a note asking the finder to treat it kindly. I took a last look at myself in it and I thought I looked tired. **,,**

Although the short narratives by Friedman and White are actually parts of longer selections, each exhibits the qualities of a good story. Whether a narrative supports the main idea of a longer essay or comprises the whole essay, there are several ingredients necessary to make it effective.

Chronological order • Most narratives follow a sequence of events as they occur in time. Friedman's narrative begins with the car-parking scene, proceeds with the action on the street, and concludes with the detective's comment on drug arrests.

Sometimes writers begin their narrative with the last event in the sequence. For example, in telling the story of Abraham Lincoln's assassination, the writer may choose to describe the shooting first, then recount the events leading to the fatal shot. This method has the advantage of focusing the reader's attention on the climactic event. Even though events are not presented in order, readers can easily figure out what happened at what time. Chaos would result, however, if a writer chose to narrate all the events at random: first the capture of John Wilkes Booth, then his preparation for the shooting, the actual murder, Lincoln's death, and finally Lincoln's activities during the fatal day.

Consistent point of view • A narrative should be presented from one, and only one, viewpoint. Once a writer chooses a narrative point of view, he or she should stick to it. Friedman chooses to tell the story of John the detective from the point of view of an outsider, a non-cop, who learns a great deal through his experiences with John, and who also reveals much about his own personality and prejudices. John's actions and remarks are always filtered through Friedman's observations. Friedman does not suddenly switch to John's point of view, showing how the detective views the writer. Had he done so, the narrative would have lost some of its objectivity. We would no longer get the sense that we were looking over Friedman's shoulder and sharing some of his reactions to the bizarre world of street crime.

Pertinent details • A narrative is effective only if it is believable, and it is believable only if sufficient concrete details are included to evoke an image in the reader's mind. A reader should see or hear an event taking place. If White had told us simply that he tried hard to get rid of the mirror, his narrative would not have had as much impact. It is the combination of realistic and image-evoking details that draws the reader into the essay. We see the junk shop where White tries to peddle the mirror. We hear the elevated train interrupt his conversation with the proprietor, see the passers-by gape at the scene, and note the reflection of White's tired face in the abandoned mirror. Writing must be concrete to be credible, and concreteness can be achieved only by means of vivid details.

These details must be relevant to the narrative, of course. If White had described — however concretely — several riders on the passing elevated train, the impact of the whole scene would have been diminished. Such a description would have been irrelevant because the riders have no connection with White and the junk-shop proprietor. But the noise of the train *does* have a connection. It adds to White's sense of futility in trying to sell the mirror.

Dialogue   •   The use of dialogue can lend drama, vividness, and immediacy to a narrative. Often the writer's presentation of a character's conversation is far more expressive than any summary or description could be. John's comments, in Friedman's essay, would sound less authentic and certainly less interesting if paraphrased by the author, skilled as he is. By presenting John's slangy and blunt comments, Friedman reveals facets of the detective's personality that no amount of description could duplicate. Dialogue reproduces speech exactly, so that the reader feels close to the narrative. Dialogue also allows the reader to come to his or her own conclusions — to make personal judgments, in other words, about the personalities of the characters and the events of the narrative.

How to Write a Narrative Essay

When you are assigned a narrative essay, begin by choosing an appropriate subject. Your narrative should be about an experience you or someone you know has undergone: a disagreement with a roommate, a parent's death, an attempt to help police capture criminals in France by using a citizen's band radio, a prank that backfired. Your subject can be an experience that is either unusual or familiar. But keep in mind that an essay written about a unique occurrence is potentially more interesting than one detailing, for example, "My Course of Study as an Occupational Therapy Major," "My Summer Job Typing Labels," or "Why I Came to College." It is true that any subject can be imaginatively treated, but more often than not, a mundane subject results in a mundane essay.

Once you have selected a general subject, you must then pinpoint a particular incident that can be effectively treated in a short essay. Your general subject might be a recent trip to Europe, for example. Some students have prepared papers on this subject in which they list every detail of their three-week itinerary. The result is an essay that reads like a date book: "Tuesday, July 7, we arrived in Italy. First we visited the Tower of Pisa, then we flew to Rome where we witnessed a Mass in St. Peter's Cathedral. It was very inspiring. We next took a train to. . . ." This approach is boring because it lacks focus and human interest, the stuff of which good narratives are made. A better method of dealing with the subject is to limit your discussion to one aspect of the trip and to focus even more specifically on a single incident. One student, for instance, wrote a successful "travel" narrative about a wedding ceremony in the midst of a war in Greece.

Although you will find it easier, in general, to limit yourself to a single incident, it is permissible to relate more than one event. If you do, make certain that the incidents are closely related and form a coherent narrative. As an example, the student essay at the end of this chapter relates several incidents: a couple of scenes describing the harassment the narrator and his family received from a crazy neighbor, an incident in court in which the narrator and his family tried to take legal action against the woman, and the surprising turn of events in the final scene. These specific incidents are closely related and integral to the story. They involve the same people and the same subject throughout, and they are all linked together to form a narrative that progresses logically and coherently.

Before you begin the actual writing process, you must determine just who your readers are going to be. Is your projected audience comprised of friends your own age and background who share your interests? Are you writing for young children who might profit from your experiences, or for older people who might like to reminisce about their college days? Will your audience be well informed about your subject, interested in your thesis, or likely to identify with you and your experience? Remember that you are not just writing for a faceless "them." You are writing for a group of individuals and you should try to imagine who they are, what their general reaction to your subject will be, and what they expect of you as a writer. If your imagined readers are of mixed ages and backgrounds, you should recognize their common denominator — the trait or interest they share with each other and with you — which will make them eager to read and accept what you have to say.

You must also determine what your narrative point of view is going to be. Are you going to tell your own story, using "I" as the narrator? Or are you going to tell someone else's story, objectively relating another person's experience without intruding into the narrative? Either perspective is proper for a narrative, but it is important that you decide which one you are going to use and that you firmly stick to that perspective. You will notice that the student essay at the end of this chapter maintains a consistent point of view throughout. The author does not suddenly switch to his neighbor's point of view, telling about how *she* lived or how *she* had been dragged to court to testify.

Once you have completed the planning stage of your essay, you are ready to start your first draft. Write about real incidents and use concrete details. The wedding essay cited previously, for instance, attempted to convey through concrete details the irony of a wedding taking place amidst a war. Without actually reading this narrative, you can assume that the writer achieved impact by means of such details as the army uniform worn by the groom, the occasional sadness in the face of the bride, and the sound of distant artillery heard above the wedding music.

Keep in mind, too, that your narrative should be presented chronologically and coherently. Because most of the narratives you will be writing are short (from

500 to 1000 words), you should begin at the point from which the rest of the narrative can logically unfold. For example, when narrating an experience you had while shark fishing, you would probably begin by setting the scene aboard the boat, then go on to describe the incident. In a short essay, it would do you little good to start by describing your hurried breakfast or your arrival at the pier. These incidents could well be relevant in an extended account, but in a short narrative you should get on board and tell your story from the logical starting point discussed earlier. This advice also holds true for your conclusion. After you have related the main incident, end at a point that logically ties up the material and states or implies your main point.

The coherence of your narrative depends on whether you stick to the main incident. Do not wander into irrelevant or distantly related areas. In the narrative on shark fishing, do not suddenly drift off into a discussion on water pollution or into a plot summary of *Jaws*. Stick to your subject. If it is worth beginning, it is also worth following to its logical end.

As you write, concentrate at all times on your purpose and the point you are making. The student who wrote about the wedding wanted to demonstrate that courage and the desire for stability persist even amid destruction and death. Without such a point, the composition probably would have been reduced to a mere newspaper description of the ceremony ("The bride wore the traditional garb of her people and looked radiant as she danced with her handsome groom . . ."). The point you make may be stated explicitly in your introduction, your conclusion, or even in the middle of your paper — or it may be implied. In the latter case, when you let the incident carry its own point, you should carefully guide the reader so that he or she draws precisely the conclusion you want drawn.

Have you

- selected an appropriate subject for your narrative?
- pinpointed one incident or two or more closely related events to narrate?
- determined your readership?
- chosen and maintained a consistent point of view?
- presented your story in a chronological, coherent, and logical way?
- made a point?

Student Essay: Trouble with a Neighbor

Stephen Ordorica

"The first time I became aware that my family was going to have trouble with our upstairs neighbor was about a year ago. It all started quite innocently one

October morning, when I found some magazines lying at our front door. They were old magazines that had come through the mail, and they were addressed to Edna Erdmann, the woman who lives above us. I had no idea why they had been placed there; after putting the magazines in front of her door, I did not give the incident a second thought.

The following afternoon we started to hear loud thumping noises on our ceiling. We thought they were due to repairs being made in the building. At three o'clock the next morning, however, the pounding resumed, and we knew the noise had nothing to do with repairs. This time the banging was louder and more frantic than the day before. My whole family was awakened by these thunderous sounds. We were all quickly dressing to investigate the reason for the deafening noise, when suddenly there was a tremendous bang at our front door. With my heart beating rapidly, and my hands shaking uncontrollably, I ran to the door expecting to be the recipient of some horrible news. I swung the door open, only to find myself looking out into a long and empty hall. Except for a big, black roach which was scurrying across the floor, there was no one there.

It was not until late that morning that I received any indication as to who did the banging. I was told by Mr. Schwartz, our neighbor, that he saw an elderly woman leaving our doorway just after he had heard the noise. By his description, I knew that it had to be Edna. I thought it best to question her about the incident, so I immediately went upstairs to her apartment. She started to yell as soon as she saw me, telling me that she was harassing us because we were burning her legs with a giant ray gun. I could not believe what I was hearing. However, I patiently tried to reassure her that we did not have a ray gun. She screamed that she had given us the magazines so that we would turn off the ray gun, and that we had not. I then realized that she was completely irrational, and logic would not convince her to stop. Therefore, we decided that we had no other alternative than to take her to court. From the time the summons was served, until the time we had to appear in court, she made our lives a nightmare. She continued banging on our ceiling and our door. In addition, she often poured large quantities of water down through our ceiling, causing the plaster to fall. Many times we would find our doorway blocked by garbage she had thrown there. Hoping it would put an end to these nerve-wracking experiences, we anxiously awaited our day in court.

It finally arrived. As she stood in front of the judge's bench, she was certainly a pathetic sight. Her bleached-blond hair was in complete disarray, and her heavy make-up made her look grotesque in the bright sunshine that poured in from the huge courtroom windows. Underneath her soiled and wrinkled dress, she wore elastic bandages on her heavy legs. Her appearance and actions were those of an unbalanced person. She waved her hands frantically as she shrilled her accusations. In a high, hysterical voice, she told the judge about the rays that were shooting up at her through our ceiling. The judge's piercing blue eyes never left her face as he listened to her story attentively. When she had concluded, the judge's face showed great sympathy and concern for her. Nevertheless, he gave her a strong warning that if she ever harassed us again, he would force her to see a psychiatrist.

The courtroom scene took place last November; since then all has been peaceful. It was such a pleasure to think that we were no longer on the mind of the crazed woman. However, what I saw this morning gave me a sickening feeling in the pit of my stomach. When I opened the door, I saw three neatly stacked magazines lying on our doormat. From where I stood I could easily read the name of the subscriber on the mailing label. In large clear letters it read: MISS EDNA ERDMANN. **,,**

Student Essay Study Questions

1. What is the point the author is trying to make?
2. Does he make his point implicitly or explicitly? Explain.
3. Is the author's attitude toward his neighbor consistent throughout the essay, or does it change?
4. Are you sympathetic toward the author? Why or why not?
5. How does the author bridge the gaps among the various incidents he relates?
6. How does the ending bring the essay full circle? What effect does this "enclosing" device have on the reader?

Assignment: *For Comprehension and Practice*

Questions for Discussion

1. For what various purposes might you write a narrative essay?
2. Imagine that you have written a letter to a friend about an incident that happened to you at college. The same incident must now be narrated in an article that will be read by strangers. How will your style differ in the two pieces?
3. How can you determine whether or not your essay has made a point?
4. Can you make a point indirectly in a narrative? That is, can you indicate what your reader should learn from your essay without explicitly telling him or her? If so, how?
5. How can identification of your audience affect the subject you choose for a narrative?

Exercises

1. Show how each of the following general subjects can be made appropriate for a narrative:

a. lions	**d.** camping
b. vegetable gardens	**e.** basketball
c. European travel	**f.** political campaigns

2. Identify the audience that might be interested in each of the following topics:
   a. learning to live with a roommate who snores

b. my unsuccessful summer as a free-lance reporter
c. my best friend's experiences learning to drive
d. how "Introductory Psychology" came to my aid in a tight situation
e. camping's not all it's cracked up to be
f. coping with subways

Essay Topics

1. Write a 500-word narrative using one of the following as your thesis sentence:
   a. At zoos I always realize that there is a distinct link between humans and animals.
   b. I am a lover of the outdoors (indoors).
   c. I enjoy (do not enjoy) cooking.
   d. I am (am not) a sports enthusiast.
2. Write a 500-word essay on one of the following:
   a. Recall a person who has meant a lot to you, and write a narrative that emphasizes the significance of your relationship.
   b. Write a narrative in which you show how your first impressions of college life compare to your later ones. (It probably will be necessary to relate more than one experience.)
   c. Write a narrative (poignant or humorous) about a favorite (or least favorite) pet.
   d. Narrate a fantasy you have had.
   e. Relate an experience you have had with someone in authority (a parent, police officer, school administrator) that made a significant impression on you.

7

Description

" The wind has gently murmured through the blinds, or puffed with feathery softness against the windows, and occasionally sighed like a summer zephyr lifting the leaves along, the livelong night. The meadow mouse has slept in his snug gallery in the sod, the owl has sat in a hollow tree in the depth of the swamp, the rabbit, the squirrel, and the fox have all been housed. The watch-dog has lain quiet on the hearth, and the cattle have stood silent in their stalls. The earth itself has slept, as it were its first, not its last sleep, save when some street sign or woodhouse door has faintly creaked upon its hinge, cheering forlorn nature at her midnight work — the only sound awake 'twixt Venus and Mars — advertising us of a remote inward warmth, a divine cheer and fellowship, where gods are met together, but where it is very bleak for men to stand. But while the earth has slumbered, all the air has been alive with feathery flakes descending, as if some northern Ceres reigned, showering her silvery grain over all the fields. (Henry David Thoreau, "A Winter Walk") "

Thoreau's brief description creates a vivid picture of the Concord woods during a snowstorm. Through the use of words and phrases that appeal to our senses, he brings the scene sharply into focus. We *see* the snow as "silvery grain over all the fields." We *feel* its "feathery softness." We *hear* the wind sighing "like a summer zephyr." We not only get a mental picture of the scene, but we sense Thoreau's attitude toward it as well. Although a certain bleakness is occasionally apparent, the overall feeling conveyed is one of tranquility and wonder. Every detail in the scene contributes to this dominant mood — an achievement essential to good descriptive writing.

What Is a Description Essay?

Description can present a scene, an object, a person, a psychological state, or a combination thereof. Regardless of the subject, however, there must be a *point* to the description. If a writer is describing a scene, he or she must know why the scene is important and how a sense of this importance can be conveyed to the reader. If a writer's purpose is to describe a scene, an object, or a person, he or she should suggest why the subject is significant or memorable. This does not mean that good descriptions can be written only about "important" or well-known subjects. It means that the description itself must treat the subject in such a way that the reader feels that some insight into the subject has been gained. The subject of Thoreau's essay is really quite ordinary — just one of countless winter descriptions written over the years. But what makes Thoreau's treatment so memorable, aside from the concrete details that bring the scene to life, is his ability to get the reader to feel that the snowy Concord woods are important in his life. If handled effectively, a description of the most ordinary subject can be a worthwhile experience for the reader.

Unlike narrative, description does not necessarily proceed chronologically, with a beginning, middle, and end in time. Instead, description scans its subject, presenting a scene as a movie camera does, from left to right, right to left, top to bottom, far to near. Here is a description of a scene that uses the far-to-near method:

" The country itself is not uncomely, despite the grime of the endless mills. It is, in form, a narrow river valley, with deep gullies running up into the hills. It is thickly settled, but not noticeably overcrowded. There is still plenty of room for building, even in the larger towns, and there are very few solid blocks. Nearly every house, big and little, has space on all four sides. Obviously, if there were architects of any professional sense or dignity in the region, they would have perfected a chalet to hug the hillsides —a chalet with a high-pitched roof, to throw off the heavy Winter snows, but still essentially a low and clinging building, wider than it was tall. But what have they done? They have taken as their model a brick set on end. This they have converted into a thing of dingy clapboards, with a narrow, low-pitched roof. And the whole they have set upon thin, preposterous brick piers. By the hundreds and thousands these abominable houses cover the bare hillsides, like gravestones in some gigantic and decaying cemetery. On their deep sides they are three, four and even five stories high; on their low sides they bury themselves swinishly in the mud. Not a fifth of them are perpendicular. They lean this way and that, hanging on to their bases precariously. And one and all they are streaked in grime, with dead and eczematous patches of paint peeping through the streaks. (H. L. Mencken, "The Libido for the Ugly") "

In one paragraph, Mencken moves from a wide view of the countryside to the peeling paint on individual houses.

In another form of description, the writer selects certain prominent features and details that contribute to the mood he or she is trying to create. This selection is not random. It includes those details the writer feels are most important to his or her purpose. This process is especially important in a brief description, where the few details must be striking and significant. In one short paragraph from *Silent Spring*, Rachel Carson establishes a dominant mood with a few well-chosen images:

> There was a strange stillness. The birds, for example — where had they gone? Many people spoke of them, puzzled and disturbed. The feeding stations in the backyards were deserted. The few birds seen anywhere were moribund; they trembled violently and could not fly. It was a spring without voices. On the mornings that had once throbbed with the dawn chorus of robins, catbirds, doves, jays, and wrens, and scores of other birds voices there was now no sound; only silence lay over the fields and woods and marsh.

Even though the description is of a bleak and "lifeless" scene, Carson uses details that make it come alive. She does not simply say "The birds weren't chirping anymore." She makes us feel their absence through references to the original vibrancy and activity of the birds.

While Thoreau's scene is "beautiful," Mencken's "ugly," and Carson's "static," all three contain precise and vivid observations; they evoke clear pictures in the reader's mind. More importantly, they create a dominant mood and make a significant point about each scene.

Another method a writer can use to create a mood or make an important point is to describe an object in some detail. Descriptions of objects rarely exist in isolation — they are almost always part of a larger picture and they should contribute significantly to the overall effect. For example, in his winter scene Thoreau vividly describes a particular snowflake that had landed on his arm: "It was one of those perfect, crystalline, star-shaped ones, six-rayed, like a flat wheel with six spokes, only the spokes were perfect little pine trees in shape, arranged around a central spangle." Thoreau is not writing about the snowflake as an exercise in pure description. Rather, he connects it to his sense of wonderment at nature's variety — a wonderment implied throughout the essay. To him the snowflake shows "that Nature has not lost her pristine vigor yet, and why should man lose heart?"

Had Mencken used the same technique, he might have focused on one object that represented the bleakness of one of the coal-mining towns. He might, for example, have described something as ordinary as a refrigerator in one of the houses. And he undoubtedly would have chosen a particularly ugly one, with its chipped paint, ill-fitting door, loose handle, soot-covered exterior, and ominous chugging sounds like those coming from the coal mines. It is pure speculation, of course, to imagine what Mencken might have included in his description. But the point is that had he chosen to focus on one object, it would have been one that fit the circumstances. He would not have described, say, a bed of bright flowers growing next to one of the shacks. That touch would not have fit in with his purpose — to show the total ugliness of the coal-mining region.

Descriptive details should contribute to the dominant mood or point the writer is making. Even when the entire description is exclusively focused on one object, there must be a point, explicit or subtle, that the writer is making. Without this underlying purpose, a description would be meaningless.

The same rule of thumb applies to descriptions of people. Such descriptions should include details of the person's physical appearance and distinguishing habits, selected in such a way that they convey the author's attitude toward the subject. Note, for example, the personal implications behind Ernest Hemingway's brief sketch of the author Gertrude Stein, whom he describes as

" very big but not tall and heavily built like a peasant woman. She had beautiful eyes and a strong German-Jewish face that also could have been Friulano and she reminded me of a northern Italian peasant woman with her clothes, her mobile face and her lovely, thick, alive immigrant hair which she put up in the same way she had probably worn it in college. She talked all the time and at first it was about people and places. "

Hemingway has carefully selected details that show Stein's impressive physical appearance and active nature. Although never explicitly stated, his fascination with Stein is also evident.

James Thurber, in a sketch of one of his former high-school teachers, creates an immediate picture when he describes her "sitting at her desk, taking the rubber band off the roll-cards, running it back upon the fingers of her right hand, and surveying us all separately with quick little hen-like turns of her head." In merely one sentence Thurber vividly portrays the teacher's nervous movements in his comparison of her to a chicken, while at the same time suggesting his *own* nervousness as a student under her scrutiny.

Philip Van Doren Stern, in his book *The Man Who Killed Lincoln*, describes the physical appearance of his villain, John Wilkes Booth, and at the same time suggests Booth's psychological state. He writes:

" His dark hair and mustache made him seem even paler than he actually was, so that the rosy light lent no color to his features. He stood alone, a silent and brooding figure, unnoticed by the passing crowds. Only his eyes, half-closed and heavy-lidded, have any indication of his reactions . . . . Booth's mouth was set in a hard grim line as these thoughts of vengeance raced through his mind. His hand clenched the edge of his cloak as he pulled it tightly around his shoulders. He had been feeding too long on his own rage — he had to have some outlet for it. "

Stern's descriptive details are physical and concrete. The reader knows what Booth looked like. But the reader also understands from the description something about Booth's mental state and what the author thinks of him. Stern's implication is that his subject is bizarre, sinister, and dangerous.

This descriptive passage, including the feelings of aversion to Booth that the author wishes to evoke in his audience, fits into Stern's overall plan for the book. Stern is describing in minute detail the assassination of Abraham Lincoln so that the reader may feel the tension of that event.

The author's point of view is an important part of the descriptive process. If Stern had wished to imply that he admired Booth, for example, instead of suggesting that he found Booth loathsome and insane, he would have chosen a different set of descriptive details to convey that impression.

Descriptive essays are used in many different ways. They might be expository, in which case the writer would explain to the reader the significance of the scenes, objects, persons, or emotional states under consideration. Or they might be persuasive. In this latter instance, the essayist would attempt to convince the reader to visit the scene being described, or to feel the same way the writer does about a certain person or object, or to identify with the writer's state of mind.

It bears repeating, however, that an author must have a *purpose* for using description in an essay. That description must support or illustrate the point the author is trying to make, and the author must be constantly aware of the reactions his or her descriptions will have on the reading audience.

The descriptive essay is a distinct composition type, and as such, can stand independently. But this mode is also a tool that can be used to enhance other types of essays. The use of description, if vivid, clear, precise, and appropriate, can make an essay stand out in a reader's mind. A point of view is more easily remembered if accompanied by a specific description than it would be if it were just presented in broad and general terms.

How to Write a Description Essay

When preparing a description essay, be sure to select a subject about which you have strong feelings. If you are deeply interested in your subject, this enthusiasm will be transmitted to the reader. If, on the other hand, you are using description merely to fulfill an assignment, this lack of interest will be conveyed.

Once you have chosen a person, scene, or object to describe, try to establish your point of view toward your topic. Do you admire your subject? Are you awed by it? Do you detest it? You should determine the perspective or attitude with which you view your subject and convey this to the reader. In addition, it is important that you stick to your point of view. Nora Ephron, in a descriptive essay about a baking contest called "Baking Off," conveys to the reader her contempt for people who spend most of their time entering contests (see p. 194). This attitude is evident throughout her essay, from her first description of the "snicky snacky Wiki Wiki Coffee Cake" to her final statement that the contestants she is describing reveal nothing "I think of as a human trait I can relate to."

In order to *maintain* the point of view you have selected, your choice of details should be appropriate. Avoid irrelevant details that do not contribute to the point or mood of the description. Ephron recreates for the reader the mood of a baking contest. Her detailed descriptions of the contestants contribute to the atmosphere she is evoking: ". . . Marjorie Johnson of Robbinsdale, Minnesota, and Mary Finnegan of Minneota, Minnesota — were seated at a little round table just off the Hilton ballroom talking about a number of things, including Tupperware. Both of them love Tupperware." If she had chosen to describe the flowers outside the convention hall, the effect would not have been the same, and her point would have been lost. She wants her readers to understand the materially oriented, intellectually empty lives she thinks these contestants lead. Flowers, however realistically described, would not have contributed to Ephron's point of view.

It is equally important to avoid trite or overused descriptive details, as they detract from the mood of the essay and are unconvincing and stale. If Ephron had described one of her characters, Marjorie Johnson, as "dull as dishwater," the effect of her words would not have been vivid and realistic, and would not have contributed to her aim.

The purpose of your descriptive details should be to create a dominant mood to convey to your readers, as Thoreau has done in "A Winter Walk," or to make a distinct point through the description, as Stern does in *The Man Who Killed Lincoln*. Both of these writers are clear about their purpose, and you should be too.

Have you . . .

- selected a subject in which you are interested, and which you think will interest your readers?
- chosen a point of view and maintained it?
- selected appropriate details that contribute to the point you wish to make and the mood you wish to evoke?
- avoided details that are irrelevant or trite and overused?
- made a clear point or created a dominant mood in your description?

Student Essay: Slow-Motion Soul-Searching on the Pequate Trail

Fred Loney

"A loud, painful shriek disrupted the quiet of the warm August night. Only an animal dying at the hands of a sadistic tormentor could have come close to reproducing that sound. The tire's death cry was ended when, upon impact, a telephone pole crushed in the driver's side of the automobile throwing the car onto the embankment. The pole, sufficiently strong to slow the car down, did not entirely impede its forward motion. The stone wall, which then made contact with the front of the car, proved more than sufficient for that task.

With the exception of the rear window all the glass in the car had broken down into proper safety glass fragments, in accordance with government regulations. A great number of these particles found their way into the eyes, mouths and hair of Mark, who was driving, and myself. The rear window was still in one piece some thirty feet down the road. The gas tank had ruptured, dumping a great deal of its high octane contents over Mark. The frame was bent. The body was disfigured beyond recognition. The engine was now only good for its few remaining salvageable parts. In short, a fourteen thousand-dollar Porsche 911 had been converted into a pile of near useless scrap in a matter of seconds.

When we started skidding, Mark had had the car going close to one hundred miles per hour. This left little more than three seconds to cover the fifty feet to the telephone pole and perhaps another second before coming to a complete stop against the wall. Four seconds is not a particularly long time. It takes longer for me to brush my teeth, and I certainly spend more time on my income tax. Yet in those seconds, questions I had pondered for years were answered.

There were no great flashes of insight and I saw no image of Christ. Every thought came to me in a well-ordered and logical manner. I remember them all clearly, though the accident was some four years ago.

Mark had brought me out in his father's car to show off his great driving skills on a rather dangerous mountain road. Mark was a gifted driver. Unfortunately, even the best of drivers are at a disadvantage when they are drunk. We were coming toward the end of the road. I looked out the window as the moonlit scenery rushed by. I looked at Mark's face, then at the speedometer on the dash. Just then Mark yelled one word in a long pleading tone, "NO!" I felt the car going into a spin. My eyes fell to the floor of the car and focused on my shoes. Right then my mind was working faster than it had ever worked before or probably will again. Yet the thoughts were well-ordered, not the drifting patterns of day-to-day thought.

With the coolness with which most television and movie spies meet their end, I addressed myself:

'Well, Fred this is it.'
'I only hope you've lived a good enough life to get into Heaven.'
'Father in Heaven make room up above, cause I'm coming your way.'
'Poor Mark.'

Time did not seem to be in any kind of hurry at all. After what seemed like a long while, the car crashed into the pole and spun round into the wall. I had not lost consciousness for even a second. Less than half a minute after the car came to a halt I had gotten out of the car, dragged Mark out and waved down a passing motorist to get help. None of this with a second thought, as if I had been in several wrecks before and was well aware of the proper procedures. Only later in the emergency room when all the excitement was over did I shiver with the thought of what might have been.

For the first and only time in my life I had been faced with what I thought to be unavoidable death. To my great surprise I had met it with a calm objectivity. I am not a particularly brave person by today's hero-oriented standards. Yet through the acceptance of what seemed inevitable and the faith in something greater than myself I not only survived the crash, but I grew because of it. **,,**

Student Essay Study Questions

1. What is the point the student is trying to make in this essay?
2. How does his selection of details contribute to this point?
3. Is he consistent in presenting his point of view to the reader?
4. What kind of audience would be interested in this essay? Why?

Assignment: *For Comprehension and Practice*

Questions for Discussion

1. What kind of audience would be interested in Thoreau's description in "A Winter Walk"?
2. When describing an object, in what situations would you include a discussion of that object's function? When would it be preferable to omit a discussion of function when describing an object?
3. For what purposes would you describe an emotional state you have experienced?
4. Why might you describe a character in an essay?
5. How could you make sure that you have made your point in an essay describing a scene? What are some hypothetical points you could make in a scenic description?
6. How can you be sure that you have established and maintained a point of view in a descriptive essay?

Exercises

1. Write a brief description, one paragraph in length, of each of the following objects. Use colorful language and try to evoke a vivid image of the object in the reader's mind:

   a. a specific table   **c.** a clock
   b. a specific automobile   **d.** a gyroscope

You may, if you wish, include mention of the object's function in your essay, if the function isn't self-evident.

2. In a paragraph each, describe the following people, telling what they look like physically, as well as what they act like and what kinds of personalities they have:

   a. a specific parent   **c.** a particular friend
   b. a specific teacher   **d.** an enemy

3. In a paragraph each, describe the following scenes:
  a. a specific sunset
  b. a grove of trees
  c. a city snowfall
  d. a traffic jam
  e. a river
  f. a city street
Try to avoid overused phrases and metaphors.
4. Describe, in a paragraph each, the following emotional states:
  a. anger
  b. frustration
  c. sadness
  d. jealousy
  e. happiness
  f. boredom
In this exercise, be sure to describe these states in relation to one specific person or one particular event.

Essay Topics

1. Describe a person who has meant a lot to you and discuss why.
2. Describe an object you are fond of, and discuss why this object is important to you.
3. Describe a scene and use it as a backdrop against which to describe an event you or someone you know has experienced.
4. Discuss a time when you were either very angry, very sad, or very happy, and describe your emotions.
Choose one topic. The length of your essay should be approximately 500 words. When writing your essay, be sure to keep in mind your purpose and prospective audience.

8

Example

" Savages we call them, because their manners differ from ours, which we think the perfection of civility; they think the same of theirs.

Perhaps, if we could examine the manners of different nations with impartiality, we should find no people so rude, as to be without any rules of politeness; nor any so polite, as not to have some remains of rudeness.

The Indian men, when young, are hunters and warriors; when old, counsellors; for all their government is by the counsel or advice of the sages; there is no force, there are no prisons, no officers to compel obedience, or inflict punishment. Hence they generally study oratory, the best speaker having the most influence. The Indian women till the ground, dress the food, nurse and bring up the children, and preserve and hand down to posterity the memory of public transactions. These employments of men and women are accounted natural and honorable. Having few artificial wants, they have abundance of leisure for improvement by conversation. Our laborious manner of life, compared with theirs, they esteem slavish and base; and the learning, on which we value ourselves, they regard as frivolous and useless. . . .

When any of them come into our towns, our people are apt to crowd round them, gaze upon them, and incommode them, where they desire to be private; this they esteem great rudeness, and the effect of the want of instruction in the rules of civility and good manners. "We have," say they, "as much curiosity as you, and when you come into our towns, we wish for opportunities of looking at you; but for this purpose we hide ourselves behind bushes, where you are to pass, and never intrude ourselves into your company. . . . (Benjamin Franklin, "Remarks on the Politeness of the Savages in North America") "

This excerpt illustrates one of the most frequently employed methods of exposition — the use of examples to support a point. Franklin bolsters his thesis statement, in the second paragraph, with several specific examples of "politeness" as practiced by "savages." In this case, the examples speak for themselves: Franklin's point is perfectly clear even without further explanation of the thesis.

The use of examples (sometimes called "exemplification") is a technique that can be used in any type of essay. This method can also constitute the main organizational pattern of an entire essay. Although the following discussion focuses on exemplification as an expository pattern, many of the points made throughout can be applied to the use of examples in any kind of essay.

What Is an Example Essay?

An essay organized by examples may feature either one very detailed illustration, or a series of illustrations in support of the writer's thesis. For example, in his essay "Shooting an Elephant," George Orwell illustrates his basic contention that British imperialistic domination of the Far East in the 1930's was futile. He says that "when the white man turns tyrant it is his own freedom that he destroys." He illustrates this point with one long, detailed description of how he, as a British police official in Burma, was forced to shoot an elephant that had gone wild and killed a native. Orwell's use of example in describing this act, committed reluctantly in order to save face before the natives who wanted and expected him to shoot the creature, conveys his thesis more effectively than any number of general statements might have.

In another essay, "Marrakech," Orwell uses a series of examples to support a similar thesis: that British domination of countries such as Morocco was immoral and futile, and that such countries would forcibly revolt against such imperialism. In one example, Orwell describes the approach of a Moroccan worker who begged from him the bread he was feeding to a gazelle in a public garden. In another example, he speaks of an occasion on which, while walking through Marrakech, he was approached by hordes of people clamoring for one of his cigarettes. He says, "None of these people, I suppose, works less than twelve hours a day, and every one of them looks on a cigarette as a more or less impossible luxury." In still another example, he describes the corpses that are carried through the streets, without coffins, covered by thousands of teeming flies. These and other dramatically detailed examples reinforce Orwell's beliefs about British imperialism in the 1930's. They also stick in the reader's mind. Without these examples, Orwell's strong feelings about his subject would lose much of their impact and vigor.

Examples should not only provide support for the main idea of the essay, but they should be appropriate to the situation as well. Orwell's examples in the essays cited previously are appropriate to his thesis. It is logical, for instance, to illustrate the idea that imperialism doesn't work with examples showing the pitiable existence of the natives in a region under imperialistic rule. Had Orwell included examples of how the Burmese or the Moroccans might have *benefited* from British occupation, his thesis would have been undercut. It was the destructive effects of imperialism on both the oppressor and the oppressed that Orwell hoped to communicate; and he does so effectively by means of carefully chosen examples.

Whether a writer uses exemplification as the major rhetorical device in an essay, or as an occasional device for greater impact, the examples must contribute to the main thrust of the piece. This is a principle that you will see at work again and again in the selections throughout this book.

How to Write an Example Essay

When you choose (or are assigned) a topic for an exemplification essay, be sure to narrow your subject and focus on the point or thesis you wish to make. Once you arrive at a thesis, you can illustrate it by means of example.

A student recently submitted a paper that begins this way: "Danger is a state of being that poses a risk. The dictionary defines it as 'exposure or liability to injury, loss, pain, or other evil.' When a person faces danger, that person experiences anxiety and fear. If the danger is very great, the person might fear for his life, and in a situation like this, he might never be quite the same again. When a person faces death, he is forced to view life as temporary, to recognize its impermanence. Danger can do this to a person. Another quality of danger is . . ." and so on. This student starts with the interesting subject of "danger," but treats it in such a general way that the essay remains as flat in tone as an entry in Webster's *Unabridged*. The reader's hands never begin to sweat because the writer has not exemplified the subject of danger in a vivid, realistic, or convincing way.

Another student, writing on the same subject, says, "When I was very young, I wondered how it would feel to be in danger. There was a curiosity within me that I knew could be satisfied only by experience, yet a deep fear always accompanied that curiosity. Then suddenly one night something happened that satisfied my curiosity and intensified my fear. . . ." The student goes on to describe the experience of being mugged.

The first student has presented a set of generalizations in place of an essay; the second has made an initial point which she supports by the immediate and sustained use of example. The second essay is far more effective than the first because it speaks vividly of people and their experiences. The writing is vibrant and realistic. The writing in the first essay, although competent, is wooden, stolid, and dull.

Examples are best when taken from real experiences you have had. You can write most convincingly about what you know best, and as a rule, you know yourself — your ideas and your experiences — more thoroughly than you know anything else.

For example, Dick Gregory, comedian, minority group spokesman, and political activist, speaks out for equal rights in his autobiography by showing how one economically underprivileged youth — himself — outgrew his life in the slums and became a success. His message is general in nature: he decries an uncaring populace which ignores, or is blind to, its hungry children, and he praises individual courage and fortitude and love in the face of great odds. His examples, however, are exclusively specific and personal. He writes in his preface:

" Richard Claxton Gregory was born on Columbus Day, 1932. A welfare case. You've seen him on every street corner in America. You knew he had rhythm by the way he snapped his cloth while he shined your shoes. Happy little black boy, the way he grinned and picked your quarter out of the air. Then he ran off and bought himself a Twinkie Cupcake, a bottle of Pepsi-Cola, and a pocketful of caramels.

You didn't know that was his dinner. And you never followed him home. "

Gregory writes of his own experiences — what he knows best. At the same time, he allows the reader to extrapolate — to follow young Richard home, and to think about how many other Richards there are in the world. Having responded personally to the specific details in this essay, the reader is then prepared to form his or her own opinions about social injustice. Like Gregory, you can draw on your own experiences, emphasizing your points by explaining how your chosen topic affects you, or indicating how your experiences may help to enlighten others.

Thus personal experience is a reliable source from which to draw examples, which in turn are likely to be the more vivid and realistic because of your familiarity with them. Depending on your purpose, however, you may also wish to draw on secondary sources — material you have either heard or read about — to support your generalizations. If you have heard a friend tell a story about an amusing incident and it is relevant to a point you are making in a paper, you may certainly refer to that story. Or, if you have read an article in a magazine that supports an idea you are discussing, by all means include this information in your essay. (In this latter case, however, it is necessary to tell your reader where this information came from, either directly in the body of your essay, or through a footnote or endnote to your paper.)

The examples you use should create a picture in the reader's mind — an image with distinctly drawn features that your audience will never forget. But you can do this only if you use specific terminology; what you describe must be real and concrete! Orwell's examples would not have been nearly so compelling had they been written with less descriptive detail. Orwell could not have evoked sympathy for the victims of oppression if he had described them merely as "poor," rather than as "poor old earth-colored bodies, bodies reduced to bones and leathery skin, bent double under the crushing weight [of loads of wood]."

To achieve the effect Orwell has demonstrated, you should visit or imagine you are visiting an actual place; witness or imagine you are witnessing a real event; see or imagine you are seeing a concrete object or person. Then record what you are observing or imagining. Note all the actual details; then select those details you feel best epitomize the scene, object, or event. Try to determine which details you feel the reader would be most interested in. Go to the zoo and note how the people react to the animals and the animals react to the people; watch your classmates eating in the cafeteria and record their reactions to the food; be observant of the world around you and try to decide which details cause the most dramatic reactions in you and your friends. Then write them down and use them as examples in your essays.

One student did just that. He went to a local zoo and recorded what he saw. He then developed a thesis that the people at the zoo acted in a less civilized way than the caged animals, and exemplified this position with the following concrete examples:

1. The people littered the ground with empty peanut shells; the gorilla neatly stacked his empty shells in a corner of his food dish.
2. The people hooted and screamed at the birds of paradise; the avians responded in measured, pleasant voices.
3. The people tossed pebbles at the alligators; the alligators ignored the people.
4. The people rode the camels endlessly around a dirt track; the camels patiently bore it.
5. The people had caged the animals; the animals hadn't imprisoned the people.

These illustrations are more fully described in the essay as a whole, but the five examples cited above aptly summarize the structure of this paper. The first four of these examples are specific; and although they contain a fact, they also imply a judgment (e.g., Gorillas are neater than humans). The final example is more general — that is, less concrete than the other four — but it is a good concluding example because it epitomizes the author's attitude towards zoos, which is the point of the paper.

Examples may be serious or humorous, depending on the purpose of your essay. One student, writing about her early religious beliefs, stated in a serious vein:

66 I never really thought much about religion when I was a child until one day our dog, a beautiful golden retriever, was shot by a local game warden for chasing deer. I prayed and prayed that Ginger would recover, but when she was in danger of dying from the wound, I understood that God wanted children to have pets so they could learn about the sorrows as well as the joys of love. When Ginger finally did recover (she lived to a ripe old age), I never forgot the lesson I learned when she was ill. It's not a very orthodox or dogmatized belief, but it brought me closer to an understanding of my religion. 99

Another student, in a more humorous mood, illustrated the proposition that "Learning to cook is more difficult than it looks" with a witty anecdote:

66 I am a chemistry major, so I thought that cooking would be a cinch for me: Mix a little bit of that, a few spoonfuls of this, a beaker full of the other thing and 'poof' — a gourmet meal.

I decided to start with the most important part of the meal — the dessert. I mixed my little bit of flour, my few spoonfuls of other ingredients, my beaker full of milk and placed the batter in well-greased baking tins and put them in the oven. I couldn't wait for the 30 minutes to elapse before peeking, so after 15 minutes I opened the oven door gently, so as not to make my cupcakes fall. I was horrified. They hadn't even begun to rise. I suddenly remembered I hadn't added the baking powder! Rather than give up, I took the pans out of the oven, the batter out of the pans, and mixed in the baking powder anyway.

Needless to say, my final cupcakes were not only flat, but leaden as well. All my chemistry training was irrelevant. The cupcakes weren't even the worst part of the meal! I suddenly had a new appreciation for my mother's culinary skills. And she hadn't even been a chemistry major. **,,**

Your examples should also be geared to the level of the audience you are appealing to. Technical or esoteric examples would not be suitable for a general audience, nor would superficial and self-evident examples be appropriate for an audience well-schooled in the subject at hand. For instance, if you are writing about faculty achievements and decided to cite illustrative examples concerning the current faculty of your college, you would not have to go into long descriptions of these faculty members if your essay is aimed at the present student body of your college. If, on the other hand, your audience were older alumni, more detailed explanatory material would be necessary.

In addition to ensuring that your examples are appropriate to your audience, you must determine whether they are relevant to your thesis and logically arranged in your paper. Examples that only indirectly relate to your subject or fall randomly throughout your essay might produce a few vivid impressions, but the total effect of the essay would be chaotic.

If you were writing a paper, for instance, about the importance of marriage in our modern, sexually "liberated" society, you would not include examples of everything from the Garden of Eden to contemporary communes. The result would probably be a hodge-podge of unrelated ideas. Rather, you should select one or several examples that specifically point up the importance of a stable marriage. These could be "negative" examples — of an acquaintance, say, whose parents were divorced early in marriage — or "positive" examples — how two unhappy people found joy after meeting and getting married. In either case, the examples must be relevant if your paper is to be effective.

Your examples must also be arranged in some kind of logical order. If, for instance, you were writing about the dangers of careless camping techniques, you could begin in roughly chronological order: failing to check on the campsite beforehand, forgetting to bring enough food and clothing, pitching the tent incorrectly, getting lost on your way out of the park, and so on. Or you could begin with your least significant example and progress to the most striking.

In this case, you might begin with your failure to bring along enough suntan lotion and end with your failure to extinguish your campfire, an oversight that resulted in a large brush fire. The arrangement of your examples in a logical fashion will not only make your essay more interesting, but it will also guide your reader through your essay and to the point you are trying to make.

Have you . . .

- arrived at a thesis you can best develop by means of exemplification?
- chosen appropriate and clear examples, from your own experience or from secondary sources, that effectively illustrate your thesis?
- presented your examples in a vivid and concrete way?
- chosen examples appropriate to your audience?
- chosen examples relevant to your subject?
- arranged your examples in a logical fashion?

Student Essay: On Being Short

Karen Eisman

"You never grow up if you are short. You may grow old, wise, distinguished, accomplished . . . no matter. People will go on treating you like a child. On your way to get the Nobel Peace Prize, somebody will offer to hold your hand crossing the street. Somebody else will probably ask you if you hadn't better use the bathroom before you leave for Sweden.

People tend to overreact to undersizedness and a life of it can make you do strange things. (I recently heard that John Wilkes Booth, at five feet eight inches, was our tallest assassin of Presidents.) Even the people who made the straphangers on subway trains had tall people in mind. Are we short people supposed to stretch our arms to reach them? Every time I get off a subway train my right arm is always longer than my left! And today, all you hear on the radio is a crazy song about the deformities of short people.

Being short can be very embarrassing. For instance, I was once asked, "How short are you?" One time my friend and I were shopping in a department store and two old women commented, "Oh look, a little girl dressed up like her mommy." It's downright appalling!!

Many times short people go unnoticed. Take as an example being served in a bank. I can remember standing in front of a teller's window in a bank for several minutes. The teller never even acknowledged my existence. She kept saying, "Next!" Finally, I threw the money at her so she had to notice me. She laughed and said, "Gee, you're so short I didn't even see you."

This is not just a woman's problem. Given two male applicants with interchangeable credentials, the taller guy is the overwhelming favorite to get the position (jockey excluded), according to a recent study. I've never seen a similar survey about the size/height ratio for women, but I do know that a lot of people tend to treat you as if an undersized brain is the inevitable complement of your cute little body.

I've taken many classes predominantly filled with the opposite sex, and these young men treat you as if you've just learned how to tie your own shoelaces. When I first met my boyfriend, he wanted to take me horseback riding, but wondered how I would get on the horse. He said, "Won't you need a ladder to get on the horse?" Needless to say, riding never became our favorite activity.

It's hard to be little in a world with so many people looking down at you. For once, I would like to sit on a bus and have my feet reach the floor without benefit of high heels. That's another problem with being short. You have to buy shoes so high that they make you walk like Frankenstein. The person that invented the platform shoe is really making a mint off us "petite people"! The result is back problems and constantly falling flat on your face.

It's not our fault that we were born a little undersized. People should accept us as we are, no matter what our size. Whenever I go to an R-rated movie with friends, I'm the one who is always questioned about age, even though I'm eighteen. Meanwhile, my seventeen-year-old friend, who is 5'7" tall, gets in with no questions asked.

Perhaps it wouldn't be so bad if all these conceptions about short people were true. (Why is it that tall people always think you are sitting down?) They should give us short people a chance. After all, "good things do come in small packages." „

Student Essay Study Questions

1. What is this student's thesis?
2. Are the examples selected to support her thesis appropriate and clear?
3. Are the examples vivid and concrete?
4. Are the examples presented in a logical way?
5. Who might comprise the audience of this essay?

Assignment: *For Comprehension and Practice*

Questions for Discussion

1. How can illustrative examples be used to clarify an ambiguous essay topic?
2. Why are generalizations usually boring, while specific examples are usually interesting?
3. How do you determine whether specific examples you have selected to support a main idea are appropriate to the audience you have envisioned?

4. What would be the effect on a reader of an essay full of generalizations, but not specific illustrations?

5. How does the use of appropriate illustrative examples in a composition indicate that you have carefully planned your essay?

Exercises

1. Write down three specific examples to illustrate each of the following thesis statements:

 a. Freshmen today are interested in preparing for careers; they are not in college merely for social reasons.

 b. Hockey can be a dangerous sport.

 c. Dogs are a nuisance.

 d. Football can help to create a cohesive feeling among students at a college or university.

 e. Candidates for political offices can benefit from lecturing to college audiences.

2. Write down a possible thesis which each of the following examples could illustrate:

 a. Milk, for example, provides the body with many nutrients.

 b. For instance, cats do not have to be walked every day.

 c. Small children, for example, rarely worry about insulting anyone.

 d. Unlike the baseball team, the football team is self-supporting.

 e. The English department, for example, requires that a major include eight four-credit courses.

 f. A college president, for example, rarely gets to know any students personally.

3. In a sentence or two, describe the audience that might appreciate each of the examples cited above.

Essay Topics

1. Write about growing up in the country (or city or suburbs), using examples from your own childhood. Be sure that the point you want to make is clear to the reader.

2. Write about a particular profession or occupation you might be interested in entering, using examples to illustrate your point.

3. Explain why you feel a particular form of student government is bad (or good), using specific examples to support your thesis.

4. Talk about your major and how you hope to follow through on it at your particular college or university. Provide illustrative examples.

5. Defend or criticize dormitory life, using specific examples.

6. Take a field trip to an interesting place near or on your campus, and compose an essay based on your observations there.

9

Definition

" . . . we have been using the word *hero* in the rather large and vague sense given to it in common usage. It is now necessary to make the term sufficiently precise to permit some check upon the position that will be subsequently developed. . . . We must rule out as irrelevant the conception of the hero as a morally worthy man, not because ethical judgments are illegitimate in history, but because so much of it has been made by the wicked. Only the making of history concerns us here, not whether it has been made well or disastrously.

The hero in history is the individual to whom we can justifiably attribute preponderant influence in determining an issue or even whose consequences would have been profoundly different if he had not acted as he did. (Sydney Hook, *The Hero in History*) "

Sydney Hook, the author of the above example, states his purpose in defining the term *hero*. That is, he intends to provide a more specific meaning of the word *hero* than is generally found in "common usage"; and in doing this, he is able to develop an argument based on the new definition. Hook first differentiates his definition of the term from other definitions by stating that a "hero" is not necessarily a "morally worthy" man. He then provides his own definition: a hero in history is one whose actions or personality affects the course of human events — for good or for evil.

In the remainder of his essay, Hook illustrates and exemplifies his definition and distinctions, and finally incorporates his definition into a discussion of the hero's place in history. Hook has a crucial point to make and he uses definition to make it forcefully. He urges that the future not be left to "heroes" such as those he describes; rather, he maintains that those interested in the preservation of democracy must take responsibility for the future.

What Is a Definition Essay?

Writers employ definition for several reasons. First, they may wish to explain a term that is unclear or ambiguous so that readers will understand precisely how that term is being used. Second, writers may want to impart information about a little-known concept. Third, they may want to define a term so that people will accept the writer's particular view of a subject. In short, writers define terms that are vague, unfamiliar, or used in a new way.

Vague or ambiguous terms • Words that mean different things to different people — words such as *love, democracy, romantic, existential, oppression, freedom* — need to be defined in order to avoid confusion. For instance, *romantic* has one meaning if it applies to an author writing in England during the early 19th century, and quite a different meaning if it refers to the atmosphere surrounding a candlelight dinner. Readers have to know what is meant by *romantic* if they are to understand the writer's use of the word in subsequent discussions.

Unfamiliar terms • Words that are likely to be entirely new to the reader must also be defined. Margaret Mead, in *Culture and Commitment, A Study of the Generation Gap,* uses definition to inform her readers about three kinds of cultures — *postfigurative, cofigurative,* and *prefigurative.* In three separate essays, she defines each of these terms by means of explanations, elaborations, and examples. Through the use of such definitions, she provides readers with a new way of understanding how different cultures develop and operate.

Familiar terms used in a new way • Any familiar term used in an unconventional way must likewise be defined. One student, for instance, wrote a paper on what it means to be an iconoclast. She began, "An iconoclast is a breaker of idols. I consider myself an iconoclast because I am a breaker of idols; however, for me the idols are not the graven images of the Bible, but the idols of materialism. I want to reject the concept that new cars, expensive homes, and color TV sets are to be worshipped and sought after. I want to be a person who does not live my life thinking that these items are to be esteemed. I know the iconoclasts do not necessarily have to erect new idols to take the place of the ones they've smashed, but I do want to set up a new ideal in which I can believe: the ideal of human understanding."

This student goes on to explain how she intends to "smash" the idols of materialism, and how she intends to pursue her own goals. Although her essay does not contain a "dictionary" definition of *iconoclasm,* the writer has effectively used a "subjective" definition in an attempt to convey her beliefs to the reader.

No matter what kind of term is being defined, a definition can serve as an introduction to a longer discussion in which an understanding of the term is crucial to overall comprehension. Or the definition can form the basis for an entire essay. Hook's definition of the hero is the basis of a longer discussion of the hero's place in history. The definition is necessary so that his readers know exactly what he means by the term. By contrast, Joan Didion, in an essay entitled "On Morality," has as her entire purpose the definition of the term *morality*. She defines it, categorizes it, and illustrates it. Her definition is not a stepping stone to a discussion of "morality" in another context, but an end in itself. In other words, she wishes her reader to understand all the connotations she sees in the term *morality* (see p. 213).

Many effective definition essays begin with a brief description of the general class to which the term belongs: "Eugenics is a *science* that . . ." and "Imagism refers to a *poetic movement* that . . .". After the class has been established, the term is then differentiated from others in its class by means of its unique characteristics: "Eugenics is a science that attempts to improve the biological character of a breed through deliberate methods adopted to that end"; and "Imagism refers to a poetic movement that is characterized by its emphasis on the presentation of a vivid picture, and on the use of common speech." In each of these cases, the writer would proceed to illustrate the definition by examples, finally concluding, perhaps, with an explanation of the overall significance of the original term defined. Philosopher Suzanne K. Langer follows this procedure in her book *Problems of Art* when she asks, "What, exactly, is a philosophical question?" She begins her definition with the statement "A philosophical question is always a demand for the *meaning* of what we are saying." She then differentiates her subject from other, similar subjects: "This makes it different from a scientific question, which is a question of fact. . . ." She proceeds to illustrate her general definition by suggesting possible philosophical questions and showing why they "demand" the meaning of what is being said. She then concludes with the major point of her essay — that asking such philosophical questions is "one of the most brilliant intellectual works of our time."

The most important thing to remember about definition essays is that the writer must either make a point about the definition or use the definition to make a point. The student who defined *iconoclasm* used her definition as a springboard for discussing her desire for improved understanding among people. This discussion is not merely tacked on at the end, but it follows logically and smoothly from the definition.

How to Write a Definition Essay

As we have noted, definition can be used as part of a longer essay, or it can function as a self-contained unit. The principles of effective definition can be applied to both types.

Whether your instructor assigns you a term to define, or you select your own, make sure its meaning is clear to you. Avoid terms that are so specialized or controversial that even knowledgeable people have trouble with them. Also avoid terms so elementary that you cannot say anything significant about them.

In addition to understanding the dictionary definitions of a given term, you should be aware of its connotations — that is, the emotional colorings and associations attached to it. If you depart from the standard meaning of the word, specifically state your new meaning, but be sure that your interpretation of a term is not so original that it distorts the standard meaning. For example, an accurate definition of *ecology* would treat the word in terms of the relationship of plant life and animal life to their environment. However, a definition which stated that the word represents "a recent movement to preserve wildlife and the beauty of nature" would be inaccurate. *Ecology* is not the same as *environmentalism* or *conservation.* In defining a term, you must work within the existing limit of the standard meaning, rather than inventing new meanings or passing along inaccurate ones.

Following is one method designed to produce a well-structured and coherent definition essay. In your first paragraph, clearly state the term you are going to define — ideally, in such a way as to catch your reader's attention. A student who wrote about the word *gourmand,* for instance, began, "I weigh 250 pounds. Some people call me 'fat,'" my friends call me 'hefty,' my mother calls me 'pleasantly overweight,' but I call myself a 'gourmand.'" The student then provided a clear, concise definition of the word: "According to the dictionary, a *gourmand* is one who enjoys eating." Then he went on to illustrate the word in terms of how it applied to him: "I enjoy good eating. In other words, I enjoy eating a lot of high quality food that is well-prepared."

In the next paragraph, differentiate between the term you are defining and other terms that are closely related. The aforementioned student began his second paragraph with "I am a *gourmand,* not a *gourmet.* Unlike a gourmet, I enjoy any kind of food — good or bad — and exercise no moderation in my eating habits." He then went on to elaborate on this distinction.

In subsequent paragraphs, you might provide specific examples to further illustrate your definition. In the essay just cited, the student gourmand described his escapade in an ice cream store, where he spent half his lunch hour selecting one quart of ice cream; he then told about his careful evaluation of a dinner menu in a Chinese restaurant and his hearty enjoyment of the meal. Finally, he described how his year-long search for the perfect pizza ended with his devouring a 14-inch pie with all the fixings — all by himself.

In the final paragraph of your essay, you could repeat the main point behind your definition. Or you might explicitly state your point, as the previous student did: "Many people look with disgust at gourmands. My doctor keeps telling me excess food causes excess weight, and excess weight causes illness. But I love being a gourmand. I am most happy and contented and pleased with the world after I have stuffed myself with good food. I and my fellow gourmands may be 'hefty,' or even 'fat,' but we are probably people least likely to start wars or destroy public property. Instead of taking out our aggressions on others, we soothe our ruffled psyches by lining our stomachs."

When preparing a definition, stick to the mode. Always keep in mind your definition and your elaboration of it. While you should use examples to illustrate your definition, do not allow the examples to overshadow it. One student, writing on totalitarianism, lost sight of her focus by getting carried away by her example. She wrote, "Totalitarianism is the state where a ruler or government refuses to allow opposition or complaint." Fair enough; but then she wrote, "My grandfather came from a totalitarian state. He lived in a country where he could not choose what he wanted to be. He hoped to become an actor, but the government wanted him to join the army; so one night, he found a rowboat and paddled across the straits separating him from freedom. Once he reached the shore, he knew there would be no turning back, so without a penny to his name, and only a few crusts of bread in his pockets, sustained by an ambition to succeed, he proceeded inland. . . ."

This essay turned out to be a warm and human story about a very appealing man, and was, in the final analysis, an excellent example of narrative. However, it does not function as a definition essay, even though the writer began in that mode. To fit the mode of definition, the entire essay must function as a definition. That is, it must expand the reader's knowledge of a term, concept, or philosophy.

In sum, be sure that your essay conveys a significant point, either implicitly or explicitly. The point may be a valid reinterpretation of a familiar term, or it may be a statement of opinion about some aspect of the term. Regardless of your method, however, remember that an essay that does not have something to say about the term becomes little more than an expanded dictionary entry.

Writing definition essays is a valuable way of learning to understand and delineate concepts. By exploring the range of meanings underlying a given term, by limiting the range to what is relevant to your purpose, and by discovering examples that pertain to the term, you are gaining valuable experience in precise and effective writing.

Have you . . .

- chosen to define a term that you fully understand?
- clearly stated what term you are going to define?
- defined the term clearly and simply?
- differentiated your term from other similar terms?
- illustrated your definition?
- made a point about your topic?
- stuck to your original purpose?

Student Essay: Tsuris

Ann Cantor

"I used the Yiddish word "Tsuris" the other day and my roommate — an Iowan — asked me what it meant. I started to explain it.

"Trouble," I said. But then I realized that this definition didn't exactly do the word justice. Yiddish terms just don't lend themselves to a one-word explanation. "Tsuris" isn't merely "trouble." It's the kind of trouble that comes on top of trouble. It's the kind of trouble my grandmother would have meant if my grandfather had broken his leg and couldn't go to work and as a result the man coming to fix the refrigerator couldn't do the repairs because he'd have to move the refrigerator and he couldn't do that because the couch was in front of it in the kitchen so my grandfather could eat soup lying down on the couch without spilling it on the rug in the living room which my grandmother had just had cleaned and the repairman was going to charge double because he had to come twice, and then my uncle Sydney called to say his daughter Tanya, the intellectual pride of the family, was quitting school to marry a circus roustabout. That's tsuris.

I used the word because I couldn't think of another word to adequately describe what I had just gone through. The computer print-out that serves as our college's student directory had just appeared and my name was listed as Ovxtann Cntos. All my class cards contained this name, too, and several of my professors had already politely asked me what nationality I was and how my name was pronounced. They had all looked puzzled, then amused, when I said "Ann." But the biggest hassle came when I tried to take a book out of the library *via* the library computer with my misspelled identification card. If there is one thing a computer will not tolerate, it is a mistake by another computer. It took me an hour to check out the book, and most of that time was spent trying to find a human who could explain my double-identity to the library computer. That's tsuris.

The word "tsuris," like most Yiddish words, connotes a gently humorous view of life. Tsuris is not just grief, but grief seen in perspective, grief seen with its ridiculous side up. The connotation of most Yiddish words reflects the Yiddish view of life: it is possible to laugh at trouble. The language reflects an optimistic view of life, despite any "tsuris" that may arise. **,,**

Student Essay Study Questions

1. How closely does this essay resemble the pattern of a definition essay as outlined in this chapter?
2. What effect is achieved by the deliberate use of a run-on sentence in the second paragraph? Explain.
3. Does the essay make a point? If so, what is it and how does the writer convey this point to the reader?
4. Does the writer veer from her main point in this essay? Explain.

Assignment: *For Comprehension and Practice*

Questions for Discussion

1. What different purposes might you have for defining terms in an essay and for writing a definition essay?

2. What subjects might be appropriate for a definition paper?

3. How do you think learning to define a term can help you in studying history? Biology? Math? Literature?

4. In writing a definition essay, why is it inappropriate merely to give a dictionary definition, then a few examples?

Exercises

1. Write a one- or two-sentence definition of each of the following terms:
- **a.** success
- **b.** failure
- **c.** gourmet
- **d.** propaganda
- **e.** cloning
- **f.** heroism

2. Prepare an outline for a definition paper on one of the terms you have defined in the previous exercise.

Essay Topic

Choose one of the following terms and define it in a 500-word essay. At the end of your paper, explain why you are (or are not) an adherent of the concept you have defined. (Look up any words that are unfamiliar to you.)
- **a.** liberalism
- **b.** conservatism
- **c.** romanticism
- **d.** realism
- **e.** materialism
- **f.** existentialism

10

Comparison and Contrast

" A simple but striking instance of the left-brain, right-brain dichotomy is the way it affects one's eye movements. The characteristic direction of these movements often yields interesting information about a person's attitude and ways of thinking. . . .

Some look quickly to the left [when asked a question]; others look first to the right. The direction of gaze of most persons is reasonably consistent (78 to 80 percent of the time in the same direction). The direction of this initial flickering shift, at the moment of pondering, permits one to classify people as "right-movers" or "left-movers."

What kinds of people glance to the left? Those who are more prone to focus on their internal subjective experiences. "Left-movers" are more readily hypnotizable, more likely to have been classical-humanistic majors in college, and are somewhat more likely to report clear visual imagery. It is significant to our understanding of creativity to note that the more readily hypnotizable person is one whose subjective experiences are rich, who accepts impulses from within, and who is capable of deep imaginative involvements.

Who are the right-movers? They tend to major in science or in "hard," quantitative subjects in college, and they are better at mathematical problems than in verbal ability. They are also quicker to identify concepts when the problem is based on words, as in this problem: "What adjective applies to the nouns — sky, ocean, eyes, jeans?"

What does the direction of a glance tell us about the way the brain functions? It implies a psychological bias — a pre-existing "set." One hemisphere is poised to act a fraction of a second before the other. In a sense, the connections of this half of the brain will take the lead in the person's psychophysiological functioning. (James H. Austin, "Eyes Left! Eyes Right!") "

This brief passage demonstrates, in miniature, how the mode of comparison and contrast works. Austin starts with a general statement about the two groups he is going to compare — those who are left-brain-oriented and those who are right-brain-oriented. He then describes each group, pointing out how the right- and the left-oriented differ. Finally, he draws a conclusion about how the brain functions.

The comparison-contrast mode is a logical choice for Austin. He is considering a subject that has two different — but comparable — parts. By discussing first one part and then the other, he is able to develop the point brought up in the thesis sentence, which is located in the first paragraph.

Not only does the entire passage elaborate Austin's thesis, but each paragraph after the first develops the topic sentence for that paragraph. These topic sentences also function as transitions, linking Austin's ideas to what has gone before, thereby giving the piece coherence and unity.

What Is a Comparison and Contrast Essay?

Writing an essay using comparison and contrast seems, at first, to be a self-evident procedure: one views two subjects and states how they are similar and how they are different. Not self-evident, however, is the fact that the writer must establish a reason for comparing the two subjects — a reason that must be presented logically and clearly to the reader. Comparison, which implies contrast as well, is a tool, a method of establishing a point. And the writer must fully understand the point he or she is going to establish before using that tool.

Writers can have many purposes for employing comparison and contrast. They can show that subjects thought to be unrelated can, in fact, share certain similarities. They can also show the reverse: that items thought to be similar are actually quite different.

For example, Norman Cousins has written an essay entitled "Two Cultures" to make a very specific point (see p. 240). He believes that if America and mankind wish to exist and progress, people will have to face up to and accept moral values and responsibilities. He illustrates this point by comparing and contrasting two groups — the scientists who take responsibility for the moral welfare of their fellow-beings and the scientists who do not. He writes:

" Some scientists, for example, see no question of conscience in lending themselves to the creation of devices for increasing the mastery of man by man. They recognize no issue of moral values in undertaking research for destructive mechanisms that no longer have anything to do with genuine national security but that can lead only to a holocaust of continental dimensions. They are neutral about breeding pathological organisms that condemn not only the living but generations yet to be born. In short, they have no difficulty in subordinating the human interest to the tribal interest.

These scientists justify their position by claiming that what they do in their laboratories is not harmful; what is harmful is what the politicians do with their work. These scientists do not accept responsibility for what others make of their theories or their discoveries. Science is pure; in devoting themselves to it, they see themselves as purists.

Other scientists, however, hold a contrasting view. They feel that they are in a better position to understand the implications and significance of what they are doing than the people who hire them to do it. Their colleagues may make proclamations in public about the morally antiseptic nature of science, but they feel that if they, the scientists, do not say openly what they know to be true, no one else will. They see no way of exempting themselves from the obligation to peer beyond the laboratory into the public arena. . . .

Just as the scientists have been divided by questions of moral priorities, so the humanists have been split by issues of human values. One group of writers and philosophers feels that questions of war and peace have become too technical and complex for them to handle. They feel that government leaders have far better sources of information and should not be subjected to pressures from the people.

Juxtaposed against them are the humanists who believe that in the making of moral judgments, the humblest citizen in the nation stands on even ground with a President. They feel, moreover, that there is something in the nature of government that makes it resistant to moral values. Men caught up in games of international realpolitik tend to delude themselves with the thought that "hard" matters of military policy are the only ones that count. History, however, is littered with the relics of civilizations whose leaders felt uncomfortable or scornful in the presence of moral questions. **,,**

The comparison-contrast format can also be used for the purpose of evaluation. A student may compare two things to show why she thinks one is "better" than another: for instance, two makes of automobiles, a sailboat vs a cabin cruiser, two courses of study. The student's point of view here is of particular importance. She should explain the situation or circumstances under which, for her, a certain thing would be preferable to another. For example, if she were comparing a pre-med program to a pre-law program, she would have to establish that pre-law was the "better" major at her school, given the absence of a biology department, and so on.

Once again, it should be emphasized that the essay must make a point. Humorist Russell Baker, in "Saturdays on Planet Libido," uses comparison and contrast to support his contention, for instance, that space movies in 1937 (during Baker's own childhood) were more intriguing than those shown today. The point of his essay is made in the conclusion, where he writes, "Even to the kiddies the prospect of sex is almost as interesting as a talking robot." Baker illustrates this contention by recalling typical scenes from one 1937-vintage science-fiction thriller, in which "the Emperor Zung leered at the helpless Velma. . . ." The author goes on to say, "We all knew too well what he wanted. He wanted to get married. This news invariably produced pandemonium in Velma's breast, signified by enchanting heavings of same, and all over the theater 11-year-olds briefly forgot to chew their Jujubes." In contrast to that earthy sort of space film, says Baker, is the modern kind in which the "evil powers that have [the heroine] at their mercy desire nothing but to pick her brain for secrets and then kill her."

Methods of Organization

There are two basic formats for the comparison-contrast essay. One is the block method, where the author first presents all the information about one of the subjects, and then all of the information about the other. In the second format, the author takes corresponding points of each subject and considers each of them separately, dealing first with point A of both subjects, then B, C, and so on. Either method is an effective means of comparing and contrasting. The outlines below will help illustrate the difference between these two approaches.

The Block Method
I.   Introduction: The purpose of this essay is to compare and contrast the pre-law program and the pre-med program at State University.
II. The pre-law program consists of
     A. Excellent history courses
     B. Excellent philosophy courses
     C. Excellent government courses
     D. Excellent advisement and a good acceptance rate for students applying to law school.
III. The pre-med program consists of
     A. Excellent biology courses
     B. Excellent chemistry courses
     C. Excellent math courses
     D. Poor advisement and poor acceptance rate for students applying to medical school.
IV. Conclusion: It can be seen that the pre-law and pre-med programs are similar in that they both consist of excellent courses. However, pre-law is a better program than pre-med in terms of advisement and student acceptance rate. Therefore, a student who has an aptitude in both areas has a better chance of succeeding in his or her career choice if he or she majors in pre-law.

The Point-by-Point Method
I.   Introduction: The purpose of this essay is to compare and contrast the pre-law program and the pre-med program at State University.
II. With regard to courses
     A. Pre-law courses are excellent
     B. Pre-med courses are excellent
III. With regard to advisement
     A. Pre-law advisement is excellent
     B. Pre-med advisement is poor

IV. With regard to the acceptance rate of students applying to professional schools
   A. Pre-law students do very well
   B. Pre-med students do very poorly
V. Conclusion: It can be seen that the pre-law and pre-med programs are similar in that they both consist of excellent courses, but pre-law is the better program than pre-med in terms of advisement and student acceptance rate. Therefore, a student who has an aptitude in both areas has a better chance of succeeding in his or her career choice if he or she majors in pre-law.

How to Write a Comparison and Contrast Essay

Whether your instructor provides a topic or you are asked to think one up yourself, it is important to determine whether there is a basis for the comparison. Make sure that the two things you are comparing have enough significant differences. Comparing a Mackintosh apple with a Red Delicious, for example, would probably result in a theme that listed a few differences of interest only to horticulturists. On the other hand, it would be absurd to discuss all the differences between an apple and a fire engine just because both are red and shiny.

To take a less farfetched example, suppose that your subject is a comparison of college dormitories and youth hostels in Europe. Even though there is only one basic similarity between the two — both provide communal sleeping quarters for young adults — that similarity could form the basis for an effective theme. In discussing the many differences between the two, you could mention the quality of the accommodations, the food (or lack of it), and the service. You could end with your strongest example: whether and in what ways the *hospitality* is the same or different in both.

By arranging your paper this way, you can effectively communicate your point to the reader: "Even though there are many differences between the two, a hostel has the same youthful spirit as a dormitory, a situation that provided me some of my most enjoyable moments in Europe." Thus you use a comparison of the two types of living arrangements to make a point about your trip. In addition, you are enlightening the reader about several aspects of European hostels.

After establishing the basis for your comparison-contrast and setting forth your purpose, you should decide on an organizational pattern. If you choose the block method, be sure that you discuss fully one subject, then the other. This pattern is an easy one to follow. If not handled carefully, however, it can result in an essay that is split down the middle. You must be sure that all the points mentioned in the discussion of subject A are brought up in the section devoted to subject B, and that you have a clear and smooth transition between the parts. Your thesis must also be clearly stated at the beginning so that the reader can see how the two parts are related.

One student wrote a successful essay by means of the block method in which he compared fraternity life with independent life:

" I live in a dorm this year. I get to study when I like, eat with whomever I like, and spend my spare time playing basketball if it suits my fancy. The rooms are small, but I can make my room as neat or as messy as I want, because I'm the only one who lives in it.

Last year I lived at the fraternity house. Every time I wanted to study, there was a meeting I had to attend. We had assigned seats at dinner, and whenever we had any free time we were expected to spend it fixing up the house. The worst part of all was the large bunk room we all slept in. It always looked like a zoo. "

A second student, writing on the same subject, failed to establish any connection between the two parts of her essay. She also shifted her point of view and so lost sight of her main point. She wrote,

" Sorority life has its advantages. My sorority plans parties every weekend and invites the members of various fraternities to attend. The men are very interested in the idea of a Sadie Hawkins party. I met one fraternity brother from Tau who asked me out after the party last week. I was late getting back and the house mother had the campus police out after me. It was wild.

Dorm life at my friend's school is very different. She told me they have fire drills twice a week and they all have to eat in the dining rooms in the dorm. The food in the dorms here is bad, too. (The sorority food isn't that fantastic either.) She concluded that I wouldn't like dormitory life at her school. "

If, on the other hand, you choose the "point-by-point" method of organization, you would discuss each aspect of both subjects as a unit, moving from point 1 of subjects A and B, to point 2, point 3, and so on. In an essay comparing your mother and father, for example, you might first discuss the basic personality of each (point 1), then their attitudes toward their children (point 2), their influences on your life (point 3), and so on. This pattern provides a back-and-forth effect that can add a touch of life and movement to your writing.

Another student, also writing on the subject of campus life, used the point-by-point method. Here is an excerpt from his essay:

" Campus living is always a matter of contrasts and choices, and one of the most important choices a sophomore must make is whether to join a fraternity or stay unaffiliated. You can choose to become a "brother" and be loyal to the group, or you can opt for the independent life. If you join a fraternity, you must be prepared for communal living: you eat together, party together, work together to keep up the appearance of the house. If, on the other hand, you maintain your individual identity, you might find yourself eating alone, sitting in the library on weekends, and spending your free time wishing you were part of a group. "

Which method should you use? It all depends on your subject. If you are comparing a relatively interesting subject with an uninteresting one, you might use the block pattern. You would discuss the duller subject first, then the more lively one. (In this kind of writing, it's usually wise to save the best until last.) The same pattern could also be used if you were comparing something the reader probably knows about with something he or she is unfamiliar with (dormitories versus youth hostels, for example). If, however, you wanted to make sharp contrasts between your items, then the point-by-point system would probably be your choice. Although this method may seem somewhat harder to handle than the block method, it usually yields more lively writing.

When comparing two items by either method, be sure to use vivid and specific examples. It's not enough to say that dormitories are clean and hostels are dirty, that the food in dorms is generally better than that in hostels, and so forth. A bare list like this would make for dull reading, indeed, and your essay would probably be much too brief. Rather, you must show by concrete example just how one facility compares with the other.

Because comparison-contrast is an essay mode of some complexity, make sure that you have made the point you set out to make. And keep in mind that your reader should clearly see this point. If you've stated your thesis at the beginning, you should probably repeat it (in different words) at the end. If you did not mention it at the start, you must let your reader know the significance of your comparison. Comparing your mother and father, for example, is simply not enough. There must be some purpose for doing so. The comparison-contrast must prove or illustrate a point: for example, how their different personalities affected the marriage; how their attitudes influenced their children; how, despite their different attitudes, they remained happily married.

Used effectively, the mode of comparison-contrast can contribute extensively to your impact as a writer.

Have you . . .

- established a purpose for your comparison and contrast essay?
- determined that comparison and contrast is a logical way to achieve this purpose?
- used one of the two basic organizational patterns?
- shown very specifically how your subjects are alike and unlike?
- illustrated your comparison-contrast with examples?
- discussed all the relevant aspects of comparison and contrast?
- proven the point you set out to make?

Student Essay: A Crush Vs. The Real Thing

Emilie Marcus

"When I was in 10th grade, I had a crush on our school's star basketball player. He didn't know I was alive, but I knew he was. As a cheerleader, I used to watch every basketball game, though I rarely knew what the score was. I had eyes only for a purple and white shirt with the number "32" on it, which spun around in mid-air, making spectacular interceptions, baskets, and fakes, and occasionally fouls, which I would bemoan louder than anyone. My best friend and I would slow down our walk home from school when we passed His house, hoping he'd be coming in or out; and we'd plan fainting fits — landing in his arms — in front of his classroom, though the only one who ever caught us was the Assistant Principal, who gave us late slips for our own history class, two floors away.

This state of affairs lasted several weeks until one basketball game when I was sitting on the sidelines watching him instead of the ball. The ball came out of nowhere and landed, full-force, right in my stomach. The crowd laughed. So did my hero. I was too embarrassed to cry out, being too much of an adolescent to want to look like a total fool, so I passed up my opportunity to faint or look injured in his presence. Somehow, as I nursed my bruised stomach and ego, the magic disappeared, and I looked at the basketball during the rest of the season.

Two years later — during my senior year — I met another basketball player, but this one wasn't a star. He loved to play, but had barely made the team. The coach put him in only when the score was so high that he couldn't spoil anything by missing a few baskets. Still, he was popular among his teammates because he was always cheerful and as good at losing as he was at winning. He did know I was alive. I was still cheering for the team, but now I stood well out of the way, and after the games we'd talk a good deal. I learned that he had taken up basketball to prove to himself that he could overcome the effects of an early-childhood case of shyness. His courage, his perseverance, and most of all, his optimism, made him special to me. I guess I fell in love — for real. With him I didn't have to plan fainting fits or hope he'd notice me walking home. He liked me for being just me.

During those basketball games, I watched the ball, knowing that he was watching it, too. And after each game was over, I knew he'd still be there. I wasn't ever hit in the stomach with a basketball again, but I knew that if I had been, he wouldn't have laughed. "

Student Essay Study Questions

1. Has the author followed the block method or the point-by-point method? Is this the most effective approach for her subject?
2. What point is the author trying to make?

3. Are her examples appropriate to her point?

4. What sort of audience would you imagine the author is addressing? Are the examples she uses appropriate to this audience?

5. Has the author demonstrated similarities as well as differences with regard to her subject?

Assignment: *For Comprehension and Practice*

Questions for Discussion

1. What are three reasons for which you might want to write a comparison-contrast essay?

2. Will the following pairs of topics make good subjects for a comparison-contrast essay? Why or why not?

    a. fascism and communism

    b. downhill skiing and cross-country skiing

    c. bowling and tennis

    d. cars and helicopters

    e. English and history as college subjects

    f. ballet and modern dance

    g. rock and classical music

    h. fraternity/sorority rushing and Phi Beta Kappa selection

    i. newspapers and magazines

What might be your purpose in comparing and contrasting each of the above pairs of subjects?

3. Which of the above topics would be more suitable to the block method of comparison-contrast, and which would be more suitable to the point-by-point method?

Exercises

1. Prepare a thesis statement for an essay comparing and contrasting three of the following sets of subjects:

    a. a BA and BS degree

    b. science writing and science-fiction writing

    c. trout fishing and deep-sea fishing

    d. motor boating and sailing

    e. sociology and anthropology

    f. living on-campus and living off-campus

2. What sets of subjects would you compare and contrast in an essay in support of each of the following thesis statements?

    a. One color stands out above all others in bringing to mind restful scenes.

    b. Educational innovations do not occur only in private schools.

c. Nearly every traveller prefers the country he or she resides in to the countries he or she has visited.
d. Going out for any varsity team is a humbling experience, but there are two teams which vie for the position of being the most humbling.
e. There is a standard of perfection for everything — even for a final exam; but most exams fall far short of this standard.

Essay Topics

Write an essay of approximately 500 words on one of the following topics:
1. Select two essays you have read this term which develop similar themes. Compare and contrast the means by which each author deals with this theme.
2. Select a character trait you admire and compare and contrast two people you know who demonstrate this trait.
3. Compare and contrast two activities with which you are familiar, and show how each contributes to the learning of good sportsmanship.
4. Make a statement about the value of having a pet, and support this statement through a comparison and contrast of two pets you or a friend have had.
5. Compare and contrast the government of the United States with that of some other government and make a concluding statement concerning the one you favor.

11

Classification and Division

" Talking evolved originally out of the increased need for the cooperative exchange of information. It grew out of the common and widespread animal phenomenon of nonverbal mood vocalization. From the typical, inborn mammalian repertoire of grunts and squeals there developed a more complex series of learnt sound signals. These vocal units and their combinations and recombinations became the basis of what we can call *information talking*. Unlike the more primitive nonverbal mood signals, this new method of communication enabled our ancestors to refer to objects in the environment and also to the past and the future as well as to the present. To this day, information talking has remained the most important form of vocal communication for our species. But, having evolved, it did not stop there. It acquired additional functions. One of these took the form of *mood talking*. Strictly speaking, this was unnecessary, because the nonverbal mood signals were not lost. We still can and do convey our emotional states by giving vent to ancient primate screams and grunts, but we augment these messages with verbal confirmation of our feelings. A yelp of pain is closely followed by a verbal signal that "I am hurt." A roar of anger is accompanied by the message "I am furious." Sometimes the nonverbal signal is not performed in its pure state but instead finds expression as a tone of voice. The words "I am hurt" are whined or screamed. The words "I am furious" are roared or bellowed. The tone of voice in such cases is so unmodified by learning and so close to the ancient nonverbal mammalian signaling system that even a dog can understand the message, let alone a foreigner from another race of our own species. The actual words used in such instances are almost superfluous. (Try snarling "good dog," or cooing "bad dog" at your pet, and you will see what I mean.) At its crudest and most intense level, mood talking is little more than a "spilling over" of verbalized sound signaling into an area of communication that is already taken care of. Its value lies in the increased possibilities it provides for more subtle and sensitive mood signaling.

A third form of verbalization is *exploratory talking*. This is talking for talking's sake, aesthetic talking, or, if you like, play talking. Just as that other form of information-transmission, picture-making, became used as a medium for aesthetic exploration, so did talking. The poet paralleled the painter. But it is the fourth type of verbalization that we are concerned with in this chapter, the kind that has aptly been described recently as *grooming talking*. This is the meaningless, polite chatter of social occasions, the "nice weather we are having" or "have you read any good books lately" form of talking. It is not concerned with the exchange of important ideas or information, nor does it reveal the true mood of the speaker, nor is it aesthetically pleasing. Its function is to reinforce the greeting smile and to maintain the social togetherness. It is our substitute for the social grooming of other primates. By providing us with a nonaggressive social preoccupa-tion, it enables us to expose ourselves communally to one another over comparatively long periods, in this way enabling valuable group bonds and friendships to grow and become strengthened. (Desmond Morris, "Four Kinds of Talking") **,,**

In "Four Kinds of Talking," Desmond Morris divides his subject into four categories and classifies the reasons for the four kinds of speech patterns that make up each of the four divisions. The unifying principle in his essay — the idea that holds the composition together, around which the four divisions evolve — is Morris's implication that all speech evolved for a reason. Morris's categories do not overlap. They are distinct from each other, although one may proceed logically from a previous one. For instance, "mood talking" and "information talking" are different categories, but the former is an offshoot of the latter.

Morris clearly intends to expand on his discussion of "grooming talking" in the remainder of the essay. In this case, his classification functions as an introduction to a longer piece.

What Is a Classification and Division Essay?

The mode of classification and division involves either the division of a group into single units or the classification of units into groups. In both cases, the purpose of an essay in this mode would be to demonstrate a unifying principle or to show a system at work.

The process of breaking down a topic into categories, and then explaining and exemplifying the categories, helps a writer to present his or her main ideas more clearly to a reader. Morris's "four kinds of talking," for instance, all contribute to an elaboration of his main idea.

A unifying principle is essential to the classification and division essay, in that it constitutes the *reason* why the items are being classified or the large group divided. The author must have a purpose for classifying and dividing items, and a specific point to make in the essay. For example, the point of Rollo May's essay, "Kinds of Power," is summed up in his conclusion:

" These five different kinds of power are obviously all present in the same person at different times. Many a businessman who exercises manipulative or competitive power at work takes on nutrient power when he comes home to his family. The question — and it is a moral one — is the proportion of each kind of power in the total spectrum of personality. No one can escape experiencing, in desire and in action, all five types of power, and only self-righteous rigidity leads one to claim that he is immune from any one of them. The goal for human development is to learn to use these different kinds of power in ways adequate to the given situation. **"**

Classification and division can be used as an essay pattern by itself, or it can function as part of a larger essay in which a certain point must be elaborated or a further explanation given. For example, in an essay called "On Being an English Major," one student used classification and division in the middle part of her essay to further explain a particular phase of her topic. That is, in order to fully explain her experience as an English major, she categorized her professors into groups that included "the scholars," "the popularizers of literature," "the sticklers for punctuation" and "the political activists."

Classification and division can also function as a general introduction to a specific topic, as we have seen in the opening sample. From several groups, an author might select one category to discuss primarily, as Desmond Morris indicates he is going to do in the opening essay.

In short, authors select the classification and division mode when they wish to be explicit in presenting to their readers all the aspects of a subject. It is often the interconnections between these various aspects that give a clue to the purpose and point of the essay.

How to Write a Classification and Division Essay

Classification and division is a process by which a group of seemingly disparate items are organized around a unifying principle. One student, for instance, categorized flowers into groups, after explaining the unifying principle underlying this process — that the flowers had been planted and placed by the curators of a museum according to a special plan. Such categorization is classification and division. Simply naming and describing each type of flower would be mere listing, not classification and division.

The student began her essay by introducing the topic and her system of classification. She wrote,

" I visited a cloister which had been turned into a medieval museum. It was spring and what struck me most were the huge numbers of flowers — all over the place. They seemed to be randomly scattered, filling up every place where there wasn't actually a wall or a building; but after I got over the initial impression, I began to see that the flowers fit into a pattern. They weren't at all randomly planted. **"**

She then proceeded to categorize the flowers and explain how each group added support to the main idea of her essay.

" The flowers were not just outside. Within the cloister were several gardens. One was an herb garden, but not just an ordinary herb garden. It was a literary herb garden. Each type of herb planted had appeared in literature. There, in one corner, was Ophelia's rosemary for remembrance, from Shakespeare's *Hamlet;* in another was Isabella's pot of basil from Boccaccio's *Decameron;* and so on. There was even a patch of Socrates' poison hemlock. There were many herbs of each type, and each had a reason for being in this garden.

In another part of the cloister were lilies — a whole internal garden of lilies. Light flowed in from a skylight and showed rows of pink lilies, white lilies, yellow lilies. Each row seemed more pious than the next, combining thoughts of religion, death, and everlasting life. The room smelt heavy with the odor of the lilies, and although the odor was beautiful, I was glad to get outside again. **"**

Finally, the categories are pulled together in her conclusion:

" Although the art and artifacts in this cloister were unusual and exquisite, the power of the museum lay in its landscaping. I came away with the feeling that I had truly experienced what it must have been like to live in a cloister. It may have been illusory, but the living flowers — and the way they were organized — gave me this feeling. **"**

Each group of flowers advances the main point of this student's essay. Had she simply listed, without a unifying principle, the kinds of flowers she saw at the museum —

tulips: red and yellow
roses: white
herbs: basil, rosemary, etc.
lilies: white, pink, yellow

the essay would not have succeeded.

In classification and division, the categories an author chooses must be distinct and non-overlapping. Each category can be broken down into smaller units, and these, in turn, can be further broken down. The divisional patterns are analogous to tree branches, with the categories becoming more and more sharply defined. And the author can stop the divisional process at any level. For example, the student essay previously cited is broken down into broad categories, the gardens. The gardens are then subdivided into smaller groups — the lilies, arranged according to color, and the herbs, grouped according to their literary reference.

In the process of dividing and classifying these groups of flowers, the writer is able to make her larger subject — the plan by which these flowers were arranged and their effect upon museum visitors — more comprehensible to the reader.

Have you . . .

- determined your reason for classifying and dividing your subject?
- established a unifying principle for your essay?
- divided and subdivided your broad subject into distinct categories or classified several objects into groups for the purpose of illustrating a specific point?
- illustrated each group or category with specific, detailed examples?
- come to a relevant conclusion based on your groups or categories?

Student Essay: I've Got My Eye on You

Fred Loney

" A major characteristic of a population in a large urban setting is the near total absence of eye contact between individuals. Although this hesitation to look into someone's eyes is not restricted to strangers on the streets (people who have lived in a city for many years often let their eyes wander when talking to close friends or business associates), it is most noticeable to an interested observer among people in public places.

Very often I make field trips as an Interested Observer into different areas to record how various kinds of people avoid eye contact. A listing and brief description of each type is humbly offered below.

1. *The Tough Guy (in the presence of even Tougher Guys)*

As the Tough Guy walks down an avenue, he approaches a few members of a Group of Tougher Guys sitting on the stoop of their building, beating rodents with their baseball bats. Rather than let his eyes accidentally meet those of the leader of this rabble, he quickly looks away and puts on the best "My Hands Are Registered as Deadly Weapons" expression he can muster. The Leader makes some snide comment at his expense in Tough Language. The Leader's cronies laugh, but the Tough Guy passes unmolested. In this situation, eye contact was avoided for the purpose of saving the Tough Guy from having to engage in a fight — and probably from having his head smashed in by a baseball bat.

2. *The Single Male and The Single Female*

There are many possibilities for eye-contact avoidance among males and females in big cities. First, there is the female walking down the street. If she is walking away from me, the male, there might be a possibility for some observation, but eye-contact avoidance is not necessary. If the female and the male are walking towards each other, however, the possibilities for eye-contact avoidance are greatly increased. Whether either avoids eye contact depends a great deal upon the relative appeal each presents to the other, and how late they are for class.

This kind of eye-contact avoidance can occur in a bar, a restaurant or some form of public transportation. It's the old "I see you pretending not to look at me. Do you see me pretending not to look at you?" game. Here, both stare at the other until one or the other looks up. They then shift their gaze to anything in the room except each other. This game always ends in a stalemate. Either one of them breaks the eye-contact avoidance and goes up to the other and starts a conversation, or they just sit it out till someone leaves.

3. *The Single Male and the Female with Boyfriend*

Here is a category replete with dangers, which I feel should be obvious to even the least experienced observer. Explanation is not needed since it is never a good idea even to try to avoid making prolonged eye contact with a girl who has her boyfriend in tow. Even the mildest of young men becomes a valiant crusader when he feels his girl is being avoided by some lecherous social scientist.

The list goes on and on. In fact there are as many examples as there are types of humans. Why are cities notorious for lack of eye contact between citizens? Why do I walk right past good friends on the street without even seeing them, when they not only see me but are doing their best to attract my attention? Why is it that every example is anything but news to city-dwellers? Fear and indifference. **,,**

Student Essay Study Questions

1. What is the point the student is trying to make?
2. Is it made directly or indirectly?
3. How does categorization of his subject help the author to make his point?
4. From what perspective is the author making his observations?
5. To whom is the writer addressing this essay?

Assignment: *For Comprehension and Practice*

Questions for Discussion

1. For what purposes would you use classification and division as an essay mode?
2. Is classification and division a more difficult mode to comprehend and execute than the previous modes discussed? Why?
3. How does classification and division differ from comparison and contrast?
4. How might the application of a system of classification and division simplify a confusing or overly broad subject? Provide examples.

Exercises

1. Classify the following items into logical groups and establish a unifying principle for doing so.
    a. members of a student radio station
    b. debaters
    c. football players
    d. fraternity members
    e. sorority members
    f. orchestra members
    g. baseball players
    h. student newspaper reporters
    i. hockey players
    j. dorm council members
    k. choir members
    l. tennis players
    m. honor society members
2. Divide the following general subjects into logical subdivisions, establishing a unifying principle for doing so.
    a. fish
    b. mammals
    c. birds

Essay Topics

Write a 500-word essay on one of the following questions:
1. Why do students join fraternities and sororities?
2. What kinds of activities comprise the extracurricular student life at your college or university?
3. What kinds of food are popular at the student cafeteria, and why?
4. How many ways are there to throw a party?
Make sure that your essay contains a unifying principle.

12

Process Analysis

"Your inquiry has set me thinking, but so far, my thought fails to materialize. I mean that, upon consideration, I am not sure that I have methods in composition. I do suppose I have — I suppose I must have — but they somehow refuse to take shape in my mind; their details refuse to separate and submit to classification and description; they remain a jumble — visible, like the fragments of glass when you look in at the wrong end of a kaleidoscope, but still a jumble. If I could turn the whole thing around and look in at the other end, why then the figures would flash into form out of chaos, and I shouldn't have any more trouble. But my head isn't right for that today, apparently. It might have been, maybe, if I had slept last night.

However, let us try guessing. Let us guess that whenever we read a sentence and like it, we unconsciously store it away in our model-chamber; and it goes with a myriad of its fellows to the building, brick by brick, of the eventual edifice which we call our style. And let us guess that whenever we run across other forms — bricks — whose color, or some other defect, offends us, we unconsciously reject these, and so one never finds them in our edifice.

Yes; one notices, for instance, that long, involved sentences confuse him, and that he is obliged to reread them to get the sense. Unconsciously, then, he rejects that brick. Unconsciously he accustoms himself to writing short sentences as a rule. At times he may indulge himself with a long one, but he will make sure that there are no folds in it, no vagueness, no parenthetical interruptions of its view as a whole; when he is done with it, it won't be a sea-serpent, with half its arches well under the water. It will be a torchlight procession.

Well, also he will notice in the course of time, as his reading goes on, that the difference between the almost right word and the right word is really a large matter — 'tis the difference between the lightning-bug and the lightning. After that, of course, that exceedingly important brick, the exact word — however, this is running into an essay, and I beg pardon. So I seemed to have arrived at this: doubtless I have methods, but they begot themselves, in which case I am only their proprietor, not their father. (Mark Twain, "The Art of Authorship") **,,**

Mark Twain, in discussing his methods of composition, humorously stumbles over his thoughts on the matter, but nonetheless comes up with a logical description of how he writes. What he has done in his comic way is *analyze* the *process* of writing.

Twain has chosen to use process analysis in this case because it is the best mode through which to answer an "inquiry" concerning his literary methods. Although part of his process is unconscious (or so he implies), enough concrete information is provided — about the storing away of sentences, for example — to allow the reader some understanding of precisely how he writes.

The major point of Twain's essay is made conclusively in the last paragraph; but note that it has been implied throughout the preceding paragraphs as well. In fact, Twain's frequent mention of his thesis functions in a transitional way, linking one paragraph to the next, and thus gives coherence to an otherwise complex essay.

What Is a Process Analysis Essay?

Process analysis could be described as an effort to see how something works by looking at its individual elements in logical order. There are several different kinds of process analysis: analysis of a physical process, whether it be natural, scientific, or mechanical; analysis of a historical process, political or social; and analysis of an individual activity.

The analysis of a natural or scientific process involves a step-by-step explanation of what is happening. Photographer and conservationist Eliot Porter, writing in a Sierra Club publication, *The Place No One Knew*, describes the process of the physical destruction of Glen Canyon on the Colorado River. In the name of "progress," a dam was erected to harness the power of the Colorado River and "develop" the area. Porter traces the effects such tampering with nature has had upon Glen Canyon and outlines the process of physical decay. He writes,

" The waters impounded by this plug of artificial stone spread back through Glen Canyon for one hundred eighty-six miles in all, inundating the sparkling river, swallowing its luminous cliffs and tapestried walls, and extinguishing far into the long, dim, distant future everything that gave it life. As the waters creep into the side canyons, enveloping one by one their mirroring pools, drowning their bright flowers, backing up their clear, sweet springs with stale flood water, a fine opaque silt settles over all, covering rocks and trees alike with a gray slimy ooze. Darkness pervades the canyons. Death and the thickening, umbrageous gloom take over where life and shimmering light were the glory of the river. **,,**

Other scientific and natural systems can be explained in this way as well. For instance, biologist Norman H. Horowitz, in an article in *Scientific American,* uses process analysis to describe in chronological order and in great detail the experiments conducted by the Viking landers to search for life on Mars and to collect data about the chemistry of the surface of the planet (see p. 000).

Process analysis can also be used to explain the workings of a mechanical object. A student recently wrote a process analysis essay in which she described the manner in which a tramway works. She used as the model for her analysis the Swiss-built tram which traverses the East River in New York City, travelling between Manhattan and Roosevelt Island. She described one part after another, explaining how each contributes to the functioning of the whole, and concluded with a description of the tram's first voyage over the water.

The analysis of a historical, sociological, or political process likewise involves a very careful and detailed description, so that the reader can understand the chronology and logic of the subject. For example, astronomer Gerald S. Hawkins and John B. White trace a historical process in "The People," a chapter of their book *Stonehenge Decoded.* The authors detail the history, in chronological order, of the various groups of early peoples who are thought to have lived on Salisbury Plain in what is now England, and who are believed to have contributed to the building of the enormous monument Stonehenge — the meaning of which is the central question of the book.

The process of individual activities can also be analyzed. We shall see, a bit later on, how an individual activity can be presented as the subject of a process analysis essay.

The purpose of writing a process analysis is to inform others of how a system or procedure works by means of a step-by-step, logical explanation, and to teach others how to understand or duplicate that process by means of a clearly explained model.

In those essays analyzing scientific, natural, or physical procedures, the purpose, as a rule, would be to enlighten others about a specialized area, to provide the readers a greater understanding of the world around them. In an essay analyzing a mechanical object, for instance, the writer might encourage the readers to understand the machine more fully so that they may duplicate it, repair it, or simply appreciate its complexity.

In detailing a historical or sociological process, the writer's purpose would be to help the reader achieve some insight into past or different societies, with the hope, perhaps, of eliciting a fuller comprehension of the present society in which we live.

Finally, by providing an explanation of an individual activity, the writer might encourage the reader to undertake such an activity, or to avoid it.

Whatever the subject matter, however, it is important to make a *point.* Why describe the process? In what way is the process important? The answers to such questions should be implicitly contained in the introduction of the essay, the conclusion, or both.

The point Eliot Porter is making in his process analysis of the physical decay of

Glen Canyon is an ecological one. He feels strongly that the damming up of rivers for political and economic reasons is wrong, and he hopes that, by showing how this "progress" has destroyed a place of natural beauty, he can prevent such events from recurring.

The point of Norman Horowitz's process analysis is to deny, on the basis of evidence collected by the Viking landers, that life exists on Mars. And the student who wrote about the New York City tramway concluded, as the point of her essay, that mass transit could be aesthetically pleasing as well as efficient.

In sum, process analysis is a useful tool for providing information to your reader, of convincing him or her of the validity, relevance, and interest of a particular field of study, of establishing a model for others to follow, or of mounting a crusade for or against a certain project. Any of these purposes can be fulfilled, so long as the *point* of the essay is clearly communicated.

How to Write a Process Analysis Essay

When you are assigned a process analysis essay, you are being asked to choose and discuss an activity, a procedure, or a system which you know something about and in which you are interested. If you are not given a specific subject on which to write, select one that genuinely intrigues you. Choose a topic about which you have something intelligent to say, something that will not seem self-evident or superficial when you start to describe it. Suppose, for instance, that you recently learned to ski, and that you found your experiences in doing so both interesting and amusing. That would be a fertile foundation on which to base an essay. One student recently submitted a process analysis essay on just this subject, as we shall see.

When you have selected your general subject — skiing, in this case — you must narrow it down to a topic specific enough to be appropriate for process analysis. The student who wrote on skiing focused her essay on the way a rope tow works, and titled her essay, "How to Cope with the Rope Tow." She began,

" The first thing you want to do if you really intend to race down that hill amidst swirling clouds of snow is to come to grips with the rope tow. It goes by you mighty fast, so you have to keep your wits about you. "

When writing your process analysis, it is essential to fully understand your subject. If you are fuzzy in your own mind about just how an object or procedure works, you cannot possibly convey any useful or clear information to your reader.

When you are convinced that you understand the process you are about to describe, continue your analysis by breaking down the process into its component steps, and then arrange the steps in sequence. Often you will find that each step must be subdivided into even smaller units if it is to be adequately explained. (In this kind of essay it is especially important to outline your ideas so that you do not leave out any steps.)

Each step or substep must be explained, in turn, as concisely and concretely as possible — preferably in separate paragraphs. If it is consistent with your purpose that you provide examples for each step, make certain that the examples are relevant to and illustrative of the steps you are trying to present. The student writing about the rope tow, for instance, continues,

" You sidestep your way up what seems to be a tremendous incline. If you're a real novice, this procedure may take some time and may result in much practice in getting up, dusting off, and putting your poles back on.

When you finally reach the bottom of the tow, the land levels off, deceptively, and you get the opportunity to stand still long enough to tuck your poles efficiently under your arm and grab the wire as it speeds by. (Be sure you have on your ski gloves or you'll find yourself with permanent grooves in your palms.) Right before you grab the wire, you place your skis in the ruts on the ground provided for this purpose. (It is absolutely necessary to point your skis *up* the hill.) "

The writer then goes on to describe the ride up as well as her disembarkment at the top of the hill. She concludes by saying,

" If you do all this, you get a chance to view the panoramas and vistas visible only to budding Olympic champions who have attained the pinnacle of the mountain. It is at about this point that you suddenly realize, with a nauseating quaver, that you won't be able to take the tow down again, but will have to rely on gravity and your own ability. "

It is particularly important in process analysis to assess the comprehension level of your intended audience with regard to the topic at hand. If you are writing a technical report on photosynthesis, you should know whether or not your audience has had an introductory biology course; and if you are describing the joys and dangers of snorkeling, it would be helpful to know whether or not the members of your audience have spent a summer collecting data with the marine biologist and oceanographer Jacques Cousteau. Conversely, you would not want to describe a clock to a watchmaker (or, for that matter, to someone who has not yet learned to tell time), and you would probably not wish to sound off on the perils of the rope tow to the captain of your college's ski team, unless you were hoping to lure that individual into reminiscences about his or her own first attempts at the sport. The writer excerpted here clearly wrote her essay for other novice skiers like herself.

Depending on your audience and your purpose, you can write your process analysis in the third person ("It works this way . . .") or the second person ("The first thing you want to do . . .").

The writer of the essay just cited has presented a logical account of her experiences on the rope tow. Her process analysis is complete in that it contains every step in the procedure. You cannot expect your reader to follow, however, if you leave out steps in your description of the process or rearrange the steps in an illogical order.

For example, if the above student had neglected to inform the reader to place his or her skis in the snow grooves meant for this purpose, the order of the steps in the process would have been noticeably disrupted. The uninitiated reader would not really understand how one got from the level ground to a position of mobility heading up the hill. And anyone attempting to follow these directions would undoubtedly have become hopelessly entangled in the rope!

Have you . . .

- chosen an interesting subject appropriate for process analysis?
- narrowed your topic down to a discussion of how some procedure, system, or object works?
- fully thought through the process in question so that you understand it completely?
- explained and illustrated each step? Are the steps logically ordered?
- omitted any steps in the process?
- made a point?

Student Essay: Candle-Making — More Than a Hobby

Ellen Cooke

"I have always loved candles. Candle-shops are among my favorite stores. The smell of faintly perfumed wax — bayberry, pine, country spice — bring back memories of a New England childhood when such smells were a part of every holiday and family get-together. The last time I visited a candle-shop, I noticed a small corner display with a sign "Do It Yourself." I suddenly envisioned a small corner of my room with country spice, pine, and bayberry wafting memories of long-gone bonfires and kitchen aromas around me, and I knew I had to become an amateur candle-maker.

The candle-making equipment, when I finally managed to carry it all home, consisted of an antique 6-candle 12″ mold, several one-pound bags of prescented and precolored wax mixed with stearic acid (to achieve dripless candles), wicking, a double-boiler and an electric burner, a wooden spoon, a candy thermometer, several antique hatpins, a bottle of rubber cement thinner, a tinfoil pan, a kitchen knife, a bottle-cleaning brush, a hunk of beeswax in a small pan, a potholder, and a book entitled *Candle-Making Made Easy*.

With this collection of materials, and a lot of paper towels — just in case — I started the process: First I threaded the mold with three strands of 24″-long wicking. I did this by carefully pushing the ends of the wicking through the holes of the mold at the end where the tips of the candles would be.

I then set one pound of the wax in the top of the double boiler (I selected pink country spice for the first batch) and placed it on the electric burner set to "Hi." While the wax was melting, I finished preparing the mold. I turned the mold over again and broke off a piece of beeswax (which I had previously warmed) and sealed the area around the tip of the candle with the beeswax to prevent leakage. I turned the mold over a final time and placed it upright (tips of candles pointing down) in a tinfoil pan. Now it was ready for pouring the wax.

The next step was to stir the wax until it was all melted and until it registered 190° on the candy thermometer. When it was ready, I poured it slowly into the mold, being careful not to make any bubbles, until it filled the mold.

The hardest part was waiting a couple of hours until the wax hardened. About an hour after I poured the wax, I cut the wicking between the tips of the candles to relieve the pressure in the mold.

When the mold was cool and the wax hardened, I cut the wax at the top of the mold into squares with a knife, and gently lifted each plug out of the mold. I held my breath as the candles emerged, attached to the plugs. They were beautiful! Smooth and perfect. I cut off the plugs and polished the candles with rubber cement thinner, and the candles were finished.

I left the candles alone for several weeks; I couldn't bear to burn them. When I finally did burn them, the room filled with the smell of country spice, and I knew that my new hobby would be mine for a long time. **,,**

Student Essay Study Questions

1. Does the writer include every detail of the process she is describing? Do you think you could follow her steps and come out with a batch of candles?
2. Are all the steps easy to follow? Are the pieces of equipment all described adequately? (In other words, has the author adequately defined her terms?)
3. Are the steps described in their proper sequence? Would you rearrange any? (Which ones and why?)
4. Does this process analysis hold your interest? Why? Would you make any changes in this essay?
5. What point is the author trying to make in this essay?

Assignment: *For Comprehension and Practice*

Questions for Discussion

1. How would you define process analysis?
2. What kinds of process analysis are there?
3. What general areas lend themselves to process analysis?

4. Why is a consideration of your prospective audience of particular importance in process analysis?
5. What various purposes might you have for writing each kind of process analysis?
6. How do you begin to organize your thoughts in preparation for a process analysis?

Exercises

Outline one of the following processes in preparation for writing a process analysis paper:
1. how a final exam is administered
2. how semester registration takes place
3. how to drive an automobile
4. how to bait a fishing hook
5. how a lake freezes

Essay Topics

Choose one of the following topics. The length of your essay should be approximately 500 words. Be sure that your purpose is clear in your own mind, and remember to assess your prospective audience.
1. Trace the process involved in the founding and organizing of a club or activity at your college or university.
2. Discuss, in a step-by-step fashion, the way a specific scientific experiment is performed. (Be sure to include your reason for doing the experiment.)
3. Trace the steps involved in preparing an assignment for one of your courses.
4. In a step-by-step analysis, describe the training of a team in a specific sport.

13

Cause and Effect

" When we moved to California, I must confess, my enthusiasm for a life in the sun was considerably dampened by the knowledge that this would also include a life on the freeway. For the first few months my husband dutifully packed me into the family car and drove me to work, a distance of around 20 miles. Then he would turn around and drive home again. Each evening he would pick me up at work and take me home. Now, my husband is a very nice guy. And the drive took him through some very pretty scenery. But he had a business of his own to deal with, and the extra 80 miles and hour and a half a day did nothing to improve his temperament. And I was beginning to feel my oats. It began with a solo marketing excursion, and then that marvelous feeling of freedom that comes with sliding behind the wheel began to take hold, and before I knew it, I was looking for a car of my own. (Deanna Sclar, *Auto Repair for Dummies*) "

Deanna Sclar is setting up a cause and effect relationship in this paragraph. She cites all the reasons that contribute to her dissatisfaction with not owning her own car, and then notes the consequence of this dissatisfaction — namely, her decision to purchase her own automobile (see p. 000).

Sclar is very clear and direct in making the link between cause and effect. Because she avoids any extraneous details, her purpose is readily apparent to the reader — that is, to demonstrate her initial feelings about being part of a freeway-oriented society, the changes in attitude that occurred, and the reasons for which these changes took place.

Sclar conveys her purpose by showing cause and effect. The point she ultimately, though subtly, makes by means of this causal analysis is that freedom and independence can be gained by driving a car of one's own.

What Is a Cause and Effect Essay?

In an essay demonstrating cause and effect, the writer describes a situation and explains to the reader the reasons why it has come about. The cause and effect essay is based on a formula: "Because X has taken place, Y has occurred." That is, the writer is interested in demonstrating why Y has taken place and what the results are. Note, too, that there may be one or more causes resulting in one or more effects.

In short, the function of cause and effect as a rhetorical mode is to enlighten the reader about the factors contributing to or resulting from a particular happening — as, for instance, writer Anne Roiphe has done in "Confessions of a Female Chauvinist Sow" (see p. 277). The *effect* Roiphe demonstrates is her self-destructive attitude of feminine superiority. The *causes* of this sexist egotism are her experiences as a child and as a young woman, during which time she was subtly taught that men are less intelligent, less honorable, and less reliable than women. In relating the effects of these causes, Roiphe is showing why something occurred.

Noted essayist George Orwell also demonstrates the results of an occurrence in his essay, "Politics and the English Language." His contention is that poor writing results from poor thinking, and that this dangerous causal relation will continue far into the future if unchecked. (See the complete essay on p. 285.)

A cause and effect essay, as with all essays, must make a point. In this case, the point is demonstrated by means of causal analysis. Roiphe's essay is a good example. By showing the reasons for her attitude of superiority over men, and by exemplifying this superiority, Roiphe demonstrates the destructiveness of such an attitude on her relationships with men, her husband in particular. She further implies that she is not alone in having this attitude. The point she ultimately makes in this cause and effect essay is that through her experiences she has learned that men and women are equal — not superior — to one another.

A cause and effect essay can be used as an explanatory device to show what has happened and why, or it can be used prophetically to show what could happen and why. Roiphe uses causal analysis to explain her actions as a "female chauvinist sow" and to explain the mistakes she made as an adult. Another writer, Martin Koughan, in "Goodbye, San Francisco," explains what *could* happen to San Francisco in the event of another major earthquake on the San Andreas fault (see p. 274).

Cause and effect may be shown in two ways: (1) *Indirectly, through description or narration* (Sclar embeds cause and effect in a description of her new life in California; and Roiphe implies a causal relationship in a series of short narratives) or (2) *Directly, through a statement of reason and result, as in X causes Y, or Y results from X* (Koughan informs the reader outright what the reasons are for an inevitable earthquake in San Francisco; and Orwell directly shows the results of poor thinking).

Cause and effect essays are aimed at readers who want an explanation — either actual or hypothetical — of events or situations. Thus the cause and effect mode can be considered an informative type of presentation.

How to Write a Cause and Effect Essay

When assigned a cause and effect essay, it is likely that you will want to sort out your goals concerning the topic before you begin to write about it. For example, if you were asked to write a causal analysis about citizens' band radios, you would have to decide among the various ways you might approach the subject. You could, for instance, show what *caused* the popularity of CB radios, or you could demonstrate the *effect* of the popularity of CB radios (such as an increase or decrease in highway safety). In short, you would have to know clearly in advance precisely the point you wish to make regarding your subject.

Suppose that you decided to focus your essay on the causes of the increasing popularity of CB radios. You might suggest in your first paragraph that your purpose in writing about CBs is to show how certain songs and films about CB radio operators (cause) have resulted in an increased interest in operating CB radios (effect). In this case, you would probably state your thesis early in the essay so that the reader understands immediately what you think is the significance of the cause and effect relationship you are describing. If your thesis is that popular music and culture have a profound effect on our lifestyles, the cause and effect relationship noted earlier could be used to support this contention.

After establishing your basic outline (thesis stated, cause and effect relationship presented in support of your thesis), you can fill in the details. As your "cause," it would be advisable to refer specifically to the "good buddy" songs and TV and film characters that have glorified the community aspect of life on the highways and encouraged other people to participate in the rituals of this activity. You would show the "effect" part of the formula by pointing to and describing the widespread advertisements for CB equipment and by citing the large number of CB radios in operation.

The final paragraph of your causal analysis should show that the cause and effect relationship you depict supports the thesis of your essay. In this case, you might conclude that the popularization of CB radios, once primarily the interest of truckers and an occasional ham operator, does, indeed, show that America is a society readily influenced by its popular culture.

In writing a causal analysis, be sure to stick to your subject. Do not wander from your main outline or add extraneous details. In other words, remember that you are dealing with cause and effect, and not some other rhetorical mode. Your CB radio essay, for example, should not be bogged down in a description of the technical aspects of radios, or in a consideration of the sorts of people who use them. Rather, it should concentrate on the cause and effect relationship you have set up.

When writing a cause and effect essay, it is particularly important not only to assess your goals, but to identify your audience as well. The complexity of your explanation will be determined by the degree to which your audience knows your subject. For example, in writing about CB radios, you might liven up your essay with a sprinkling of CB jargon, but the amount of jargon you use should vary according to the familiarity of your audience with such language. Similarly, the level of technicality with which you describe the influence of CB radios should be appropriate to your audience.

Your cause and effect essay can either be formal or informal in style, depending upon your subject, purpose, and audience. For example, your essay on CB radios would probably be informal, since you would be dealing with popular culture; an essay on the causes of drug addiction would be more serious, however, and would therefore be more appropriately written in a formal tone.

Have you . . .

- established a purpose for considering cause and effect?
- arrived at a thesis?
- assessed your audience?
- illustrated both "cause" and "effect"?
- come to a conclusion?
- kept to the mode?
- maintained an appropriate rhetorical style?

Student Essay: Hunting

Andrew Nitze

"Friends and acquaintances have been outraged by the fact that I hunt. They ask me why I find it necessary to indulge myself with such a "superficial reassurance of my masculinity" at the expense of an animal's life. They tell me that beyond the senseless killing of the animal, the detrimental effects of hunting may be seen in the hunter. More often than not, I am unable to dispel their misconceptions. Their assumption is that the hunter approaches hunting as a sport. Hunting, for me, is not a sport, but a ritual.

It is a ritual through which I attempt to overcome many of the internal barriers urban existence has placed between me and nature.

The gratification of the confrontation and kill is not simply that of successfully utilizing one's reflexes and hunting skills. I have never conceived of hunting as a test. This is the most prominent misconception about hunting. I do not hunt as a means of reaffirming the superiority of my intelligence and acquired skills over the instincts of an animal. If that were so, hunting would only serve to further man's alienation from animals and the natural environment. By hunting I do not wish to dominate nature, but rather to revel in it. To hunt and kill an animal reaffirms the fact that man is not removed from nature, but dependent upon it for his very sustenance.

One cannot hope to attain a relationship with an animal simply through passive observation or by viewing films or looking at photographs. In stalking an animal one must seek to understand it. This understanding leads to a form of respect. Thus, ironically, by stalking and killing an animal one may most fully experience its life. Perhaps the most profound description of this relationship between the hunter and his prey may be found in the cave drawings of primitive man. The "Wounded Bison," done in approximately 15,000 B.C., is a cave painting in Altamira, Spain. It depicts the dying animal collapsed on the ground, its legs no longer capable of supporting its body's weight. Its head is lowered in defense. The most striking features of the painting are the power and dignity of the creature in its final agony. This painting, like many others found in the caves of Southern France and Spain, was created during the rituals preceding and following the hunt. From such a painting one can see that the hunter is the least indifferent to the beauty of the life he will sacrifice. By killing it he has experienced it as an individual, not passively but with enormous intensity. Only from a feeling of this intensity could works such as the "Wounded Bison" be conceived.

Today, food, our most basic need taken from nature, is presented for most of us in the supermarket as a mass-produced and seldom organic substance. We have removed ourselves from a relationship of respect for the food we require in order to survive and, by extension, for the earth that produced it. It is commonly recognized, in our current appreciation of the lost lifestyle of the North American Indian and his cultural values, that it is possible to hunt and kill an animal while being extremely sensitive to its spirit and, indeed, while feeling a real kinship to it.

Obviously, there are contrasting attitudes and practices concerning reverence for the life of animals — for example, the Buddhists' abstinence from the consumption of any meat, sometimes even of eggs, milk, or milk products. In this country, however, the evaluation that must be made would compare the meat-eating hunter's attitude with that of the meat-eater who causes the slaughter of animals by buying in the supermarket the pink, plastic-encased pork, lamb, or beef that can evoke no emotion, no self-examination, because it retains so little to remind one of the wonder of life in the animal from whom such flesh was taken. Thus, I can defend my hunting by stating that it is a result of my desire to recover some of the closeness of nature that existence in an urban or suburban environment does not provide. ,,

Student Essay Study Questions

1. What is the "cause" in this essay? What is the "effect"?
2. The cause and effect relationship in this essay is subtly presented. Is this student's subtlety an asset to his writing? Why or why not?
3. Do you find the student's reasoning on this subject convincing?
4. Do you think the student sounds defensive in his first paragraph? Does his tone change throughout the essay?

Assignment: *For Comprehension and Practice*

Questions for Discussion

1. What is the function of a cause and effect essay?
2. Can you think of any specific uses for a cause and effect essay?
3. How does causal analysis differ from process analysis?
4. What is the difference between the subject of a cause and effect essay and its thesis?
5. Why is audience assessment so important in preparing a cause and effect essay?
6. What tone is the most appropriate for a cause and effect essay?

Exercises

Outline a cause and effect paper on one of the following subjects. Be sure to arrive at a thesis.
1. getting poor grades
2. making friends
3. choosing a major
4. getting a summer job
5. learning to use the library

Essay Topics

Write a 500-word essay showing cause and effect on one of the following topics:
1. television viewing
2. being a varsity athlete
3. being an organization or club leader
4. being a good scholar
5. smoking
6. raising cats
Be sure to make a point in your essay.

14

Persuasion

" The ability to write with sense and style has decreased and ought to be improved. There are an infinite number of cultural reasons for this form of educational illiteracy but policy decisions are more responsible than the effects of television or whatever social abstraction can be invoked. It ought to be fairly plain that the decline in writing ability coincides with the kind and amount of teaching that governs it.

In the last decade the following have occurred: Composition courses have been dropped at universities and never undertaken in high schools. Senior faculty, anxious to assert their professionalism, have refused to teach writing. Few institutions have kept a required course in freshman writing. Professors of English or literature have been replaced by technicians whose work is not connected directly to classroom performance: the "remedial" class is a kind of Sunday school on campus.

For a number of reasons, none of them good, the amount of writing demanded in the classroom has dropped sharply. The theory behind this is that students can't do it (that is, they are minorities, disadvantaged, culturally inexperienced); won't do it (they remember the 1960's); and shouldn't have to do it (that is, faculty are somewhat nervous about course enrollment). It's not much of a theory.

The facts, I think, are that students like and respect hard work; that minorities are especially anxious to do well and resent educational ploys; and, most important of all, that the teaching of writing is the single most important aspect of higher education. (Ronald Berman, "On Writing Good") "

In this selection, which appeared as part of a newspaper editorial, Ronald Berman states a point of view and sets out to prove it through persuasive argument. His thesis is that student ability to write has declined and should be improved through the effective teaching of composition in college.

Berman concisely and clearly informs the reader of his purpose in the thesis statement. In the excerpt cited and throughout the piece, he provides background and examples to illustrate the state of illiteracy as it currently exists. He also offers explicit suggestions as to why and how the situation should be improved.

Berman never veers from his purpose, and his arguments are persuasive because they appear valid and well-reasoned. In addition, Berman wisely addresses those opposed to his point of view — those who would argue that remedial writing is more useful than teaching composition, those who fear that it isn't popular with students, those who refuse to believe that a decline in the quality of instruction in composition has resulted in a decline in literacy, as well as those who seek to blame other factors such as television — and, by anticipating their objections to his argument, effectively refutes their position.

Berman argues with force. But it is his prerogative to twist an arm or two in presenting a persuasive argument — as long as he doesn't twist the facts.

What Is a Persuasion Essay?

Writers use persuasive argument to convince an audience of the validity of their position on a certain issue. The intent is to persuade the audience to believe and think as the writer does. The method used is logical reasoning.

The subject of a persuasive argument is often a controversial one, in that the writer may be attempting to convince people to reverse their opinions. A writer may, for example, try to persuade the members of one political party to support the candidate of another.

At other times, however, an essayist might simply be attempting to rouse people out of their lethargy or ignorance. One writer, for instance, found herself in the position of trying to educate her college community to the health dangers of adopting wild campus squirrels as pets. Such a position would be controversial only if the audience has a vested interest in squirrels.

On still other occasions, a writer may be arguing a position similar to that held by the reader, but in a way which is new to the reader. In this case, the writer is not dealing with a controversial issue, but audience opposition might be encountered just the same. For example, the writer and the audience might agree on the issue of banning hockey at the local ice rink during times of general skating, but each might hold a different opinion on how to enforce the regulation.

One place you are certain to find persuasive essays is the editorial section of the newspaper, whether in student or professional publications. Articles of this nature take a position on an issue (generally a controversial one) in an attempt to convince readers to believe in and support a certain point of view.

Persuasive argument is perhaps the most formal and structured of the essay modes thus far discussed. Indeed, a logical structure is required in convincing an audience of a particular point of view. There are two basic ways of reasoning in an persuasive essay, both equally effective but differing in structure. One method involves deductive logic, and the other, inductive logic.

Deductive Logic

Deductive logic is a pattern of reasoning that uses supposed truths as evidence to arrive at — or "infer" — other truths.

The form of such deductive arguments is called the *syllogism,* which is comprised of two statements of supposed truths (known as "premises") and a conclusion. Deductive argumentation is "conclusive" argumentation, which means that the writer bases his or her conclusions only on the evidence presented in the premises. That is, the conclusion follows from the premises. If the premises are true, then the conclusion will be true as well; in fact, if the premises are true, then it will be impossible for the conclusion not to be true. Let us consider an example of deductive logic:

Premise 1: **All students taking composition at the local community college are freshmen.**

Premise 2: **Freshmen at the college have to declare their major field of study.**

Conclusion: **Therefore, all students taking composition at the local community college have to declare their major field of study.**

The conclusion of this argument is based solely on the premises, or evidence, stated. The argument is therefore conclusive. No evidence unstated in the premises is needed to arrive at the conclusion. Moreover, the statements in the syllogism are arranged in such a way that the conclusion *follows* from the premises.

Now, let us look at a syllogism in which the conclusion does not follow from the premises:

Premise 1: **All students taking work-study programs at the local community college are sophomores.**

Premise 2: **All students at the college have to file for graduation.**

Conclusion: **Therefore, all students filing for graduation have to take work-study programs.**

This argument is not a conclusive deductive argument because the conclusion does *not* follow from the premises.

Deductive arguments can be used in writing to prove a point to the reader. A conclusive argument is difficult to contradict. The reader can readily be convinced to share the writer's point of view — unless, of course, the reader has evidence that the premises themselves are untrue. In order to be effective, a deductive argument must have a valid conclusion as well as premises based on truth. Certainly a valid, honest argument is more effective — and meaningful — than a valid but dishonest one. The purposes of a writer would seldom justify basing his or her arguments on known falsehoods.

Hypothetical Syllogism • Another form of deductive argument is a conditional type called "hypothetical syllogism." In this kind of argument, containing a series of "if . . . then" statements, the last part (or "consequent") of each premise is identical to the first part (or "antecedent") of the following premise. This kind of reasoning is used to arrive at a conclusion based on a series of interdependent conditional statements.

Following is an example of a hypothetical syllogism:

Premise 1:   **If I am to be a pre-med student, I have to take four science courses next term.**
Premise 2:   **If I have to take four science courses next term, I shall not have time for a music course this term.**
Conclusion: **Therefore, if I take a music course this term, I can't be pre-med.**

Note that each statement is dependent on the previous statement and that the second half of the first statement ("I have to take four science courses next term") is the same as the first half of the second statement.

A student might employ a hypothetical syllogism in an essay to demonstrate the consequences of a series of related occurrences.

Indirect Argument • A third process by which a conclusion can be derived is the use of indirect argument, another form of deductive logic. In this type of inference, the writer presents a number of propositions. One of these is true, but which one is not known. The correct proposition is proven true by the process of elimination, which demonstrates that all but one proposition can be seen to be false. For example, the writer might prove, by elimination, that a certain suspect in a mystery case is responsible for a murder. Every other suspect can be eliminated from suspicion if provided with alibis. The criminal would be known by the lack of a demonstrable alibi.

Inductive Logic

A good argument need not be deductive. There are other forms of inference as well. Inductive reasoning, or the scientific method, enables the writer to make generalizations based on or verified by accurate data gleaned from observing the actual world. In induction, that is, the writer uses observed information, or data, about specific objects in order to make generalizations about the other members of that class of objects.

For example, it can be asserted that a lighted match applied to propane gas will start a fire. This generalization can be made on the basis of the many documented instances in which a lighted match has ignited propane gas; furthermore, there have been no documented cases in which propane gas, when lit by a match, has not resulted in fire. Although we could never document *every* case of combustion resulting from the combination of lighted matches and propane, we have sufficient evidence to assume that the rule will always hold true. We can therefore make a generalization about the whole class of propane gas based on a sampling of just part of that class. This is an example of induction.

Arguing from Probabilities   •   In inductive reasoning, if the generalization made is thought always to occur, as in the case of the lighted match and propane gas, that generalization is called a "uniform generalization." When there is a *good chance,* but it is not *absolutely certain,* that a generalization will be true, it is called a "statistical generalization." Statistical generalizations are made on the basis of mathematical probability — in other words, on the assumption that, based on past statistical evidence, there is a good chance that a certain event will occur under certain circumstances. For example, each time a coin is flipped, there is a 50 percent chance that heads will turn up. Based on this statistic, it is probable that if we flipped a coin 100 times, heads would come up 50 times. However, it is not *absolutely* certain that this will be true; therefore, in this case we can speak only in terms of probabilities.

To be effective, an argument based on probabilities must build on accurate and self-evident or well-documented evidence.

Arguing from Analogies   •   Another method of inductive reasoning is argument by analogy. With this type of logic, the writer demonstrates the validity or falsity of a position by comparing it to a similar position stated in an identical manner. For example, in demonstrating the foolishness of the argument that "We should ban taverns because some people get drunk," the writer might argue that this statement is analogous to the statement "We should ban marriage because some people commit adultery." It is clear that the second statement is foolish; given that, the arguer can demonstrate by analogy that the first statement is foolish also.

Argument by analogy can be a useful tool in rhetoric. But it is important for the writer to assess the nature of his or her audience when drawing analogies, in order to be able to determine precisely what will make a suitable analogy.

How to Write a Persuasion Essay

The expansion of a logical formula into an essay is merely a matter of filling out your underlying plan — that is, adding definitions, explanations, background, and illustrative examples to a pattern of reasoning.

Using Deduction in an Essay

Suppose you wanted to prove that the drama club has an adverse effect on student life at your school, and you wanted to arrive at this conclusion deductively. You would first set up your deductive syllogism, stating your premises and arriving at your conclusion. You might argue as follows:

Premise 1: **The quality of student life at Jenkins College depends on student happiness and academic work.**
Premise 2: **The drama club adversely affects student happiness and academic work.**
Conclusion: **Therefore, the drama club has an adverse affect on the quality of student life at Jenkins College.**

Your argument would be valid and conclusive, because your conclusion follows your premises; that is, it is based exclusively on the premises you include in the argument.

This format can be used as the basis for your essay. Your syllogism includes a definition of terms and a thesis. All that remains is to write an introductory paragraph that states the objectives of your paper and to provide examples that illustrate the premises of your argument. In this case, such examples might be that (1) the drama club makes many students unhappy because it selects only a few student members from the many who try out and (2) that it is injurious to academic performance because it forces its members to rehearse for many hours, thereby taking essential time away from studies.

Using Induction in an Essay

When you want to present an argument based on observations you have made, you would do so by expanding the inductive process into an essay. You would begin by presenting your observations and then drawing conclusions about them. An inductive essay about the benefits of television-watching might, for instance, be based on the following outline:

A. TV has enriched my mind in the field of sociology. Over the past few years I've watched many documentaries (provide specific examples here) and gained information about other people and countries.
B. TV has enriched my mind in the field of science. I've seen moon landings and programs on biology and chemistry (provide examples).
C. TV has introduced me to literature. I've heard book reviews and seen dramatizations (provide examples) that have inspired me to read more.

These observations would constitute your data. Your conclusion would follow:

It can be seen, in view of the examples cited, that television has enriched my mind and is thus beneficial.

Avoiding Fallacies

When presenting an argument in an essay, it is often an easy matter to commit an error in logic or a mistake in reasoning. Such errors are called "fallacies." Fallacies can impede the presentation of your ideas by muddling up the process by which you are presenting them; and they can provide your opponents, those whom you are trying to convince to accept your arguments, with reasons for disbelieving your conclusions. An awareness of certain logical fallacies could aid you in keeping your reasoning logical and conclusive. Following are several logical fallacies that commonly occur in student essays.

Formal Fallacies •   A formal fallacy is an error in the *form* of the argument. One such formal fallacy is the "fallacy of composition," which erroneously suggests that what is true of any part of a thing is also true of the whole. One student, for example, wrote an irate essay in which he claimed that every history professor he had studied under taught Marxism. On this shaky basis, he concluded that the college was a Marxist institution. You can clearly see that this conclusion is absurd: the college as a whole cannot be said to have the same political attitude as that held by its individual members.

The reverse situation, the "fallacy of division," is another common error of reasoning to be aware of. In this case, what is true of the whole is erroneously assumed to be true for each component of the whole. For example, another student wrote that her school was committed to expanding its enrollment. She concluded that each department was expanding in like manner and erroneously reasoned that her own major department would soon be overcrowded and impersonal. Her conclusion is not necessarily true. What is true of the whole is not necessarily true of its parts.

Still another formal fallacy you should avoid is the "fallacy of irrelevant conclusion." This is committed when you arrive at a conclusion that you have not adequately demonstrated. For example, one may try to argue that college is not necessary and in the process wind up demonstrating that college is expensive. This conclusion may be true, but it is not what the writer intended to prove. Thus, a fallacy has been committed.

You should also avoid the "non sequitur," a formal fallacy occasionally known as "argumentative leap." In this case, a writer leaves out a step or premise in the reasoning process. Note, for example, the following argument:

I can fit a history course into my schedule. I will thus have enough credits to minor in history.

The second statement may at first seem reasonable until one realizes that the writer has not stated the premise "if I take the history course." The writer has thus committed an argumentative leap.

Linguistic Fallacy • The second general category of logical errors consists of "linguistic fallacies." This kind of error results from using words imprecisely. If, by accident, a word with two meanings is not adequately defined, the writer is said to have committed a "fallacy of ambiguity." If the writer does this purposely, he or she is engaging in the "fallacy of equivocation." If two people inadvertently intend the same word to mean two different things, and each thinks the other means what he or she does, then they are committing a "fallacy of verbal issue."

In all of these cases, adequate definition of terms would suffice to eliminate the problem.

Material Fallacies • The third general category of logical errors consists of "material fallacies." These are the result of premises that are mistakenly assumed to be true.

The first type of material fallacy to avoid is the "slogan," which is used to convey a false impression about a subject. Slogans rarely encompass the whole truth about a subject, but they delude the reader into thinking that they can. Slogans are often used as propaganda, as George Orwell demonstrates in *Animal Farm:* The slogan "All animals are equal" seems to make sense to the animals initially, but it does not convey the entire truth, which is that "All animals are equal, but some animals are more equal than others." Slogans are so pat, so cut and dried that they often defy discussion or contradiction — but on closer analysis they can usually be seen as a form of false reasoning.

Another material fallacy to steer clear of is "arguing in a circle." In this case, the conclusion is used as a premise, such that the arguer assumes the truth of the conclusion in formulating his or her premises. For example, this statement:

We know John is a sophomore because he takes chemistry, and we know he's taking chemistry because he's a sophomore.

is a case of circular reasoning. The steps in this process are not arranged as a syllogism (All sophomores take chemistry; John is a sophomore; therefore, John is taking chemistry.), but are ordered in such a way that the truth of the conclusion is dependent on the truth of the premises, and the premises depend for their truth on the validity of the conclusion. Circular arguing does not advance the knowledge of the reader or the position of the arguer. Rather, this fallacy depends for its success on the length and complexity of the argument. If the argument involves many parts, the reader or listener might neglect to notice that the writer or arguer has merely *assumed* the truth of his or her premises.

A third material fallacy to beware of occurs when an arguer uses a position held by his or her opponent to turn the argument against this opponent. Such an argument, called "ad hominem" ("to the man"), attempts to "prove" a point by personally attacking the opponent rather than the argument or position held by that person.

Although it is possible to get away with certain logical fallacies or errors in reasoning, particularly if you have an unsophisticated audience, your powers of clear thinking and intellectual honesty would suffer in the process. Writing clearly, concisely, and to the point involves being accurate, logical, consistent, and honest in presenting your ideas. And if you keep the aforementioned logical fallacies in mind, you will be better able to avoid errors in reasoning when planning and writing your essays.

Emotional Appeals

Arguments that draw irrelevant conclusions or present irrelevant evidence, though they may at times appear effective because they depend for their success on the fears, prejudices, and inclinations of the opposition, are really emotional appeals — and should be avoided. For example, if a builder is arguing against the construction of a building on a particular site on the grounds that the site is a marsh and the planned building would surely sink, and he attempts to enlist the support of the neighbors by reminding them that the construction will bring dirt and noise and disruption to their neighborhood, he is committing an emotional appeal. That is, he is arguing an irrelevant point (his real point being that the construction to which he has committed himself will result in financial loss to himself) which he hopes will appeal to the fears of his opponents, rather than relying on the force of his logic.

Emotionally charged arguments that appeal to hearts, rather than heads, do not constitute good writing or thinking. Try to avoid the use of emotional appeal in convincing your readers to accept your point of view. A reasoned argument in favor of child care, for example, is really more persuasive than a description of the cute five-year-olds who populate day-care centers. Moreover, a clear and logical presentation of your ideas on this matter will better bear the weight of close reader analysis.

Winning Your Point

Persuasive argumentation requires tact as well as logical skill to be effective. It is important that you avoid offending your audience by the tone of your essay. If you are condescending in your approach, you will alienate your audience — even if your logic is impeccable. Your readers, if alienated, will search hard for counter-arguments to your ideas, and they will ferret out flaws in your reasoning process. Remember that very few issues have a clear-cut right and wrong. If you recognize and admit the fact that the controversial issue you are discussing has two sides, and that both positions have their merits, your opponents are more likely to be attentive to your views. It is easier to win converts through respect for their point of view than it is to shame them into relinquishing a belief. Thus your best position relative to your reader, particularly if you are facing opposition, is to get him or her to regard your ideas with an open mind. The only way to achieve this end is to avoid an offensive tone.

In writing a persuasive essay, it is important, perhaps more so than in any other essay mode, to assess your readers and gauge their reactions. Know which side of an issue the members of your audience are likely to uphold, and learn how firmly entrenched they are in their position. Be aware of potential opposition and hostility so you can counter it, and have knowledge of those in agreement with your views so you can build on their support. Then prepare your essay accordingly.

If you are facing an uphill battle in getting your ideas across to your reader, begin your essay by avowing an awareness of the position of your opponents. Consider (and, when possible, refute) counterarguments in your essay, and when you cannot refute a point, concede it; admit that there is some strength in your opponent's stand. Then come back with a strong assertion and defense of your own point of view.

When preparing a persuasive argument, you have a purpose: you are attempting to convince your reader to adopt your point of view on an issue. Try to convey your purpose and the reasoning behind it to your audience; but remember, too, that audience "conversions" do not always happen at once. If you have convinced your opposition even to read and consider your viewpoint, you are well on your way to winning your point.

Have you . . .

- chosen a position to defend and stated it clearly?
- chosen to present your position in a deductive or inductive argument?
- provided background information?
- defined your terms?
- provided support for your statements?
- made your point clearly and firmly?
- refuted the opposition?
- checked for fallacies?
- avoided blatant emotional appeals?
- avoided an offensive tone?
- assessed your audience?

Student Essay: The Case for an All-Volunteer Army

Ann Weber

"I read an article the other day that frightened me. It was a report of a new clamor to reinstitute the draft during peace time. The armed forces, the article reasoned, were being filled with unqualified personnel and our level of defensive readiness could be maintained only if the draft were reinstituted. I would like to state the case for those opposed to a comeback of the draft.

First, the draft represents an interruption in the lives of young people setting out on careers. Even if drafting is deferred until after college, many people would find an interruption of their graduate education or of a new job to be an insurmountable loss. The time spent in the armed forces could never be made up, and the draftee would lose the edge in the competition for jobs and career advancements.

This brings me to the second point. Drafting unwilling personnel into the armed forces does not make them good soldiers. A dissatisfied, unhappy soldier cannot perform as effectively as someone who wants to be there, even if he were initially judged more "qualified."

It has been argued that the present system of no-draft has resulted in an army exclusively made up of the poor and undereducated. If this is true, it is up to the government to increase incentives — more interesting army jobs, higher salaries, better fringe benefits, better housing, greater educational benefits — in order to attract a wider variety of people to enlist. It is not an answer to force "qualified" people to serve who do not want to be there and for whom such enforced service will mean professional hardship and unhappiness.

It has also been said that all people should spend some time serving their country. I agree with this statement, but I do not agree that "service" necessarily means *armed* service. In a democratic society, "service" can take the form of whatever an individual does best. Professors of history, carpenters, musicians, and bankers strengthen the fabric of our country; all can "serve" better without guns.

I am not a pacifist, and I do believe in the armed services; but I do not agree that everyone ought to be forced to serve during peace time any more than I think that all people ought to be forced to teach school simply because I believe in the value of education.

The draft is backward-looking and does not make any sense. Those that are proposing it have obviously not thought out the issue from the point of view of the potential draftee. **,,**

Student Essay Study Questions

1. Is this an inductive or a deductive argument? Explain.
2. Does this essay progress in an orderly and systematic fashion?
3. Does the author provide adequate examples to support the points she is making?
4. Does she refute potential objections?
5. Does the writer use analogy in her reasoning? Explain.
6. Is there an instance in which the writer is arguing *ad hominem?* Where?
7. Are you convinced by the author to accept her point of view? Explain.

Assignment: *For Comprehension and Practice*

Questions for Discussion

1. Discuss whether each position stated below could be more effectively defended through inductive or deductive reasoning and why:

    a. College students are more liberal than their parents.

    b. College athletics help to alleviate the pressures on students.

    c. The high density of pre-med and pre-law students in college today is the result of an uncertain economic climate in the country as a whole.

    d. Competitive intercollegiate sports, debating, and other activities prepare students for competition in life.

2. What is the difference between deductive and inductive reasoning?

3. Why should you attempt to imagine the kind of audience you will have when preparing a persuasive argument?

4. Why is it important to control the tone of your persuasive argument?

5. What are some of the most common logical flaws in persuasive arguments?

Exercises

1. Outline an essay based on one of the following topics, first as an inductive argument, and then as a deductive argument:

    a. Can the honor system really work?

    b. Are college students really preparing for life?

    c. Is religion an important aspect of campus life?

2. Exchange outlines with another member of the class and check each other's outline for errors in reasoning and lack of clarity.

Essay Topics

Write a 500-word persuasion essay on one of the following subjects:

1. Support or refute the statement "College is not for everyone."

2. Argue for (or against) the notion that the federal government should support private as well as public higher education.

3. State whether you feel that sororities and fraternities are beneficial or detrimental to campus life. Defend your position.

4. Support or attack the contention that children today watch too much television.

15

The Research Paper

Often the material you include in your assigned essays comes from your own experience and observations. At other times, however, you will be asked to pursue a subject that cannot be written "off the top of your head." In addition to "research," this topic may call for more work in organization and careful presentation than other papers have required. For this reason, research papers are often assigned at the end of a writing course, after basic skills and tools of rhetoric have been mastered.

Finding a Suitable Topic

In many composition courses, students are given a series of topics from which they must select one to write about. These topics are often of a general nature (solar energy, ecology, religious cults, etc.), so the student is expected to focus on a specific question pertaining to that topic.

In other situations, students are expected to come up with original subjects for a research paper. In this case, they must select their own general topics and then focus their attention on proving an aspect of the topic or on answering a question pertaining to it.

Whichever is your case, you must consider several factors in the process of deciding your subject: you should choose a topic (from the instructor's suggestions or from your own general reading and knowledge) about which you have some familiarity or in which you have some interest. If you are interested in solar energy, have followed recent news items about it in periodicals, and would like to learn even more about it, this is a good subject to select. Conversely, if you have no interest whatsoever in the subject of religious cults and have never cared to read articles about them, you are unlikely to muster up the enthusiasm necessary to do a good job on a research paper devoted to that topic.

You should also consider the manageability of the topic you are in the process of selecting. (This is particularly important when choosing an original topic, since in most cases instructors have considered manageability when assigning topics.) Is the subject one that can be discussed in some depth in 10 to 15 pages? For that matter, can discussion of the topic be *limited* to 10 or 15 pages? Is the subject one you understand? Are the books and articles you will be reading on this subject likely to be comprehensible to you?

A topic such as "Man's Quest for Food" is obviously too broad to be interesting or manageable in 10 to 15 pages; you could barely scratch the surface of such a topic. Where, for instance, would you begin your research? Under "food" in the dictionary? Nor would it be entirely feasible to explore "pins" as the subject of a research paper. Although one could imagine a discussion of the origin and history of the pin, it does not seem a subject likely to intrigue many writers — or readers. It might also be difficult to determine the significance of such a limited topic.

Another factor to consider in arriving at a general subject, or deciding which of several assigned general topics to select, is the availability of information about the topic. What resources are at hand concerning the subject? A subject such as "endangered species," for instance, can easily be researched in current periodicals and other books. But you would be foolish to try to obtain information on a subject about which little was written — the early manuscripts of Caxton, for example — or about which it would take a special trip, say to England to discover relevant information.

When you select a broad subject (or when you have found one on your own) ask yourself what is important about that subject, why you feel it is interesting and what point do you want to make about it. Then formulate the answer in a sentence and let that sentence be your thesis. At this stage, your thesis is a preliminary one that should guide your research. During the actual writing of the paper, your thesis can be refined.

For instance, suppose you had selected as your topic the autobiographical influences on Ernest Hemingway's novels. (This alone is not a thesis but a general subject.) First, you might do some reading in the area and ask yourself what you want to say about the influences of Hemingway's life on his art. You might then read a biography of Ernest Hemingway, noting those instances in which he used his actual experiences as the basis for certain fictional pieces. Next, as a means of further narrowing your topic, you might explore the fact that Catherine Barkley, the heroine of *A Farewell to Arms,* is based in part on a real-life nurse (Agnes von Kurowsky, who attended Hemingway in Italy when he was wounded during World War I) and in part on Hemingway's first two wives (Hadley, with whom he lived in Paris in the 1920's, and Pauline). By guiding your research in this way, you will have successfully focused your paper on a manageable subject.

Research and Early Planning

Once you have narrowed your topic to a manageable size and focused your ideas about the subject, you are ready to begin your research.

How to Begin and Where to Go

The place to start is your college library. First, look up your subject in the card catalogue. (Remember, *every* book is listed in the card catalogue three times — according to title, author, and subject. Allow yourself the maximum opportunity to find a given book by using all three categories when possible.) Notice that there are brief notes indicating what the book is about in each of these card catalogue entries. Try, by means of this information, to amass a group of books with a wide variety of approaches to your subject. For example, if you were doing the Hemingway/Catherine paper, you would want to read, in addition to the novel you are dealing with *(A Farewell to Arms),* whatever nonfiction prose Hemingway wrote concerning the time he spent in Paris *(A Moveable Feast),* as well as critical biographies containing information on the Milan and Paris experiences (such as Carlos Baker's *Ernest Hemingway: A Life Story*), other critical biographies on the people Hemingway knew in Paris (such as Andrew Turnbull's *Scott Fitzgerald*), and, finally, other writers' accounts of the same time period (such as Gertrude Stein's *The Autobiography of Alice B. Toklas*). You will find some of these books by looking up "Ernest Hemingway" in the subject card catalogue; others will turn up in the bibliographies of your first batch of books. If you need help, consult your librarian; it is his or her job to direct you to the resources you need.

Another source of information and material is your library's reference room. Here, you will find encyclopedias (such as *Britannica* and *Americana*), biographical dictionaries (such as *Who's Who*), abstracts (such as *Biological Abstracts, Dissertation Abstracts, Dissertation Abstracts International,* and *Comprehensive Dissertation Index*), and bibliographies and indexes (such as *Bibliographic Index, Biography Index,* the *MLA Bibliography, The Subject Guide to Books in Print,* and *The Readers' Guide to Periodical Literature*) — all of which contain information that may be pertinent to your subject. Some of these resources list books, others list periodicals, and some list both. Certain of these indexes, bibliographies, and abstracts are constantly growing, with a new volume published yearly or even monthly, whereas others are fairly complete but have supplements which appear from time to time containing entries for recently published articles and books. Ask your librarian to direct you to the indexes and bibliographies relevant to your topic. For instance, for your Hemingway paper you might want to check the *MLA Bibliography* or the *Readers' Guide to Periodical Literature* to find current and historical articles about *A Farewell to Arms* and its relation to Hemingway's life. You might even want to find out what the critics said about this novel at the time it was published, in 1929.

When you have compiled a good-sized bibliography from the card catalogue, abstracts, and indexes in your library, seek out the book-length works in the stacks and locate the articles in the periodical room. This last resource contains journals, magazines, and newspapers — both current and historic — as well as certain periodicals on microfilm.

Taking Notes

As you read through the material you've collected and take notes on it, make sure that your information is well organized and clear. Some students like to keep 3 x 5 note cards for each source they consult, putting the bibliographic information (title, author, publisher, location of publisher, date of publication, page number, and library call number) on one side of a card, and the notes themselves on the other. Other students prefer using a page in a notebook for each source they consult, placing the bibliographic information at the top of the page and the notes themselves underneath. Whichever method you choose, be sure to keep in mind the following list of hints:

1. Keep an accurate record of the bibliographic information. Include the library call number (if it's a library book), and the location in which you found the book (the college library, the town library, your friend's book shelf) so you can retrieve it easily if you have to.
2. Whenever you make a notation from the book, jot down the page number on which the information appeared. (One way to keep a consistent and accurate record is to write the page number at the top of the card or page, before anything else.)
3. Make sure you include quotation marks if your note is taken exactly as it appears in the source. If you are paraphrasing, you do not need quotation marks. In either case, if you use the information in your paper, you will need to footnote the source.

Your note cards will look something like this:

Bibliography card

```
Baker, Carlos. Ernest Hemingway: A Life Story.  New York:
     Bantam, 1969. (978 pages)
In college library, call number:  _____
General remarks:  This is a critical biography. Baker con-
nects the events in Hemingway's life with events in his
works.
```

Note cards

```
Baker, p. 65
Hemingway, wounded in a hospital in Milan, meets the
beautiful nurse Agnes von Kurowsky, 1918.
```

Baker, p. 69
"By the middle of August, Ernest was 'wildly' in love with
Agnes von Kurowsky."
" 'You had a great case on her,' Elsie another nurse re-
called later on."

Baker, p. 76
". . . the unconsummated love affair with Agnes had matured
him faster than anything else had done."
"The memory of the north of Italy in 1918 would stay with
him all the rest of his life."

```
Baker, p. 245
Baker writes, in regard to the composing of A Farewell to
Arms, "Hemingway had been trying for years to make fictional
use of his war experiences of 1918." Baker further notes
that "the story [of Hemingway's love affair with Agnes] was
aching to be told."
```

The advantage of using 3 x 5 cards is that when you organize your essay, you can reorder your notes to correspond to the sections of your paper.

Compiling Information

Making a Plan • The organization of your material is a key task in writing a term paper. Begin by formulating your thesis — the point you are trying to make — into a sentence or group of sentences, and state it in an introductory paragraph. For instance, if you were writing on the Hemingway subject cited earlier, your introductory paragraph might look something like this:

```
Ernest Hemingway published A Farewell to Arms in 1929. Ac-
cording to his biographer, Carlos Baker, the book met with
enormous critical success. One of the most interesting as-
pects of the book is that it contains several important
episodes which parallel documented events in Hemingway's
own life, and as such, can be considered "a novel with a
heavy autobiographical content."[1]
```

Another, perhaps more common, way of beginning your research paper is to introduce the subject in your first paragraph and state the thesis in your second paragraph. For example, you could precede the paragraph just cited with a quotation, which could serve to introduce your topic:

```
It has been written of Ernest Hemingway that ". . .the
memory of the north of Italy in 1918 would stay with him
all the rest of his life"; and so it did.  A Farewell to
Arms is a testament to its staying power.
```

Next, think of the various stages of development needed to prove this thesis and state these steps as the main points of your research paper plan. Each step should be incorporated as a topic sentence into the successive sections of your paper. For example, the steps involved in proving your thesis about *A Farewell to Arms* might be the following:

1. The basis of the book is Ernest Hemingway's war experiences as a soldier in Italy in 1918.
2. Ernest is pictured in the book as Lt. Frederick Henry. The main female character of the book, Catherine Barkley, is modeled on an early girlfriend of Hemingway's, Agnes von Kurowsky. Other characters in the book, such as Dr. Rinaldi, are likewise modeled on people Hemingway knew at this time.
3. The Catherine/Henry episodes also bear resemblances to experiences Hemingway had with his first wife, Hadley, and his second wife, Pauline.

Using Research Material • Think of the information you have gathered in your research as *evidence* to support the steps you are using to prove your main point. Thus, to prove Step 1 (that the basis of the book is Hemingway's war experiences as a soldier in Italy in 1918), you would first describe the war scenes in *A Farewell to Arms*. Then you would cite Hemingway's actual war experiences, as described by Baker in his biography. You might also cite any published letters written by Hemingway during that period. In short, you will want to go through all your reference notes and place into the "step 1" category any information from any source relating to these war experiences.

Do the same for the other steps in your plan as well: organize all your relevant material into the appropriate categories. Any material that does not fit into any of your steps should be excluded from your paper. You will not impress anyone with your scholarship if you include irrelevant material. Such information will simply cloud your purpose. If you have placed each note on a separate 3 x 5 card, you would then simply arrange your stack of cards in the order of the steps on your essay plan.

After you have outlined the ideas in your paper and organized your research notes, you need only a statement that ties your efforts together such that your main point is proven by means of your research; then your research paper plan is complete. In the Hemingway paper you might conclude,

```
Although the story line in A Farewell to Arms is certainly
fictional (no real characters named Catherine Barkley and
Lt. Henry lived and died in quite the same circumstances as
they do in the book), there are, nonetheless, enough sim-
ilarities between incidents and characters in the book and
corresponding incidents and characters in Hemingway's life
to demonstrate the presence of autobiographical overtones
in this novel--to prove, in fact, that "the story ached
to be told."
```

The First Draft

After you have plotted the plan of your paper, it is time to work up a first draft. In writing a research paper, you should plan to use the tools you have been learning and practicing in earlier sections of this book. Whichever modes or methods fit your plan should be employed. For instance, in writing about Hemingway's autobiographical influences in *A Farewell to Arms,* you would probably include various modes of development: process analysis (to show Hemingway's writing process in *A Farewell to Arms*), description (of Hemingway's family, friends, and characters), narrative (to relate the incidents in Hemingway's life and novel), comparison and contrast (to compare the real-life occurrences with the fictional ones), and so on.

In addition, consider carefully your *purpose* in writing this paper. Are you trying to convince your readers to accept a point of view? To teach them something? To answer a question? Moreover, who are your readers? Are you aiming this paper at your fellow students? Your instructor? Or are you planning to try to publish this essay in a literary journal? Be sure to assess your audience. How much do your readers know — or care to know — about Hemingway? Also make certain the tone of your paper is suitable to both your purpose and your audience.

Keep in mind, too, that your organization must be logical; that is, it must help you accomplish your purpose in undertaking to write the research paper. In trying to prove your contention about Hemingway and *A Farewell to Arms*, for example, don't wander off the topic into an irrelevant description of Hemingway's short stories.

Be sure, too, that your paragraphs are coherent and that each advances your thesis; also make certain that you connect each paragraph to the one preceding with a transitional sentence. Finally, check your punctuation, diction, and grammar. It is always helpful at this stage, in fact, to read your paper aloud, and to have a friend read it through as well.

Avoiding Plagiarism

When it comes time to include your research information as evidence to support the steps you have taken to prove your main point, it is of particular importance that you do so very carefully, to avoid the problem of plagiarism. If you include a direct quotation *or a paraphrase* of someone else's material without a footnote, or if it is not clear where your own ideas end and your sources begin, you run the risk of being accused of academic dishonesty, with all the attendant consequences.

Let us look, for example, at two ways of including the research notes cited earlier in an essay — the correct way, with a clear delineation made between the student's views and those of his or her sources; and the incorrect way, with this distinction blurred.

This is the correct way:

> Carlos Baker, Hemingway's biographer, writes of Hemingway's composition of <u>A Farewell to Arms</u>: "He had been trying for years to make fictional use of his war experiences of 1918."[1] Baker continues by saying that "the story ached to be told" about Hemingway's wounding in Italy and his love affair with the nurse who attended him, Agnes von Kurowsky.[2] A careful reader can compare certain descriptions of Catherine Barkley, the heroine of <u>A Farewell to Arms</u>, with descriptions of Agnes in Baker's book, and see how influential the real-life character was in the creation of the fictitious one.

Here, the writer has carefully noted direct quotations and paraphrases, and it is clear to the reader that the last sentence in the paragraph is the student's own work.

Now, the incorrect way:

> I believe that the heroine of <u>A Farewell to Arms</u>, Catherine Barkley, was modeled after Agnes von Kurowsky, a nurse who tended him in Italy when he was wounded.[1] The story of Hemingway's war experiences in Italy in 1918 make up the basis of <u>A Farewell to Arms</u>. It is a story which "ached to be told."[2]

In this paragraph, it is hard to tell the student's ideas from those of the sources. It is difficult to tell what the footnote citations refer to, where the information has come from, and how much factual material is involved. Even if the footnotes are accurate in their bibliographical information, the reader is still confused as to whether the quoted material or the paraphrased material is being footnoted. The student's use of source material here borders on plagiarism at worst, confusion at best. Clarity would have been assured, however, if the writer had cited his or her source in the course of the paragraph, rather than simply referring to it in the footnote. In this way, the reader could easily have seen who is responsible for which words and ideas.

Students often claim that they do not have to cite sources for "common knowledge," and to some extent this is true; but "common knowledge" does not usually extend to specific facts about a subject. If you write something "off the top of your head," the chances are it is general information, not specific. If you think you know something because you remember having "read it somewhere," however, you are obliged to find the "somewhere" and include it in your notes. Even if your information comes from a lecture or a conversation, such information should be annotated.

Footnote and Bibliography Forms

Footnotes • Accurate documentation of your notes is a painstaking but necessary process. It is important to remember that *every* time you cite a source, whether a quotation or a paraphrase, you must annotate it. If you place the notes at the bottom of each page of your essay, they are called *footnotes;* if you gather them all together at the end of your paper, they are called *endnotes.* Both footnotes and endnotes are numbered consecutively (from 1 on) throughout the paper.

A footnote or endnote indication number should be typed ½ space above the line, *following* the material you are annotating. (Footnote or endnote numbers are always placed outside all punctuation, including quotation marks.) For example:

Carlos Baker said this was a story that "ached to be told."[1]

Baker also said Hemingway's war experiences would stay with him forever.[2]

Obviously, quotation marks are used to indicate direct quotations. However, if you are quoting a passage of more than a few lines, you do not use quotation marks. Instead, you should single-space, indent, and separate the quotation from the rest of the text, like this:

Carlos Baker wrote,

> Whether it was for this reason or some other,
> the wind and rain of a season of thaw were
> always afterwards associated in his mind with
> the prospect of imminent disaster.[3]

This passage indicates that . . . .

Quoted material should be worded *exactly* as it appears in your source, punctuation included. If you leave out a word or phrase, indicate its absence by means of an ellipsis, or 3 dots. For example:

```
Baker wrote, "Whether . . . for this reason . . ."
```

If you leave out a whole sentence, or if you are leaving out some words at the end of a sentence, indicate it by ellipses and a period, or 4 dots. For example:

```
Baker wrote, "it was for this reason . . . ."
```

Make sure that your elimination of material doesn't alter the sense of the quotation. If on the other hand you add anything to a quoted passage, you must insert it in brackets. For example:

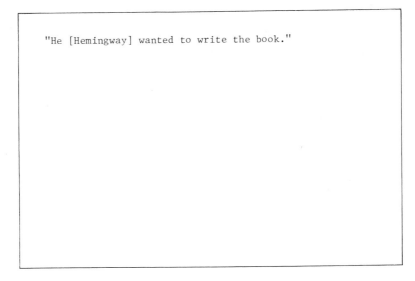

```
"He [Hemingway] wanted to write the book."
```

If you are using a particular text as the basis for your paper, and you often quote selections from this book throughout, cite the text the first time you use it and indicate in the note that henceforth you will refer to it parenthetically. After your first reference, you can then simply place the page number of the passage you are quoting in parentheses after the quotation. For example, the first time you quote material from *A Farewell to Arms* in the Hemingway paper, you would footnote it in this way:

```
Miss Barkley was quite tall.  She wore what seemed to me to
be a nurse's uniform, was blonde and had a tawny skin and
gray eyes.  I thought she was very beautiful.1


_____

1Ernest Hemingway, A Farewell to Arms.  (New York: Scrib-
ner's, 1957), p. 18.  All future references to this book
will be noted by page number.
```

Then, from this point on you would annotate quotations from the book as follows:

```
" 'Good luck,' Catherine said.   'Thank you very much' "
(p. 278).
```

(Note that the parenthetical page number appears *within* the final punctuation.)

In preparing footnotes or endnotes, the following forms should be followed:

Book with single author:

```
1Ernest Hemingway, A Farewell to Arms (New York: Scribner's,
1957), p. 73.
```

Book with multiple authors:

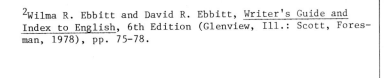

```
²Wilma R. Ebbitt and David R. Ebbitt, Writer's Guide and
Index to English, 6th Edition (Glenview, Ill.: Scott, Fores-
man, 1978), pp. 75-78.
```

Cite edition number when relevant. Also include the state name if the city is not well known.

Translations or edited works:

```
³Thomas More, Utopia, ed. and trans. H. V. S. Ogden (New
York: Appleton-Century-Crofts, 1949), p. 81.
```

Multiple-volume works:

[4]Sir Thomas Malory, _Works_, ed. Eugene Vinaver, 3 vols.
(Oxford: Clarendon, 1947), Vol. III, p. 1123.

Chapter or short works in book by single author:

[5]Ernest Hemingway, "In Another Country," in _The Snows of
Kilimanjaro and Other Stories_ (New York: Scribners, 1961),
p. 68.

Works or articles in collections or anthologies:

[6]Flannery O'Connor, "The Displaced Person," in <u>Classics of Modern Fiction</u>, 2nd ed., ed. Irving Howe (New York: Harcourt Brace Jovanovich, 1972), p. 473.

Article in magazine:

[7]Jeffrey Stein, "Spy Versus Spy in Washington," <u>Saturday Review</u>, May 26, 1979, p. 13.

Article in newspaper:

[8]"Report Cites Decline in Research Support," <u>Princeton Weekly Bulletin</u>, May 14, 1979, p. 1, col. 3.

Article in journal:

[9]R. M. Lumiansky, "Comedy and Theme in the Chester <u>Harrowing of Hell</u>," <u>Tulane Studies in English</u>, X (1960), p. 5.

Lectures

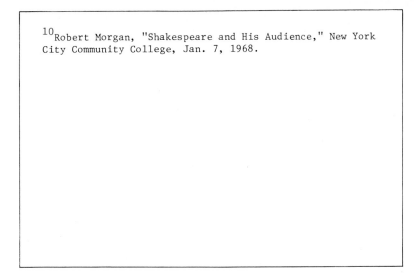

[10]Robert Morgan, "Shakespeare and His Audience," New York
City Community College, Jan. 7, 1968.

Second reference to cited work

[11]Hemingway, p. 78.

If you have used more than one book by the same author, or if you are citing two authors with the same surname, your second reference should be as follows:

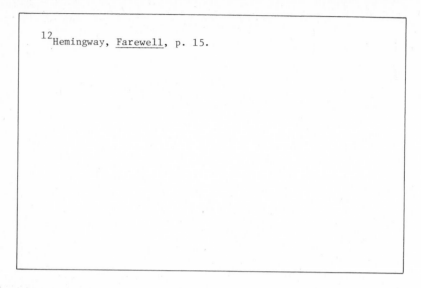

^{12}Hemingway, _Farewell_, p. 15.

You should prepare your notes with care. It is extremely important to be accurate when citing references.

The preceding section devoted to documentation should assist you in preparing most freshman term papers. If you need more extensive information on this subject, however, you should consult *The MLA Handbook* (New York: Modern Language Association, 1977), or James D. Lester, *Writing Research Papers*, 3rd ed. (Glenview, Ill.: Scott, Foresman, 1980).

The Bibliography • In addition to annotating your paper, you should indicate to your reader all the sources you used in thinking out your paper, whether or not they found their way into your notes. These sources (books and articles) comprise your bibliography, a list which is placed at the end of your paper.

Bibliographic listings are made alphabetically, and their format is slightly different from that of footnotes and endnotes. Some common bibliographic entries are as follows:

Book with single author:

Hemingway, Ernest. A Farewell to Arms. New York: Scribner's, 1957.

A second book by the same author:

----------The Sun Also Rises. New York: Scribner's, 1954.

Book with multiple authors:

> Ebbitt, Wilma R., and David R. Ebbitt. <u>Writer's Guide and Index to English</u>, 6th ed. Glenview, Ill.: Scott, Foresman, 1978.

Translations or edited works:

> More, Thomas. <u>Utopia</u>. Translated and edited by H. V. S. Ogden. New York: Appleton-Century-Crofts, 1949.

Multiple volume works:

```
Malory, Sir Thomas.  Works.  Edited by Eugene Vinaver.
    3 vols.  Oxford:  Clarendon, 1947.
```

Chapter or short work in book by single author:

```
Hemingway, Ernest.  "In Another Country."  The Snows of
    Kilimanjaro and Other Stories.  New York:  Scribner's,
    1961, pp. 65-71.
```

Work or article in collection or anthology:

O'Connor, Flannery. "The Displaced Person." <u>Classics of
     Modern Fiction</u>. 2nd ed. Edited by Irving Howe. New
     York: Harcourt Brace Jovanovich, 1972, pp. 469-511.

Article in magazine:

Stein, Jeffrey. "Spy Versus Spy in Washington." <u>Saturday
     Review</u>. May 26, 1972, pp. 13-16.

Article in newspaper:

```
"Report Cites Decline in Research Support."  Princeton
    Weekly Bulletin.  14 May 1979, p. 1, col. 3.
```

Article in journal:

```
Lumiansky, R. M.  "Comedy and Theme in the Chester Har-
    rowing of Hell."  Tulane Studies in English, X (1960),
    5-13.
```

Lectures

```
Morgan, Robert.  "Shakespeare and His Audience."  New York
     City Community College.  7 Jan. 1968.
```

This is only a partial list of types of bibliographical entries, but it should be sufficient for most freshman term papers. If you need more extensive bibliographical information, however, you can consult *The MLA Handbook* or *Writing Research Papers.*

Revising the Paper

When preparing your research paper in a final-draft form, you should consider the same elements as you would when revising any paper: grammar, spelling, sentence structure, punctuation, paragraph structure, organization, style, diction. But you must also remain aware of certain items specific to research papers — namely, the reliability of your research material and the accuracy of your footnotes and bibliographical information. To facilitate the revisions of your final draft, use the following checklist as a guide.

Have you . . .

- selected your subject with care?
- narrowed your topic to a manageable thesis?
- stated your thesis in a clear, straightforward manner?
- thoroughly researched your topic in the reserve room, the card catalogue, the stacks, the research room, and the periodical room of your library?
- taken notes accurately and thoroughly?
- organized your information logically, including relevant material and excluding extraneous material?
- incorporated your research material accurately, to avoid confusion or plagiarism?
- accurately annotated all quoted and paraphrased material?
- gathered all your sources into a bibliography?
- correctly observed notation and bibliography forms?
- revised your paper for grammar, punctuation, spelling, and diction?

Also refer to this checklist as you read through the sample student research paper that follows. Can you offer the author of this paper any constructive criticism?

"Pulitzer Prize-Winning Poet Found Dead":

The Puzzle of Anne Sexton's Death

PULITZER PRIZE-WINNING POET FOUND DEAD

WESTON, Mass., Oct. 6 (AP)--Anne Sexton, a Pulitzer Prize-winning
poet whose work was preoccupied with death, has been found dead at
her home and may have taken her own life, police said. She was 45.

Mrs. Sexton, who was recently divorced from her husband Alfred,
was found Friday inside a car with its engine idling, parked in her
garage. She was pronounced dead on the scene . . . . (The Washington Star)[1]

Anne Sexton's untimely death in 1974 puzzled her admirers and

the readers of her poems. Like many poets, Sexton wrote about her

beliefs, her pains, her experiences. Unlike many poets, she seemed

to have views which were universal. She appeared, through her

poetry, to be an ordinary human being, like all of us. Her suicide,

then, was disturbing to the readers who identified with her. To

begin to understand her self-destructive act, it is necessary to

learn what her life was like and what made it so bad that she

committed suicide. It is important to know where and how she

lived, who her family and friends were, whatever we can about her

insanity, why she wrote the poems she did and what these poems

were about, and what the critics thought about her work.

She was born to Ralph C. and Mary G. Harvey on November 9,

1928. She grew up in Wellesley, Massachusetts, with the renowned

poet Sylvia Plath (who also committed suicide in 1963).[2] After

2

her marriage to Alfred Sexton at the age of nineteen, Anne went to college and also did some fashion modeling, only to be dissatisfied with all these activities. She wanted to be a homemaker.[3] She bore two daughters, Linda and Joy. Soon after she had her second daughter, she suffered a mental breakdown and was hospitalized. She felt that the baby would die and it would be her fault. She started hearing voices that were imaginary. After a month in the hospital and frequent visits with a psychiatrist, she left the hospital, but shortly thereafter she made several attempts at suicide. She was in and out of hospitals, battling insanity, for seven years.[4]

Sexton started writing poetry as a form of therapy, a treatment suggested by her doctor. To Bedlam and Part Way Back, published in 1960, was the result of her "home therapy."[5] In one of her poems, "Ringing the Bells," which she read in a movie she made about herself called Anne Sexton, she described her experiences in the mental institution. She wrote,

> And this is the way they ring
> the bells in Bedlam.
> And this is the bell-lady
> who comes each Tuesday
> morning
> to give us music lessons
> and because the attendants
> make you go
> and because we mind by
> instinct, like bees caught in the wrong
> hive, we are the circle of the
> crazy ladies. . .[6]

Reason for Sexton's writing poetry

Subjects of Sexton's poetry discussed: theme of insanity

3

Note student's smooth incorporation of direct and indirect quotations into paper.

In a second poem, a prayer called "For the Year of the Insane," she gave another gloomy picture of life in an institution:

> All this is death
> In the mind there is a thin alley called death
> and I move through it
> as through water.
> My body is useless.
> It lies curled up like a dog on a carpet.
> It has given up.[7]

In this poem Anne Sexton seemed perplexed because she was told that she was insane; she appeared to herself, however, to be the same woman she had always been.

In the film, too, Sexton presented herself as totally sane, though her face showed the pangs of her life. She was a pretty woman in spite of her imperfect complexion. Her light blue eyes were set deep and ringed with dark shadows. Her lashes and brows were dark brown; black bags hung limply under each eye. In the film her eyes never seemed to look directly at the viewer; they wandered. Her forehead was wrinkled with care and the creases deepened each time she tried to stress a point. She had withered, dry lips, and dimples which ran down each side of her face to form a double chin. Her short, dark hair curled limply inward towards her neck. She was tall and thin. Everything about her seemed natural and pleasant; she had a good sense of humor. She seemed a normal mother and a normal wife, with two children, a dog, and a

4

station wagon. The film also indicated that Sexton had a strong belief in God.

When her life was flowing smoothly after her bout with so-
called madness, she wrote a play, possibly autobiographical, dealing with insanity. It was called Mercy Street.[8] The suicidal
heroine, Daisy Cullen, is in a mental institution and is separated
from her child. She seeks help from God, much like Sexton herself.[9]
Sexton's husband Alfred disliked the play because he felt that it
laid bare their relationship. In particular, he objected to a
scene in which Daisy Cullen remembers making love for the first time
to her own husband. Alfred Sexton became enraged, saying, "You
can't expose me like that! Everyone is looking at me."[10] Sexton's
two teenage daughters, Joy and Linda, wanted to see the play, but
Sexton was afraid to let them because of her husband's reaction.[11]

In her poetry Sexton insisted on a need for God and religion.
Perhaps she needed this belief to give her strength to cope with
her life. She had had no early religious training; she attended
public schools and her parents were not religiously inclined,
though her great-grandfather, who was the governor of Maine, held
his own Sunday services regularly. She said in an interview with
Margaret Ferrari, "I have this terrible need for God. For
Jesus."[12] Although her need for God was somewhat evident in some

**Theme of
religion**

of her early works, the need showed more in The Book of Folly, published in 1972. There was a section in this book called "The
Jesus Papers." It dealt with Christ, Sexton's belief in him, and
his crucifixion.[13] In The Book of Folly Sexton wrote,

> I want the heaven to descend and sit in My dinner plate
> and so do you.
> I want God to put his Steaming arms around Me
> and so do you.
> Because we need.
> Because we are sore creatures.[14]

Her need was clearly shown in this excerpt. She talked of Jesus
as the man she wanted him to be, and not what he was supposed to
be. She had "transformed Him from a Jesus who'd condemn her to
one who wouldn't. He was her creation. . . ."[15]

The last work Sexton published before her death, The Death
Notebooks, also centered on religious themes. Sexton indicates
that since she could not find herself after a lifelong search, she
found God instead and believed in him.[16] In one of her poems
entitled "With Mercy for the Greedy" Sexton wrote,

> True. There is
> a beat Jesus.
> He is frozen to his bones like a
> chunk of beef.
> How desperately he wanted to pull
> his arms in.
> How desperately I touch his vertical
> and horizontal axes!
> But I can't. Need is not quite
> belief.[17]

6

Her poetry and attitudes towards God were said to be blasphemous, even though the intention of good was there.[18] In The Awful Rowing Towards God, a book she wrote but failed to publish before her death, her view of religion seemed simplified.[19]

Sexton published six works. They included To Bedlam and Part Way Back (1960); All My Pretty Ones (1962), which won her a Pulitzer Prize; and Love Poems (1969). In Love Poems she spoke of male/female relationships and reflected her own insecurities. Her marriage ended in divorce the year of her death.[20]

She also published Transformations (1972), which was an amusing attempt to rewrite Grimm's Fairytales. Her other works included The Book of Folly (1974), and The Death Notebooks (1974).

Anne Sexton's works, which dealt mainly with herself, her problems, and her surroundings, received mixed critical reactions. On the whole it was praised; it was labeled as disgraceful only by those critics who couldn't handle her honesty. Martin Dodsworth, in his article "Puzzlers," wrote, "Sexton is the most promising poet to have appeared in some time."[21] Thomas P. McDonnell said that Sexton's poetry possessed a type of stillness, ". . . stillness not of tranquillity but ineffably at the point of fear itself."[22]

Scope of Sexton's work

**Critical reactions to her work.
(Note smooth transitions throughout.)**

7

Sexton's own critical view

Sexton, herself, believed in her own gift of poetry. She felt that a poet is born with talent. It isn't something one can learn. The gift can be developed, but it must be there first.

Sexton said that she worked best in quiet surroundings. And she worked hard. She revised some of her poems as many as three hundred times.[23] She admitted that Robert Lowell was a strong influence in her life, though she did not copy his style.[24] Sexton said that she started each poem with a strong emotion and then worked around it. Expand, expand, cut, cut, expand, expand, cut, cut, is the way a Sexton poem was born.[25] Sexton said, "the great feeling after writing a poem is even better than that after sex. . . ."[26] She kept a rejection drawer for all the sets of lines she couldn't use.[27] One critic said she came to understand herself through her work.[28] Sexton tried to master life with all its complexities through writing.[29]

Purpose of paper repeated; question of reason for suicide answered. Paper comes full circle.

Why would someone with such a great gift, who had achieved success as a poet and who seemed to have everything to live for, commit suicide? There have been many theories. Sexton's The Death Notebooks begins with a quotation from Ernest Hemingway: "Look you con man, make a living out of your death."[30] Some thought that was exactly what Sexton did. She spoke and wrote of death openly and honestly and did not fear it. She accepted the

8

fact that she would die some day and decided to exercise control
over the event.[31] Others theorized that during the last years of
her life she wanted to be with God. Still others thought her
divorce early during the year of her death pained her.

In the film on Sexton, the poet seemed to favor life over
death. She said that she wanted to live because of all she had.
Therefore, her motives for suicide are unclear. Maxine Kuman,
Sexton's friend and a Pulitzer Prize-winning poet in her own
right, dined with Sexton the day of her death. "It was all so
sudden. She showed no sign," Kuman said.[32] Kuman also felt
Sexton's suicide was not provoked by her divorce.[33] Margaret
Ferrari speculated, "Sexton often longed of joining her friend
Plath in her death,"[34] though Plath's death took place thirteen
years before Sexton's.

In October 1976, Sexton was scheduled to appear at a series
of poetry readings called "5:45 interludes," but she died before
the readings. In her place friends gathered in a "Tribute to Anne."
Her friends, including Erica Jong and Kurt Vonnegut, read her
poetry.[35]

Why she killed herself will perhaps always remain a mystery
to her friends and readers. It is evident that she led a hard,
painful life, replete with nervous breakdowns, insanity, divorce,

**Conclusion:
writer sums up
paper**

9

and the relatively early deaths of her mother and father. She
hated wars and politics and found both hard to deal with during
her lifetime; yet she also had much to live for. Perhaps the
theory that she wanted to control her own destiny makes the most
sense after all. If she had predetermined her own death, "Live or
Die" and The Death Notebooks were her way of saying so. In one
passage Sexton wrote she said, "This is my death, and it will
profit me to understand it."[36]

10

Endnotes

[1]Associated Press, "Pulitzer Prize-Winning Poet Anne Sexton Found Dead," The Washington Star, 6 October 1974, p. 6.

[2]Margaret Ferrari, "Between Death and God," America, 9 November 1974, p. 281.

[3]Beatrice Berg, "Oh, I Was Very Sick," The New York Times, 9 November 1969, p. 8.

[4]Berg, p. 7.

[5]Associated Press, "Anne Sexton Dies; Pulitzer Poet, 45," The New York Times, 5 October 1974, p. 65.

[6]Anne Sexton, National Educational Television, 1966 (30 min., sound).

[7]Anne Sexton, "For the Year of the Insane," Harpers, June 1965, p. 68.

[8]Berg, p. 1.

[9]Berg, p. 7.

[10]Berg, p. 7.

[11]Berg, p. 7.

[12]Ferrari, p. 281.

[13]Anne Sexton, The Book of Folly (Boston: Houghton Mifflin, 1972), p. 93.

[14]Sexton, Folly, p. 102.

Student has chosen to use endnotes. Notes could also be written as footnotes at bottom of each page.

Note form: footnote number is indented and positioned ½ space higher than entry.

11

[15]Ferrari, p. 282.

[16]Sandra Gilbert, "Jubilant Anne," The Nation, 14 September 1974, p. 164.

[17]Anne Sexton, All My Pretty Ones (Boston: Houghton Mifflin, 1962), p. 22.

[18]Ferrari, p. 282.

[19]P. Ward, "Anne Sexton: Rowing Towards God," Christian Today, 27 August 1976, p. 18.

[20]Berg, p. 7.

[21]Martin Dodsworth, "Puzzlers," Encounters, March 1965, p. 86.

[22]Thomas P. McDonnell, "Light in a Dark Journey," America, 22 November 1969, p. 729.

[23]William Packard, The Craft of Poetry (New York: Doubleday, 1974), p. 19.

[24]Packard, p. 19.

[25]Packard, p. 22.

[26]Packard, p. 22.

[27]Packard, p. 22.

[28]Barbara Kelves, "Art in Poetry," Paris Review, Summer 1971, p. 60.

[29]Ferrari, p. 281.

12

[30] Anne Sexton, The Death Notebooks (Boston: Houghton Mifflin, 1974), Preface.

[31] Gilbert, p. 164.

[32] "Pulitzer Prize-Winning Poet Anne Sexton Found Dead," p. 6.

[33] "Pulitzer prize-Winning Poet Anne Sexton Found Dead," p. 6.

[34] Ferrari, p. 281.

[35] Associated Press. "Friends of Anne Sexton Pay Tribute in Poetry," The New York Times, 29 October 1974, p. 2.

[36] Sexton, The Death Notebooks, p. 11.

13

Bibliography

Note form of alphabetical entries: each starts at left margin and runovers are indented.

<u>Anne Sexton</u>. National Educational Television, 1966. (Sound, 30 min.)

Associated Press. "Anne Harvey Sexton." <u>The Washington Post</u>, 6 October 1974, p. 6.

----------. "Anne Sexton Dies; Pulitzer Prize Poet, 45." <u>The New York Times</u>, 5 October 1974, p. 65.

Additional works by same author indicated by broken lines.

----------. "Friends of Anne Sexton Pay Tribute in Poetry." <u>The New York Times</u>, 29 October 1974, p. 2.

----------. "Pulitzer Prize-Winning Poet Anne Sexton Found Dead." <u>The Washington Star</u>, 6 October 1974, p. 6.

Berg, Beatrice. "Oh, I Was Very Sick." <u>The New York Times</u>, 9 November 1969, pp. 1, 7f.

Dodsworth, Martin. "Puzzlers." <u>Encounters</u>, March 1965, p. 86.

Ferrari, Margaret. "Between Death and God." <u>America</u>, 9 November 1974, pp. 281.

Gilbert, Sandra. "Jubilant Anne." <u>The Nation</u>, 14 September 1974, pp. 163.

Howard, Richard. "Five Poets." <u>Poetry</u>, 9 November 1974, pp. 281ff.

Jong, Erica. "Remembering Anne Sexton." <u>The New York Times</u>, p. 1.

14

Kelves, Barbara. "Art in Poetry." <u>Paris Review</u>, Summer 1971,
   pp. 58-61.

McDonnell, Thomas. "Light in a Dark Journey." <u>America</u>,
   22 November 1969, pp. 729ff.

Meinke, Peter. "The Poet as a Loser." <u>New Republic</u>, 22 June 1974,
   p. 27.

Packard, William. <u>The Craft of Poetry</u>. New York: Doubleday,
   1974.

Sexton, Anne. <u>All My Pretty Ones</u>. Boston: Houghton Mifflin,
   1960.

----------. <u>The Book of Folly</u>. Boston: Houghton Mifflin, 1972.

----------. <u>The Death Notebooks</u>. Boston: Houghton Mifflin,
   1974.

----------. "For the Year of the Insane." <u>Harpers</u>, June 1965,
   p. 68.

Swenson, May. "The Poetry of Three Women." <u>Nation</u>, 23 February
   1963, pp. 164ff.

Ward, P. "Anne Sexton: Rowing Towards God." <u>Christian Today</u>,
   27 August 1976, pp. 18f.

Zeweig, Paul. "The Making and Unmaking." <u>Partisan Review</u>, XL
   (1973), pp. 227ff.

Assignment: *For Comprehension and Practice*

Study Questions

1. How can you arrive at a suitable thesis once you have selected your general topic?

2. What are some of the ways you can ferret out information for a research topic?

3. How can you avoid confusion and plagiarism when incorporating research material into your research paper draft?

4. Why do you think footnote and bibliography information is organized the way it is?

Exercises

1. Organize the following research material (from Calvin S. Hall, *A Primer of Freudian Psychology*) into a paragraph in which you are trying to define the psychological term "regression." Be sure to make clear the distinction between quoted material, paraphrase, and your own words.

   a. p. 95: "Having reached a certain stage of development, a person may retreat to an earlier level because of fear. This is called *regression*."

   b. p. 96: Hall says some forms of regression seem like everyday activities because they are so common. Dreaming is a common type of regression.

2. Put the following notation information into proper endnote or footnote form:

   a. p. 19: William James in "Address at the Emerson Centenary in Concord." In a book edited by Milton Konvitz and Stephen Whicher called *Emerson*. Published by Prentice-Hall, Inc., Englewood Cliffs, N.J., 1962.

   b. p. 43: F. Scott Fitzgerald's *The Great Gatsby*, 1953, Charles Scribner's Sons, N.Y.

   c. p. ix, in the Introduction to *Henry James*, edited with an introduction by Leon Edel, published by Vintage Books in 1956, in N.Y.

3. Put the same information into proper bibliography form.

Research Paper Topics

Write a research paper of 10 to 15 pages in length on one of the following topics:

   1. The History of Solar Energy
   2. Seals as an Endangered Species
   3. The Land Grant Act
   4. The Rise of Cults in America
   5. The Emergence of Pro-Hockey as the New National Sport
   6. The History of the Gas Crisis
   7. The Nobel Prize and Its Origins
   8. The San Andreas Fault: Does It Pose a Real Threat to California?
   9. The Influence of the Films of Charles Chaplin on those of Woody Allen
   10. Art Deco

Some of these topics are specific, some general. If you choose a general topic, be sure to narrow it down so that your paper makes a point.

Part Three

Readings

16

Narrative Essays

Riverboat Heroes

Mark Twain

Mark Twain, born Samuel Langhorne Clemens (1835-1910), is one of America's outstanding humorists. He is best known for his novels *The Adventures of Tom Sawyer, The Adventures of Huckleberry Finn, A Connecticut Yankee in King Arthur's Court,* and for his humorous essays and stories, many of which he presented in lectures around the United States and in several foreign countries. Twain spent his youth in Hannibal, Missouri, and was a pilot on a riverboat on the Mississippi River just before the Civil War. *Old Times on the Mississippi* is an account of his riverboat experiences. "Riverboat Heroes" (editor's title) is from "Sounding," a chapter in *Old Times.*

Before narrating this tale, Twain explains that at low tide, members of the riverboat crew "sound" the channel to find the deepest sections of the river for the boat to pass through.

One trip a pretty girl of sixteen spent her time in our pilot-house with her uncle and aunt, every day and all day long. I fell in love with her. So did Mr. Thornburg's cub, Tom G———. Tom and I had been bosom friends until this time; but now a coolness began to arise. I told the girl a good many of my river adventures, and made myself out a good deal of a hero; Tom tried to make himself appear to be a hero, too, and succeeded to some extent, but then he always had a way of embroidering. However, virtue is its own reward, so I was a barely perceptible trifle ahead in the contest. About this time something happened which promised handsomely for me: the pilots decided to sound the crossing at the head of 21. This would occur about nine or ten o'clock at night, when the passengers would be still up; it would be Mr. Thornburg's watch, therefore my chief would have to do the sounding. We had a perfect love of a sounding-boat — long, trim, graceful, and as fleet as a greyhound; her thwarts were cushioned; she carried twelve oarsmen; one of the mates was always sent in her to transmit orders to her crew, for ours was a steamer where no end of "style" was put on.   /1

We tied up at the shore above 21, and got ready. It was a foul night, and the river was so wide, there, that a landsman's uneducated eye could discern no opposite shore through such a gloom. The passengers were alert and interested; everything was satisfactory. As I hurried through the engine-room, picturesquely gotten up in storm toggery, I met Tom, and could not forbear delivering myself of a mean speech: —   /2

"Ain't you glad *you* don't have to go out sounding?"

Tom was passing on, but he quickly turned, and said, —

"Now just for that, you can go and get the sounding-pole yourself. I was going after it, but I'd see you in Halifax, now, before I'd do it."   /3

"Who wants you to get it? *I* don't. It's in the sounding-boat."

"It ain't, either. It's been new-painted; and it's been up on the ladies' cabin guards two days, drying."   /4

I flew back, and shortly arrived among the crowd of watching and wondering ladies just in time to hear the command:

"Give way, men!"   /5

I looked over, and there was the gallant sounding-boat booming away, the unprincipled Tom presiding at the tiller, and my chief sitting by him with the sounding-pole which I had been sent on a fool's errand to fetch. Then that young girl said to me, —   /6

"Oh, how awful to have to go out in that little boat on such a night! Do you think there is any danger?"   /7

I would rather have been stabbed. I went off, full of venom, to help in the pilot-house. By and by the boat's lantern disappeared, and after an interval a wee spark glimmered upon the face of the water a mile away. Mr. Thornburg blew the whistle in acknowledgment, backed the steamer out, and made for it. We flew along for a while, then slackened steam and went cautiously gliding toward the spark. Presently Mr. Thornburg exclaimed, —   /8

"Hello, the buoy-lantern's out!"

He stopped the engines. A moment or two later he said, —

"Why, there it is again!"   /9

So he came ahead on the engines once more, and rang for the leads. Gradually the water shoaled up, and then began to deepen again! Mr. Thornburg muttered: —

"Well, I don't understand this. I believe that buoy has drifted off the reef. Seems to be a little too far to the left. No matter, it is safest to run over it, anyhow."   /10

So, in that solid world of darkness we went creeping down on the light. Just as our bows were in the act of plowing over it, Mr. Thornburg seized the bell-ropes, rang a startling peal, and exclaimed, —

"My soul, it's the sounding-boat!"   /11

A sudden chorus of wild alarms burst out far below — a pause — and then a sound of grinding and crashing followed. Mr. Thornburg exclaimed, —

"There! the paddle-wheel has ground the sounding-boat to lucifer matches! Run! See who is killed!"   /12

I was on the main deck in the twinkling of an eye. My chief and the third mate and nearly all the men were safe. They had discovered their danger when it was too late to pull out of the way; then, when the great guards overshadowed them a moment later, they were prepared and knew what to do; at my chief's order they sprang at the right instant, seized the guard, and were hauled aboard. The next moment the sounding-yawl swept aft to the wheel and was struck and splintered to atoms. Two of the men and the cub Tom, were missing — a fact which spread like wildfire over the boat. The passengers came flocking to the forward gangway, ladies and all, anxious-eyed, white-faced, and talked in awed voices of the dreadful thing. And often and again I heard them say, "Poor fellows! poor boy, poor boy!"   /13

By this time the boat's yawl was manned and away, to search for the missing. Now a faint call was heard, off to the left. The yawl had disappeared in the other direction. Half the people rushed to one side to encourage the swimmer with their shouts; the other half rushed the other way to shriek to the yawl to turn about. By the callings, the swimmer was approaching, but some said the sound showed failing strength. The crowd massed themselves against the boiler-deck railings, leaning over and staring into the gloom; and every faint and fainter cry wrung from them such words as "Ah, poor fellow, poor fellow! is there *no* way to save him?"   /14

But still the cries held out, and drew nearer, and presently the voice said pluckily, —

"I can make it! Stand by with a rope!"   /15

What a rousing cheer they gave him! The chief mate took his stand in the glare of a torch-basket, a coil of rope in his hand, and his men grouped about him. The next moment the swimmer's face appeared in the circle of light, and in another one the owner of it was hauled aboard, limp and drenched, while cheer on cheer went up. It was that devil Tom.   /16

The yawl crew searched everywhere, but found no sign of the two men. They probably failed to catch the guard, tumbled back, and were struck by the wheel and killed. Tom had never jumped for the guard at all, but had plunged head-first into the river and dived under the wheel. It was nothing; I could have done it easy enough, and I said so; but everybody went on just the same, making a wonderful to-do over that ass, as if he had done something great. That girl couldn't seem to have enough of that pitiful "hero" the rest of the trip; but little I cared; I loathed her, anyway.   /17

Review Questions

1. How does Twain use understatement for humorous effect?
2. What effect does the riverboat jargon have on the narrative? Is this jargon easily understood in the context of the tale? Explain.

3. What is the point of the narrative?

4. How does the narrator project his personality in this selection? What kind of person do you think the narrator is?

5. What effect does the mingling of narration and dialogue have on the story? Does the dialogue sound natural?

Early Punishment

Richard Wright

Richard Wright (1908-1960), author of many stories, novels, and essays, was most productive during the 1930's, 40's, and 50's. His force as a writer lay in his exposure of the poisonous effect of a racially prejudiced environment. His books include *Uncle Tom's Children*, a collection of stories (1938); *Twelve Million Black Voices*, a photo essay (1941); *Black Power* (1954); and *Native Son*, his most famous novel (1940).

The selection included here is an excerpt from Wright's autobiography, *Black Boy* (1945), detailing his youth in the South. The dramatic intensity of Wright's first-person narrative is compelling, yet free from self-pitying pathos.

One winter morning in the long-ago, four-year-old days of my life I found myself standing before a fireplace, warming my hands over a mound of glowing coals, listening to the wind whistle past the house outside. All morning my mother had been scolding me, telling me to keep still, warning me that I must make no noise. And I was angry, fretful, and impatient. In the next room Granny lay ill and under the day and night care of a doctor and I knew that I would be punished if I did not obey. I crossed restlessly to the window and pushed back long fluffy white curtains — which I had been forbidden to touch — and looked yearningly out into the empty street. I was dreaming of running and playing and shouting, but the vivid image of Granny's old, white, wrinkled, grim face, framed by a halo of tumbling black hair, lying upon a huge feather pillow, made me afraid.   /1

The house was quiet. Behind me my brother — a year younger than I — was playing placidly upon the floor with a toy. A bird wheeled past the window and I greeted it with a glad shout.   /2

"You better hush," my brother said.

"You shut up," I said.   /3

My mother stepped briskly into the room and closed the door behind her. She came to me and shook her finger in my face.   /4

"You stop that yelling, you hear?" she whispered. "You know Granny's sick and you better keep quiet!"   /5

I hung my head and sulked. She left and I ached with boredom.

"I told you so," my brother gloated.

"You shut up," I told him again.   /6

I wandered listlessly about the room, trying to think of something to do, dreading the return of my mother, resentful of being neglected. The room held nothing of interest except the fire and finally I stood before the shimmering embers, fascinated by the quivering coals. An idea of a new kind of game grew and took root in my mind. Why not throw something into the fire and watch it burn? I looked about. There was only my picture book and my mother would beat me if I burned that. Then what? I hunted around until I saw the broom leaning in a closet. That's it . . . Who would bother about a few straws if I burned them? I pulled out the broom and tore out a batch of straws and tossed them into the fire and watched them smoke, turn black, blaze, and finally become white wisps of ghosts that vanished. Burning straws was a teasing kind of fun and I took more of them from the broom and cast them into the fire. My brother came to my side, his eyes drawn by the blazing straws.   /7

"Don't do that," he said.

"How come?" I asked.

"You'll burn the whole broom," he said.

"You hush," I said.

"I'll tell," he said.

"And I'll hit you," I said.   /8

My idea was growing, blooming. Now I was wondering just how the long fluffy white curtains would look if I lit a bunch of straws and held it under them. Would I try it? Sure. I pulled several straws from the broom and held them to the fire until they blazed; I rushed to the window and brought the flame in touch with the hems of the curtains. My brother shook his head.   /9

"Naw," he said.   /10

He spoke too late. Red circles were eating into the white cloth; then a flare of flames shot out. Startled, I backed away. The fire soared to the ceiling and I trembled with fright. Soon a sheet of yellow lit the room. I was terrified; I wanted to scream but was afraid. I looked around for my brother; he was gone. One half of the room was now ablaze. Smoke was choking me and the fire was licking at my face, making me gasp.   /11

I made for the kitchen; smoke was surging there too. Soon my mother would smell that smoke and see the fire and come and beat me. I had done something wrong, something which I could not hide or deny. Yes, I would run away and never come back. I ran out of the kitchen and into the back yard. Where could I go? Yes, under the house! Nobody would find me there. I crawled under the house and crept into a dark hollow of a brick chimney and balled myself into a tight knot. My mother must not find me and whip me for what I had done. Anyway, it was all an accident; I had not really intended to set the house afire. I had just wanted to see how the curtains would look when they burned. And neither did it occur to me that I was hiding under a burning house.   /12

Presently footsteps pounded on the floor above me. Then I heard screams. Later the gongs of fire wagons and the clopping hoofs of horses came from the direction of the street. Yes, there was really a fire, a fire like the one I had seen one day burn a house down to the ground, leaving only a chimney standing black. I was stiff with terror. The thunder of sound above me shook the chimney to which I clung. The screams came louder. I saw the image of my grandmother lying helplessly upon her bed and there were yellow flames in her black hair. Was my mother afire? Would my brother burn? Perhaps everybody in the house would burn! Why had I not thought of those things before I fired the curtains? I yearned to become invisible, to stop living. The commotion above me increased and I began to cry. It seemed that I had been hiding for ages, and when the stomping and screaming died down I felt lonely, cast forever out of life. Voices sounded near-by and I shivered.   /13

"Richard!" my mother was calling frantically.   /14

I saw her legs and the hem of her dress moving swiftly about the back yard. Her wails were full of an agony whose intensity told me that my punishment would be measured by its depth. Then I saw her taut face peering under the edge of the house. She had found me! I held my breath and waited to hear her command me to come to her. Her face went away; no, she had not seen me huddled in the dark nook of the chimney. I tucked my head into my arms and my teeth chattered.   /15

"Richard!"

The distress I sensed in her voice was as sharp and painful as the lash of a whip on my flesh.   /16

"Richard! The house is on fire. Oh, find my child!"

Yes, the house was afire, but I was determined not to leave my place of safety. Finally I saw another face peering under the edge of the house; it was my father's. His eyes must have become accustomed to the shadows, for he was now pointing at me.   /17

"There he is!"

"Naw!" I screamed.

"Come here, boy!"

"Naw!"

"The house is on fire!"

"Leave me 'lone!"   /18

He crawled to me and caught hold of one of my legs. I hugged the edge of the brick chimney with all of my strength. My father yanked my leg and I clawed at the chimney harder.   /19

"Come outta there, you little fool!"

"Turn me loose!"   /20

I could not withstand the tugging at my leg and my fingers relaxed. It was over. I would be beaten. I did not care any more. I knew what was coming. He dragged me into the back yard and the instant his hand left me I jumped to my feet and broke into a wild run, trying to elude the people who surrounded me, heading for the street. I was caught before I had gone ten paces.   /21

From that moment on things became tangled for me. Out of the weeping and the shouting and the wild talk, I learned that no one had died in the fire. My brother, it seemed, had finally overcome enough of his panic to warn my mother, but not before more than half the house had been destroyed. Using the mattress as a stretcher, Grandpa and an uncle had lifted Granny from her bed and had rushed her to the safety of a neighbor's house. My long absence and silence had made everyone think, for a while, that I had perished in the blaze.   /22

"You almost scared us to death," my mother muttered as she stripped the leaves from a tree limb to prepare it for my back.   /23

I was lashed so hard and long that I lost consciousness. I was beaten out of my senses and later I found myself in bed, screaming, determined to run away, tussling with my mother and father who were trying to keep me still. I was lost in a fog of fear. A doctor was called — I was afterwards told — and he ordered that I be kept abed, that I be kept quiet, that my very life depended upon it. My body seemed on fire and I could not sleep. Packs of ice were put on my forehead to keep down the fever. Whenever I tried to sleep I would see huge wobbly white bags, like the full udders of cows, suspended from the ceiling above me. Later, as I grew worse, I could see the bags in the daytime with my eyes open and I was gripped by the fear that they were going to fall and drench me with some horrible liquid. Day and night I begged my mother and father to take the bags away, pointing to them, shaking with terror because no one saw them but me. Exhaustion would make me drift toward sleep and then I would scream until I was wide awake again; I was afraid to sleep. Time finally bore me away from the dangerous bags and I got well. But for a long time I was chastened whenever I remembered that my mother had come close to killing me.   /24

Review Questions

1. What is the major point Wright is making in this narrative?
2. How does he convey this point through the incident he relates?
3. How does the mixture of dialogue and narrative contribute to the effectiveness of the piece?
4. What is the author's attitude toward the other members of his family? What is his attitude toward himself? Is his adult attitude toward himself, reflected in the memories of his childhood, the same as the attitude he had toward himself as a child?
5. What audience do you think the author is addressing?

Pencils Down

Andrew Ward

Andrew Ward (1946-   ) is an essayist and short-story writer whose pieces have appeared in *Audience, Redbook, The New York Times, American Heritage,* and *The Atlantic Monthly.* Born in Chicago, he attended Oberlin College and the

Rhode Island School of Design; he now lives in New Haven, Connecticut, with his wife and son.

"Pencils Down" is taken from his book *Fits and Starts* (1978), a humorous account of his attempts to cope with growing up. The essay details several of his frustrating encounters with the American educational system.

Everything will be going fine and then suddenly I will have that dream again, the one in which I am walking across a campus and a classmate runs by me, waving his arms and shouting, "Come on! You're late!"   /1

"Late?" I call after him. "Late for what?"

"Late for what!" he exclaims. "Late for Bretko's final!"

In spite of myself, I begin to lope after him. "Bretko? Who's Bretko?"

"Jesus Christ!" he says as we dash toward the classroom building, "where have you *been* all semester? Professor Bretko! Phosphates and Positivism! Come on!"   /2

It is just when we reach the classroom, where the final in a course I have never heard of on a subject I know nothing about is already in progress, that I wake up in a tangle of bedding, my eyes bulging like eggs in the dark.   /3

The first real test I remember taking was at a solemn little pedagogic enterprise called the Lab School, to which the faculty of the University of Chicago sent its children and in which it tested out some of its educational theories. I spent four years guinea-pigging my way through the Lab School, but I don't remember very much about it. I do remember a wide, saintly kindergarten teacher who cured my stuttering ("Now, take your time, Andy," she would say as I stammered before her, "we have all the time in the world"). And I remember Miss Mums, a siren of a second-grade teacher with a flamboyant bust who used to hop up and down whenever one of us answered her correctly. I still think the university was on to something when it hired Miss Mums; most of us did our best to keep her perpetually hopping before us.   /4

In any case, sometime during the second grade a group of pale young men with attaché cases arrived at the school and established themselves in a little room which was usually devoted to hearing tests. We were called in one by one "to have a little fun," as Miss Mums put it, "with some nice big men." Some of us didn't want to have a little fun. One boy, whose mother made him wear some sort of prophylactic powder in his hair, threw up in the hallway when his turn came, and had to spend the rest of the day with the nurse.   /5

When it came my turn, I walked down to the testing room and stood silently in the doorway, waiting to be noticed, which was my way of announcing myself in those days. I was finally beckoned in by a man with thick glasses that made his eyes look like fish suspended in ice.   /6

"Now, Mark," he said brightly, "if you'll just take your seat right here, we can all start playing with blocks."   /7

Much too polite to correct him about my name, I took my seat at a table around which four men with note pads loomed attentively. I was given six red plastic cubes and told, with many winks and nods, to do whatever I felt like doing with them. In truth, I didn't feel like doing anything with them. I was old enough to know that you couldn't build anything with six cubes. But the men looked so eager that I decided to do what I could, which was to line them all up into a row, then into two rows of three, then into three rows of two. The three rows of two seemed to go over very big. I could see out of the corner of my eye that they had begun to jot furiously, nodding to themselves as if entire life philosophies were being confirmed before their eyes.   /8

I shoved the blocks around a while longer and finally leaned back. There was a pause, and then suddenly one of the men rose to his feet agitatedly and jabbed his pencil into the fish-eyed man's ribs.

"See? What did I tell you?"   /9

"You never told me *anything!*" the fish-eyed man hissed back, shoving the pencil aside. There was a scene, and in the confusion I got down off my chair and made my way back to Miss Mums's room. "Now," she asked me as I sat down at my desk, "wasn't that fun?"

"Yes," I said, and she gave a little hop.   /10

My parents seem to have had me down for college *in utero.* I remember working on a geography report about Bolivia when I was in the third grade and my mother standing over me with an anxious look and declaring, "They're going to count this for college."   /11

As far as she was concerned, they were going to count everything for college. She used college in her disciplinary warnings the way some mothers used Santa Claus. This had the effect of simultaneously trivializing and exalting my academic labors. On the one hand, I could not believe that my knowledge that Bolivia was the only country in the world to lynch two successive heads of state from the same lamppost was going to count for anything in college. On the other hand, I could sometimes imagine a tweedy admissions officer leaning back and asking, "By the way, Andrew, what country was it that lynched two successive heads of state from the same lamppost?"   /12

"I believe that was Bolivia, sir."

"Excellent! Oh, excellent! Andrew, I believe you and Harvard are going to get along very nicely."   /13

I never did very well in school; in fact, the further along I got the worse I did, until by senior year in high school I was just squeaking through. I ascribe this to a difficulty I've always had with admitting to ignorance. It is hard to learn anything when you are constantly trying to look as though you know it already. I would rarely ask a question, for instance, unless it was to demonstrate, in its expression, a precocious knowledge of the subject under discussion. I would always start off my questions with, "Wouldn't you say that . . . ," knowing full well that the teacher probably would, and would congratulate me for my insight. In what were commonly known as bullshit courses, this worked in my favor. In math and science, in which I had no ability or interest, it got me nowhere.   /14

I did pretty well on my English and history college boards, and miserably in math and science, as was my pattern. My parents had me sign up for every testing date there was, and I swung at the ball in such varying locales as Danbury State Teachers College, Tom's School of Business Success, and most of the high school auditoriums in southwestern Connecticut.   /15

Oberlin College was my first choice, naturally enough, because my parents went there, and my brother, and all my aunts and uncles; because my grandfather was head of its art department, and my father was one of its trustees. Oberlin had strict admissions standards in those days, and there was considerable doubt on my parents' part that I would manage to gain admittance.   /16

When I had my admissions interview in a hotel suite in New York, I had just received a D in chemistry, a course I had to pass in order to suit the science requirement, since I had all but flunked biology the year before. After several genial inquiries as to my family's health and whereabouts, the admissions officer proved remarkably encouraging. He hinted that I would be admitted under what he called Oberlin's "Tom Sawyer Program," which permitted students with "asymmetrical aptitudes," as he put it, to get in. He could not keep from wincing as his eyes descended on row upon row of D's and C's in my high school record, but he emphasized and reemphasized the positive side: high marks in art and English, soloist in the chorus, good attendance; and as the interview drew to a close, I got the impression that he was far more eager for me to go to Oberlin College than I was. As he waited with me for the elevator in the foyer outside his suite, he held my coat for me while I attempted, in vain, to get my second arm into its sleeve. We waltzed around in this way for some time, and as I finally stepped into the elevator, still lunging about for my elusive sleeve, he looked at me with the game, pained expression of a man at a dinner party who must smack his lips over something repugnant.   /17

Oberlin didn't turn out to be quite what I had in mind, and vice versa. As I went along, I had more and more trouble getting to class, until eventually I lost all track of where I was supposed to be, and when. Sometimes I would catch a glimpse of someone dimly familiar and follow him to his next class, in the hope that it would turn out to be one of my own. It never did turn out to be one of my own, but in this way I attended some fascinating lectures on subjects ranging from a historical review of the Albanian nation-state to the topical poetry of Po Chü-i.   /18

I was well into my third, last-ditch semester at Oberlin College before I finally managed to pinpoint my problem: I couldn't read. Not that I couldn't have stood up before a Wednesday Assembly and read aloud from my geology text in a clear, authoritative voice, making myself heard unto the last rows of Finney Chapel. It was just that to my own ears I wouldn't have been making any sense at all.   /19

As finals week approached, I tried to overcome this disability by locking myself into my room in the dormitory, laying out my study materials in the lone beam of my Tensor desk lamp, and sitting there, hunched over my open textbook with a yellow felt-tip pen at the ready to indicate important passages. I sat that way for hours at a time, waiting for the words over which my eyes passed to form phrases, sentences, ideas, and succeeding only in an occasional flicker of recognition, enough to link perhaps twenty words together — "The exercise begins a rather extensive study to be continued in later sections of Chapter XXI" — but never enough to gain me a foothold. /**20**

I was reduced to hoping that it was all penetrating my mind on a subconscious level, and I would tidily underline what I could only assume was important — headings, captions, opening and closing sentences, anything resembling a list, numbers, and sometimes a central sentence, a few of which, I figured, were probably important, too. /**21**

Underlining accomplished several purposes. It gave me something to do, it demarcated the pages I had already gone through (I had no other way of knowing), and it hid from whoever might duck into my room the fact that I was, in effect, an illiterate, and had no business going to college. /**22**

My last final at Oberlin was in Geology I, a course I took because it was touted to have been designed for the scientifically inept. This touting did not, however, seem to have originated with the geology department. If there is more to know about rocks than was included in Geology I, I don't want to hear about it. By the time I took the final, I had missed all but seven of my classes, and had received an F on my research paper, a study of the Greenwich, Connecticut, reservoir system which I based on a water company comic book starring a character made out of drainpipe named Wally Water. /**23**

I took the exam with some fifty other geology cadets in a dark, gothic room overlooking Tappan Square. The proctor, a work-booted geology major, handed out the test questions and the blue books, and, stopwatch raised, signaled to us to begin. /**24**

The questions must have been mimeographed minutes before, because the ink still smelled sweet and dizzying. The first and second questions rang no bells at all, and as I read them my pen felt icy and useless in my fingers. In the third question I could barely make out the following: ". . . bituminous coal and discuss its suitability as a fuel. Use illustrations to explain your answer where necessary." /**25**

It was as if I had stumbled into someone else's identity. I didn't know anything about rocks. I didn't know anything about science. Why were they asking me these things? I stared up at the blackboard, where the proctor was already chalking up how much time we had left. He squinted back at me with suspicion, and I swerved my gaze ceilingward, as if searching for the appropriate phrasing with which to set down my brimming knowledge. /**26**

Coal. What did I know about coal? I thought of black lung, carbon paper, the coal heap in my parents' basement in Chicago. Then, for a moment, a phrase sprang to my mind from an eighth-grade science text: "Coal results from the deterioration and mineralization of prehistoric tropical rain forests." /**27**

Quickly, before it sank back out of reach, I opened my blue book and began to write. "Coal results from the deterioration and mineralization of prehistoric tropical rain forests. Coal deposits are apt to be found in those places where prehistoric tropical rain forests once stood. Thus, coal mines in present use are located in these places." /**28**

"Coal," I continued boldly, "contains some of the chemical elements of prehistoric tropical rain forests, but usually not all of them. Those that remain are those which have survived and, in a sense, resulted from, the deterioration and mineralization of prehistoric tropical rain forests."   /**29**

That got me through three pages of large, loopy script. All around me, my classmates were filling one blue book after another. One girl across the room wrote the ink out of one pen, hurled it to the floor, and furiously scrawled on with another. All I could hear in the room was the steady scrape of pens and the rapid flutter of pages.   /**30**

To drive home my point, I decided to deliver on a few illustrations. Carefully, but with a certain graphic flair, I drew

1) a rain forest with arrows signifying "trees," "scrub vegetation," "sun," and "topsoil,"
2) a rain forest deteriorating,
3) a deteriorated rain forest making its way underground,
4) a coal mine in full operation labeled, "Thousands of years later," and,
5) a black lump labeled "resultant coal ore fragment."   /**31**

These led to another drawing illustrating the chemical breakup of coal. I drew a circle and divided it into three parts, labeled, "sulfur," "carbon," and "other." Coal was suitable as a fuel, I noted, because it burned.   /**32**

As I underlined all my headings and captions I wondered about my alternatives. I could claim that I had overdosed on No-Doz, that I was reeling, hallucinating, unable to think. I could hand in a blank blue book, copy out a C-level set of answers in another blue book that evening, hand it in the next morning, and elegantly apologize for the mixup. I could feign a fainting spell or an epileptic fit or psychosomatic paralysis of my right hand. I could accuse the earnest, chalk-faced girl beside me of cheating and storm out of the door, or punch out the proctor in a rebellious frenzy, becoming, overnight, a campus legend.   /**33**

But it gradually became obvious to me that the college simply wanted me to answer these questions. Otherwise, I reasoned, they would not be asking them. And it was just as obvious that if I couldn't answer their questions, I had no business being there. Somehow, in the rustle of the testing room, this hit me like a revelation. I wanted to get up then, find the professor, and explain, "Say, sir. I didn't *realize* any of this." He would understand. It must have happened before.   /**34**

I looked at two of my friends a few rows away, both busily writing. At these times my friends seemed strangely distant and unfamiliar. They were each into their third or fourth blue book. What in God's name were they writing about?   /**35**

The hinge of my jaw ached and trembled, and as I yawned, the floor took on a soft, inviting look. I put down my pen and stretched out my legs and wondered if it would be all right if I just stretched out for a little while on the scuffed, hardwood floor, closed my eyes, and slept.   /**36**

"Pencils down," the proctor commanded, chopping at the air with his hand.   /**37**

A resolute, perspiring girl in the front row raised her hand and asked if she could "just finish one last sentence."   /**38**

The proctor nodded and a score of heads and hands ducked back down to finish sentences. I sat still for a moment, and then scribbled one last sentence, "Coal remains one of the most popular forms of fuel in use today."   /**39**

"All right, that's it," the proctor declared, and everyone groaned and stretched and stacked up blue books. I signed mine with a bold hand, but glancing over my five pages I knew it was at last all over for me at Oberlin College. All that remained was one last explosion of red-inked exclamations expressing regret, alarm, and grave concern for my future.   /**40**

Review Questions

1. The events of the essay occurred well in advance of the writing of the essay; therefore, the author can comment in retrospect on these events. Find several examples which illustrate that Ward is viewing his childhood and adolescence with the eyes of an adult, and discuss what effect such detached commentary has on the reader.

2. Ward uses examples, similes, and metaphors in humorous ways. Find some instances of these and discuss how they create a cumulative comic effect.

3. How does Ward tie together many different incidents with a single narrative theme?

4. How does Ward establish the characters of the people he mentions in the essay?

5. What is the point of Ward's narrative? Does he make it directly or indirectly?

The Elephant's Child

Shana Alexander

Shana Alexander (1925-   ), a journalist, has written for *Life* and *Newsweek*, and has been an editor of *McCall's*. She has broadcast over CBS on such programs as *Spectrum* and *60 Minutes* and is the author of *Anyone's Daughter* (1979) and *Talking Woman*. She is an observer of the modern scene.

"The Elephant's Child," part of which is reprinted here, was first published in *Life*, May 11, 1962, and was collected in *Talking Woman* (1977). An example of a narrative written in the third person by an outside observer, it reports the birth of a baby elephant in the city zoo in Portland, Oregon.

Despite what you may have read, O Best Beloved, the Elephant's Child is born with his trunk fully developed and firmly attached. It is pink-tipped and hairy and, when the Child is hungry, it makes a noise like a leaky balloon. But your ignorance, Best Beloved, is most understandable: until this spring, a baby elephant had not been seen in these parts for almost half a century, not even by other elephants.   /1

Today there are 301 elephants in the United States. Three hundred of them were born in the wilds, plucked from their native jungles at a tender age, and caught their first glimpse of America through the stout bars of a shipping crate. But the 301st elephant first saw the light of day on Saturday, May 14, 1962, over the transom of the maternity ward in the city zoo in Portland, Oregon. There, at 5:58 A.M., after lying-in for twelve weeks in an accouchement fit for a czarina, a ten-year-old Siamese elephant named Belle sounded one final blast through her trunk and then quietly gave birth to her first calf. He was the color of boiled veal and hairy all over from wrinkled rump to tip of his eight-inch trunk. . . .   /2

At the start of their vigil, participants in The Great Portland Elephant Watch were a group of healthy, alert, eager animal experts and reporters. They lounged in the hay pile swapping elephant tales; they read avidly through the scant elephant literature available; they catnapped occasionally, and rose often to poke, fondle, and feed the female herd. Sometimes they played poker; Belle's liver pills and antibiotic capsules made excellent chips. They dined on one hundred pounds of peanuts which a Portland nut merchant had sent to Belle, drank innumerable half-cups of coffee (the second half invariably was saved for the expectant mother) and watched TV.   /3

The zoo switchboard was swamped with more than 500 Belle calls a day. Many callers were people in betting pools seeking hot tips on the likeliest day and hour of the birth. Others were amateur obstetricians offering hot tips to the zoo men. Fill the enclosure with teak logs, suggested one, so Belle "would feel at home in the jungle." Another affirmed that all elephant babies are stillborn, but come to life if the rest of the herd is allowed to toss the infant back and forth with their trunks. A number of callers said it was well known that the gestation period of an elephant is three, or six or nine years, so the Elephant Watch might as well go home. This particular suggestion soon came to have a strong attraction for the Watchers. They grew irritable, groggy, emotionally strung out, itchy from the hay, and sickest of all of the overpowering smell of elephant. After a few hours in Belle's snugly warmed maternity ward, each heavy lungful of air seemed to weigh on the diaphragm like another rancid dumpling.   /4

A private 20-by-20-foot concrete maternity chamber was in readiness for Belle, if necessary, but [Dr.] Maberry preferred to leave her with the other pregnant females. Elephants are herd animals by nature, and the doctor believed that the companionship of Belle's ladies-in-waiting would reassure her. . . .   /5

"Preservation of the young is the greatest instinct of all wild animals," Maberry says. "But if you interfere, they'll often switch and try to destroy the young. The best procedure is to keep your mouth shut and your eyes open." Nevertheless, Maberry felt a certain amount of human intervention was essential.   /6

On the afternoon of Thursday, January 18, Belle had a sudden seizure. She moved away from Rosy, Pet, and Tuy Hoa to the opposite end of the enclosure. The seizure lasted two and one half minutes, then subsided.   /7

That night Belle's temperature remained steady, but the temperature outside the elephant house dropped to 20° and an icy wind swirled snow along the deserted pathways of the zoo. Inside, Maberry, his aides, and the waiting press sipped black coffee and walked the floor. So did Belle. From time to time, Thonglaw charged the bars of his cage with a force that shook the building. Once he trumpeted so fiercely he roused the guard at the zoo gates a quarter-mile away. At 5:10 A.M., Belle moved off alone again and squealed in the grip of a mighty spasm. This one lasted four minutes. Half an hour later, she had a third attack. An elephant in labor exerts about four times the force of a horse, and Belle's pains must have been gargantuan. Every time Belle squealed, the other elephants crowded close to Belle's flanks and petted her with their trunks.   /8

By morning all was quiet again. When there was absolutely no change in Belle's behavior throughout the rest of the long day, the six-man team decided to seek the advice of the one man on earth known to have delivered an elephant in captivity, Dr. Eremanno Bronzini of the Rome zoo. The Portland phone company eagerly agreed to put through a conference call gratis. A high school Italian teacher was rushed to the zoo to translate. Then it turned out that Dr. Bronzini had no telephone. Finally, in London, the frantic callers roused Dr. Emmanuel Amoroso of the Royal Veterinary College. Dr. Amoroso had seen many elephants born in African jungle compounds, and he said that Belle's labor might last twelve hours, since this would be her first baby. He added that the cord would break automatically, and he told Maberry not to worry about tying the umbilical knot; Belle would do that job herself, with her trunk. He warned the Portland team to remain on the *qui vive* because, once Belle got into high gear, "it will be a rather precipitous birth."   /9

Alas, it was about as precipitous as a glacier crossing the polar ice cap. On Friday, January 19, Maberry and Metcalfe ran the first electrocardiograms ever reported on an elephant. Belle's great fifty-pound heart was thumping steadily at about thirty-eight beats per minute; fetal heartbeat was eighty-five. On Monday, at 2:20 P.M., Belle trumpeted loudly twice. It seemed as though she had entered the acute stage of labor at last, but in retrospect Maberry feels that these early symptoms were false labor stimulated by the unsettling presence of so many pop-eyed journalists.   /10

For some reason, Belle always suffered most on Thursdays. After the first pains on Thursday, January 18, she slept little, ate little, drank little, and spent most of her time executing a curious, three-legged rocking motion. She kept her left rear leg half-cocked — whether to fend off meddlesome medics or just to relieve the well-known leg cramps of pregnancy, no one but Belle knew for sure. Blood tests showed that Belle was becoming slightly anemic, so her diet was fortified twice daily with a pailful of diluted molasses. Belle took each dose with a single slurp of her trunk and downed it with the ecstatic expression of a child swallowing cough medicine on a TV commercial.   /11

The next Thursday, January 25, Belle suffered several unusually severe contractions and for some hours stopped eating and drinking altogether. When Maberry and Metcalfe attempted to obtain a second blood sample, Belle bellowed and charged. The doctors ducked back outside the steel bars just in the nick of time. "She snapped three steel chains just as if they were thread," Maberry said later.   /12

The following Thursday, February 1, Belle had her worst night yet. She rocked and walked the floor all night long. One of her elephant midwives always paced alongside and kept the miserable beast company, while the other two lay down and slept, snoring loudly through their trunks.   /13

The next night, Maberry put down his bedroll just outside the bars. When Belle's pains appeared to become especially severe, she lay down flat and little Pet knelt beside her and gently massaged Belle's belly with her knee for fifteen or twenty minutes. During the massages, both elephants made odd snorting sounds. Pet even tried half-sitting on Belle's head. Later Belle half-sat on Pet. Nothing seemed to help. When the pains were sharpest, all four elephants crowded close together and cried in unison. Sometimes the muscles between Belle's eyes knotted into a tremendous bulge, and tears rolled down her trunk. Though Maberry could see very severe muscular contractions, the baby's kicking was no longer apparent. The doctor thought the baby probably couldn't kick because he was now holding in a vertical position, almost directly head down.   /14

By then, the assembled newsmen were also bellowing loudly. In a rout of journalism by science, the reporters were banished from the elephant house and armed guards were posted to assure Belle's privacy. Maberry wanted to do everything in his power to prevent having a premature baby elephant on his hands.   /15

On the evening of Friday, April 13, all was quiet in the elephant house of the Portland Zoological Gardens. At midnight, Dr. Maberry made his regular check on bulging Belle and, noticing nothing at all unusual, he bedded down in the massive pile of hay which had served him as his uneasy and tickly resting place for three months. At 12:45 A.M., the veterinarian was roused by an urgent telephone call: across town a pet poodle was gravely ill. Leaving the regular night guard on duty at the elephant house, Maberry drove to the stricken dog's bedside. As he was reviving the poisoned poodle, the zoo guard telephoned and reported that Belle had suddenly begun thrashing around in her cage. She was throwing water over her head with her trunk, and her three elephant midwives appeared greatly agitated. Maberry got back to his outsize patient by 2 A.M.   /16

This time there was no question that acute labor was under way at last. Belle was bellowing oddly, her eyes were wide and bulging, she was continually straining and pushing against the walls and bars, throwing her head from side to side, alternately kneeling and standing. The veterinarian quickly telephoned Zoo Director Jack Marks and summoned two more keepers to help him control the three rambunctious midwives. By 5:30 A.M., these excited females were still squealing shrilly, but Belle had quit bellowing and was busy rapidly crossing and uncrossing her hind legs. While all this was going on, the human observers thought it the better part of prudence to remain watching from outside the bars.   /17

At 5:56 A.M., Belle suddenly began spinning rapidly and silently in circles, pivoting on her forefeet. After two solid minutes of this dervishing — abruptly at 5:58 A.M. — hind feet first and backside front, Belle's 225-pound infant quietly dropped in a heap to the floor and gazed about with bright red but wide-open eyes. As he lay huddled under Belle's great belly, the mother swiftly knotted or clamped the umbilical stump with her trunk. When Pet and 5,000-pound Tuy Hoa strolled over and tried to sit down on the newcomer, the guards quickly prodded all three of the ponderous ex-midwives outside to their open-air patio.   /18

Belle gave her newborn son a couple of swift kicks in his fuzzy flanks. Slowly but firmly, he rose up on his stout legs. Gently shoving him with her trunk and forelegs, Belle nudged his head around to her breast. At 6:30, the baby took his first swallow of elephant milk, a thin liquid which is said to taste like diluted coconut milk. He much enjoyed his first breakfast, though part of it was lost dribbling down the fringes of his hairy chops. Occasionally his tiny, flabby, pink-tipped trunk seemed to quiver with gourmet appreciation, and he emitted high squeals of delight.   /19

At 7 A.M., excited Zoo Director Marks was on the telephone, proclaiming the blessed event to reporters, when he collapsed to the floor in a dead faint. He was rushed to the hospital, put to bed for a couple of hours, and then sent home to rest. On the way home, he insisted on stopping at the zoo to see how Belle was doing.   /20

A few hours later, a brilliant spring sun was shining over Portland, a blue elephant flag fluttered from a shopping center flagpole, and the city's children were trooping to the zoo grounds to view the newborn elephant child, and also to take part in the annual Easter egg-rolling contest on the zoo lawn. Inside the elephant house, the newcomer was alternately nursing and stumping sturdily back and forth through his mother's legs. Belle's owner, Morgan Berry, finally dashed in from Seattle, clutching a tape measure. His baby elephant, he reported proudly, stands thirty-five inches high, measures forty-six inches at the chest, fifty-three inches at the abdomen, and eight inches at the trunk. Later he announced that Belle and the little fellow could be purchased for $30,000, and the people of Portland immediately started a fund-raising drive to meet the price.   /21

At 10 A.M., Keeper Tucker forked Belle her morning meal of hay, bread, apples, and so forth, and she devoured the mess with gusto. After twenty-one months of pregnancy, she appeared within four hours to have returned completely to her old, sweet-tempered, high-spirited, gentle-hearted self. So indeed had Dr. Maberry. The lines of fatigue and tension from attending a 6,000-pound female through three months of on-and-off labor had vanished from his face. As Maberry, Belle, and baby lounged amid the hay wisps regarding one another with an air of total contentment and fulfillment of a job well-done, the director of the egg-rolling contest poked his head through the doorway. He suggested that Belle, as Portland's first lady, should have the honor of stepping out onto the lawn and rolling out the day's first Easter egg.   /22

"I don't think so," said Maberry. "Belle has already rolled her egg for today."   /**23**

Review Questions

1. "The Elephant's Child" is narrated in the third person. How does the effect of this essay differ from that created by narrative essays written in the first person?
2. What is the point Alexander is trying to make in this essay?
3. The introductory paragraphs of this essay contain references to Rudyard Kipling's "The Elephant's Child" in the *Just So Stories*. What tone do these references to a children's story impart to the essay?
4. How does Alexander develop and present the personalities of the elephants and their human attendants? With whom does she have the most sympathy?
5. What is the most exciting part of the narration?

17

Description Essays

The Death of the Moth

Virginia Woolf

Virginia Woolf (1882-1941) began her literary career as a critic for the *Times Literary Supplement* and continued writing essays until her death. She is best known as a novelist, however. Among her best known titles are *The Voyage Out,* which appeared in 1915, followed by *Night and Day* (1919), *Jacob's Room* (1922), *Mrs. Dalloway* (1925), and *To the Lighthouse* (1927).

The following essay illustrates Woolf's characteristic concern about the essential nature of things and events rather than their superficial appearance.

Moths that fly by day are not properly to be called moths; they do not excite that pleasant sense of dark autumn nights and ivy-blossom which the commonest yellow underwing asleep in the shadow of the curtain never fails to rouse in us. They are hybrid creatures, neither gay like butterflies nor sombre like their own species. Nevertheless the present specimen, with his narrow hay-coloured wings, fringed with a tassel of the same colour, seemed to be content with life. It was a pleasant morning, mid-September, mild, benignant, yet with a keener breath than that of the summer months. The plough was already scoring the field opposite the window, and where the share had been, the earth was pressed flat and gleamed with moisture. Such vigour came rolling in from the fields and the down beyond that it was difficult to keep the eyes strictly turned upon the book. The rooks too were keeping one of their annual festivities; soaring round the tree-tops until it looked as if a vast net with thousands of black knots in it has been cast up into the air; which, after a few moments sank slowly down upon the trees until every twig seemed to have a knot at the end of it. Then, suddenly, the net would be thrown into the air again in a wider circle this time, with the utmost clamour and vociferation, as though to be thrown into the air and settle slowly down upon the tree-tops were a tremendously exciting experience.   /1

The same energy which inspired the rooks, the ploughmen, the horses, and even, it seemed, the lean bare-backed downs, sent the moth fluttering from side to side of his square of the window-pane. One could not help watching him. One was, indeed, conscious of a queer feeling of pity for him. The possibilities of pleasure seemed that morning so enormous and so various that to have only a moth's part in life, and a day moth's at that, appeared a hard fate, and his zest in enjoying his meagre opportunities to the full, pathetic. He flew vigorously to one corner of his compartment, and, after waiting there a second, flew across to the other. What remained for him but to fly to a third corner and then to a fourth? That was all he could do, in spite of the size of the downs, the width of the sky, the far-off smoke of houses, and the romantic voice, now and then, of a steamer out at sea. What he could do he did. Watching him, it seemed as if a fibre, very thin but pure, of the enormous energy of the world had been thrust into his frail and diminutive body. As often as he crossed the pane, I could fancy that a thread of vital light became visible. He was little or nothing but life.   /2

Yet, because he was so small, and so simple a form of the energy that was rolling in at the open window and driving its way through so many narrow and intricate corridors in my own brain and in those of other human beings, there was something marvellous as well as pathetic about him. It was as if someone had taken a tiny bead of pure life and decking it as lightly as possible with down and feathers, had set it dancing and zig-zagging to show us the true nature of life. Thus displayed one could not get over the strangeness of it. One is apt to forget all about life, seeing it humped and bossed and garnished and cumbered so that it has to move with the greatest circumspection and dignity. Again, the thought of all that life might have been had he been born in any other shape caused one to view his simple activities with a kind of pity.   /3

After a time, tired by his dancing apparently, he settled on the window ledge in the sun, and the queer spectacle being at an end, I forgot about him. Then, looking up, my eye was caught by him. He was trying to resume his dancing, but seemed either so stiff or so awkward that he could only flutter to the bottom of the window-pane; and when he tried to fly across it he failed. Being intent on other matters I watched these futile attempts for a time without thinking, unconsciously waiting for him to resume his flight, as one waits for a machine, that has stopped momentarily, to start again without considering the reason for its failure. After perhaps a seventh attempt he slipped from the wooden ledge and fell, fluttering his wings, on to his back on the window-sill. The helplessness of his attitude roused me. It flashed upon me that he was in difficulties; he could no longer raise himself; his legs struggled vainly. But, as I stretched out a pencil, meaning to help him to right himself, it came over me that the failure and awkwardness were the approach of death. I laid the pencil down again.   /4

The legs agitated themselves once more. I looked as if for the enemy against which he struggled. I looked out of doors. What had happened there? Presumably it was midday, and work in the fields had stopped. Stillness and quiet had replaced the previous animation. The birds had taken themselves off to feed in the brooks. The horses stood still. Yet the power was there all the same, massed outside indifferent, impersonal, not attending to anything in particular. Somehow it was opposed to the little hay-coloured moth. It was useless to try to do anything. One could only watch the extraordinary efforts made by those tiny legs against an oncoming doom which could, had it chosen, have submerged an entire city, not merely a city, but masses of human beings; nothing, I knew, had any chance against death. Nevertheless after a pause of exhaustion the legs fluttered again. It was superb this last protest, and so frantic that he succeeded at last in righting himself. One's sympathies, of course, were all on the side of life. Also, when there was nobody to care or to know, this gigantic effort on the part of an insignificant little moth, against a power of such magnitude, to retain what no one else valued or desired to keep, moved one strangely. Again, somehow, one saw life, a pure bead. I lifted the pencil again, useless though I knew it to be. But even as I did so, the unmistakable tokens of death showed themselves. The body relaxed, and instantly grew stiff. The struggle was over. The insignificant little creature now knew death. As I looked at the dead moth, this minute wayside triumph of so great a force over so mean an antagonist filled me with wonder. Just as life had been strange a few minutes before, so death was now as strange. The moth having righted himself now lay most decently and uncomplainingly composed. O yes, he seemed to say, death is stronger than I am.   /5

Review Questions

1. What type of description is this?
2. What is Woolf's purpose in writing this description?
3. Does Woolf create an image? How?
4. Why does the author include references to herself in this essay?

Knoxville: Summer, 1915

James Agee

James Agee (1909-1955), born in Knoxville, was an American poet, novelist, screenwriter, and critic. He is best known for his book of poems, *Permit Me Voyage* (1934); his classic study of a poor sharecropper family, *Let Us Now Praise*

Famous Men (1941); and the screenplays for *The African Queen* and *The Quiet One.*

The following description essay is the beginning section of his Pulitzer Prize novel, *A Death in the Family* (1957), which was published after his death. It embodies Agee's distinctive knack for rich description.

We are talking now of summer evenings in Knoxville, Tennessee, in the time that I lived there so successfully disguised to myself as a child. It was a little bit mixed sort of block, fairly solidly lower middle class, with one or two juts apiece on either side of that. The houses corresponded: middle-sized gracefully fretted wood houses built in the late nineties and early nineteen hundreds, with small front and side and more spacious back yards, and trees in the yards, and porches. These were softwooded trees, poplars, tulip trees, cottonwoods. There were fences around one or two of the houses, but mainly the yards ran into each other with only now and then a low hedge that wasn't doing very well. There were few good friends among the grown people, and they were not poor enough for the other sort of intimate acquaintance, but everyone nodded and spoke, and even might talk short times, trivially, and at the two extremes of the general or the particular, and ordinarily nextdoor neighbors talked quite a bit when they happened to run into each other, and never paid calls. The men were mostly small businessmen, one or two very modestly executives, one or two worked with their hands, most of them clerical, and most of them between thirty and forty-five.   /**1**

But it is of these evenings, I speak.   /**2**

Supper was at six and was over by half past. There was still daylight, shining softly and with a tarnish, like the lining of a shell; and the carbon lamps lifted at the corners were on in the light, and the locusts were started, and the fire flies were out, and a few frogs were flopping in the dewy grass, by the time the fathers and the children came out. The children ran out first hell bent and yelling those names by which they were known; then the fathers sank out leisurely in crossed suspenders, their collars removed and their necks looking tall and shy. The mothers stayed back in the kitchen washing and drying, putting things away, recrossing their traceless footsteps like the lifetime journeys of bees, measuring out the dry cocoa for breakfast. When they came out they had taken off their aprons and their skirts were dampened and they sat in rockers on their porches quietly.   /**3**

It is not of the games children play in the evening that I want to speak now, it is of a contemporaneous atmosphere that has little to do with them: that of the fathers of families, each in his space of lawn, his shirt fishlike pale in the unnatural light and his face nearly anonymous, hosing their lawns. The hoses were attached at spiggots that stood out of the brick foundations of the houses. The nozzles were variously set but usually so there was a long sweet stream of spray, the nozzle wet in the hand, the water trickling the right forearm and the peeled-back cuff, and the water whishing out a long loose and low-curved cone, and so gentle a sound. First an insane noise of violence in the nozzle, then the still irregular sound of adjustment, then the smoothing into steadiness and a pitch as accurately tuned to the size and style of stream as any violin. So many qualities of sound out of one hose: so many choral differences out of those several hoses that were in earshot. Out of any one hose, the almost dead silence of the release, and the short still arch of the separate big drops, silent as a held breath, and the only noise the flattering noise on leaves and the slapped grass at the fall of each big drop. That, and the intense hiss with the intense stream; that, and that same intensity not growing less but growing more quiet and delicate with the turn of the nozzle, up to that extreme tender whisper when the water was just a wide bell of film. Chiefly, though, the hoses were set much alike, in a compromise between distance and tenderness of spray (and quite surely a sense of art behind this compromise, and a quiet deep joy, too real to recognize itself), and the sounds therefore were pitched much alike; pointed by the snorting start of a new hose; decorated by some man playful with the nozzle; left empty, like God by the sparrow's fall, when any single one of them desists: and all, though near alike, of various pitch; and in this unison. These sweet pale streamings in the light lift out their pallors and their voices all together, mothers hushing their children, the hushing unnaturally prolonged, the men gentle and silent and each snail-like withdrawn into the quietude of what he singly is doing, the urination of huge children stood loosely military against an invisible wall, and gentle happy and peaceful, tasting the mean goodness of their living like the last of their suppers in their mouths; while the locusts carry on this noise of hoses on their much higher and sharper key. The noise of the locust is dry, and it seems not to be rasped or vibrated but urged from him as if through a small orifice by a breath that can never give out. Also there is never one locust but an illusion of at least a thousand. The noise of each locust is pitched in some classic locust range out of which none of them varies more than two full tones: and yet you seem to hear each locust discrete from all the rest, and there is a long, slow, pulse in their noise, like the scarcely defined arch of a long and high set bridge. They are all around in every tree, so that the noise seems to come from nowhere and everywhere at once, from the whole shell heaven, shivering in your flesh and teasing your eardrums, the boldest of all the sounds of night. And yet it is habitual to summer nights, and is of the great order of noises, like the noises of the sea and of the blood of her precocious grandchild, which you realize you are hearing only when you catch yourself listening. Meantime from low in the dark, just outside the swaying horizons of the hoses, conveying always grass in the damp of dew and its strong green-black smear of smell, the regular yet spaced noises of the crickets, each a sweet cold silver noise three-noted, like the slipping each time of three matched links of a small chain.   /4

But the men by now, one by one, have silenced their hoses and drained and coiled them. Now only two, and now only one, is left, and you see only ghostlike shirt with the sleeve garters, and sober mystery of his mild face like the lifted face of large cattle enquiring of your presence in a pitchdark pool of meadow; and now he too is gone; and it has become that time of evening when people sit on their porches, rocking gently and talking gently and watching the street and the standing up into their sphere of possession of the trees, of birds hung havens, hangars. People go by; things go by. A horse, drawing a buggy, breaking his hollow iron music on the asphalt; a loud auto; a quiet auto; people in pairs, not in a hurry, scuffling, switching their weight of aestival body, talking casually, the taste hovering over them of vanilla, strawberry, pasteboard and starched milk, the image upon them of lovers and horsemen, squared with clowns in hueless amber. A street car raising its iron moan; stopping, belling and starting; stertorous; rousing and raising again its iron increasing moan and swimming its gold windows and straw seats on past and past and past, the bleak spark crackling and cursing above it like a small malignant spirit set to dog its tracks; the iron whine rises on rising speed; still risen, faints; halts; the faint stinging bell; rises again, still fainting, lifting, lifts, faints forgone: forgotten. Now is the night one blue dew.   /5

Now is the night one blue dew, my father has drained, he has coiled the hose.
Low on the length of lawns, a frailing of fire who breathes.
Content, silver, like peeps of light, each cricket makes his comment over and over in
    the drowned grass.
A cold toad thumpily flounders.
Within the edges of damp shadows of side yards are hovering children nearly sick
    with joy of fear, who watch the unguarding of a telephone pole.
Around white carbon corner lamps bugs of all sizes are lifted elliptic, solar systems.
    Big hardshalls bruise themselves, assailant: he is fallen on his back,
    legs squiggling.
Parents on porches: rock and rock: From damp strings morning glories hang their
    ancient faces.
The dry and exalted noise of the locusts from all the air at once enchants
    my eardrums.   /6

On the rough wet grass of the back yard my father and mother have spread quilts. We all lie there, my mother, my father, my uncle, my aunt, and I too am lying there. First we were sitting up, then one of us lay down, and then we all lay down, on our stomachs, or on our sides, or on our backs, and they have kept on talking. They are not talking much, and the talk is quiet, of nothing in particular, of nothing at all in particular, of nothing at all. The stars are wide and alive, they seem each like a smile of great sweetness, and they seem very near. All my people are larger bodies than mine, quiet, with voices gentle and meaningless like the voices of sleeping birds. One is an artist, he is living at home. One is a musician, she is living at home. One is my mother who is good to me. One is my father who is good to me. By some chance, here they are, all on this earth; and who shall ever tell the sorrow of being on this earth, lying, on quilts, on the grass, in a summer evening, among the sounds of night. May God bless my people, my uncle, my aunt, my mother, my father, oh, remember them kindly in their time of trouble; and in the hour of their taking away.   /7

After a little I am taken in and put to bed. Sleep, soft smiling, draws me unto her: and those receive me, who quietly treat me, as one familiar and well-beloved in that home: but will not, oh, will not, not now, not ever; but will not ever tell me who I am.   /8

Review Questions

1. What point is the author making in this essay?
2. How does Agee's choice of descriptive details contribute to this point? Be specific.
3. Why do you suppose the author describes the evening — especially supper time — rather than some other part of the day?
4. What audience do you think Agee is addressing?

An Enduring Spirit

N. Scott Momaday

N. Scott Momaday (1934-   ) was born in Lawton, Oklahoma. He received his B.A. from the University of New Mexico and his M.A. and Ph.D. from Stanford University. He is the author of several books of poetry, literary criticism, and a novel, *House Made of Dawn*, which won the Pulitzer Prize for fiction in 1969. The theme running throughout his work is that of the enduring spirit of his Indian forebears and their close ties to the land.

In this selection, from the Introduction to *The Way to Rainy Mountain*, Momaday describes his grandmother and her pervasive hold on his imagination.

My grandmother had a reverence for the sun, a holy regard that now is all but gone out of mankind. There was a wariness in her, and an ancient awe. She was a Christian in her later years, but she had come a long way about, and she never forgot her birthright. As a child she had been to the Sun Dances; she had taken part in those annual rites, and by them she had learned the restoration of her people in the presence of Tai-me. She was about seven when the last Kiowa Sun Dance was held in 1887 on the Washita River above Rainy Mountain Creek. The buffalo were gone. In order to consummate the ancient sacrifice — to impale the head of a buffalo bull upon the medicine tree — a delegation of old men journeyed into Texas, there to beg and barter for an animal from the Goodnight herd. She was ten when the Kiowas came together for the last time as a living Sun Dance culture. They could find no buffalo; they had to hang an old hide from the sacred tree. Before the dance could begin, a company of soldiers rode out from Fort Sill under orders to disperse the tribe. Forbidden without cause the essential act of their faith, having seen the wild herds slaughtered and left to rot upon the ground, the Kiowas backed away forever from the medicine tree. That was July 20, 1890, at the great bend of the Washita. My grandmother was there. Without bitterness, and for as long as she lived, she bore a vision of deicide.   /1

Now that I can have her only in memory, I see my grandmother in the several postures that were peculiar to her: standing at the wood stove on a winter morning and turning meat in a great iron skillet; sitting at the south window, bent above her beadwork, and afterwards, when her vision failed, looking down for a long time into the fold of her hands; going out upon a cane, very slowly as she did when the weight of age came upon her; praying. I remember her most often at prayer. She made long, rambling prayers out of suffering and hope, having seen many things. I was never sure that I had the right to hear, so exclusive were they of all mere custom and company. The last time I saw her she prayed standing by the side of her bed at night, naked to the waist, the light of a kerosene lamp moving upon her dark skin. Her long, black hair, always drawn and braided in the day, lay upon her shoulders and against her breasts like a shawl. I do not speak Kiowa, and I never understood her prayers, but there was something inherently sad in the sound, some merest hesitation upon the syllables of sorrow. She began in a high and descending pitch, exhausting her breath to silence; then again and again — and always the same intensity of effort, of something that is, and is not, like urgency in the human voice. Transported so in the dancing light among the shadows of her room, she seemed beyond the reach of time. But that was illusion; I think I knew then that I should not see her again.   /2

Houses are like sentinels in the plain, old keepers of the weather watch. There, in a very little while, wood takes on the appearance of great age. All colors wear soon away in the wind and rain, and then the wood is burned gray and the grain appears and the nails turn red with rust. The windowpanes are black and opaque; you imagine there is nothing within, and indeed there are many ghosts, bones given up to the land. They stand here and there against the sky, and you approach them for a longer time than you expect. They belong in the distance; it is their domain.   /3

Once there was a lot of sound in my grandmother's house, a lot of coming and going, feasting and talk. The summers there were full of excitement and reunion. The Kiowas are a summer people; they abide the cold and keep to themselves, but when the season turns and the land becomes warm and vital they cannot hold still; an old love of going returns upon them. The aged visitors who came to my grandmother's house when I was a child were made of lean and leather, and they bore themselves upright. They wore great black hats and bright ample shirts that shook in the wind. They rubbed fat upon their hair and wound their braids with strips of colored cloth. Some of them painted their faces and carried the scars of old and cherished enmities. They were an old council of warlords, come to remind and be reminded of who they were. Their wives and daughters served them well. The women might indulge themselves; gossip was at once the mark and compensation of their servitude. They made loud and elaborate talk among themselves, full of jest and gesture, fright and false alarm.

They went abroad in fringed and flowered shawls, bright beadwork and German silver. They were at home in the kitchen, and they prepared meals that were banquets. /4

There were frequent prayer meetings, and great nocturnal feasts. When I was a child I played with my cousins outside, where the lamplight fell upon the ground and the singing of the old people rose up around us and carried away into the darkness. There were a lot of good things to eat, a lot of laughter and surprise. And afterwards, when the quiet returned, I lay down with my grandmother and could hear the frogs away by the river and feel the motion of the air. /5

Now there is a funeral silence in the rooms, the endless wake of some final word. The walls have closed in upon my grandmother's house. When I returned to it in mourning, I saw for the first time in my life how small it was. It was late at night, and there was a white moon, nearly full. I sat for a long time on the stone steps by the kitchen door. From there I could see out across the land; I could see the long row of trees by the creek, the low light upon the rolling plains, and the stars of the Big Dipper. Once I looked at the moon and caught sight of a strange thing. A cricket had perched upon the handrail, only a few inches away from me. My line of vision was such that the creature filled the moon like a fossil. It had gone there, I thought, to live and die, for there, of all places, was its small definition made whole and eternal. A warm wind rose up and purled like the longing within me. /6

The next morning I awoke at dawn and went out on the dirt road to Rainy Mountain. It was already hot, and the grasshoppers began to fill the air. Still, it was early in the morning, and the birds sang out of the shadows. The long yellow grass on the mountain shone in the bright light, and a scissortail hied above the land. There, where it ought to be, at the end of a long and legendary way, was my grandmother's grave. Here and there on the dark stones were ancestral names. Looking back once, I saw the mountain and came away. /7

Review Questions

1. What is the point that Momaday is trying to make in this piece?
2. How does he use description to make this point?
3. What exactly is he describing?
4. What audience would you imagine Momaday is addressing?
5. How does Momaday's sense of nostalgia become apparent in this essay?

Baking Off

Nora Ephron

Nora Ephron (1941-   ) is a New York City-based essayist whose writing has been published in *New York* magazine, *The New Yorker, The New York Times Book*

Review, Ms., and *Rolling Stone.* She is the author of *Wallflower at the Orgy,* and *Crazy Salad,* (1975), a collection of essays about women, in which "Baking Off" is included.

In "Baking Off," Ephron describes a cooking contest, which she implies is typical of the kind of activity in which certain women spend much of their time participating. Ephron's disdain for such activities is evident through the sarcasm in this piece.

Roxanne Frisbie brought her own pan to the twenty-fourth annual Pillsbury Bake-Off. "I feel like a nut," she said. "It's just a plain old dumb pan, but everything I do is in that crazy pan." As it happens, Mrs. Frisbie had no cause whatsoever to feel like a nut: it seemed that at least half the 100 finalists in the Bake-It-Easy Bake-Off had brought something with them — their own sausages, their own pie pans, their own apples. Edna Buckley, who was fresh from representing New York State at the National Chicken Cooking Contest, where her recipe for fried chicken in a batter of beer, cheese, and crushed pretzels had gone down to defeat, brought with her a lucky handkerchief, a lucky horseshoe, a lucky dime for her shoe, a potholder with the Pillsbury Poppin' Fresh Doughboy on it, an Our Blessed Lady pin, and all of her jewelry, including a silver charm also in the shape of the doughboy. Mrs. Frisbie and Mrs. Buckley and the other finalists came to the Bake-Off to bake off for $65,000 in cash prizes; in Mrs. Frisbie's case, this meant making something she created herself and named Butterscotch Crescent Rolls — and which Pillsbury promptly, and to Mrs. Frisbie's dismay, renamed Sweet 'N Creamy Crescent Crisps. Almost all the recipes in the finals were renamed by Pillsbury using a lot of crispy snicky snacky words. An exception to this was Sharon Schubert's Wiki Wiki Coffee Cake, a name which ought to have been snicky snacky enough; but Pillsbury, in a moment of restraint, renamed it One-Step Tropical Fruit Cake. As it turned out, Mrs. Schubert ended up winning $5,000 for her cake, which made everybody pretty mad, even the contestants who had been saying for days that they did not care who won, that winning meant nothing and was quite beside the point; the fact was that Sharon Schubert was a previous Bake-Off winner, having won $10,000 three years before for her Crescent Apple Snacks, and in addition had walked off with a trip to Puerto Vallarta in the course of this year's festivities. Most of the contestants felt she had won a little more than was really fair. But I'm getting ahead of the story.   /1

The Pillsbury Company has been holding Bake-Offs since 1948, when Eleanor Roosevelt, for reasons that are not clear, came to give the first one her blessing. This year's took place from Saturday, February 24, through Tuesday, February 27, at the Beverly Hilton Hotel in Beverly Hills. One hundred contestants — 97 of them women, 2 twelve-year-old boys, and 1 male graduate student — were winnowed down from a field of almost 100,000 entrants to compete for prizes in five categories: flour, frosting mix, crescent main dish, crescent dessert, and hot-roll mix. They were all brought, or flown, to Los

Angeles for the Bake-Off itself, which took place on Monday, and a round of activities that included a tour of Universal Studios, a mini-version of television's *Let's Make a Deal* with Monty Hall himself, and a trip to Disneyland. The event is also attended by some 100 food editors, who turn it from a mere contest into the incredible publicity stunt Pillsbury intends it to be, and spend much of their time talking to each other about sixty-five new ways to use tuna fish and listening to various speakers lecture on the consumer movement and food and the appliance business. General Electric is co-sponsor of the event and donates a stove to each finalist, as well as the stoves for the Bake-Off. . . .   /2

"The Bake-Off is America," a General Electric executive announced just minutes before it began. "It's family. It's real people doing real things." Yes. The Pillsbury Bake-Off is an America that exists less and less, but exists nonetheless. It is women who still live on farms, who have six and seven children, who enter county fairs and sponsor 4-H Clubs. It is Grace Ferguson of Palm Springs, Florida, who entered the Bake-Off seventeen years in a row before reaching the finals this year, and who cooks at night and prays at the same time. It is Carol Hamilton, who once won a trip on a Greyhound bus to Hollywood for being the most popular girl in Youngstown, Ohio. There was a lot of talk at the Bake-Off about how the Bake-It-Easy theme had attracted a new breed of contestants this year, younger contestants — housewives, yes, but housewives who used whole-wheat flour and Granola and sour cream and similar supposedly hip ingredients in their recipes and were therefore somewhat more sophisticated, or urban, or something-of-the-sort than your usual Bake-Off contestant. There were a few of these — two, to be exact: Barbara Goldstein of New York City and Bonnie Brooks of Salisbury, Maryland, who actually visited the Los Angeles County Art Museum during a free afternoon. But there was also Suzie Sisson of Palatine, Illinois, twenty-five years old and the only Bundt-pan person in the finals, and her sentiments about life were the same as those that Bake-Off finalists presumably have had for years. "These are the beautiful people," she said, looking around the ballroom as she waited for her Bundt cake to come out of the oven. "They're not the little tiny rich people. They're nice and happy and religious types and family-oriented. Everyone talks about women's lib, which is ridiculous. If you're nice to your husband, he'll be nice to you. Your family is your job. They come first."   /3

I was seven years old when the Pillsbury Bake-Off began, and as I grew up reading the advertisements for it in the women's magazines that were lying around the house, it always seemed to me that going to a Bake-Off would be the closest thing to a childhood fantasy of mine, which was to be locked overnight in a bakery. In reality, going to a Bake-Off *is* like being locked overnight in a bakery — a very bad bakery. I almost became sick right there on Range 95 after my sixth carbohydrate-packed sample — which happened, by coincidence, to be a taste of the aforementioned Mrs. Frisbie's aforementioned Sweet 'N Creamy Crescent Crisps.   /4

But what is interesting about the Bake-Off — what is even significant about the event — is that it is, for the American housewife, what the Miss America contest used to represent to teen-agers. The pinnacle of a certain kind of achievement. The best in field. To win the Pillsbury Bake-Off, even to be merely a finalist in it, is to be a great housewife. And a creative housewife. "Cooking is very creative." I must have heard that line thirty times as I interviewed the finalists. I don't happen to think that cooking is very creative — what interests me about it is, on the contrary, its utter mindlessness and mathematical certainty. "Cooking is very relaxing" — that's my bromide. On the other hand, I have to admit that some of the recipes that were concocted for the Bake-Off, amazing combinations of frosting mix and marshmallows and peanut butter and brown sugar and chocolate, were practically awe-inspiring. And cooking, it is quite clear, is only a small part of the apparently frenzied creativity that flourishes in these women's homes. . . . /5

On Monday morning at exactly 9 a.m., the one hundred finalists marched four abreast into the Hilton ballroom, led by Philip Pillsbury, former chairman of the board of the company. The band played "Nothin' Says Lovin' Like Somethin' from the Oven," and when it finished, Pillsbury announced: "Now you one hundred winners can go to your ranges."   /6

Chaos. Shrieking. Frenzy. Furious activity. Cracking eggs. Chopping onions. Melting butter. Mixing, beating, blending. The band perking along with such carefully selected tunes as "If I Knew You Were Coming I'd Have Baked a Cake." Contestants running to the refrigerators for more supplies. Floor assistants rushing dirty dishes off to unseen dishwashers. All two hundred members of the working press, plus television's Bob Barker, interviewing any finalist they could get to drop a spoon. At 9:34 a.m., Mrs. Lorraine Walmann submitted her Cheesy Crescent Twist-Ups to the judges and became the first finalist to finish. At 10 a.m., all the stoves were on, the television lights were blasting, the temperature in the ballroom was up to the mid-nineties, and Mrs. Marjorie Johnson, in the course of giving an interview about her house to the Minneapolis *Star*, had forgotten whether she had put one cup of sugar or two into her Crispy Apple Bake. "You know, we're building this new house," she was saying. "When I go back, I have to buy living-room furniture." By 11 a.m., Mae Wilkinson had burned her skillet corn bread and was at work on a second. Laura Aspis had lost her potholder. Barbara Bellhorn was distraught because she was not used to California apples. Alex Allard was turning out yet another Honey Drizzle Cake. Dough and flour were all over the floor. Mary Finnegan was fussing because the crumbs on her Lemon Cream Bars were too coarse. Marjorie Johnson was in the midst of yet another interview on her house. "Well, let me tell you," she was saying, "the shelves in the kitchen are built low. . . ." One by one, the contestants, who were each given seven hours and four tries to produce two perfect samples of their recipes, began to finish up and deliver one tray to the judges and one tray to the photographer. There were samples everywhere, try this, try that, but after six tries, climaxed by Mrs. Frisbie's creation, I stopped sampling. The overkill was unbearable: none of the recipes seemed to contain one cup of sugar when two would do, or a delicate cheese when Kraft American would do, or an actual minced onion when instant minced onions would do. It was snack time. It was convenience-food time. It was less-work-for-Mother time. All I could think about was a steak.   /7

By 3 p.m., there were only two contestants left — Mrs. Johnson, whose dessert took only five minutes to make but whose interviews took considerably longer, and Bonnie Brooks, whose third sour-cream-and-banana cake was still in the oven. Mrs. Brooks brought her cake in last, at 3:27 p.m., and as she did, the packing began. The skillets went into brown cartons, the measuring spoons into barrels, the stoves were dismantled. The Bake-Off itself was over — and all that remained was the trip to Disneyland, and the breakfast at the Brown Derby . . . and the prizes.   /8

And so it is Tuesday morning, and the judges have reached a decision, and any second now, Bob Barker is going to announce the five winners over national television. All the contestants are wearing their best dresses and smiling, trying to smile anyway, good sports all, and now Bob Barker is announcing the winners. Bonnie Brooks and her cake and Albina Flieller and her Quick Pecan Pie win $25,000 each. Sharon Schubert and two others win $5,000. And suddenly the show is over and it is time to go home, and the ninety-five people who did not win the twenty-fourth annual Pillsbury Bake-Off are plucking the orchids from the centerpieces, signing each other's programs, and grumbling. They are grumbling about Sharon Schubert. And for a moment, as I hear the grumbling everywhere — "It really isn't fair." . . . "After all, she won the trip to Mexico" — I think that perhaps I am wrong about these women: perhaps they are capable of anger after all, or jealousy, or competitiveness, or something I think of as a human trait I can relate to. But the grumbling stops after a few minutes, and I find myself listening to Marjorie Johnson. "I'm so glad I didn't win the grand prize," she is saying, "because if you win that, you don't get to come back to the next Bake-Off. I'm gonna start now on my recipes for the next year. I'm gonna think of something really good." She stopped for a moment. "You know," she said, "it's going to be very difficult to get back to normal living."   /9

Review Questions

1. How does Ephron's descriptions of what goes on at the Bake-Off contribute to her point?
2. How does Ephron use character description?
3. What other kind of description (besides character description) does she use?
4. Is Ephron consistent in the kind of mood she evokes in this essay?
5. What is the meaning of the last sentence in the essay?

18

Example Essays

Slang Origins

Woody Allen

Woody Allen (1935-   ), comedian, writer, movie director, star, and comic philosopher of our age, has published two books, *Getting Even* (1971) and *Without Feathers* (1975), and many essays in *The New Yorker*. His films include *Sleeper, Love and Death, Annie Hall, Interiors,* and *Manhattan.*

"Slang Origins" is a satiric essay in the mode of exemplification. Allen illustrates his purpose in this selection with a series of imaginary origins for certain expressions in our language.

How many of you have ever wondered where certain slang expressions come from? Like "She's the cat's pajamas," or to "take it on the lam." Neither have I. And yet for those who are interested in this sort of thing I have provided a brief guide to a few of the more interesting origins.   /1

Unfortunately, time did not permit consulting any of the established works on the subject, and I was forced to either obtain the information from friends or fill in certain gaps by using my own common sense.   /2

Take, for instance, the expression "to eat humble pie." During the reign of Louis the Fat, the culinary arts flourished in France to a degree unequaled anywhere. So obese was the French monarch that he had to be lowered onto the throne with a winch and packed into the seat itself with a large spatula. A typical dinner (according to DeRochet) consisted of a thin crêpe appetizer, some parsley, an ox, and custard. Food became the court obsession, and no other subject could be discussed under penalty of death. Members of a decadent aristocracy consumed incredible meals and even dressed as foods. DeRochet tells us that M. Monsant showed up at the coronation as a weiner, and Etienne Tisserant received papal dispensation to wed his favorite codfish. Desserts grew more and more elaborate and pies grew larger and larger until the minister of justice suffocated trying to eat a seven-foot "Jumbo Pie." *Jumbo* pie soon became *jumble* pie and "to eat a jumble pie" referred to any kind of humiliating act. When the Spanish seamen heard the word *jumble*, they pronounced it "humble," although many preferred to say nothing and simply grin.   /3

Now, while "humble pie" goes back to the French, "take it on the lam" is English in origin. Years ago, in England, "lamming" was a game played with dice and a large tube of ointment. Each player in turn threw dice and then skipped around the room until he hemorrhaged. If a person threw seven or under he would say the word "quintz" and proceed to twirl in a frenzy. If he threw over seven, he was forced to give every player a portion of his feathers and was given a good "lamming." Three "lammings" and a player was "kwirled" or declared a moral bankrupt. Gradually any game with feathers was called "lamming" and feathers became "lams." To "take it on the lam" meant to put on feathers and later, to escape, although the transition is unclear.   /4

Incidentally, if two of the players disagreed on the rules, we might say they "got into a beef." This term goes back to the Renaissance when a man would court a woman by stroking the side of her head with a slab of meat. If she pulled away, it meant she was spoken for. If, however, she assisted by clamping the meat to her face and pushing it all over her head, it meant she would marry him. The meat was kept by the bride's parents and worn as a hat on special occasions. If, however, the husband took another lover, the wife could dissolve the marriage by running with the meat to the town square and yelling, "With thine own beef, I do reject thee. Aroo! Aroo!" If a couple "took to the beef" or "had a beef" it meant they were quarreling.   /5

Another marital custom gives us that eloquent and colorful expression of disdain, "to look down one's nose." In Persia it was considered a mark of great beauty for a woman to have a long nose. In fact, the longer the nose, the more desirable the female, up to a certain point. Then it became funny. When a man proposed to a beautiful woman he awaited her decision on bended knee as she "looked down her nose at him." If her nostrils twitched, he was accepted, but if she sharpened her nose with pumice and began pecking him on the neck and shoulders, it meant she loved another.   /6

Now, we all know when someone is very dressed up, we say he looks "spiffy." The term owes its origin to Sir Oswald Spiffy, perhaps the most renowned fop of Victorian England. Heir to treacle millions, Spiffy squandered his money on clothes. It was said that at one time he owned enough handkerchiefs for all the men, women and children in Asia to blow their noses for seven years without stopping. Spiffy's sartorial innovations were legend, and he was the first man *ever* to wear gloves on his head. Because of *extra*-sensitive skin, Spiffy's underwear had to be made of the finest Nova Scotia salmon, carefully sliced by one particular tailor. His libertine attitudes involved him in several notorious scandals, and he eventually sued the government over the right to wear earmuffs while fondling a dwarf. In the end, Spiffy died a broken man in Chichester, his total wardrobe reduced to kneepads and a sombrero.   /**7**

Looking "spiffy," then, is quite a compliment, and one who does is liable to be dressed "to beat the band," a turn-of-the-century expression that originated from the custom of attacking with clubs any symphony orchestra whose conductor smiled during Berlioz. "Beating the band" soon became a popular evening out, and people dressed up in their finest clothes, carrying with them sticks and rocks. The practice was finally abandoned during a performance of the *Symphonie fantastique* in New York when the entire string section suddenly stopped playing and exchanged gunfire with the first ten rows. Police ended the melee but not before a relative of J. P. Morgan's was wounded in the soft palate. After that, for a while at least, nobody dressed "to beat the band."   /**8**

If you think some of the above derivations questionable, you might throw up your hands and say, "Fiddlesticks." This marvelous expression originated in Austria many years ago. Whenever a man in the banking profession announced his marriage to a circus pinhead, it was the custom for friends to present him with a bellows and a three-year supply of wax fruit. Legend has it that when Leo Rothschild made known his betrothal, a box of cello bows was delivered to him by mistake. When it was opened and found not to contain the traditional gift, he exclaimed, "What are these? Where are my bellows and fruit? Eh? All I rate is fiddlesticks!" The term "fiddlesticks" became a joke overnight in the taverns amongst the lower classes, who hated Leo Rothschild for never removing the comb from his hair after combing it. Eventually "fiddlesticks" meant any foolishness.   /**9**

Well, I hope you've enjoyed some of these slang origins and that they stimulate you to investigate some on your own. And in case you were wondering about the term used to open this study, "the cat's pajamas," it goes back to an old burlesque routine of Chase and Rowe's, the two nutsy German professors. Dressed in oversized tails, Bill Rowe stole some poor victim's pajamas. Dave Chase, who got great mileage out of his "hard of hearing" specialty, would ask him:

CHASE: Ach, Herr Professor. Vot is dot bulge under your pocket?
ROWE: Dot? Dot's de chap's pajamas.
CHASE: The cat's pajamas? Ut mein Gott?   /**10**

Audiences were convulsed by this sort of repartee and only a premature death of the team by strangulation kept them from stardom.   /**11**

Review Questions

1. Where does Allen state his alleged purpose in this essay?

2. Is this his real purpose in the essay? Does he have a more important reason for writing this piece?
3. What is Allen satirizing?
4. How do Allen's examples further his aims?
5. Is the sequence of examples logical or does it seem random and chaotic?
6. What makes this essay funny?

Fear — The Great Enemy

Eleanor Roosevelt

Eleanor Roosevelt, (1884-1962), the wife of President Franklin D. Roosevelt, was a great woman in her own right, being a writer, diplomat, and champion of youthful and liberal causes during a long and fruitful political and personal life.

"Fear — The Great Enemy," has been taken from her book *You Learn by Living* (1960). It is an essay in which Mrs. Roosevelt states, in her simple and direct way, what she considers to be the important values in life. She supports her point through exemplification.

Fear has always seemed to me to be the worst stumbling block which anyone has to face. It is the great crippler. Looking back, it strikes me that my childhood and my early youth were one long battle against fear.   /1

I was an exceptionally timid child, afraid of the dark, afraid of mice, afraid of practically everything. Painfully, step by step, I learned to stare down each of my fears, conquer it, attain the hard-earned courage to go on to the next. Only then was I really free.   /2

Of all the knowledge that we acquire in life this is the most difficult. But it is also the most rewarding. With each victory, no matter how great the cost or how agonizing at the time, there comes increased confidence and strength to help meet the next fear.   /3

I do not know any way of doing this except through self-discipline. In educational circles there is always a great deal of talk about how much discipline should be imposed. I do not know the answer, but I do know that the discipline one imposes on oneself is the only sure bulwark one has against fear. It is a lesson I had to learn at a painfully early age.   /4

My grandmother brought me up from the time I was seven. Because she had been overindulgent with her own children, she decided that my younger brother and I must be taught to obey. She proceeded on the theory that it is wiser to say "no" than "yes" to children.   /5

She believed that a daily cold sponge bath kept one from catching cold and I took cold sponge baths for years. She believed that if I caught cold or had a headache it was a result of my own foolishness and that I should be expected to keep myself in good health. All this was spartan treatment and it was, I think, carried to excess, but I must confess that even today I feel that I am responsible for using common sense in keeping myself in good health.   /6

All this was imposed discipline. I learned in time that when I wanted very much to do things I was more than apt to be told "no." So I learned self-discipline as a kind of defense. I learned to protect myself from disappointment by not asking for what I wanted.   /7

There were things I wanted so much, things like love and affection. I was conscious, as only a very young girl can be, of the fact that I did not have the looks of my aunts or my beautiful mother. I was the ugly duckling. I had such an intense longing for approval and love that it forced me to acquire self-discipline. Undoubtedly, this stood me in good stead in later life but I had to attain it much earlier than most people do.   /8

I had to make a difficult choice: I was afraid of everything, but, on the other hand, I wanted to do things that would win me the affection I craved. So I had to stare down my fears.   /9

I can remember vividly an occasion when I was living in my grandmother's house on Thirty-seventh Street in New York City. One of my aunts was ill and asked for some ice, which was kept in the icebox out of doors in the back yard.   /10

I was so frightened that I shook. But I could not refuse to go. If I did that, she would never again ask me to help her and I could not bear not to be asked.   /11

I had to go down alone from the third floor in the dark, creeping through the big house, which was so hostile and unfamiliar at night, in which unknown terrors seemed to lurk. Down to the basement, shutting a door behind me that cut me off from the house and safety. Out in the blackness of the back yard.   /12

I suffered agonies of fear that night. But I learned that I could face the dark and it never again held such horror for me.   /13

I think my grandmother quite unwittingly let fears take root in me because she left so many questions unanswered. She never told me anything, but she allowed me to read anything I wanted in the library, which held a great many books. A number of them were on theological subjects, which did not attract me, though I still remember the terror aroused by the Gustave Doré illustrations of the Bible.   /14

Reading all the way through Dickens and Scott, I came upon much material which I could not understand. Although I lived in the family with young uncles and aunts, they did not consider it their business to tell me much about life. As a result, I would face members of my family at awkward moments with questions which they did not want to answer. The book I was reading would promptly disappear. No matter how much I looked or asked, no one had seen it. I never realized that it had been removed, so I went on searching. As I grew in knowledge, I would find the book again and understand what I had been reading and why my questions had not been answered.   /15

I can remember one day coming home from the class which was my source of information on many subjects, chiefly from other children, all of whom were well-brought-up little girls. I said to my grandmother, "What is the meaning of whore? It is in the Bible."   /16

"It is not a word that little girls should use," she told me severely.   /17

Later on, my school friends enlightened me.   /18

The fact of being free to read while not being able to understand what I was reading only whetted my curiosity. While I cannot say my grandmother enlightened me, her negative method made me seek enlightenment on many subjects she was far from wanting me to know about.   /19

I remember once being sent to a church fair and being given money to spend. Instead, I spent my money for a ticket to *Tess of the d'Urbervilles*, which my young aunts had seen. I had been told that I was too young to go.   /20

But the withholding of information from a child either frustrates him or makes him seek it for himself. And the trouble with the latter method is that it is apt to make the child feel both guilty and dishonest.   /21

I found myself enmeshed in a series of lies, trying to explain why I brought nothing home from the fair. At length, it was easier to own up and take my punishment. Stealing and lying, they told me, were unforgivable sins. For three days, no one spoke to me. To a child who wanted above everything else to be loved, this was a terrible punishment.   /22

None the less, I went on lying, more or less, out of fear, until I went to boarding school abroad at fifteen. I can remember now the wonder and the freedom I experienced when I realized that I could start with a clean slate, that there was nothing to be afraid of.   /23

Through most of my early life that childish fear persisted, the terror of displeasing the people I lived with. I look back now with amazement on the dreadful day after I was married. Franklin had given me one of his precious first editions to look at. In some inconceivable way, I tore one page a little. I held it in my hands, while cold shivers went up and down my spine. Finally, I made myself tell him what I had done. He looked at me with bewilderment and some amusement. "If you had not done it, I probably would. A book is made to be read, not to be held." What I had dreaded I don't know, but I remember my vast relief. That was the beginning of my becoming more mature about my fears of displeasing people.   /24

The encouraging thing is that *every* time you meet a situation, though you may think at the time it is an impossibility and you go through the tortures of the damned, once you have met it and lived through it you find that forever after you are freer than you ever were before. If you can live through that you can live through anything. You gain strength, courage, and confidence by *every* experience in which you really stop to look fear in the face. You are able to say to yourself, "I lived through this horror. I can take the next thing that comes along."   /25

The danger lies in refusing to face the fear, in not daring to come to grips with it. If you fail anywhere along the line it will take away your confidence. You must make yourself succeed every time. *You must do the thing you think you cannot do.*   /26

Like too many people of my generation I grew up with a fear of insanity and no real understanding of it. During the First World War, I was living in Washington, where my husband was Assistant Secretary of the Navy. The Red Cross asked me to visit St. Elizabeth's Hospital, where the Navy had a big installation for boys who had gone temporarily or permanently insane.   /27

I cannot do this, I thought. I was terrified of insanity. Then I realized that I was the Assistant Secretary's wife. This was my job. I had to do it whether I could do it or not.   /28

The first time I went to the ward with the doctor, he unlocked a door, we went in, and then he locked it behind us. Locked in with the insane! I wanted to bang at the door, to get out. But I was ashamed of myself. I would not have shown my terror for the world.   /29

It was a long ward with men, some of them in cubicles chained to their beds, and a strange sound permeating the whole place. The men were talking and mumbling to themselves, not conversation, just private thoughts revealed in an endless series of monologues.   /30

At the end of the ward, standing where the sun coming through the window touched his golden hair, stood a handsome young man. He did not see us. He saw nothing but some private vision of his own. He kept muttering.   /31

"What is he saying?" I asked the doctor.

"He keeps repeating the orders at Dunkirk to go to the shelters."

"Will he get over it?"

"I don't know," the doctor said flatly.   /32

I watched the boy struggling with his private hell and my imaginary fear seemed shameful. It was one more hurdle to climb over but it had to be done. That, at least, I need never fear again.   /33

One thing I learned by those visits to the Naval Hospital helped me enormously later on. Over and over, I met women there, young and old, who were obliged to confront situations they had never conceived of. They had to face the fact that their husbands or sons were temporarily or permanently affected mentally by the war. They met the problem in different ways, of course, most of them courageously, some of them magnificently. Often I became involved in the fate of a particular boy and some of them I followed for years after they left the hospital. To see how people could face what seemed to be an insurmountable disaster was a tremendous lesson.   /34

Review Questions

1. What is Eleanor Roosevelt's point in this essay?
2. Which examples best convey Roosevelt's point to her readers?
3. Are the examples arranged in a logical way? Explain.
4. Are the examples consistent in tone?

The Music of This Sphere

Lewis Thomas

Lewis Thomas (1917-   ) a physician and scientist, is president of Memorial Sloan-Kettering Cancer Center in New York. He has served on the faculties of the University of Minnesota, NYU-Bellevue Medical Center, and Yale Medical School. He is also a member of the National Academy of Sciences.

In addition to his scientific accomplishments, Dr. Thomas has published a series of essays on science in *The New England Journal of Medicine,* some of which were collected in *The Lives of a Cell* (1974) and *The Snail and the Medusa* (1979). These essays, comprising Dr. Thomas's observations of the world around him, are as easily appreciated for their style and content by the layman as by the scientist. "The Music of This Sphere" is an exemplification essay.

It is one of our problems that as we become crowded together, the sounds we make to each other, in our increasingly complex communication systems, become more random-sounding, accidental or incidental, and we have trouble selecting meaningful signals out of the noise. One reason is, of course, that we do not seem able to restrict our communication to information-bearing, relevant signals. Given any new technology for transmitting information, we seem bound to use it for great quantities of small talk. We are only saved by music from being overwhelmed by nonsense.   /1

It is a marginal comfort to know that the relatively new science of bioacoustics must deal with similar problems in the sounds made by other animals to each other. No matter what sound-making device is placed at their disposal, creatures in general do a great deal of gabbling, and it requires long patience and observation to edit out the parts lacking syntax and sense. Light social conversation, designed to keep the party going, prevails. Nature abhors a long silence.   /2

Somewhere, underlying all the other signals, is a continual music. Termites make percussive sounds to each other by beating their heads against the floor in the dark, resonating corridors of their nests. The sound has been described as resembling, to the human ear, sand falling on paper, but spectrographic analysis of sound records has recently revealed a high degree of organization in the drumming; the beats occur in regular, rhythmic phrases, differing in duration, like notes for a tympani section.   /3

From time to time, certain termites make a convulsive movement of their mandibles to produce a loud, high-pitched clicking sound, audible ten meters off. So much effort goes into this one note that it must have urgent meaning, at least to the sender. He cannot make it without such a wrench that he is flung one or two centimeters into the air by the recoil.   /4

There is obvious hazard in trying to assign a particular meaning to this special kind of sound, and problems like this exist throughout the field of bioacoustics. One can imagine a woolly-minded Visitor from Outer Space, interested in human beings, discerning on his spectrograph the click of that golf ball on the surface of the moon, and trying to account for it as a call of warning (unlikely), a signal of mating (out of the question), or an announcement of territory (could be).   /5

Bats are obliged to make sounds almost ceaselessly, to sense, by sonar, all the objects in their surroundings. They can spot with accuracy, on the wing, small insects, and they will home onto things they like with infallibility and speed. With such a system for the equivalent of glancing around, they must live in a world of ultrasonic batsound, most of it with an industrial, machinery sound. Still, they communicate with each other as well, by clicks and high-pitched greetings. Moreover, they have been heard to produce, while hanging at rest upside down in the depths of woods, strange, solitary, and lovely bell-like notes.   /6

Almost anything that an animal can employ to make a sound is put to use. Drumming, created by beating the feet, is used by prairie hens, rabbits, and mice; the head is banged by woodpeckers and certain other birds; the males of deathwatch beetles make a rapid ticking sound by percussion of a protuberance on the abdomen against the ground; a faint but audible ticking is made by the tiny beetle *Lepinotus inquilinus,* which is less than two millimeters in length. Fish make sounds by clicking their teeth, blowing air, and drumming with special muscles against tuned inflated air bladders. Solid structures are set to vibrating by toothed bows in crustaceans and insects. The proboscis of the death's-head hawk moth is used as a kind of reed instrument, blown through to make high-pitched, reedy notes.   /7

Gorillas beat their chests for certain kinds of discourse. Animals with loose skeletons rattle them, or, like rattlesnakes, get sounds from externally placed structures. Turtles, alligators, crocodiles, and even snakes make various more or less vocal sounds. Leeches have been heard to tap rhythmically on leaves, engaging the attention of other leeches, which tap back, in synchrony. Even earthworms make sounds, faint staccato notes in regular clusters. Toads sing to each other, and their friends sing back in antiphony.   /8

Birdsong has been so much analyzed for its content of business communication that there seems little time left for music, but it is there. Behind the glossaries of warning calls, alarms, mating messages, pronouncements of territory, calls for recruitment, and demands for dispersal, there is redundant, elegant sound that is unaccountable as part of the working day. The thrush in my backyard sings down his nose in meditative, liquid runs of melody, over and over again, and I have the strongest impression that he does this for his own pleasure. Some of the time he seems to be practicing, like a virtuoso in his apartment. He starts a run, reaches a midpoint in the second bar where there should be a set of complex harmonics, stops, and goes back to begin over, dissatisfied. Sometimes he changes his notation so conspicuously that he seems to be improvising sets of variations. It is a meditative, questioning kind of music, and I cannot believe that he is simply saying, "thrush here."   /9

The robin sings flexible songs, containing a variety of motifs that he rearranges to his liking; the notes in each motif constitute the syntax, and the possibilities of variation produce a considerable repertoire. The meadow lark, with three hundred notes to work with, arranges these in phrases of three to six notes and elaborates fifty types of song. The nightingale has twenty-four basic songs, but gains wild variety by varying the internal arrangement of phrases and the length of pauses. The chaffinch listens to other chaffinches, and incorporates into his memory snatches of their songs.   /10

The need to make music, and to listen to it, is universally expressed by human beings. I cannot imagine, even in our most primitive times, the emergence of talented painters to make cave paintings without there having been, near at hand, equally creative people making song. It is, like speech, a dominant aspect of human biology.   /11

The individual parts played by other instrumentalists — crickets or earthworms, for instance — may not have the sound of music by themselves, but we hear them out of context. If we could listen to them all at once, fully orchestrated, in their immense ensemble, we might become aware of the counterpoint, the balance of tones and timbres and harmonics, the sonorities. The recorded songs of the humpback whale, filled with tensions and resolutions, ambiguities and allusions, incomplete, can be listened to as a *part* of music, like an isolated section of an orchestra. If we had better hearing, and could discern the descants of sea birds, the rhythmic tympani of schools of mollusks, or even the distant harmonics of midges hanging over meadows in the sun, the combined sound might lift us off our feet.   /12

There are, of course, other ways to account for the songs of whales. They might be simple, down-to-earth statements about navigation, or sources of krill, or limits of territory. But the proof is not in, and until it is shown that these long, convoluted, insistent melodies, repeated by different singers with ornamentations of their own, are the means of sending through several hundred miles of undersea such ordinary information as "whale here," I shall believe otherwise. Now and again, in the intervals between songs, the whales have been seen to breach, leaping clear out of the sea and landing on their backs, awash in the turbulence of their beating flippers. Perhaps they are pleased by the way the piece went, or perhaps it is celebration at hearing one's own song returning after circumnavigation; whatever, it has the look of jubilation.   /13

I suppose that my extraterrestrial Visitor might puzzle over my records in much the same way, on first listening. The 14th Quartet might, for him, be a communication announcing, "Beethoven here," answered, after passage through an undersea of time and submerged currents of human thought, by another long signal a century later, "Bartok here."   /14

If, as I believe, the urge to make a kind of music is as much a characteristic of biology as our other fundamental functions, there ought to be an explanation for it. Having none at hand, I am free to make one up. The rhythmic sounds might be the recapitulation of something else — an earliest memory, a score for the transformation of inanimate, random matter in chaos into the improbable, ordered dance of living forms. Morowitz has presented the case, in thermodynamic terms, for the hypothesis that a steady flow of energy from the inexhaustible source of the sun to the unfillable sink of outer space, by way of the earth, is mathematically destined to cause the organization of matter into an increasingly ordered state. The resulting balancing act involves a ceaseless clustering of bonded atoms into molecules of higher and higher complexity, and the emergence of cycles for the storage and release of energy. In a nonequilibrium steady state, which is postulated, the solar energy would not just flow to the earth and radiate away; it is thermodynamically inevitable that it must rearrange matter into symmetry, away from probability, against entropy, lifting it, so to speak, into a constantly changing condition of rearrangement and molecular ornamentation. In such a system, the outcome is a chancy kind of order, always on the verge of descending into chaos, held taut against probability by the unremitting, constant surge of energy from the sun.   /**15**

If there were to be sounds to represent this process, they would have the arrangement of the Brandenburg Concertos for my ear, but I am open to wonder whether the same events are recalled by the rhythms of insects, the long, pulsing runs of birdsong, the descants of whales, the modulated vibrations of a million locusts in migration, the tympani of gorilla breasts, termite heads, drumfish bladders. A "grand canonical ensemble" is, oddly enough, the proper term for a quantitative model system in thermodynamics, borrowed from music by way of mathematics. Borrowed back again, provided with notation, it would do for what I have in mind.   /**16**

Review Questions

1. What does Thomas mean by "music"?
2. What does Thomas mean by "it would do for what I have in mind" at the end of the essay?
3. What point is Thomas trying to convey?
4. How is he using his many examples to help convey that point?

The American Tradition of Winning

George Plimpton

George Plimpton (1927-   ) is a contemporary writer and journalist whose essays have appeared in such magazines as *Esquire, Sports Illustrated, Horizon,* and *Vogue,* and whose many books include several about sports, written from the point of view of an insider. Plimpton actually participated as an amateur in such professional sports leagues as golf, boxing, baseball, and football. He also founded *The Paris Review.*

"The American Tradition of Winning," which first appeared in United Airlines' *Mainliner* magazine, contains many pertinent examples to support the author's view of the American preoccupation with sports.

Involvement with sports, as participant or observer in the stands, is supposed to provide a healthy uplift . . . largely by identification with winning. Chief Justice Warren once offered a pertinent observation: "At the breakfast table," he said, "I always open the newspaper to the sports page first. The sports page records people's accomplishments. The front page has nothing but man's failures."   /1

I have never been comfortable with that comment — since in fact the sports page lists far more failures, losers, and also-rans than any other page in a newspaper short of the stock market listings on a Black Friday.   /2

The reason for this is obvious enough: for every winner there is a loser; in the case of tournaments, with rafts of contestants entered, only one winner can emerge. Since there are so many losers, sport has not been a release at the breakfast table, but a type of daily agony. The fan looks at the paper in the morning and he probably starts off his day (unless he possesses the magnanimity of a Chief Justice) by feeling punk. Imagine being a Washington Capitals hockey fan. At this writing the team has lost 26 straight games!   /3

The problem, of course, is that these things are taken very seriously. It was not always so. Back in the 1870s, in the infancy of football, President White of Cornell once rather testily denied the request of an undergraduate football squad to travel to the Midwest to play a Michigan team. "I will not permit 30 men to travel 400 miles," he said, "merely to agitate a bag of wind." One can scarcely imagine what the good president would have said, and the height to which his eyebrows would have arched, had his undergraduate student body turned up with the team and requested to travel out there simply to *watch* a bag of wind being agitated.   /4

Since then a near-symbiotic relationship has developed between the player and the fan in the stands watching him — that phrase, "I just die with the Chiefs (or the Rams, or the Mets, or whatever)" . . . the fan's forefinger raised to denote that his team (and he) are Number One, the "we did it, we did it," and the self-satisfied smiles on the faces of people coming down the stadium ramps after their teams have won. We seem to require the personal assurance of an idol's triumph in the highly dramatic situation that sports provides — and a loser too, someone to jeer at and feel superior to . . . the substitute scapegoat for the tyrant down the hall who has the key to the executive washroom.   /5

All of this is probably natural enough, and understandable — but then the fan in his intensity for a win begins to take on the same desperate excesses that sometimes the athlete must indulge in to play at his best. His team loses and he crumples up the sports page and throws it at the family cat. In the stands the fan becomes as competitive as a man striving for a championship.   /6

Unfortunately, the champion is so often driven by a set of impulses and persuasions that are not necessarily desirable or attractive. Billie Jean King, who drove herself to championships with 40/200 vision, a bad set of knees and a famous tendency to eat too much ice cream, has said that many topflight tennis players have never become true winners because they are *afraid* to be . . . to accept the ugliness of those responsibilities — not only the grim determination to become the champion, but also the enmity and jealousy that comes with attaining the top. Her close pal Rosemary Casals called off their friendship ostensibly because she could not accept the idea of being friendly with someone whose position she coveted.   /7

Sad and interesting — friendships disbanded, everything put aside to win. But then surely it is the athlete's prerogative to do so: the choice is personal; reputation, livelihood, the future, and so forth are obvious determinants.   /8

It is difficult, however, to understand how such intensity applies to a *fan* (unless he has bet his wife and that family cat on the outcome of a game). Yet the honest emphasis on supporting a winner has become an obsession to such a point (witness the Soviet hockey series in which the visitors' anthem was booed, obscenities in Russian held aloft on signs, objects thrown and generally a type of bellicosity in the air that awed witnesses felt was almost palpable) that editorial writers surveying the national character, get fidgety and begin worrying once again about the win-at-all-cost grip that seizes American fans and so often makes them louts.   /9

I remember John Gordy, the All-Pro Detroit offensive guard, talking about it: "The snowballs come down with rocks in them. I've seen these guys who are sedate businessmen, and they've got a Caddy out in the parking lot, and a big house in Grosse Pointe to drive home to, and a wine cellar, and all they have to worry about are their golf handicaps — and I've seen these guys hanging over the runways with the hair hanging down into their eyes, and their faces blood-red, screaming insults, like you were a bug and they wanted to exterminate you. . . . When something like that happens to you, and the pain, and all the grief of losing, you come off the field and you want to get to your family, and you hurry through the tunnel to get away from the crowd, and you hear them screaming at you, and you think about where you can go to eat in a place where nobody knows you, and all the time you're wondering how you can be *hated* so much for going out there and trying your best."   /**10**

What seems to be missing is a sense of perspective — an appreciation that there is much more of a feast going on at an athletic contest besides the matter of winning. One would hope for vision that is panoramic rather than focussed, so that the occasion itself can be relished . . . the skills, the pageantry, the incidentals (Marianne Moore, the poet laureate of the Brooklyn Dodgers, was entranced by the behavior of the Ebbets Field pigeons). . . .   /**11**

Jim Murray, the great West Coast sports columnist, addressed one of his books to readers who did not need "larger-than-life heroics all the time. They can take their sport with a squirt of humor and a twist of irreverence."   /**12**

In the spirit of this attitude I remember some years back, in the heat of a hectic football game at Harvard Stadium, a pigeon (Marianne Moore would have exclaimed in delight!) landed on the four-yard line — turning as soon as he put down and setting out toward the goal line with great determination, his neck bobbing in his haste. But then indecision, or perhaps something startling in the grass, diverted his attention, and he stopped a foot or two short. He revolved, peering here and there . . . and suddenly that immense crowd focussed on him, neighbors nudging each other and remarking on the pigeon's vacillation just at the brink of the goal line: megaphones went up, cries of "Go, bird, go!" erupted from one side of the stadium and, "Hold that pigeon!" from the Harvard side.   /13

Odd, I cannot remember whether he crossed the line or not, but I recall that the vast good-natured attention given the bird seemed from that point on to infuse the crowd's reaction to the game itself — chauvinism muted, skills enjoyed. A sudden sensibility reflected, if only for a time, President White of Cornell's long-past suspicion of undue emphasis on "agitating a bag of wind."   /14

Review Questions

1. What is the tone of this essay? Is it formal, informal, proper, or slangy? Explain.
2. What is Plimpton's thesis?
3. Which are the two or three most vivid examples he uses to illustrate his thesis? What makes them vivid?
4. Would this essay have been as effective if Plimpton had used one extended example rather than several examples?
5. What is the point Plimpton is making in this essay?
6. What effect is achieved by closing the essay with the same image as that used to open it?

19

Definition Essays

On Morality

Joan Didion

Joan Didion (1934-   ) was born in Sacramento, California, and educated at the University of California, Berkeley. She has served as editor of *Vogue* magazine and the *National Review,* and as a columnist for the *Saturday Evening Post.* She was awarded *Vogue's* "Prix de Paris" in 1956, and a Bread Loaf fellowship in 1963. Her articles have also appeared in *Holiday* magazine and *Harper's.* Her books of essays include *Slouching Toward Bethlehem* (1968), in which "On Morality" appeared, and most recently *The White Album* (1979). She has also written two novels, including *Play It As It Lays* and *A Book of Common Prayer.*

As it happens I am in Death Valley, in a room at the Enterprise Motel and Trailer Park, and it is July, and it is hot. In fact it is 119°. I cannot seem to make the air conditioner work, but there is a small refrigerator, and I can wrap ice cubes in a towel and hold them against the small of my back. With the help of the ice cubes I have been trying to think, because *The American Scholar* asked me to, in some abstract way about "morality," a word I distrust more every day, but my mind veers inflexibly toward the particular.   /1

Here are some particulars. At midnight last night, on the road in from Las Vegas to Death Valley Junction, a car hit a shoulder and turned over. The driver, very young and apparently drunk, was killed instantly. His girl was found alive but bleeding internally, deep in shock. I talked this afternoon to the nurse who had driven the girl to the nearest doctor, 185 miles across the floor of the Valley and three ranges of lethal mountain road. The nurse explained that her husband, a talc miner, had stayed on the highway with the boy's body until the coroner could get over the mountains from Bishop, at dawn today. "You can't just leave a body on the highway," she said. "It's immoral."   /2

It was one instance in which I did not distrust the word, because she meant something quite specific. She meant that if a body is left alone for even a few minutes on the desert, the coyotes close in and eat the flesh. Whether or not a corpse is torn apart by coyotes may seem only a sentimental consideration, but of course it is more: one of the promises we make to one another is that we will try to retrieve our casualties, try not to abandon our dead to the coyotes. If we have been taught to keep our promises — if, in the simplest terms, our upbringing is good enough — we stay with the body, or have bad dreams.   /3

I am talking, of course, about the kind of social code that is sometimes called, usually pejoratively, "wagon-train morality." In fact that is precisely what it is. For better or worse, we are what we learned as children: my own childhood was illuminated by graphic litanies of the grief awaiting those who failed in their loyalties to each other. The Donner-Reed Party, starving in the Sierra snows, all the ephemera of civilization gone save that one vestigial taboo, the provision that no one should eat his own blood kin. The Jayhawkers, who quarreled and separated not far from where I am tonight. Some of them died in the Funerals and some of them died down near Badwater and most of the rest of them died in the Panamints. A woman who got through gave the Valley its name. Some might say that the Jayhawkers were killed by the desert summer, and the Donner Party by the mountain winter, by circumstances beyond control; we were taught instead that they had somewhere abdicated their responsibilities, somehow breached their primary loyalties, or they would not have found themselves helpless in the mountain winter or the desert summer, would not have given way to acrimony, would not have deserted one another, would not have *failed*. In brief, we heard such stories as cautionary tales, and they still suggest the only kind of "morality" that seems to me to have any but the most potentially mendacious meaning.   /4

You are quite possibly impatient with me by now; I am talking, you want to say, about a "morality" so primitive that it scarcely deserves the name, a code that has as its point only survival, not the attainment of the ideal good. Exactly. Particularly out here tonight, in this country so ominous and terrible that to live in it is to live with antimatter, it is difficult to believe that "the good" is a knowable quantity. Let me tell you what it is like out here tonight. Stories travel at night on the desert. Someone gets in his pickup and drives a couple of hundred miles for a beer, and he carries news of what is happening, back wherever he came from. Then he drives another hundred miles for another beer, and passes along stories from the last place as well as from the one before; it is a network kept alive by people whose instincts tell them that if they do not keep moving at night on the desert they will lose all reason. Here is a story that is going around the desert tonight: over across the Nevada line, sheriff's deputies are diving in some underground pools, trying to retrieve a couple of bodies known to be in the hole. The widow of one of the drowned boys is over there; she is eighteen, and pregnant, and is said not to leave the hole. The divers go down and come up, and she just stands there and stares into the water. They have been diving for ten days but have found no bottom to the caves, no bodies and no trace of them, only the black 90° water going down and down and down, and a single translucent fish, not classified. The story tonight is that one of the divers has been hauled up incoherent, out of his head, shouting — until they got him out of there so that the widow could not hear — about water that got hotter instead of cooler as he went down, about light flickering through the water, about magma, about underground . nuclear testing.   /5

That is the tone stories take out here, and there are quite a few of them tonight. And it is more than the stories alone. Across the road at the Faith Community Church a couple of dozen old people, come here to live in trailers and die in the sun, are holding a prayer sing. I cannot hear them and do not want to. What I can hear are occasional coyotes and a constant chorus of "Baby the Rain Must Fall" from the jukebox in the Snake Room next door, and if I were also to hear those dying voices, those Midwestern voices drawn to this lunar country for some unimaginable atavistic rites, *rock of ages cleft for me,* I think I would lose my own reason. Every now and then I imagine I hear a rattlesnake, but my husband says that it is a faucet, a paper rustling, the wind. Then he stands by a window, and plays a flashlight over the dry wash outside.   /6

What does it mean? It means nothing manageable. There is some sinister hysteria in the air out here tonight, some hint of the monstrous perversion to which any human idea can come. "I followed my own conscience." "I did what I thought was right." How many madmen have said it and meant it? How many murderers? Klaus Fuchs said it, and the men who committed the Mountain Meadows Massacre said it, and Alfred Rosenberg said it. And, as we are rotely and rather presumptuously reminded by those who would say it now, Jesus said it. Maybe we have all said it, and maybe we have been wrong. Except on that most primitive level — our loyalties to those we love — what could be more arrogant than to claim the primacy of personal conscience? ("Tell me," a rabbi asked Daniel Bell when he said, as a child, that he did not believe in God. "Do you think God cares?") At least some of the time, the world appears to me as a painting by Hieronymus Bosch; were I to follow my conscience then, it would lead me out onto the desert with Marion Faye, out to where he stood in *The Deer Park* looking east to Los Alamos and praying, as if for rain, that it would happen: "*. . . let it come and clear the rot and the stench and the stink, let it come for all of everywhere, just so it comes and the world stands clear in the white dead dawn.*"   /7

Of course you will say I do not have the right, even if I had the power, to inflict that unreasonable conscience upon you; nor do I want you to inflict your conscience, however reasonable, however enlightened, upon me. ("We must be aware of the dangers which lie in our most generous wishes," Lionel Trilling once wrote. "Some paradox of our nature leads us, when once we have made our fellow men the objects of our enlightened interest, to go on to make them the objects of our pity, then of our wisdom, ultimately of our coercion.") That the ethic of conscience is intrinsically insidious seems scarcely a revelatory point, but it is one raised with increasing infrequency; even those who do raise it tend to *segue* with troubling readiness into the quite contradictory position that the ethic of conscience is dangerous when it is "wrong," and admirable when it is "right." /8

You see I want to be quite obstinate about insisting that we have no way of knowing — beyond that fundamental loyalty to the social code — what is "right" and what is "wrong," what is "good" and what "evil." I dwell so upon this because the most disturbing aspect of "morality" seems to me to be the frequency with which the word now appears; in the press, on television, in the most perfunctory kinds of conversation. Questions of straightforward power (or survival) politics, questions of quite indifferent public policy, questions of almost anything: they are all assigned these factitious moral burdens. There is something facile going on, some self-indulgence at work. Of course we would all like to "believe" in something, like to assuage our private guilts in public causes, like to lose our tiresome selves; like, perhaps, to transform the white flag of defeat at home into the brave white banner of battle away from home. And of course it is all right to do that; that is how, immemorially, things have gotten done. But I think it is all right only so long as we do not delude ourselves about what we are doing, and why. It is all right only so long as we remember that all the *ad hoc* committees, all the picket lines, all the brave signatures in *The New York Times,* all the tools of agitprop straight across the spectrum, do not confer upon anyone any *ipso facto* virtue. It is all right only so long as we recognize that the end may or may not be expedient, may or may not be a good idea, but in any case has nothing to do with "morality." Because when we start deceiving ourselves into thinking not that we want something or need something, not that it is a pragmatic necessity for us to have it, but that it is a *moral imperative* that we have it, then is when we join the fashionable madmen, and then is when the thin whine of hysteria is heard in the land, and then is when we are in bad trouble. And I suspect we are already there. /9

Review Questions

1. How does Didion's anecdotal style help her define her term?
2. Is her definition of "morality" a unique one? Would such a definition be consistent with the dictionary definition of the term?
3. What other terms does Didion define (either explicitly or implicitly)?
4. What is the point Didion is making?

For a New Definition of Lunacy

Sydney J. Harris

Sydney J. Harris (1917-   ) is a journalist, born in London and educated in Chicago. He worked on Chicago newspapers and later became a syndicated columnist. Of his many books, his most recent include *The Best of Harris* (1975), from which this definition essay was taken, and *Winners and Losers* (1972).

In disclosing more about her family life and background, Stalin's daughter declared that, in her opinion, her father was not "insane" when he ordered the political purges of the 1930s, although he may have become paranoid a decade later.   /1

I think the world of the future — if there is to be one — will require a new definition of the word *insane*. Heretofore, we have looked upon insanity as a mental aberration; it seems to me that there is something called "moral insanity" as well.   /2

There is no doubt that Stalin was out of his mind in his last years, or that Hitler was a psychopath from the moment he entered the Munich beer cellar in the 1920s. But what of the men around them? What of the cool, plausible, efficient functionaries who did their dreadful bidding?   /3

In some ways, indeed, it is easier to forgive a lunatic like Hitler than a Goering, a Goebbels, a Himmler or an Eichmann. He was possessed by a demon burning in his brain; they had no such excuse for their coldly bestial behavior. Likewise, the men around Stalin who helped murder all the Old Bolsheviks were morally insane.   /4

Our current definition of lunacy is too narrow, too clinical, too conventional, to serve as a socially useful yardstick in judging the actions of public figures. True, we are all reservoirs of private wickedness, and it takes no Shadow to know what evil lurks in the hearts of men.   /5

But public wickedness on a mass scale is not just quantitatively larger; it is qualitatively different. To be unjust, to be cruel, even to kill, for personal reasons, seems part of the defect we were born with; to kill thousands, and even millions, of people impersonally, simply because they are kulaks or capitalists or Poles or Jews, is a form of moral insanity.   /6

In his book, *Functionaries,* F. William Howton defines such men as those who "view their work entirely in terms of a job well done — without stopping to consider whether or not the job ought to be done." Eichmann was just doing his job, taking orders, carrying out the function assigned him.   /7

To divorce ends from means, to dehumanize oneself so that a child shipped to a gas chamber means no more than a sausage slipped into a casing, may not be insanity in the medical sense of the term — but if there is a moral norm in human conduct, what else can we call such a diabolic departure from the norm?   /8

Review Questions

1. Has Harris effectively defined a familiar term in a new way?
2. What is the old definition of the word "insane"? (Look it up in a dictionary.)
3. How does Harris illustrate his new definition?
4. What type of audience is Harris addressing?
5. What is Harris' point in this definition?

Psychobabble

R. D. Rosen

R. D. Rosen (1949-   ) was born in Chicago and educated at Brown and Harvard.
He has been an assistant editor of *Playboy,* a chef, a teacher of writing, and an arts
editor and columnist for the *Boston Phoenix.* His articles have appeared in *New
Times* and *New Republic,* and he is the author of *Me and My Friends, We No
Longer Profess Any Graces: A Premature Memoir* (1971), and *Psychobabble: Fast
Talk and Quick Cure in the Era of Feeling* (1977). A slightly altered version of the
following essay is the first chapter of the last book listed.

While having drinks recently with a young woman I had not seen for some time,
I asked how things were going and received this reply: "I've really been getting in
touch with myself lately. I've struck some really deep chords." I recoiled slightly at
the grandeur of her remarks, but she proceeded, undaunted, to reel out a string
of broad psychological insights with an enthusiasm attributable less to her Tequila
Sunrises than to the confessional spirit that is sweeping America.   /1

I could not help thinking that I disappointed her with my inability to summon
more lyricism and intensity in my own conversation. Now that reticence has gone
out of style, I sensed an obligation to reciprocate her candor but couldn't bring
myself to use the popular catch phrases of revelation. Would she understand if I
said that instead of striking deep chords I had merely tickled the ivories of my
psychic piano? That getting my head together was not exactly the way in which I
wanted to describe what was going on above *my* neck? Surely it wouldn't do any
good if I resorted to more precise, but pompously clinical, language and admitted
that I was well on my way to resolving my attitude toward my own maternal
introject.   /2

"Whenever I see you," she said brightly, "it makes me feel very good inside.
It's a real high-energy experience."   /3

So what was wrong with me that I couldn't feel the full voltage of our meeting.
Unable to match her incandescence, I simply agreed, "Yes, it's good to see you,
too," then fell silent.   /4

Finally she said, her beatific smile widening, "But I can really dig your silence.
If you're bummed out, that's OK."   /5

If anything characterizes the cultural life of the Seventies in America, it is an
insistence on preventing failures of communication. Everything must now be
spoken. The Kinsey Report, Masters and Johnson, *The Joy of Sex* and its
derivatives; the *Playboy* Advisor, the *Penthouse* Forum, *Oui's* Sex Tapes;
contraception; Esalen and the human potential movement; the democratization
of psychotherapy — all these various oils have helped lubricate the national
tongue. It's as if the full bladder of civilization's squeamishness has finally burst.
The sexual revolution, this therapeutic age, has culminated in one profuse, steady

stream of self-revelation, confessed profligacy and publicized domestic trauma . . . .   /6

One hears it everywhere, like endless panels of a Feiffer cartoon. In restaurants distraught lovers lament, "I wish I could get into your head." A man on a bus says to his companion, "I just got back from the coast. What a different headset!" The latest reports from a corrupt Esalen provide us with new punch lines: A group leader there intones that "it's beautiful if you're unhappy. Go with the feeling . . . You gotta be you 'cause you're you and you gotta be, and besides, if you aren't gonna be you who else's gonna be you, honey. . . . This is the Aquarian Age and the time to be oneself, to love one's beauty, to go with one's process."   /7

Are you sufficiently laid back to read this article? Will it be a heavy experience, or merely the mock?   /8

It's time we lend a name to this monotonous patois, this psychological patter, whose concern is to faithfully catalog the ego's condition: Psychobabble. As Psychobabble begins to tyrannize conversations everywhere, it is difficult to avoid, and there is an embarrassment involved in not using it in the presence of other Psychobabblers that is akin to the mild humiliation experienced by American tourists in Paris who cannot speak the native language. It is now spoken by magazine editors, management consultants, sandal makers, tool and die workers and Ph.D.s in clinical psychology alike. What the sociologist Philip Rieff in the mid-Sixties called "Psychological Man," that mid-20th century victim of his own interminable introspection, has become Psychobabbler, the victim of his own inability to describe human behavior with anything but platitudes.   /9

Psychobabble seems to have emerged toward the end of the Sixties, distilled from the dying rad/lib dialects of political activism and the newly thriving language of the human potential movement with its Fritz Perls of wisdom. Activism was acquiring more and more of a therapeutic cast, and the radical battles, once fought exclusively in the real political world, were now being enacted in the individual psyche. T-groups, encounter groups, sensitivity training, group gropes, drama and primal therapies all helped shape the trend. Two years ago, when Jerry Rubin proclaimed in *Psychology Today* that he was going back to his body, where the real wars of liberation were taking place, those who hadn't already preceded him now clamored to trade in their political critiques for therapeutic ideals. The disaffected were saying "Off the pigs" one day and "Man, I really feel tense, don't mess with my head" the next.   /10

Of course, this is not the first time in our history that psychological ideas have dominated national conversation. The old Psychobabble, however, was really just the wholesale use of Freudian terms, less banter than a sort of intellectual one-upmanship. In post-World War II America, Freudian terminology was embraced by liberal magazines, novelists and enough of the middle class so that the growing demand for psychoanalysis easily outdistanced the supply of doctors.   /11

As one Boston psychoanalyst, who has practiced for over 30 years, says, "After the war, everyone was talking simplistically about the Oedipus complex. It

was the rage. Everyone had the idea that knowledge itself would make you free."
Now he has to listen to the new Psychobabble. A social worker patient in his 30s,
himself a group leader, eagerly responded at the beginning of therapy to each
interpretation his analyst made by saying, "I hear you, I hear you."   /**12**

"I'm sorry," said the doctor, "I didn't know you were a little deaf."

"I'm not. I *hear* you. It means I comprehend."

"Well, *what* do you comprehend?

The patient paused. "Jesus," he replied, "I don't know."   /**13**

Psychobabble, the psychoanalyst says, "is just a way of using candor in order
not to be candid." The dangers of the old Psychobabble were remarked upon as
early as 1929 in an article by Joseph Jastrow in *The Century* entitled "The
Freudian Temper and Its Menace to the Lay Mind." In it, Jastrow quotes a
Boston analyst, Dr. Myerson of Beacon Street: "Everybody talks glibly of
repression, complexes, sublimation, wish fulfillment and subconsciousness as if
they really understood Freud and what he was talking about. Gentle reader, let
me say this, that with the exception of a few professional philosophers,
psychologists, psychiatrists and psychoanalysts, I have not met a dozen people
who knew more than the terms of Freud."   /**14**

The new Psychobabblers, however, don't even seem to know the terms — of
Freud, Jung, Adler, or any body of psychological thought. Their language seems
to free-float in some linguistic atmosphere, a set of repetitive verbal formalities
that kills off the very spontaneity, candor and understanding it pretends to
promote. It's an idiom that reduces psychological insight and therapeutic
processes to a collection of standardized insights, that provides only a limited
lexicon to deal with an infinite variety of problems. "Uptight" is a word now used
to describe an individual who is experiencing anything from mild uneasiness to a
clinical depression. To ask someone why he or she refers to another as being
"hung-up" produces a reply along the lines of: *"Why?* Man, he's just *hung-up."*
Oddly, those few psychiatric terms borrowed by Psychobabble are used
recklessly. One is no longer fearful: one is *paranoid.* The adjective is applied to
the populace with a generosity that must confuse real clinical paranoiacs.
Increasingly, people describe their moody friends as *manic-depressives* and
almost anyone you don't like is psychotic, or at least *schizzed-out.*   /**15**

The Cult of Candor, and particularly its language, Psychobabble, is a feature
of contemporary decorum, a form of *politesse,* a signal to others that one is ready
to talk a certain kind of turkey, to engage in *real dialogue.* And real dialogue, it
turns out, is often no more than a monologue. When I asked a man to whom I had
just been introduced at a party recently, "How do you do?" he responded by
describing, with an utter disrespect for brevity, his relationship with his wife.
Confession is the new handshake.   /**16**

If Psychobabble were a question of language alone, the worst one could say
about it is that it is just another example of the corrosion and unimaginativeness
of spoken English. But the prevalence of Psychobabble reflects more than a mere
"loss for words." It indicates that, in an era when the national gaze has turned
inward, and in a country that needs therapy perhaps more than any other,

Americans still have enormous difficulty in understanding the depth of their psychological problems, perhaps even in understanding that psychological problems *have* depth.   /**17**

Even among the well-analyzed and congenitally content there is a tendency to believe in the new ethos of "being oneself" and in the promises of total liberation. This trend has been well-documented in some excellent books during the last ten years. In his recent *Social Amnesia: A Critique of Conformist Psychology from Adler to Laing,* leftist historian Russell Jacoby noted that the reasons for this current occupation with self and individuality go beyond the voluntary desire to be spiritualized: "The more the development of late capitalism renders obsolete or at least suspect the real possibilities of self, self-fulfillment and actualization, the more they are emphasized as if they could spring to life through an act of will alone." For instance, here's an advertisement from *Publishers Weekly* for Martin Shepard's latest book, *The Do-It-Yourself Psychotherapy Book:* "This book will save you thousands of dollars and give you control of your own life and your best self. *No More* Paid Advisors, Sex Hangups, Feelings of Inferiority, Psychosomatic Illness, Guilt. *Enjoy* More Personal Power, Boundless Sensual Pleasure, New-Found Self Reliance. Your Birthright of Health, New Lifestyles."   /**18**

This notion that psychological growth may be achieved through an act of sheer ego that takes into account neither history nor one's own unconscious leads to a kind of narcissism, perfectly embodied by our previously quoted Esalen group leader in this conversation reported in a *Village Voice* article: /**19**

> "Leo," said Miriam, "you have to realize the important thing is living in the present moment. You have to be fully aware in the now, that's the trick."
>
> "Beautiful," said Shirley, "beautiful. It's just like the Aquarian Age."
>
> "Shirley," said Leo, "you've got to stop that Aquarian Age stuff. If this is the Aquarian Age, we're in trouble, we've been screwed by Nixon, we've been screwed by Ford, and we're letting Kissinger screw everyone he wants."
>
> "I don't understand politics," said Shirley. "I don't know anything about politics, so I don't feel as if I'd been screwed. It's not part of my reality, so it's not true for me."   /**20**

Psychobabble has insinuated itself into many American art forms, and in most cases this is no surprise. That we can now hear it on *The Bob Newhart Show,* in which Newhart plays a Chicago psychotherapist, seems only fitting for a medium that unerringly reflects mid-cult values. In rock music, the incidence of Psychobabble is high, which is only natural for an art form whose audience does not prize it above all for its ability to elucidate and whose requirements of rhyme and comprehensibility do not encourage the refinement of insights (ideas are normally at the mercy of "love/above," "out tonight/treat her right" couplets). But it is interesting to note that the English progressive rock group Gentle Giant has a song called "Knots," based on R. D. Laing's book, that the American group

The Flock has a new cut titled "My O.K. Today," inspired by their reading of *I'm O.K.! You're O.K.!* and that lines like Todd Rundgren's "Get your trip together, be a real man" abound more than ever. But the most eloquent Psychobabbler in rock music today is John Denver, who, fresh from Erhard Seminars Training in California, now sounds like the Fritz Perls posters that adorned the walls of student cells in 1971. From his *Rolling Stone* interview of last May: /21

> How far out it is to be a bird and fly around the trees. I am what I've always wanted to be and that is the truth. And I think — in fact, it's not what I think, but I observe that if people were to really take a good look at themselves, they are exactly the way that they have always wanted to be. . . . My experience is that if I can tell you the truth, just lay it out there, then I have totally opened up a space for you to be who you are and that it really opens up all the room in the world for us to do whatever we want to do in regard to each other. If I don't like you, I'll tell you. And that's great.   /22

As for contemporary films that deal in Psychobabble (*Alice Doesn't Live Here Anymore, Diary of a Mad Housewife, I Love You, Alice B. Toklas* and others), one is always tempted to praise highly those that capture the essence of Psychobabble dialogues, simply on the basis of verisimilitude. Because film and also rock music are to some extent engaged in *representing* the way people talk, and not in analyzing why, they are easy targets to attack for using Psychobabble. One has to look elsewhere to find a medium that has truly suffered at the hands of Psychobabble.   /23

Such a victim is American publishing (although one might also say it victimizes itself). Psychobabble's influence on publishing in this country has been disastrous, and the number of Psychobabble books offered to the public with a solemnity reserved for great works is astounding. Seventeen years ago, Alfred Kazin derided the Myth of Universal Creativity engendered by the Freud craze, "the assumption," as he put it, "that every idle housewife was meant to be a painter and that every sexual deviant is really a poet." The time has never been more propitious than now for ordinary citizens to spill their beans in print. To an older and still mistaken belief that you only had to be neurotic to create has been added the more recent societal sanction — that, according to the Cult of Candor, it is virtuous to reveal to as many people as possible the tragedies and erotic and emotional secrets of one's private life. It seems that all one needs today in order to become a bona fide author is a few months of therapy and an ability to compose grammatical sentences.   /24

Books written in Psychobabble almost always seem "touchingly human," as the phrase goes, but in their simplification of human problems they engage in what Jacoby has called (referring to the neo-Freudians, to whom Psychobabblers are indebted) "the monotonous discovery of common sense." They present revelation uninformed by history, unmediated by ideology; like verbal home movies.   /25

Now this tendency has flowered in the garden of rampant Psychobabble. In the newly released book *Intimate Feedback: A Lover's Guide to Getting in Touch with Each Other* by Barrie and Charlotte Hopson (Simon & Schuster), we are offered these startling insights, quintessentially Psychobabble: /**26**

> Who am I? This is a question which has always been central to man's awareness of himself.
> Human existence is exemplified by one person trying to communicate with others.
> When couples say that they have nothing new to learn about each other, this is due to stereotyped communication patterns, unless they really do not like one another and have no interest in their partner.   /**27**

Last winter, Delacorte Press published an autobiographical account by Harry C. Lyon Jr. entitled *It's Me and I'm Here!* Even the title, all too reminiscent of Transactional Analysis' bible, *I'm O.K.! You're O.K.!,* suggested a giddy infatuation with self-actualization — and the contents did not disappoint. Lyon was raised bourgeois, attended West Point, bedded women by subtle coercion and then realized that he was living by a morality that directed emotional traffic without getting him anywhere. Off to Esalen, naturally. In the book's foreword, human potential psychologist Carl Rogers tells us that he "became thoroughly convinced that [Lyon] was 'for real.'" Lyon concurs in his own introduction: /**28**

> Look, my life has been exciting. It has been strange and painful, and I don't know quite what to make of it myself. But I want you to touch it — touch me — because I so much want to reach you. I want you to feel that pain and joy I have felt. . . .   /**29**

It's Me and I'm Here! is just another tale told by an ego tumescent with spiritual pride.   /**30**
What Psychobabble encourages in the way of shoddy thinking, and this is easily observed in recent books written in Psychobabble, is the propensity to interpret psychological characteristics as conscious choices or determined purely by culture instead of functions also of the unconscious, instinctual life. In *Harper's* magazine's "Wraparound" section on "Masculinity" a couple of months ago, one woman wrote: /**31**

> I chose lesbianism because I'm a female chauvinist. The strongest reason for my female chauvinism is woman's innate respect for life, unshared by men, I believe, because men do not bear or nurture living things.   /**32**

It is not uncommon these days to hear people speak about their homosexuality as a "preferred" form of sexual life or defend their three divorces because "marriage simply doesn't work anymore" — all as if what one is, what has become of one, has been nothing more than a *moral* choice, a decision to participate in a prevailing and attractive ideology; as if the instinctual life of one's childhood and the concept of repression have nothing to do with it, outdated "Freudian" ideas designed to undermine one's will, one's ability to do and be exactly what one wants. Even the existence of the unconscious has fallen out of favor, now just some quaint notion that only complicates the breezy formulations of Psychobabble. Pop psych culture has seized on the Laingian assertion that there isn't even a difference of degree anymore between "sanity" and "insanity"; one can choose between them like a grocery shopper at the frozen food section. Note, for instance, the way that Psychobabble obscures the subtle, but existing distinctions between pathology and habit. Psychobabble describes anyone with a commitment or highly developed interest as a *freak*. A composer is a *music-freak*, a writer a *word-freak*, a cyberneticist a *computer-freak* — as though one's profession is in fact just one's chosen perversion or stimulant.   /33

We now have the ideals of "the totally liberated person" and "doing your own thing," concepts that dislodge the goals of human growth from the sources of the conflicts that impede it. Take Louise Diane Campanelli, whose recent book, *Sex and All You Can Eat* (Lyle Stuart), is a masterpiece of the banality of liberation. Repulsed by her husband's obesity, she went out and had, at last count, 62 lovers. Her psychiatrist, himself a Psychobabbler, has provided an introduction in which he tells us that the book's theme "concerns the poignant life story of a young woman of foreign parentage who is caught in a clash of cultures, as well as in an identity crisis." From his description, it sounds like Henry James. "As her psychiatrist," he concludes with all the solicitude of a child's piano teacher, "I can say with confidence that she has come a long way. She still has a long way to go."   /34

Campanelli herself begins by reassuring her readers that:

> There is a tremendous amount of adultery going on in America today. Going on, indeed, at this very minute. Yes, while you read, thousands upon thousands of couples are coupling in hotel and motel rooms, in the rear seats of automobiles, and in "his" or "her" bedroom because the spouse is safely away.   /35

By the book's end, she has refined her perceptions: "Adultery has changed my life. . . . One thing I've learned is that there are very few men and women in our society who are true to another person 24 hours a day, 365 days a year."   /36

If women are testing their independence and making domestic jailbreaks, then many men are certainly suffering as a result. Male response has been in many quarters a sudden and useful self-scrutiny, culminating here and there in pedantic apologies. (In America, where movements spring up overnight like fast-food outlets, the New Femininity must be met with a New Masculinity; all God's children gotta have ideology.) In the case of the pseudonymous Albert Martin and his recent *One Man, Hurt* (Macmillan), though, there is only a bewildered lament. His wife of 20 years asked him for a divorce in 1972. He couldn't understand why she didn't love him, but readers of his 278-page account will no doubt get some idea. Martin, in reality a New York public relations executive by another name, has a very one-dimensional understanding of his failed marriage and yearns, in interminable paragraphs, for an uncluttered security in the face of this threat to his male's worldview, one he is not in the least capable of modifying to accommodate his wife's side of the story. His writing has all the flair of a personal letter dashed off at 3:00 in the morning. *One Man, Hurt* is self-justification dressed as compassion — and reading it only inspired respect for his ex-wife for not having felt similarly compelled to burden the reading public with her grievances.   /37

When Martin tries to be reflective (which requires a great effort), he pawns his troubles off on external forces:

> I think there are bad times to be certain things in history. It was bad to be a witch in Salem in the 1700s, bad to be a Negro in America before May 1954 [and it's a joy being one now, Al?], bad to be a polio victim the year before they discovered the vaccine. And I know it is bad to be in marital trouble in America today because the times have never been worse for getting effective help.   /38

The implied equation of his predicament with religious persecution, racial injustice and severe physical handicap is an indication of how little Martin is willing to understand the nature of marriage, and his in particular. *One Man, Hurt* is further proof that there is today a publishing house (and its promotion and advertising department) ready to hear anybody's complaint.   /39

The publishing industry's enthusiasm for Psychobabble of the above variety as well as of the more explicitly therapeutic strain (*How To Be Your Own Best Friend, How To Be Awake & Alive, When I Say No, I Feel Guilty*) — a story in itself — was foreshadowed during the past five or six years by the success of confessional books. To name but a few, Gestalt Therapy "refounder" Fritz Perls' *In and Out the Garbage Pail* was a lesson in incontinent narcissism ("I am becoming a public figure," he announces on page 1); R. D. Laing's *Knots* made relationships seem irresistibly complex; Nancy Friday gave women's sexual fantasies a good name with *My Secret Garden* and *Forbidden Flowers;* Erica Jong aired her own fantasies in too-touted *Fear of Flying;* and an equally overrated book, Nigel Nicolson's tribute to his famous parents, Harold Nicolson and Vita Sackville-West, in *Portrait of a Marriage,* endowed the polymorphous perverse with historical dignity.   /40

Now that the genre has been appropriated by every other divorcee, adulterer and successfully therapized individual, there may be no end in sight to the number of truisms published as striking revelation, to the prurience parading as sociology. The apparently insatiable American appetite for Psychobabble in print may be an indication of several things: That this society has become so atomized that the emotional strength once derived from communities and the extended family can now only be obtained from books; that the simple conviction in the noble savagery of freely playing emotions and the unqualified virtues of "liberation" has now displaced an understanding of the difficult, dialectical nature of psychological growth and change; that a country with a paltry sense of its own short national history (and therefore an imperialist disregard for the history of other, older nations) breeds citizens who cannot grasp the importance of their own private history and childhood and so act as if they were free to select any form of enlightenment that they find appealing.   /41

The popularity of Psychobabble has eclipsed the public taste for literature, in which there are surely more compelling answers to human problems than there are to be found in the books I've mentioned and those like them. Novelists are slowly going out of business while small-town gurus appear on talk shows to exchange insights with Joey Bishop.   /42

Please! No more books by unhappy housewives crying, "I've just got to be me!" No more 33-year-old ad agency executives telling me how they make men want to get into their pants at the singles bar! No more divorced men screaming for justice! No more daydreams of Great Danes with searching tongues! Enough!   /43

This very week in the bookstores, one can find on the hard-cover nonfiction shelf *Your Inner Conflicts — How To Solve Them; How to Give and Receive Advice; How To Live With Another Person; Free to Love; Creating and Sustaining Intimacy in Marriage; Stand Up, Speak Out, Talk Back* and countless others. The field of self-help and confession is becoming so specialized that before long we might well have Psychobabble books written on the thinnest pretexts: *How to Grocery Shop Without Having an Anxiety Attack, How To Achieve Transference in Elevators, You CAN Marry Your Mother, The Promiscuous Coleus.*   /44

Words themselves do not "cure" a person, and words themselves, even the most virulent Psychobabble, cannot make one "sick." However, in the absence of more profound understandings of what we feel and why we feel it, Psychobabble deludes many people into thinking they need not examine themselves with anything but its dull instruments. The danger of Psychobabble is that it anesthetizes curiosity, numbs the desire to know. And, in that state, emotional growth is eventually stunted, no matter how many times one repeats, "I've just got to go with my feelings." Knowledge itself may not free anyone, but the lack of it only reinforces the chains.   /45

Language may, in the end, prove too inadequate to systematically describe wants, desires and emotional states in general. Even the borders delineated by clinical terminology blur badly in the face of actual human behavior. The best one can do now is challenge Psychobabble by declining courteously to accept its usage, as did a young man I know who grew up in a suburb with a group of peers who were "morbidly sensitive to each other's feelings, you know the kind. They'd get into these psychosensitive moods." He dated a girl from the group who one day asked him point-blank if he was getting his head together.   /46

"Yes," he replied. "I can feel it congealing."   /47

Review Questions

1. How does Rosen arrive at his definition?
2. What are some examples he provides of the concept "psychobabble"?
3. What is Rosen's attitude toward his subject?
4. Rosen is coining and defining a new word in this essay. Do you think he is right when he says there is a need for such a word?
5. What is Rosen's main point in this essay?

What Is Eros?

Rollo May

Rollo May (1909-   ), an Ohio-born psychoanalyst, was educated at Oberlin College, the Union Theological Seminary, and Columbia University. He has taught in several colleges and has been a fellow of the American Psychological Association. Among his many books are *Love and Will* (1969), from which this definition of "eros" is excerpted, and *Power and Innocence* (1972).

Eros in our day is taken as a synonym for "eroticism" or sexual titillation. *Eros* was the name given to a journal of sexy arcana, containing "Aphrodisiac Recipes" and posing such weighty question-and-answer articles as, "Q: How Do the Porcupines Do It? A: Carefully." One wonders whether everyone has forgotten the fact that eros, according to no less an authority than St. Augustine, is the power which drives men toward God. Such gross misunderstandings would tend to make the demise of eros unavoidable: for in our overstimulated age we have no need for titillation which no longer titillates. It is essential, therefore, that we clarify the meaning of this crucial term.   /1

Eros created life on the earth, the early Greek mythology tells us. When the world was barren and lifeless, it was Eros who "seized his life-giving arrows and pierced the cold bosom of the Earth," and "immediately the brown surface was covered with luxuriant verdure." This is an appealing symbolic picture of how Eros *incorporates* sex — those phallic arrows which pierce — as the instrument by which he creates life. Eros then breathed into the nostrils of the clay forms of man and woman and gave them the "spirit of life." Ever since, eros has been distinguished by the function of giving the spirit of life, in contrast to the function of sex as the release of tension. Eros was then one of the four original gods, the others being Chaos, Gaea (mother earth), and Tartarus (the dark pit of Hades below the earth). Eros, says Joseph Campbell, is always, regardless of guise, the progenitor, the original creator from which life comes.   /2

Sex can be defined fairly adequately in physiological terms as consisting of the building up of bodily tensions and their release. Eros, in contrast, is the experiencing of the personal intentions and meaning of the act. Whereas sex is a rhythm of stimulus and response, eros is a state of being. The pleasure in sex is described by Freud and others as the reduction of tension; in eros, on the contrary, we wish not to be released from the excitement but rather to hang on to it, to bask in it, and even to increase it. The end toward which sex points is gratification and relaxation, whereas eros is a desiring, longing, a forever reaching out, seeking to expand.   /3

All this is in accord with the dictionary definitions. *Webster's* defines sex (coming from the Latin *sexus,* meaning "split") as referring to "physiological distinctions. . . . the character of being male or female, or . . . the distinctive functions of male or female." Eros, in contrast, is defined with such terms as "ardent desire," "yearning," "aspiring self-fulfilling love often having a sensuous quality." The Latins and Greeks had two different words for sex and love, as we do; but the curious thing to our ears is how rarely the Latins speak of *sexus.* Sex, to them, was no issue; it was *amor* they were concerned about. Similarly, everyone knows the Greek word *eros,* but practically no one has ever heard of their terms for "sex." It is φῦλον, the word from which we derive the zoological term "phylon," tribe or race. This is an entirely different stem from the Greek word *philia,* which means love in the sense of friendship.   /4

Sex is thus a zoological term and is rightly applied to all animals as well as human beings. Kinsey was a zoologist, and appropriately to his profession, he studied human sexual behavior from a zoological point of view. Masters is a gynecologist and studies sex from the viewpoint of sexual organs and how you manage and manipulate them: sex, then, is a pattern of neurophysiological functions and the sexual problem consists of what you do with organs.   /5

Eros, on the other hand, takes wings from human imagination and is forever transcending all techniques, giving the laugh to all the "how to" books by gaily swinging into orbit above our mechanical rules, making love rather than manipulating organs.   /6

For eros is the power which *attracts* us. The essence of eros is that it draws us from ahead, whereas sex pushes us from behind. This is revealed in our day-to-day language when I say a person "allures" me or "entices" me, or the possibilities of a new job "invite" me. Something in me responds to the other person, or the job, and pulls me toward him or it. I participate in forms, possibilities, higher levels of meaning on neurophysiological dimensions but also on aesthetic and ethical dimensions as well. As the Greeks believed, knowledge and even ethical goodness exercise such a pull. Eros is the drive toward union with what we belong to — union with our own possibilities, union with significant other persons in our world in relation to whom we discover our own self-fulfillment. Eros is the yearning in man which leads him to dedicate himself to seeking *arête,* the noble and good life.   /7

Sex, in short, is the mode of relating characterized by tumescence of the organs (for which we seek the pleasurable relief) and filled gonads (for which we seek satisfying release). But eros is the mode of relating in which we do not seek release but rather to cultivate, procreate, and form the world. *In eros, we seek increase of stimulation.* Sex is a need, but eros is a desire; and it is this admixture of desire which complicates love. In regard to our preoccupation with the orgasm in American discussions of sex, it can be agreed that the aim of the sex act in its zoological and physiological sense is indeed the orgasm. But the aim of eros is not: eros seeks union with the other person in delight and passion, and the procreating of new dimensions of experience which broaden and deepen the being of both persons. It is common experience, backed up by folklore as well as the testimony of Freud and others, that after sexual release we tend to go to sleep — or, as the joke puts it, to get dressed, go home, and *then* go to sleep. But in eros, we want just the opposite: to stay awake thinking of the beloved, remembering, savoring, discovering ever-new facets of the prism of what the Chinese call the "many-splendored" experience.   /8

It is this urge for union with the partner that is the occasion for human tenderness. For eros — not sex as such — is the source of tenderness. Eros is the longing to establish union, full relationship. This may be, first, a union with abstract forms. The philosopher Charles S. Peirce sat alone in his house in Milford, Connecticut working out his mathematical logic, but this did not prevent his experiencing eros; the thinker must be "animated by a true eros," he wrote, "for the task of scientific investigation." Or it may be a union with aesthetic or philosophical forms, or a union with new ethical forms. But it is most obvious as the pull toward the union of two individuals sexually. The two persons, longing, as all individuals do, to overcome the separateness and isolation to which we all are heir as individuals, can participate in a relationship that, for the moment, is not made up of two isolated, individual experiences, but a genuine union. A sharing takes place which is a new *Gestalt,* a new being, a new field of magnetic force.   /9

Review Questions

1. How does May define "eros" in terms of the general class to which the word belongs?
2. How does he differentiate this term from others of its class?
3. How does May illustrate his definition?
4. What point is May making in this essay?
5. What audience is May addressing?

20

Comparison and Contrast Essays

Meaningful Relationships

Russell Baker

Russell Baker (1925-   ) began his career in journalism in 1947 as a staff member of the *Baltimore Sun*. He stayed with *The Sun* until 1953, eventually attaining the position of London Bureau Chief. He then joined *The New York Times*, where he served in the Washington D.C. Bureau and in 1962 began publishing his "Observer" column. "Observer" is still published by *The Times* and is also nationally syndicated.

Baker has published several collections of newspaper articles in book form. He has also written fiction and contributed articles to various periodicals, including *The New York Times Magazine, Saturday Evening Post, Sports Illustrated, Life, Look,* and *Mademoiselle*. The piece included here appeared in *The Times* in March 1978.

I heard of a man and woman recently who had fallen in love. "Hopelessly in love" was the woman's antique phrase for it. I hadn't realized people still did that sort of thing jointly. Nowadays the fashion is to fall in love with yourself, and falling in love with a second party seems to be generally regarded as bad form.   /1

It may be, of course, that many people are still doing it, but simply not admitting it publicly, perhaps on the assumption that it is a shameful act, as adultery used to be. Nowadays people discuss their adultery with strangers at parties and on airplanes, and not long ago I saw a married couple chatting about theirs on television, the way people used to discuss their car-repair problems.   /2

A possible explanation, I suppose, is that, in an age when the fashion is to be in love with yourself, confessing to being in love with somebody else is an admission of unfaithfulness to one's beloved. The truth is probably more complicated.   /3

Consider, for example, the situation of Ed and Jane, a hypothetical modern couple who see each other across a crowded room, feel inexplicable sensations not reducible to computer printouts and make human contact. After conventional preliminary events, they will naturally want to express what exists between them.   /4

Jane may announce that they "relate" beautifully. Ed may boast about how gratifyingly they "communicate." The beauty of their "relating" and the gratifications of their "communicating" may induce them to "establish a relationship."   /5

Why it is always a "relationship" they establish, and never a "communicationship," I don't know, but "relationship" is the universally approved term. On days when things go badly, they do not have a lover's quarrel. Instead, Jane says that Ed is not "relating" and Ed says that Jane is not "communicating."   /6

On days when things go well they boast about how "fulfilling" their "relationship" is. Ed and Jane do not dream of living happily ever after. They are more like the Bell telephone system. They aspire to heavy communicating in a fulfilling relationship.   /7

In fact, they are probably afraid of falling in love; and if, in spite of everything, they nevertheless do fall in love, they are too embarrassed to tell anybody. Why? One reason is that it is such an out-of-date thing to do. Falling in love is not scientific. It cannot be described in the brain-numbing jargon of sociology. It can only be described in the words of song writers. People in Cole Porter's antique old songs were always falling in love, and worse, talking about romance. Romance! Astaire and Rogers in a penthouse, and other such musty stuff. We have moved on to Mick Jagger, to John Lennon, who urged everybody to do it in the road instead of in the penthouse.   /8

Falling in love is archaic, like cookouts and tail fins on your Plymouth. Communicating, relating, experiencing fulfilling relationships — these are what up-to-date boys and girls engage in.   /9

When disaster strikes, it is not "the end of a love affair" to make them blue, but "the destruction of our relationship" to make them yearn for new "therapeutic experience."   /10

This grotesque terminology in which Americans now discuss what used to be called affairs of the heart is curious not only for its comic pseudoscientific sound, but also for the coolness with which it treats a passion formerly associated with heat. It takes a very cool pair of cats to talk about the grandest of passions as though it were only an exercise in sociology. Imagine Dante filling pages about the satisfactory nature of communicating with Beatrice, or Juliet raving on through five acts about her fulfilling relationship with Romeo.   /11

The way people talk, of course, reflects the way they think, and this avoidance of the language of love probably reflects a wish to avoid the consuming single-minded commitment to love to which the old words led, often no doubt to the dismay of people who uttered them. Why in our time we should tread so gingerly to avoid commitment to love to the second party is the subject for a monograph. Perhaps it comes from a fear of living too fully, perhaps from the current cultural fashion conditioning us to believe that whatever interferes with self-love will lead to psychic headache.   /12

Whatever the explanation, it is a bleak era for love, which makes it a time of dull joys, small-bore agonies and thin passions. "I could not love thee, dear, so much, lov'd I not honor more," the poet once could write. Today he could only say, "I could not have so fulfilling a relationship with thee, dear, had I not an even more highly intensified mental set as regards the absurd and widely discredited concept known as honor."   /13

Review Questions

1. What is the subject of Baker's comparison?
2. Does he use the block method or the point by point method of comparison?
3. Does Baker favor one subject of the comparison over the other? Does he ever waver in this preference? Explain.
4. What is the point Baker is trying to make?

Grant and Lee: A Study in Contrasts

Bruce Catton

Bruce Catton (1899-1978), a journalist and historian specializing in the Civil War, was a newspaper reporter and the editor of *American Heritage* magazine. His historical writing earned him both a Pulitzer Prize and a National Book Award. Of his many books, the best-known include *A Stillness at Appomattox* (1953), *Waiting for the Morning Train: An American Boyhood* (1972), and *Gettysburg: The Final Fury* (1974).

The following essay is an excellent example of how comparison and contrast can be used as the basis for an entire essay.

When Ulysses S. Grant and Robert E. Lee met in the parlor of a modest house at Appomattox Court House, Virginia, on April 9, 1865, to work out the terms for

Bruce Catton, "Grant and Lee: A Study in Contrasts" from *The American Story*, ed. Earl Schenck Miers, © 1956 by Broadcast Music, Inc. Used by permission of the copyright holder.

the surrender of Lee's Army of Northern Virginia, a great chapter in American life came to a close, and a great new chapter began.   /1

These men were bringing the Civil War to its virtual finish. To be sure, other armies had yet to surrender, and for a few days the fugitive Confederate government would struggle desperately and vainly, trying to find some way to go on living now that its chief support was gone. But in effect it was all over when Grant and Lee signed the papers. And the little room where they wrote out the terms was the scene of one of the poignant, dramatic contrasts in American history.   /2

They were two strong men, these oddly different generals, and they represented the strengths of two conflicting currents that, through them, had come into final collision.   /3

Back of Robert E. Lee was the notion that the old aristocratic concept might somehow survive and be dominant in American life.   /4

Lee was tidewater Virginia, and in his background were family, culture, and tradition . . . the age of chivalry transplanted to a New World which was making its own legends and its own myths. He embodied a way of life that had come down through the age of knighthood and the English country squire. America was a land that was beginning all over again, dedicated to nothing much more complicated than the rather hazy belief that all men had equal rights and should have an equal chance in the world. In such a land Lee stood for the feeling that it was somehow of advantage to human society to have a pronounced inequality in the social structure. There should be a leisure class, backed by ownership of land; in turn, society itself should be keyed to the land as the chief source of wealth and influence. It would bring forth (according to this ideal) a class of men with a strong sense of obligation to the community; men who lived not to gain advantage for themselves, but to meet the solemn obligations which had been laid on them by the very fact that they were privileged. From them the country would get its leadership; to them it could look for the higher values — of thought, of conduct, of personal deportment — to give it strength and virtue.   /5

Lee embodied the noblest elements of this aristocratic ideal. Through him, the landed nobility justified itself. For four years, the Southern states had fought a desperate war to uphold the ideals for which Lee stood. In the end, it almost seemed as if the Confederacy fought for Lee; as if he himself was the Confederacy . . . the best thing that the way of life for which the Confederacy stood could ever have to offer. He had passed into legend before Appomattox. Thousands of tired, underfed, poorly clothed Confederate soldiers, long since past the simple enthusiasm of the early days of the struggle, somehow considered Lee the symbol of everything for which they had been willing to die. But they could not quite put this feeling into words. If the Lost Cause, sanctified by so much heroism and so many deaths, had a living justification, its justification was General Lee.   /6

Grant, the son of a tanner on the Western frontier, was everything Lee was not. He had come up the hard way and embodied nothing in particular except the eternal toughness and sinewy fiber of the men who grew up beyond the mountains. He was one of a body of men who owed reverence and obeisance to no one, who were self-reliant to a fault, who cared hardly anything for the past but who had a sharp eye for the future.   /7

These frontier men were the precise opposites of the tidewater aristocrats. Back of them, in the great surge that had taken people over the Alleghenies and into the opening Western country, there was a deep, implicit dissatisfaction with a past that had settled into grooves. They stood for democracy, not from any reasoned conclusion about the proper ordering of human society, but simply because they had grown up in the middle of democracy and knew how it worked. Their society might have privileges, but they would be privileges each man had won for himself. Forms and patterns meant nothing. No man was born to anything, except perhaps to a chance to show how far he could rise. Life was competition.   /8

Yet along with this feeling had come a deep sense of belonging to a national community. The Westerner who developed a farm, opened a shop, or set up in business as a trader, could hope to prosper only as his own community prospered — and his community ran from the Atlantic to the Pacific and from Canada down to Mexico. If the land was settled, with towns and highways and accessible markets, he could better himself. He saw his fate in terms of the nation's own destiny. As its horizons expanded, so did his. He had, in other words, an acute dollars-and-cents stake in the continued growth and development of his country.   /9

And that, perhaps, is where the contrast between Grant and Lee becomes most striking. The Virginia aristocrat, inevitably, saw himself in relation to his own region. He lived in a static society which could endure almost anything except change. Instinctively, his first loyalty would go to the locality in which that society existed. He would fight to the limit of endurance to defend it, because in defending it he was defending everything that gave his own life its deepest meaning.   /10

The Westerner, on the other hand, would fight with an equal tenacity for the broader concept of society. He fought so because everything he lived by was tied to growth, expansion, and a constantly widening horizon. What he lived by would survive or fall with the nation itself. He could not possibly stand by unmoved in the face of an attempt to destroy the Union. He would combat it with everything he had, because he could only see it as an effort to cut the ground out from under his feet.   /11

So Grant and Lee were in complete contrast, representing two diametrically opposed elements in American life. Grant was the modern man emerging; beyond him, ready to come on the stage, was the great age of steel and machinery, of crowded cities and a restless burgeoning vitality. Lee might have ridden down from the old age of chivalry, lance in hand, silken banner fluttering over his head. Each man was the perfect champion of his cause, drawing both his strengths and his weaknesses from the people he led.   /12

Yet it was not all contrast, after all. Different as they were — in background, in personality, in underlying aspiration — these two great soldiers had much in common. Under everything else, they were marvelous fighters. Furthermore, their fighting qualities were really very much alike.   /13

Each man had, to begin with, the great virtue of utter tenacity and fidelity. Grant fought his way down the Mississippi Valley in spite of acute personal discouragement and profound military handicaps. Lee hung on in the trenches at Petersburg after hope itself had died. In each man there was an indomitable quality . . . the born fighter's refusal to give up as long as he can still remain on his feet and lift his two fists.   /14

Daring and resourcefulness they had, too; the ability to think faster and move faster than the enemy. These were the qualities which gave Lee the dazzling campaigns of Second Manassas and Chancellorsville and won Vicksburg for Grant.   /15

Lastly, and perhaps greatest of all, there was the ability, at the end, to turn quickly from war to peace once the fighting was over. Out of the way these two men behaved at Appomattox came the possibility of a peace of reconciliation. It was a possibility not wholly realized, in the years to come, but which did, in the end, help the two sections to become one nation again . . . after a war whose bitterness might have seemed to make such a reunion wholly impossible. No part of either man's life became him more than the part he played in their brief meeting in the McLean house at Appomattox. Their behavior there put all succeeding generations of Americans in their debt. Two great Americans, Grant and Lee — very different, yet under everything very much alike. Their encounter at Appomattox was one of the great moments of American history.   /16

Review Questions

1. Has Catton used the block method or the point by point method in this essay?
2. What is the significance of the comparison Catton is making?
3. What is Catton's attitude toward Lee? Toward Grant? How do you know this?
4. How does Catton use the contrasts between Grant and Lee to epitomize the reasons for the Civil War?
5. What final point does Catton make in his essay?

The Discovery of What it Means to Be an American

James Baldwin

James Baldwin (1924-   ) is a novelist and essayist whose primary themes include the tensions experienced by blacks, artists, and homosexuals in America and abroad. His novels include *Go Tell It on the Mountain* (1953), *Giovanni's Room*

(1956), and *Another Country* (1962). He also wrote a drama *(Blues for Mr. Charlie),* and several pieces of short fiction, some of which were collected in *Going to Meet the Man* (1966). His books of essays include *Notes of a Native Son* (1955); *Nobody Knows My Name* (1961); *The Fire Next Time* (1963), which first appeared in *The New Yorker;* and *No Name in the Street* (1972).

"The Discovery of What it Means to Be an American" was first published in *The New York Times Book Review* in 1959, and reappeared in *Nobody Knows My Name.* There are several comparisons made in this essay, although the primary comparison is of white and black Americans in Europe.

"It is a complex fate to be an American," Henry James observed, and the principal discovery an American writer makes in Europe is just how complex this fate is. America's history, her aspirations, her peculiar triumphs, her even more peculiar defeats, and her position in the world — yesterday and today — are all so profoundly and stubbornly unique that the very word "America" remains a new, almost completely undefined and extremely controversial proper noun. No one in the world seems to know exactly what it describes, not even we motley millions who call ourselves Americans.   /1

I left America because I doubted my ability to survive the fury of the color problem here. (Sometimes I still do.) I wanted to prevent myself from becoming *merely* a Negro; or, even, merely a Negro writer. I wanted to find out in what way the *specialness* of my experience could be made to connect me with other people instead of dividing me from them. (I was as isolated from Negroes as I was from whites, which is what happens when a Negro begins, at bottom, to believe what white people say about him.)   /2

In my necessity to find the terms on which my experience could be related to that of others, Negroes and whites, writers, and non-writers, I proved, to my astonishment, to be as American as any Texas G.I. And I found my experience was shared by every American writer I knew in Paris. Like me, they had been divorced from their origins, and it turned out to make very little difference that the origins of white Americans were European and mine were African — they were no more at home in Europe than I was.   /3

The fact that I was the son of a slave and they were the sons of free men meant less, by the time we confronted each other on European soil, than the fact that we were both searching for our separate identities. When we had found these, we seemed to be saying, why, then, we would no longer need to cling to the shame and bitterness which had divided us so long.   /4

It became terribly clear in Europe, as it never had been here, that we knew more about each other than any European ever could. And it also became clear that, no matter where our fathers had been born, or what they had endured, the fact of Europe had formed us both, was part of our identity and part of our inheritance.   /5

I had been in Paris a couple of years before any of this became clear to me. When it did, I, like many a writer before me upon the discovery that his props have all been knocked out from under him, suffered a species of breakdown and was carried off to the mountains of Switzerland. There, in that absolutely alabaster landscape, armed with two Bessie Smith records and a typewriter, I began to try to re-create the life that I had first known as a child and from which I had spent so many years in flight.   /6

It was Bessie Smith, through her tone and her cadence, who helped me to dig back to the way I myself must have spoken when I was a pickaninny, and to remember the things I had heard and seen and felt. I had buried them very deep. I had never listened to Bessie Smith in America (in the same way that, for years, I would not touch watermelon), but in Europe she helped to reconcile me to being a "nigger."   /7

I do not think that I could have made this reconciliation here. Once I was able to accept my role — as distinguished, I must say, from my "place" — in the extraordinary drama which is America, I was released from the illusion that I hated America.   /8

The story of what can happen to an American Negro writer in Europe simply illustrates, in some relief, what can happen to any American writer there. It is not meant, of course, to imply that it happens to them all, for Europe can be very crippling, too; and, anyway, a writer, when he has made his first breakthrough, has simply won a crucial skirmish in a dangerous, unending and unpredictable battle. Still, the breakthrough is important, and the point is that an American writer, in order to achieve it, very often has to leave this country.   /9

The American writer, in Europe, is released, first of all, from the necessity of apologizing for himself. It is not until he *is* released from the habit of flexing his muscles and proving that he is just a "regular guy" that he realizes how crippling this habit has been. It is not necessary for him, there, to pretend to be something he is not, for the artist does not encounter in Europe the same suspicion he encounters here. Whatever the Europeans may actually think of artists, they have killed enough of them off by now to know that they are as real — and as persistent — as rain, snow, taxes or businessmen.   /10

Of course, the reason for Europe's comparative clarity concerning the different functions of men in society is that European society has always been divided into classes in a way that American society never has been. A European writer considers himself to be part of an old and honorable tradition — of intellectual activity, of letters — and his choice of a vocation does not cause him any uneasy wonder as to whether or not it will cost him all his friends. But this tradition does not exist in America.   /11

On the contrary, we have a very deep-seated distrust of real intellectual effort (probably because we suspect that it will destroy, as I hope it does, that myth of America to which we cling so desperately). An American writer fights his way to one of the lowest rungs on the American social ladder by means of pure bull-headedness and an indescribable series of odd jobs. He probably *has* been a "regular fellow" for much of his adult life, and it is not easy for him to step out of that lukewarm bath.   /12

We must, however, consider a rather serious paradox: though American society is more mobile than Europe's, it is easier to cut across social and occupational lines there than it is here. This has something to do, I think, with the problem of status in American life. Where everyone has status, it is also perfectly possible, after all, that no one has. It seems inevitable, in any case, that a man may become uneasy as to just what his status is.   /13

But Europeans have lived with the idea of status for a long time. A man can be as proud of being a good waiter as of being a good actor, and in neither case feel threatened. And this means that the actor and the waiter can have a freer and more genuinely friendly relationship in Europe than they are likely to have here. The waiter does not feel, with obscure resentment, that the actor has "made it," and the actor is not tormented by the fear that he may find himself, tomorrow, once again a waiter.   /14

This lack of what may roughly be called social paranoia causes the American writer in Europe to feel — almost certainly for the first time in his life — that he can reach out to everyone, that he is accessible to everyone and open to everything. This is an extraordinary feeling. He feels, so to speak, his own weight, his own value.   /15

It is as though he suddenly came out of a dark tunnel and found himself beneath the open sky. And, in fact, in Paris, I began to see the sky for what seemed to be the first time. It was borne in on me — and it did not make me feel melancholy — that this sky had been there before I was born and would be there when I was dead. And it was up to me, therefore, to make of my brief opportunity the most that could be made.   /16

I was born in New York, but have lived only in pockets of it. In Paris, I lived in all parts of the city — on the Right Bank and the Left, among the bourgeoisie and among *les misérables,* and knew all kinds of people, from pimps and prostitutes in Pigalle to Egyptian bankers in Neuilly. This may sound extremely unprincipled or even obscurely immoral: I found it healthy. I love to talk to people, all kinds of people, and almost everyone, as I hope we still know, loves a man who loves to listen.   /17

This perpetual dealing with people very different from myself caused a shattering in me of preconceptions I scarcely knew I held. The writer is meeting in Europe people who are not American, whose sense of reality is entirely different from his own. They may love or hate or admire or fear or envy this country — they see it, in any case, from another point of view, and this forces the writer to reconsider many things he had always taken for granted. This reassessment, which can be very painful, is also very valuable.   /18

This freedom, like all freedom, has its dangers and its responsibilities. One day it begins to be borne in on the writer, and with great force, that he is living in Europe as an American. If he were living there as a European, he would be living on a different and far less attractive continent.   /19

This crucial day may be the day on which an Algerian taxi-driver tells him how it feels to be an Algerian in Paris. It may be the day on which he passes a café terrace and catches a glimpse of the tense, intelligent and troubled face of Albert

Camus. Or it may be the day on which someone asks him to explain Little Rock and he begins to feel that it would be simpler — and, corny as the words may sound, more honorable — to go to Little Rock than sit in Europe, on an American passport, trying to explain it.   /20

This is a personal day, a terrible day, the day to which his entire sojourn has been tending. It is the day he realizes that there are no untroubled countries in this fearfully troubled world; that if he has been preparing himself for anything in Europe, he has been preparing himself — for America. In short, the freedom that the American writer finds in Europe brings him, full circle, back to himself, with the responsibility for his development where it always was: in his own hands.   /21

Even the most incorrigible maverick has to be born somewhere. He may leave the group that produced him — he may be forced to — but nothing will efface his origins, the marks of which he carries with him everywhere. I think it is important to know this and even find it a matter for rejoicing, as the strongest people do, regardless of their station. On this acceptance, literally, the life of a writer depends.   /22

The charge has often been made against American writers that they do not describe society, and have no interest in it. They only describe individuals in opposition to it, or isolated from it. Of course, what the American writer is describing is his own situation. But what is *Anna Karenina* describing if not the tragic fate of the isolated individual, at odds with her time and place?   /23

The real difference is that Tolstoy was describing an old and dense society in which everything seemed — to the people in it, though not to Tolstoy — to be fixed forever. And the book is a masterpiece because Tolstoy was able to fathom, and make us see, the hidden laws which really governed this society and made Anna's doom inevitable.   /24

American writers do not have a fixed society to describe. The only society they know is one in which nothing is fixed and in which the individual must fight for his identity. This is a rich confusion, indeed, and it creates for the American writer unprecedented opportunities.   /25

That the tensions of American life, as well as the possibilities, are tremendous is certainly not even a question. But these are dealt with in contemporary literature mainly compulsively; that is, the book is more likely to be a symptom of our tension than an examination of it. The time has come, God knows, for us to examine ourselves, but we can only do this if we are willing to free ourselves of the myth of America and try to find out what is really happening here.   /26

Every society is really governed by hidden laws, by unspoken but profound assumptions on the part of the people, and ours is no exception. It is up to the American writer to find out what these laws and assumptions are. In a society much given to smashing taboos without thereby managing to be liberated from them, it will be no easy matter.   /27

It is no wonder, in the meantime, that the American writer keeps running off to Europe. He needs sustenance for his journey and the best models he can find.

Europe has what we do not have yet, a sense of the mysterious and inexorable limits of life, a sense, in a word, of tragedy. And we have what they sorely need: a new sense of life's possibilities.   /**28**

In this endeavor to wed the vision of the Old World with that of the New, it is the writer, not the statesman, who is our strongest arm. Though we do not wholly believe it yet, the interior life is a real life, and the intangible dreams of people have a tangible effect on the world.   /**29**

Review Questions

1. How do you know that the subjects of Baldwin's comparison and contrast in this essay are black and white Americans?
2. How do the experiences of black Americans in Europe differ from those of white Americans in Europe?
3. In what ways are the experiences of black Americans and white Americans the same?
4. What point is Baldwin ultimately trying to make? Does he succeed?
5. Is there a secondary set of subjects being compared and contrasted in the essay? What are they?
6. Has Baldwin used the point-by-point method of comparison or the block method? Explain.

Two Cultures

Norman Cousins

Norman Cousins (1912-   ), who recently stepped down as editor of *Saturday Review*, began his career in journalism as the editor of *Current History* in 1935. He became editor of *Saturday Review* in 1942. His essays have appeared primarily in *Saturday Review*, and he has written several books, including *The Celebration of Life* (1974) and *Anatomy of an Illness as Perceived by the Patient* (1979).

"Two Cultures," which appeared in *Saturday Review*, contains two comparisons: the old scientists versus humanists dichotomy, and a newer split, those who believe in moral responsibility versus those who do not.

A generation of scientists and humanists has come of age since C. P. Snow first called attention, in his book *The Two Cultures*, to the gap between the two groups. He was troubled by what he regarded as a wall of separation between those who were trained to think systematically and those who nurtured themselves in the world of the creative imagination. Sir Charles claimed that the two cultures had the greatest difficulty in understanding each other; that each had very little curiosity about what the other was doing; and that as a consequence, both had insufficient respect for each other at a time of mutual challenge.   /1

The same charge certainly cannot be made today. Whatever rift may once have existed between scientists and humanists has been substantially closed. Indeed, as the special articles in *SR*'s December 10 issue on "God and Science" clearly demonstrated, the scientists have lost their feeling of strangeness even in the presence of theologians. The sciences have been de-mystified for the humanists; and the humanities have become less extraneous to the scientists. The ivory tower and the laboratory are no longer zones of isolation from which the occupants stare balefully at one another but are points of departure for a rounded view of life. Language, which at one time was the means for performing the rituals of detachment, is being used today for defining a common purpose.   /2

The old gap between the two cultures, however, has been replaced by an even more serious division within the sciences and the humanities themselves. The separation between two intellectual worlds has given way to a profound philosophical cleavage that now cuts across all disciplines. It is a cleavage of values reflecting the differences in the way truth is perceived and pursued; differences in the way the world is understood; differences, more implicit than explicit perhaps, in the way the individual sees his obligations to society.   /3

Some scientists, for example, see no question of conscience in lending themselves to the creation of devices for increasing the mastery of man by man. They recognize no issue of moral values in undertaking research for destructive mechanisms that no longer have anything to do with genuine national security but that can lead only to a holocaust of continental dimensions. They are neutral about breeding pathological organisms that condemn not only the living but generations yet to be born. In short, they have no difficulty in subordinating the human interest to the tribal interest.   /4

These scientists justify their position by claiming that what they do in their laboratories is not harmful; what is harmful is what the politicians do with their work. These scientists do not accept responsibility for what others make of their theories or their discoveries. Science is pure; in devoting themselves to it, they see themselves as purists.   /5

Other scientists, however, hold a contrasting view. They feel that they are in a better position to understand the implications and significance of what they are doing than the people who hire them to do it. Their colleagues may make proclamations in public about the morally antiseptic nature of science, but they feel that if they, the scientists, do not say openly what they know to be true, no one else will. They see no way of exempting themselves from the obligation to peer beyond the laboratory into the public arena.   /6

Perhaps the prime example of this latter group would be the scientists who wrote a letter to President Truman early in 1945, imploring him to recognize that the atomic bomb was not merely a highly devastating weapon but a suicidal device of mass incineration that could bring down civilization itself. They urged that before dropping the bomb on a live target, the United States carry out a demonstration of the power of the bomb under the auspices of the International Red Cross. On the basis of that demonstration, an ultimatum could be issued and Japan itself would have the choice of surrendering or being subjected to nuclear war. But the President decided against such a test. Claims were later made that Japan had no interest in ending the war and that were it not for the atomic bomb, it would have been necessary for the United States to invade the Japanese mainland, with a consequent loss of hundreds of thousands of American lives. These claims, however, do not square with the fact that Japan had asked the Soviet Union to use its good offices to inquire about U.S. peace terms. The Soviet Union did not meet this request. The United States knew about the affair because it had intercepted the coded message from Tokyo to Moscow. Several months earlier, the Soviet Union, on prodding from the United States, had agreed to enter the war in the Far East. As soon as we knew we could end the war by ourselves, because of the atomic bomb, we wanted to be able to polish off Japan before the agreed-upon Russian entry. The purpose was to prevent the Soviet Union from establishing a claim on the occupation of Japan. Hence the U.S. decision to use the atomic bomb — not once but twice — in going for the knockout blow.   /7

Since the end of World War II, many of the atomic scientists have continued to exercise their sense of responsibility by staying together and by trying to persuade the American people that modern warfare makes traditional concepts of victory and defeat obsolete, and that national security is to be achieved not through the pursuit of force, but through the control of it.   /8

Just as the scientists have been divided by questions of moral priorities, so the humanists have been split by issues of human values. One group of writers and philosophers feels that questions of war and peace have become too technical and complex for them to handle. They feel that government leaders have far better sources of information and should not be subjected to pressures from the people.   /9

Juxtaposed against them are the humanists who believe that in the making of moral judgments, the humblest citizen in the nation stands on even ground with a President. They feel, moreover, that there is something in the nature of government that makes it resistant to moral values. Men caught up in games of international realpolitik tend to delude themselves with the thought that "hard" matters of military policy are the only ones that count. History, however, is littered with the relics of civilizations whose leaders felt uncomfortable or scornful in the presence of moral questions.   /10

Two hundred years ago, a great nation was founded on the idea that the strength of a country begins with moral concepts, the truth of which is confirmed in the natural response of human beings and in the history of the race. If we want that nation to go on for another two hundred years, we will dispense with the nonsense that moral values are incidental and that the national interest can stand apart from the human interest.   /11

Review Questions

1. Why does Cousins include the first comparison and how does he use it?
2. Is Cousins using the block method of comparison or the point-by-point method?
3. What is Cousins' point of view in this essay?
4. Does he side with either group in his main comparison?
5. Do you agree with Cousins' point of view? Why?

21

Classification and Division Essays

Some American Types

Max Lerner

Max Lerner (1902-   ) was born in Russia and became a U.S. citizen in 1907. Educated at Yale, Washington University in St. Louis, and Robert Brookings Graduate School, Lerner has had a varied career, working at different times as an author, lecturer, professor, editor (*Nation*, 1936-1938), radio commentator, columnist, and academic dean.

Lerner's books include *America as a Civilization* (1957) from which the following essay was taken, *It Is Later Than You Think* (1943), and *Ideas as Weapons* (1939).

Seventeenth-century England produced a number of books on *Characters* depicting English society through the typical personality patterns of the era. Trying something of the same sort for contemporary America, the first fact one encounters is the slighter emphasis on a number of character types than stand out elsewhere in Western society: to be sure, they are to be found in America as well, but they are not characteristically American. One thinks of the scholar, the aesthete, the priest or "parson," the "aristocratic" Army officer, the revolutionary student, the civil servant, the male schoolteacher, the marriage broker, the courtesan, the mystic, the saint. Anyone familiar with European literature will recognize these characters as stock literary types and therefore as social types. Each of them represents a point of convergence for character and society.

Anyone familiar with American literature will know that it contains stock portraits of its own which express social types. I want to use these traditional types as backdrops and stress some of the social roles that are new and still in process of formation.   /1

Thus there is the *fixer,* who seems an organic product of a society in which the middleman function eats away the productive one. He may be public-relations man or influence peddler; he may get your traffic fine settled, or he may be able — whatever the commodity — to "get it for you wholesale." He is contemptuous of those who take the formal rules seriously; he knows how to cut corners — financial, political, administrative, or moral. At best there is something of the iconoclast in him, an unfooled quality far removed from the European personality types that always obey authority. At worst he becomes what the English call a "spiv" or cultural procurer.   /2

Related to the fixer is the *inside dopester,* as Riesman has termed him. He is oriented not so much toward getting things fixed as toward being "in the know" and "wised up" about things that innocents take at face value. He is not disillusioned because he has never allowed himself the luxury of illusions. In the 1920s and 1930s he consumed the literature of "debunking"; in the current era he knows everything that takes place in the financial centers of Wall Street, the political centers of Capitol Hill, and the communications centers of Madison Avenue — yet among all the things he knows there is little he believes in. His skepticism is not the wisdom which deflates pretentiousness but that of the rejecting man who knows ahead of time that there is "nothing in it" whatever the "it" may be. In short, he is "hep."   /3

Another link leads to the *neutral* man. He expresses the devaluing tendency in a culture that tries to avoid commitments. Fearful of being caught in the crosscurrents of conflict that may endanger his safety or status, he has a horror of what he calls "controversial figures" — and anyone becomes "controversial" if he is attacked. As the fixer and the inside dopester are the products of a middleman's society, so the neutral man is the product of a technological one. The technician's detachment from everything except effective results becomes — in the realm of character — an ethical vacuum that strips the results of much of their meaning.   /4

From the neutral man to the *conformist* is a short step. Although he is not neutral — in fact, he may be militantly partisan — his partisanship is on the side of the big battalions. He lives in terror of being caught in a minority where his insecurity will be conspicuous. He gains a sense of stature by joining the dominant group, as he gains security by making himself indistinguishable from that group. Anxious to efface any unique traits of his own, he exacts conformity from others. He fears ideas whose newness means they are not yet accepted, but once they are firmly established he fights for them with a courage born of the knowledge that there is no danger in championing them. He hates foreigners and immigrants. When he talks of the "American way," he sees a world in which other cultures have become replicas of his own.   /5

It is often hard to distinguish the conformist from the *routineer.* Essentially he is a man in uniform, sometimes literally, always symbolically. The big public-service corporations — railroads, air lines, public utilities — require their employees to wear uniforms that will imprint a common image of the enterprise as a whole. City employees, such as policemen and firemen, wear uniforms. Gas-station attendants, hotel clerks, bellhops, must similarly keep their appearance within prescribed limits. Even the sales force in big department stores or the typists and stenographers in big corporations tend toward the same uniformity. There are very few young Americans who are likely to escape the uniform of the Armed Services. With the uniform goes an urge toward pride of status and a routineering habit of mind. There is the confidence that comes of belonging to a large organization and sharing symbolically in its bigness and power. There is a sense of security in having grooves with which to move. This is true on every level of corporate business enterprise, from the white-collar employee to "the man in the gray flannel suit," although it stops short of the top executives who create the uniforms instead of wearing them. Even outside the government and corporate bureaus there are signs of American life becoming bureaucratized, in a stress on forms and routines, on "going through channels."   /6

Unlike the conformist or routineer, the *status seeker* may possess a resourceful energy and even originality, but he directs these qualities toward gaining status. What he wants is a secure niche in a society whose men are constantly being pulled upward or trodden down. Scott Fitzgerald has portrayed a heartbreaking case history of this character type in *The Great Gatsby,* whose charm and energy are invested fruitlessly in an effort to achieve social position. The novels of J. P. Marquand are embroideries of a similar theme, narrated through the mind of one who already has status and is confronted by the risk of losing it. At various social levels the status seeker becomes a "joiner" of associations which give him symbolic standing.   /7

Review Questions

1. What is the unifying theme underlying Lerner's categorizations?
2. Is there an order to these categorizations? Explain.
3. Are the categories distinct types?
4. What is the tone of the essay?
5. What audience do you think Lerner is addressing? Why?

Kinds of Humor

C. S. Lewis

C(live) S(taples) Lewis (1898-1963) was born in Ireland and educated at Oxford in England. A medievalist who taught at Cambridge, Lewis's writings focus on Christian tenets and mythology. His writings include the series for children, *The*

Chronicles of Narnia (1952-1956); *The Allegory of Love* (1936), about medieval romantic love; and *The Screwtape Letters* (1942), an ironic treatment of the theme of salvation, from which the following selection was taken. "Kinds of Humor" illustrates well the mode of classification and division.

I divide the causes of human laughter into Joy, Fun, the Joke Proper, and Flippancy. You will see the first among friends and lovers reunited on the eve of a holiday. Among adults some pretext in the way of Jokes is usually provided, but the facility with which the smallest witticisms produce laughter at such a time shows that they are not the real cause. What that real cause is we do not know. Something like it is expressed in much of that detestable art which the humans call Music, and something like it occurs in Heaven — a meaningless acceleration in the rhythm of celestial experience, quite opaque to us. Laughter of this kind does us no good and should always be discouraged. Besides, the phenomenon is of itself disgusting and a direct insult to the realism, dignity, and austerity of Hell.   /1

Fun is closely related to Joy — a sort of emotional froth arising from the play instinct. It is very little use to us. It can sometimes be used, of course, to divert humans from something else which the Enemy would like them to be feeling or doing: but in itself it has wholly undesirable tendencies; it promotes charity, courage, contentment, and many other evils.   /2

The Joke Proper, which turns on sudden perception of incongruity, is a much more promising field. I am not thinking primarily of indecent or bawdy humour, which, though much relied upon by second-rate tempters, is often disappointing in its results. The truth is that humans are pretty clearly divided on this matter into two classes. There are some to whom "no passion is as serious as lust" and for whom an indecent story ceases to produce lasciviousness precisely in so far as it becomes funny: there are others in whom laughter and lust are excited at the same moment and by the same things. The first sort joke about sex because it gives rise to many incongruities; the second cultivate incongruities because they afford a pretext for talking about sex. If your man is of the first type, bawdy humour will not help you — I shall never forget the hours which I wasted (hours to me of unbearable tedium) with one of my early patients in bars and smoking rooms before I learned this rule. Find out which group the patient belongs to — and see that he does *not* find out.   /3

The real use of Jokes or Humour is in quite a different direction, and it is specially promising among the English, who take their "sense of humour" so seriously that a deficiency in this sense is almost the only deficiency at which they feel shame. Humour is for them the all-consoling and (mark this) the all-excusing, grace of life. Hence it is invaluable as a means of destroying shame. If a man simply lets others pay for him, he is "mean"; if he boasts of it in a jocular manner and twits his fellows with having been scored off, he is no longer "mean" but a comical fellow. Mere cowardice is shameful; cowardice boasted of with humorous exaggerations and grotesque gestures can be passed off as funny. Cruelty is shameful — unless the cruel man can represent it as a practical joke. A thousand bawdy, or even blasphemous, jokes do not help towards a man's damnation so much as his discovery that almost anything he wants to do can be done, not only without the disapproval but with the admiration of his fellows, if only it can get itself treated as a Joke. And this temptation can be almost entirely hidden from your patient by that English seriousness about Humour. Any suggestion that there might be too much of it can be represented to him as "Puritanical" or as betraying a "lack of humour."   /4

But flippancy is the best of all. In the first place it is very economical. Only a clever human can make a real Joke about virtue, or indeed about anything else; any of them can be trained to talk *as if* virtue were funny. Among flippant people the Joke is always assumed to have been made. No one actually makes it; but every serious subject is discussed in a manner which implies that they have already found a ridiculous side to it. If prolonged, the habit of Flippancy builds up around a man the finest armour plating against the Enemy that I know, and it is quite free from the dangers inherent in the other sources of laughter. It is a thousand miles away from joy; it deadens, instead of sharpening, the intellect; and it excites no affection between those who practise it.   /5

Review Questions

1. What subject is Lewis categorizing, and how does he do so?
2. What is the underlying theme holding this categorization together?
3. What is the tone of this essay?
4. How does irony function in this essay?
5. What audience is Lewis addressing in this piece?

Different Types of Composers

Aaron Copland

Aaron Copland (1900-   ) is a renowned pianist and composer, having written music for orchestra, ballet, stage, film, voice, and chamber groups. Copland is also a lecturer and teacher. He has lectured on contemporary music at the New School for Social Research in New York, and has taught poetry at Harvard. He has also been on the faculty of the Berkshire Music Center, and has conducted his own works in the United States, Europe, and Latin America.

Copland's honors include membership in the American Academy of Arts and Letters, the National Institute of Arts and Letters, and the American Society of Composers. He has received a Guggenheim Foundation Fellowship, a Pulitzer Prize in Music, and has been awarded the Presidential Medal of Freedom.

Among his writings are four books: *Music and Imagination* (1952), *What to Listen For in Music* (1957), *New Music* (1968), and *Copland on Music* (1976). The essay to follow is an example of classification and division.

I can see three different types of composers in musical history, each of whom conceives music in a somewhat different fashion.   /1

The type that has fired public imagination most is that of the spontaneously inspired composer — the Franz Schubert type, in other words. All composers are inspired, of course, but this type is more spontaneously inspired. Music simply wells out of him. He can't get it down on paper fast enough. You can almost tell this type of composer by his prolific output. In certain months, Schubert wrote a song a day. Hugo Wolf did the same.   /2

In a sense, men of this kind begin not so much with a musical theme as with a completed composition. They invariably work best in the shorter forms. It is much easier to improvise a song than it is to improvise a symphony. It isn't easy to be inspired in that spontaneous way for long periods at a stretch. Even Schubert was more successful in handling the shorter forms of music. The spontaneously inspired man is only one type of composer, with his own limitations.   /3

Beethoven symbolizes the second type — the constructive type, one might call it. This type exemplifies my theory of the creative process in music better than any other, because in this case the composer really does begin with a musical theme. In Beethoven's case there is no doubt about it, for we have the notebooks in which he put the themes down. We can see from his notebooks how he worked over his themes — how he would not let them be until they were as perfect as he could make them. Beethoven was not a spontaneously inspired composer in the Schubert sense at all. He was the type that begins with a theme; makes it a germinal idea; and upon that constructs a musical work, day after day, in painstaking fashion. Most composers since Beethoven's day belong to this second type.   /4

The third type of creator I can only call, for lack of a better name, the traditionalist type. Men like Palestrina and Bach belong in this category. They both exemplify the kind of composer who is born in a particular period of musical history, when a certain musical style is about to reach its fullest development. It is a question at such a time of creating music in a well-known and accepted style and doing it in a way that is better than anyone has done it before you.   /5

Beethoven and Schubert started from a different premise. They both had serious pretensions to originality: After all, Schubert practically created the song form single-handed; and the whole face of music changed after Beethoven lived. But Bach and Palestrina simply improved on what had gone before them.   /6

The traditionalist type of composer begins with a pattern rather than with a theme. The creative act with Palestrina is not the thematic conception so much as the personal treatment of a well-established pattern. And even Bach, who conceived forty-eight of the most varied and inspired themes in his *Well Tempered Clavichord*, knew in advance the general formal mold that they were to fill. It goes without saying that we are not living in a traditionalist period nowadays.   /7

One might add, for the sake of completeness, a fourth type of composer — the pioneer type: men like Gesualdo in the seventeenth century, Moussorgsky and Berlioz in the nineteenth, Debussy and Edgar Varese in the twentieth. It is difficult to summarize the composing methods of so variegated a group. One can safely say that their approach to composition is the opposite of the traditionalist type. They clearly oppose conventional solutions of musical problems. In many ways, their attitude is experimental — they seek to add new harmonies, new sonorities, new formal principles. The pioneer type was the characteristic one at the turn of the seventeenth century and also at the beginning of the twentieth century, but it is much less evident today.   /8

Review Questions

1. Though Copland does not explicitly state what his purpose is in categorizing composers, his essay does imply a purpose. What do you think his purpose in writing this essay is?
2. What are the three major categories Copland mentions? How do they differ?
3. Why does Copland add a fourth category?
4. Does Copland imply any preferences for one or another type of composer?
5. Is it necessary to be familiar with the composers' work to understand Copland's essay?

Thinking as a Hobby

William Golding

William Golding (1911-   ) was born in Cornwall, England and educated at Oxford. He has been a settlement house worker, a teacher, and a participant in experimental theater.

Golding's writing includes several novels, among them *Lord of the Flies* (1954), *The Inheritors* (1955), *Pincher Martin* (1956), *The Spire* (1964), and *The Pyramid* (1967). In addition, he has written many short pieces and plays. The classification and division essay included here first appeared in *Holiday* magazine in August, 1961.

While I was still a boy, I came to the conclusion that there were three grades of thinking; and since I was later to claim thinking as my hobby, I came to an even stranger conclusion — namely, that I myself could not think at all.   /1

I must have been an unsatisfactory child for grownups to deal with. I remember how incomprehensible they appeared to me at first, but not, of course, how I appeared to them. It was the headmaster of my grammar school who first brought the subject of thinking before me — though neither in the way, nor with the result he intended. He had some statuettes in his study. They stood on a high cupboard behind his desk. One was a lady wearing nothing but a bath towel. She seemed frozen in an eternal panic lest the bath towel slip down any farther; and since she had no arms, she was in an unfortunate position to pull the towel up again. Next to her crouched the statuette of a leopard, ready to spring down at the top drawer of a filing cabinet labeled A-AH. My innocence interpreted this as the victim's last, despairing cry. Beyond the leopard was a naked, muscular gentleman, who sat, looking down, with his chin on his fist and his elbow on his knee. He seemed utterly miserable.   /2

Some time later, I learned about these statuettes. The headmaster had placed them where they would face delinquent children, because they symbolized to him the whole of life. The naked lady was the Venus of Milo. She was Love. She was not worried about the towel. She was just busy being beautiful. The leopard was Nature, and he was being natural. The naked, muscular gentleman was not miserable. He was Rodin's Thinker, an image of pure thought. It is easy to buy small plaster models of what you think life is like.   /3

I had better explain that I was a frequent visitor to the headmaster's study, because of the latest thing I had done or left undone. As we now say, I was not integrated. I was, if anything, disintegrated; and I was puzzled. Grownups never made sense. Whenever I found myself in a penal position before the headmaster's desk, with the statuettes glimmering whitely above him, I would sink my head, clasp my hands behind my back and writhe one shoe over the other.   /4

The headmaster would look opaquely at me through flashing spectacles.   /5

"What are we going to do with you?"   /6

Well, what *were* they going to do with me? I would writhe my shoe some more and stare down at the worn rug.   /7

"Look up, boy! Can't you look up?"   /8

Then I would look up at the cupboard, where the naked lady was frozen in her panic and the muscular gentleman contemplated the hindquarters of the leopard in endless gloom. I had nothing to say to the headmaster. His spectacles caught the light so that you could see nothing human behind them. There was no possibility of communication.   /9

"Don't you ever think at all?"   /10

No, I didn't think, wasn't thinking, couldn't think — I was simply waiting in anguish for the interview to stop.   /11

"Then you'd better learn — hadn't you?"   /12

On one occasion the headmaster leaped to his feet, reached up and plonked Rodin's masterpiece on the desk before me.   /13

"That's what a man looks like when he's really thinking."   /14

I surveyed the gentleman without interest or comprehension.   /15

"Go back to your class."   /16

Clearly there was something missing in me. Nature had endowed the rest of the human race with a sixth sense and left me out. This must be so, I mused, on my way back to the class, since whether I had broken a window, or failed to remember Boyle's Law, or been late for school, my teachers produced me one, adult answer: "Why can't you think?"   /17

As I saw the case, I had broken the window because I had tried to hit Jack Arney with a cricket ball and missed him; I could not remember Boyle's Law because I had never bothered to learn it; and I was late for school because I preferred looking over the bridge into the river. In fact, I was wicked. Were my teachers, perhaps, so good that they could not understand the depths of my depravity? Were they clear, untormented people who could direct their every action by this mysterious business of thinking? The whole thing was incomprehensible. In my earlier years, I found even the statuette of the Thinker confusing. I did not believe any of my teachers were naked, ever. Like someone born deaf, but bitterly determined to find out about sound, I watched my teachers to find out about thought.   /18

There was Mr. Houghton. He was always telling me to think. With a modest satisfaction, he would tell me that he had thought a bit himself. Then why did he spend so much time drinking? Or was there more sense in drinking than there appeared to be? But if not, and if drinking were in fact ruinous to health — and Mr. Houghton was ruined, there was no doubt about that — why was he always talking about the clean life and the virtues of fresh air? He would spread his arms wide with the action of a man who habitually spent his time striding along mountain ridges.   /19

"Open air does me good, boys — I know it!"   /20

Sometimes, exalted by his own oratory, he would leap from his desk and hustle us outside into a hideous wind.   /21

"Now, boys! Deep breaths! Feel it right down inside you — huge draughts of God's good air!"   /22

He would stand before us, rejoicing in his perfect health, an open-air man. He would put his hands on his waist and take a tremendous breath. You could hear the wind, trapped in the cavern of his chest and struggling with all the unnatural impediments. His body would reel with shock and his ruined face go white at the unaccustomed visitation. He would stagger back to his desk and collapse there, useless for the rest of the morning.   /23

Mr. Houghton was given to high-minded monologues about the good life, sexless and full of duty. Yet in the middle of one of these monologues, if a girl passed the window, tapping along on her neat little feet, he would interrupt his discourse, his neck would turn of itself and he would watch her out of sight. In this instance, he seemed to me ruled not by thought but by an invisible and irresistible spring in his nape.   /24

His neck was an object of great interest to me. Normally it bulged a bit over his collar. But Mr. Houghton had fought in the First World War alongside both Americans and French, and had come — by who knows what illogic? — to a settled detestation of both countries. If either country happened to be prominent in current affairs, no argument could make Mr. Houghton think well of it. He would bang the desk, his neck would bulge still further and go red. "You can say what you like," he would cry, "but I've thought about this — and I know what I think!"   /25

Mr. Houghton thought with his neck.   /26

There was Miss Parsons. She assured us that her dearest wish was our welfare, but I knew even then, with the mysterious clairvoyance of childhood, that what she wanted most was the husband she never got. There was Mr. Hands — and so on.   /27

I have dealt at length with my teachers because this was my introduction to the nature of what is commonly called thought. Through them I discovered that thought is often full of unconscious prejudice, ignorance and hypocrisy. It will lecture on disinterested purity while its neck is being remorselessly twisted toward a skirt. Technically, it is about as proficient as most businessmen's gold, as honest as most politicians' intentions, or — to come near my own preoccupation — as coherent as most books that get written. It is what I came to call grade-three thinking, though more properly, it is feeling, rather than thought.   /28

True, often there is a kind of innocence in prejudices, but in those days I viewed grade-three thinking with an intolerant contempt and an incautious mockery. I delighted to confront a pious lady who hated the Germans with the proposition that we should love our enemies. She taught me a great truth in dealing with grade-three thinkers; because of her, I no longer dismiss lightly a mental process which for nine-tenths of the population is the nearest they will ever get to thought. They have immense solidarity. We had better respect them, for we are outnumbered and surrounded. A crowd of grade-three thinkers, all shouting the same thing, all warming their hands at the fire of their own prejudices, will not thank you for pointing out the contradictions in their beliefs. Man is a gregarious animal, and enjoys agreement as cows will graze all the same way on the side of a hill.   /29

Grade-two thinking is the detection of contradictions. I reached grade two when I trapped the poor, pious lady. Grade-two thinkers do not stampede easily, though often they fall into the other fault and lag behind. Grade-two thinking is a withdrawal, with eyes and ears open. It became my hobby and brought satisfaction and loneliness in either hand. For grade-two thinking destroys without having the power to create. It set me watching the crowds cheering His Majesty the King and asking myself what all the fuss was about, without giving me anything positive to put in the place of that heady patriotism. But there were compensations. To hear people justify their habit of hunting foxes and tearing them to pieces by claiming that the foxes liked it. To hear our Prime Minister talk about the great benefit we conferred on India by jailing people like Pandit Nehru and Gandhi. To hear American politicians talk about peace in one sentence and refuse to join the League of Nations in the next. Yes, there were moments of delight.   /30

But I was growing toward adolescence and had to admit that Mr. Houghton was not the only one with an irresistible spring in his neck. I, too, felt the compulsive hand of nature and began to find that pointing out contradiction could be costly as well as fun. There was Ruth, for example, a serious and attractive girl. I was an atheist at the time. Grade-two thinking is a menace to religion and knocks down sects like skittles. I put myself in a position to be converted by her with an hypocrisy worthy of grade three. She was a Methodist — or at least, her parents were, and Ruth had to follow suit. But, alas, instead of relying on the Holy Spirit to convert me, Ruth was foolish enough to open her pretty mouth in argument. She claimed that the Bible (King James Version) was literally inspired. I countered by saying that the Catholics believed in the literal inspiration of Saint Jerome's *Vulgate,* and the two books were different. Argument flagged.   /31

At last she remarked that there were an awful lot of Methodists, and they couldn't be wrong, could they — not all those millions? That was too easy, said I restively (for the nearer you were to Ruth, the nicer she was to be near to) since there were more Roman Catholics than Methodists anyway; and they couldn't be wrong, could they — not all those hundreds of millions? An awful flicker of doubt appeared in her eyes. I slid my arm round her waist and murmured breathlessly that if we were counting heads, the Buddhists were the boys for my money. But Ruth had *really* wanted to do me good, because I was so nice. She fled. The combination of my arm and those countless Buddhists was too much for her.   /32

That night her father visited my father and left, red-cheeked and indignant. I was given the third degree to find out what had happened. It was lucky we were both of us only fourteen. I lost Ruth and gained an undeserved reputation as a potential libertine.   /33

So grade-two thinking could be dangerous. It was in this knowledge, at the age of fifteen, that I remember making a comment from the heights of grade two, on the limitations of grade three. One evening I found myself alone in the schoolhall, preparing it for a party. The door of the headmaster's study was open. I went in. The headmaster had ceased to thump Rodin's Thinker down on the desk as an example to the young. Perhaps he had not found any more candidates, but the statuettes were still there, glimmering and gathering dust on top of the cupboard. I stood on a chair and rearranged them. I stood Venus in her bath towel on the filing cabinet, so that now the top drawer caught its breath in a gasp of sexy excitement. "A-ah!" The portentous Thinker I placed on the edge of the cupboard so that he looked down at the bath towel and waited for it to slip.   /34

Grade-two thinking, though it filled life with fun and excitement, did not make for content. To find out the deficiencies of our elders bolsters the young ego but does not make for personal security. I found that grade two was not only the power to point out contradictions. It took the swimmer some distance from the shore and left him there, out of his depth. I decided that Pontius Pilate was a typical grade-two thinker. "What is truth?" he said, a very common grade-two thought, but one that is used always as the end of an argument instead of the beginning. There is a still higher grade of thought which says, "What is truth?" and sets out to find it.   /35

But these grade-one thinkers were few and far between. They did not visit my grammar school in the flesh though they were there in books. I aspired to them, partly because I was ambitious and partly because I now saw my hobby as an unsatisfactory thing if it went no further. If you set out to climb a mountain, however high you climb, you have failed if you cannot reach the top.   /36

I *did* meet an undeniably grade-one thinker in my first year at Oxford. I was looking over a small bridge in Magdalen Deer Park, and a tiny mustached and hatted figure came and stood by my side. He was a German who had just fled from the Nazis to Oxford as a temporary refuge. His name was Einstein.   /37

But Professor Einstein knew no English at that time and I knew only two words of German. I beamed at him, trying wordlessly to convey by my bearing all the affection and respect that the English felt for him. It is possible — and I have to make the admission — that I felt here were two grade-one thinkers standing side by side; yet I doubt if my face conveyed more than a formless awe. I would have given my Greek and Latin and French and a good slice of my English for enough German to communicate. But we were divided; he was as inscrutable as my headmaster. For perhaps five minutes we stood together on the bridge, undeniable grade-one thinker and breathless aspirant. With true greatness, Professor Einstein realized that any contact was better than none. He pointed to a trout wavering in midstream.   /38

He spoke: *"Fisch."*   /39

My brain reeled. Here I was, mingling with the great, and yet helpless as the veriest grade-three thinker. Desperately I sought for some sign by which I might convey that I, too, revered pure reason. I nodded vehemently. In a brilliant flash I used up half of my German vocabulary. *"Fisch. Ja. Ja."*   /40

For perhaps another five minutes we stood side by side. Then Professor Einstein, his whole figure still conveying good will and amiability, drifted away out of sight.   /41

I, too, would be a grade-one thinker. I was irreverent at the best of times. Political and religious systems, social customs, loyalties and traditions, they all came tumbling down like so many rotten apples off a tree. This was a fine hobby and a sensible substitute for cricket, since you could play it all the year round. I came up in the end with what must always remain the justification for grade-one thinking, its sign, seal and charter. I devised a coherent system for living. It was a moral system, which was wholly logical. Of course, as I readily admitted, conversion of the world to my way of thinking might be difficult, since my system did away with a number of trifles, such as big business, centralized government, armies, marriage. . . .   /42

It was Ruth all over again. I had some very good friends who stood by me, and still do. But my acquaintances vanished, taking the girls with them. Young women seemed oddly contented with the world as it was. They valued the meaningless ceremony with a ring. Young men, while willing to concede the chaining sordidness of marriage, were hesitant about abandoning the organizations which they hoped would give them a career. A young man on the first rung of the Royal Navy, while perfectly agreeable to doing away with big business and marriage, got as red-necked as Mr. Houghton when I proposed a world without any battleships in it.   /43

Had the game gone too far? Was it a game any longer? In those prewar days, I stood to lose a great deal, for the sake of a hobby.   /44

Now you are expecting me to describe how I saw the folly of my ways and came back to the warm nest, where prejudices are so often called loyalties, where pointless actions are hallowed into custom by repetition, where we are content to say we think when all we do is feel.   /45

But you would be wrong. I dropped my hobby and turned professional.   /46

If I were to go back to the headmaster's study and find the dusty statuettes still there, I would arrange them differently. I would dust Venus and put her aside, for I have come to love her and know her for the fair thing she is. But I would put the Thinker, sunk in his desperate thought, where there were shadows before him — and at his back, I would put the leopard, crouched and ready to spring.   /47

Review Questions

1. What is Golding's main point in this essay?
2. How does his use of classification help to prove this point?
3. What is the tone of Golding's essay?
4. Is he directing this essay toward a particular audience? Can you imagine what the characteristics of this audience might be?
5. Do you think Golding really considers himself a grade-one thinker? Explain.

22

Process Analysis Essays

Getting Ready for a Cow

E. B. White

E(lwyn) B(rooks) White (1899-   ) was born in Mt. Vernon, New York and educated at Cornell University. He has had a long career as a writer, beginning as a reporter and continuing as a freelance writer. He has contributed many pieces to *The New Yorker* and *Harper's*.

His books, three of them for children, include *Stuart Little* (1945), *Charlotte's Web* (1952), *The Trumpet of the Swan* (1970, a revised version of William Strunk Jr.'s *Elements of Style* (1959), and *One Man's Meat*, a collection of essays written in the 1930's and 40's, in which "Getting Ready for a Cow" appears. White was awarded the Laura Ingalls Wilder Award for children's books in 1970, and the National Medal for Literature in 1971.

This month an event is scheduled to take place here which is the culmination of four years of preparation. I am going to get a cow. Perhaps I should put it the other way round — a cow is going to get me. (I suspect I am regarded hereabouts as something of a catch.)

To establish a herd, even to establish a herd of one, is a responsibility which I do not lightly assume. For me this is a solemn moment, tinged with pure eagerness. I have waited a long time for this cow, this fateful female whom I have yet to meet. Mine has been a novitiate in which I have groomed myself faithfully and well for the duties of a husbandryman; I feel that now, at the end of these years, I have something to offer a cow.   /1

Of course I could have got a cow immediately on arriving here in the country. There is no law against a man getting a cow before he, or she, is ready. I see by *Life* magazine that Chic Johnson, the Helzapoppin farmer of Putnam County, N.Y., established his herd by "buying the World's Fair Borden Exhibit." This struck me as a rather clearcut case of a man who was perhaps not ready for his cows. He probably had not even had himself tested for Bangs. "At the dairy," said the article, describing a party the actor was throwing, "cows were milked and ridden bareback." Mr. Johnson was photographed in the act of trying to strike up an acquaintance with one of his own cows, but I noticed she had averted her gaze. He was wearing shorts and a jockey cap. From the photograph I judged that the cows were in clean, modern quarters, and there seemed to be a great many of them (I counted forty cows and ten milkmaids — enough to keep an actor in cream); but I think probably it will suit me better to have one cow with whom I am well acquainted than a barnful of comparative strangers in all stages of lactation.   /2

I knew from the very first that some day there would be a cow here. One of the first things that turned up when we bought the place was a milking stool, an old one, handmade, smooth with the wax finish which only the seat of an honest man's breeches can give to wood. A piece of equipment like that kicking around the barn is impossible to put out of one's mind completely. I never mentioned the name "cow" in those early days, but I knew that the ownership of a milking stool was like any other infection — there would be the period of incubation and then the trouble itself. The stool made me feel almost wholly equipped — all I needed was the new plank floor under the cow, the new stanchion, the platform, the curb, the gutter, the toprail, the litter alley, the sawdust, the manger, the barn broom, the halter, the watering pail, the milk pail, the milk cans, the brushes, the separator, the churn, the cow, and the ability to milk the cow.   /3

And there was the barn itself, egging me on. There it stood, with the old tie-ups intact. Every morning the sun rose, climbed, and shone through the south windows into the deserted stalls, scarred and pitted from bygone hooves. I tried not to look. But everytime I walked past I admired the ingenious construction of the homemade stanchions, set in a solid wooden curb and locked with pegs and tumblers, everything handhewn by a man who had fashioned, with ax and chisel, whatever he had needed for himself and his creatures. Men familiar with the habits and desires of cows have advised me to take those old stanchions out because of their rigidity, which is too confining for a cow, and I have already begun the work, but not without many misgivings and a feeling of guilt. The urge to remodel, the spirit of demolition, are in the blood of all city people who move to the country, and must be constantly guarded against. I have seen too many cases of farmhouses being torn limb from limb by a newly arrived owner, as though in fright or in anger.   /4

There is something bumptious in the common assumption that an old house or an old barn must be hacked to pieces before it is a fit place in which to settle.

The city man coming suddenly to the country customarily begins his new life by insulting someone else's old one; he knocks blazes out of his dwelling house, despite its having served former owners well for a hundred years or more. My own house is about a hundred and forty years old — three times my age — yet I, a mere upstart, approached it as though it didn't know its business and weren't quite fit for me the way it was, when the truth, as I now see it, was that I was not quite fit for *it*. Quite aside from the expense and inconvenience of razing one's newly acquired home, there is a subtle insult in the maneuver, the unmistakable implication that the former inhabitants lived either in squalor or in innocence, and that one's neighbors, in houses of similar design and appointments, are also living in squalor or innocence. Neither is true. But the demolition goes right ahead. The place of a newly arriving city man always looks more like a battleground than a home: earthworks are thrown up around the foundation wall, chimneys are reduced to rubble, and on the front lawn a cement mixer appears, with its little wheels and big round abdomen. It would be a comical sight if it were not so dispiriting.   /5

I don't know why people act in this panicky way. I do know for a fact that a man can't know the quality of his home until he has lived in it a year or two; and until he knows its good and bad qualities how can he presume to go about remodeling it? In the frenzy of resettlement one often does queer things and lives to regret his mistakes. When I go into my neighbors' "unimproved" houses in the dead of winter and feel how comfortable they are and cheerful, the sills banked with spruce boughs, the little heating stoves standing in candid warmth in the middle of the room, the geraniums and flowering maples blazing away in tin cans on the sunny shelf above the sink, with no pipes to freeze under the floors and no furnace around which huddle full ash cans like gloomy children, I always chuckle over the commotion city people make in their determination that their farmhouse shall be "livable." They have no idea how livable a farmhouse can be if you let it alone. We have too many preconceptions, anyway, about life and living. There is nothing so expensive, really, as a big, well-developed, full-bodied pre-conception.   /6

But as far as my cow was concerned, it was not so much any hesitancy at ripping things up and changing things around, not so much a matter of equipment and housing; it was simply that I felt the need of a personal probationary period. If a man expects his cow to have freshened before he gets her she has a right to expect that some important change will have been worked in him too. I didn't want a cow until I could meet her on her own ground, until I was ready, until I knew almost as much about the country as she did — otherwise it would embarrass me to be in her presence. I began this probation in 1938. For more than a year I kept my cow in the hindmost region of my thoughts. It was almost two years before I even allowed myself to dwell on her form and face. Then I began to lay the groundwork of my herd.   /7

My first move was to purchase fifteen sheep and a case of dynamite. The sheep, I figured, would improve my pasture, and the dynamite would keep me out of mischief in the meantime. Before they were done, the sheep managed to serve another useful purpose: I had no desire to have a cow on the place until I had learned how an udder worked, and my first lambing time taught me a lot about that. The way to learn to sail a big boat is first to sail a little one, because the little one is so much harder to manage. The same is true of udders. I can milk a sheep now, with her small cleverly concealed udder, and so I have no hesitancy about going on to a large and more forthright bag. The dynamite also turned out to have a second purpose — it had the advantage of letting people know something was going on around here.   /8

That fall when we dynamited for my cow was a great time. I set out to revive a run-out hayfield, and while I was at it I thought I would remove the rocks. I hadn't the slightest notion of what I was getting into, except that I knew I was establishing a cow, and, true to form, thought first of demolition. The rocks didn't look like much when I made my preliminary survey, but I discovered as time went on that a rock is much like an iceberg — most of it is down-under. A very great deal of spadework had to be done around the horse-size rocks before you could hook on to them with the team, and of course the others had to be drilled before they could be exploded. Hand drilling is tedious business, but I didn't have sense enough to charter an air-drill, which I learned later I could have done. The cow receded. There were days when I almost forgot her, so engrossed did I become in the amazing turn which my probation had taken. It was the end of summer; the days were hot and bright. Across the broad field, newly plowed, would come the exultant warning cry of "Fie-ah!" Then the breathless pause, then the blast, and the dunnage and rock fragments flying into the sun, than another pause and the sound of falling wreckage.   /9

Although the field had been turned over by the plow, the fragmentation from the blasting left it looking more like a gravel pit than a seedbed. There was a tremendous lot of work to be done just hauling away the debris after the bombing was over. The plowman hooked his team to the drag and I borrowed a tractor and another drag from a neighbor, and together we went at it. Day after day we loaded the drags, hauled them to the edge of the woods, and tossed the rocks off, creating a kind of hit and miss stone wall. I learned to throw the chain over a big rock with a "rolling holt," back the tractor up to it, and ease the rock on to the drag by giving it a nudge of power. The cow seemed a long way off, but I held her firmly in my thoughts, as a soldier holds the vision of home and peace through a long campaign in a foreign land. Rivers of sweat flowed into the dry, chewed-up soil, mountains of granite slogged along the dragways, all to achieve, in some remote time, the blade of new grass, the tiny jet of yellow milk. The whole thing seemed like a strangely tangential episode, as if I had wandered off on an idiot's holiday.   /10

And after the rocks had been torn from the earth and removed, then there was the matter of dressing the field. Having no cow, I had no dressing, except a small amount of sheep manure and hen manure which would be needed for the gardens. The field would need thirty or forty spreader loads. After much exploring, some dressing was located in a barn cellar within reasonable trucking distance, and for some days I lived close to a dung fork. This phase of the work had a cow smell and seemed somehow closer to the main issue.   /11

All winter the land and I lay waiting. In spring the frost opened cracks and seams in the field to receive the seed. I marked out courses with guide stakes and sowed the long lanes, working on a windless morning. The rains of spring never descended that year, and summer ushered in one of the most blistering droughts on record. The new grass drooped, the weeds jumped up and sang. The result of a year's labor seemed meager, doubtful. But it turned out that there was established in spite of the dry season what a farmer calls a good bottom. As soon as it got half a chance the field picked up miraculously. This summer, under benign rains, it has become a sweetly rolling green, like something Grant Wood might have sent me.   /12

Meantime the sheep had been at work in the pasture, quietly, with no dynamite. Their golden hooves had channeled among the rocks and ferns, and they had fertilized easily as they went. The time was approaching when I might take unto myself a cow. I began to see her as a living being who was growing closer to me, whose path and mine were soon to cross. I began having the sort of daydreams I used to have at fifteen: somewhere in the world (I would think) is the girl who is some day to be my wife. What is she doing? Where is she? What is she like?   /13

Of course there was still the matter of the barn — a fit place for this dream creature to spend her winter nights. The thought of a concrete floor flashed through my mind, and was quickly gone. I had invested in one concrete floor when I built my henhouse, and one concrete floor is enough for any man's lifetime. The sensible thing would be to lay a good smooth plank floor, with a six-inch platform, and perhaps a gutter. I turned, as one always does turn in any critical time, to the mail order catalogue and began a study of floor plans — stalls and gutters and curbs and stanchions and rails and partitions. I learned about stanchions, stanchion anchors, alignment devices; I began to pit the high curb against the low curb, the single post stall against the double. One evening after dark I went to the barn with a two-foot rule and a flashlight and measured up the job, working carefully and late, in pitch black except for the concentrated beam of the flash — an odd tryst, as I think back on it, but part of my beautiful romance. When I returned to the house I made a plan, drawn to scale, showing a maternity pen, three stalls, a raised platform, an eleven-inch curb hollowed out to six inches at the anchor point, and a gate, everything worked out to the inch. The platform is to be cut on the bias — a long stall (4 foot 10) at one end, in case my lovely girl turns out to be an Amazon, a medium-size stall (4 foot 4) for a medium-size bride, and a short stall (3 foot 8) for the heifer which will inevitably bless this marriage.   /14

There have been setbacks and reverses. Priorities worked against me and I soon found out that barn furnishings were almost unobtainable. I sent to Sears for their Russet Cow Halter, 32D449, the one with the adjustable crown and the brown hardware to match her eyes and hair, but they returned the money, with a grim note, Form Number 7, rubber stamped. Where they got the rubber for the stamp I have no idea.   /15

Tomorrow the carpenter arrives to start tearing out the old floor. When the last stanchion is anchored and the last brushful of whitewash has been applied to wall and rafter, I shall anoint myself and go forth to seek my love. This much I know, when the great day comes and she and I come marching home and pause for a moment in the barnyard before the freshly whitened door, *she's* got to carry *me* across the threshold. I'm tired.   /16

Review Questions

1. What is the "process" that White describes in this essay?
2. What purpose do you think he has in describing this process?
3. Does White reveal anything about himself in his process analysis? Explain.
4. What audience would you imagine White is addressing?

How to Shop for a Used Car

Deanna Sclar

Deanna Sclar described herself as an "urban cliff-dweller" before she moved to California. Once there, she discovered she needed her own car to get to work. She decided to learn all about cars, and the results of her efforts include not only a mastery of the car she drives, but her book, *Auto Repair for Dummies* (1976). The following selection from this book exemplifies process analysis.

You should have a good idea of what you want, and how much you are prepared to pay, before you go shopping. Read the ads, look at the "blue book," car-watch a bit on the street, and talk to people who own the cars you like for a firsthand view of the pleasures and problems associated with that particular model.   /1

Be wary of the following kinds of cars:

1 Car models that have gone completely out of production unless the one you want was so widely sold that there are still lots of parts available. Of course you may want to buy an Edsel as a collector's item. . . .

2 Cars with engines that have been modified. If a major change has been made by the owner, find out what went wrong with the original equipment and ask a professional what damage the defective part might have done to other parts of the car.

3 Sports cars with racing modifications. Most of these souped-up darlings are miserable in stop-and-go traffic and at lower speeds. Many have been worn out by leading fast lives and aren't good for anyone anymore.

4 Very new cars that are up for sale. These may be lemons or might have been wrecked.

5 Any car that has been in a wreck. Although the car may have been

completely restored, it's possible that the frame is bent and less stable, that the spot welds may not hold, or that the steering may be damaged. And remember, even though you may be convinced that the car has been restored and is as good as new, when the times comes for *you* to sell it, you may have trouble finding a buyer who feels the same way.

6 Station wagons owned by traveling salespeople, fleet cars, police cars, ex-taxis, etc. As I've mentioned before, these are usually driven hard and may be worn out.   /2

Now that you know what you *don't* want, figure out a general range of makes and models that appeal to you. Go for a pre-1970 car if possible. Although there are many good cars made since then, generally speaking the '60s were way ahead in terms of construction and materials. Don't limit your choice to just one car. But if you have a favorite brand, go to a dealer who sells new cars of that make, because they will tend to have more used cars of the same kind that they have taken as trade-ins. Follow these guidelines: /3

Do your shopping during daylight hours. Floodlights tend to make cars look more exotic, and they can hide a lot of damage, especially to the underbody of the car.   /4

If you are looking for a trade-in on your old car, park it about half a block away and *walk* to the dealer's lot. This is a good procedure to follow even if you are shopping for a new car. Most dealers will appraise your old car to decide how much they are going to have to give you in trade for it (whether you say you want to trade it in or not). They'll tack that onto the price they'd like to get for the car you are looking at. It is better to get a nice low price on the car you want and *then* talk trade-ins, so keep your car an unknown quantity until you are ready to deal.   /5

Shop several places. Buying a car is like hiring a mechanic for an expensive repair job. Establish that you are shopping around. They will be more eager to offer you a good deal to keep you out of the hands of the competition.   /6

Make it clear that you are looking for a car in *fine condition* and that you value condition over price. This will prevent the dealer from trying out the lemons on you. They will know that you are going to be very upset if they sell you a car that is not in good shape.   /7

Check each car that you really like, and road-test it according to the instructions in the next part of this chapter. It will help you to identify the cars that you want to consider and will impress the dealer a lot, especially if you are female. If you can, bring a friend to help you test the car.   /8

Visit several dealers this way. Then go back to the car you liked best and tell the dealer that you are there to buy if the deal is good. (In all of this, it is wise to remember that you want to *buy,* not *be sold,* a car.)   /9

Now is the time to trot out your trade-in and deal for the best price. It is your turn to be the car dealer here, so talk up your old car. Say that you've had better offers (even if you haven't) if you feel your car is being undervalued. And it will be undervalued at first. That's car trading. Tell the dealer that you know that the "blue book" value is above what was offered and that you know what other dealers are selling your model for. Eventually you will reach a price that is less than you'd like to get but more than the original offer. If the new price seems in line, take it.   /10

Before you drive the deal home, tell the dealer that you want to take his car to a mechanic to have it checked. Dealers will usually let you do this, although some may have reservations about letting the car off the lot overnight.   /11

Do have the car checked by a mechanic. It shouldn't cost more than $20 to $30, and a mechanic has the ability to *hear* things you'd miss, a sixth sense to diagnose them, and the hoists and equipment to check the car fully. Unless the mechanic is a personal buddy, don't tell where you got the car.   /12

If a dealer refuses to let you take the car to a mechanic for a checkup or refuses to consider any kind of guarantee, RUN! If he has no faith in your chances of happiness with that car, he probably knows what he is *not* talking about.   /13

This is not meant to replace having a professional mechanic check a car you are ready to buy. But it is the best way to determine whether the car is worth considering, and it may be your only chance if you are buying from a private party who has a lot of other interested people waiting to view the car. Besides, as I've already pointed out, it will impress the dealers no end, and possibly prevent them from trying to sell you a car that is not in good shape.   /14

When Herb and I went looking for Sylvester, I had the most marvelous time checking out the prospects. Most used-car dealers we encountered tended to be "old-boy" types, who were convinced that the only thing the "little lady" would be interested in was the color of the car. When I asked one of them to open the hood, he said, "Will you know what you're looking at if I do?" That fellow's eyes popped as I wrenched open the master cylinder and poked around. "What is she doing?" he asked my husband in astonishment. "Oh, she's a mechanic," Herb replied. "I'm just along for the ride." The salesman wiped his brow. "Now I've seen everything," he murmured. After I got through telling him what was wrong with the car and what it would probably cost to fix it we left.   /15

Review Questions

1. Does Sclar's process analysis seem complete?
2. Are there social judgments made in this essay, which is ostensibly a forthright "how-to-do-it" essay? Explain.
3. Is there a feminist point of view embedded in this essay? Explain.
4. Does Sclar have a point to make? Explain.
5. How does Sclar's use of process analysis contribute to her purpose?
6. How does Sclar's humorous style affect the reader's perception of the essay? Explain.

My Search for Roots: A Black American's Story

Alex Haley

Alex Haley (1921-   ) is a journalist and writer who was born in Ithaca, New York. His writings have appeared in *The New York Times Magazine, Harper's, Atlantic,* and the *Reader's Digest.* His most famous book, *Roots: The Saga of an American Family* (1976) won a National Book Award in 1977 and a citation from the Pulitzer Prize Committee. He is also the author, with Malcolm X, of *The Autobiography of Malcolm X* (1965).

In this article, which appeared at the same time as *Roots,* Haley explains the process of writing his book.

My earliest memory is of Grandma, Cousin Georgia, Aunt Plus, Aunt Liz and Aunt Till talking on our front porch in Henning, Tenn. At dusk, these wrinkled, graying old ladies would sit in rocking chairs and talk, about slaves and massas and plantations — pieces and patches of family history, passed down across the generations by word of mouth. "Old-timey stuff," Mamma would exclaim. She wanted no part of it.   /1

The furthest-back person Grandma and the others ever mentioned was "the African." They would tell how he was brought here on a ship to a place called "Naplis" and sold as a slave in Virginia. There he mated with another slave, and had a little girl named Kizzy.   /2

When Kizzy became four or five, the old ladies said, her father would point out to her various objects and name them in his native tongue. For example, he would point to a guitar and make a single-syllable sound, *ko.* Pointing to a river that ran near the plantation, he'd say "Kamby Bolongo." And when other slaves addressed him as Toby — the name given him by his massa — the African would strenuously reject it, insisting that his name was "Kin-tay."   /3

Kin-tay often told Kizzy stories about himself. He said that he had been near his village in Africa, chopping wood to make a drum, when he had been set upon by four men, overwhelmed, and kidnapped into slavery. When Kizzy grew up and became a mother, she told her son these stories, and he in turn would tell *his* children. His granddaughter became my grandmother, and she pumped that saga into me as if it were plasma, until I knew by rote the story of the African, and the subsequent generational wending of our family through cotton and tobacco plantations into the Civil War and then freedom.   /4

At 17, during World War II, I enlisted in the Coast Guard, and found myself a messboy on a ship in the Southwest Pacific. To fight boredom, I began to teach myself to become a writer. I stayed on in the service after the war, writing every single night, seven nights a week, for eight years before I sold a story to a magazine. My first story in the Digest was published in June 1954: "The Harlem Nobody Knows." At age 37, I retired from military service, determined to be a full-time writer. Working with the famous Black Muslim spokesman, I did the actual writing for the book *The Autobiography of Malcolm X.*   /5

I remembered still the vivid highlights of my family's story. Could this account possibly be documented for a book? During 1962, between other assignments, I began following the story's trail. In plantation records, wills, census records, I documented bits here, shreds there. By now, Grandma was dead; repeatedly I visited other sources, most notably our encyclopedic matriarch, "Cousin Georgia" Anderson in Kansas City, Kan. I went as often as I could to the National Archives in Washington, and the Library of Congress, and the Daughters of the American Revolution Library.   /6

By 1967, I felt I had the seven generations of the U.S. side documented. But the unknown quotient in the riddle of the past continued to be those strange, sharp, angular sounds spoken by the African himself. Since I lived in New York City, I began going to the United Nations lobby, stopping Africans and asking if they recognized the sounds. Every one of them listened to me, then quickly took off. I can well understand: me with a Tennessee accent, trying to imitate African sounds!   /7

Finally, I sought out a linguistics expert who specialized in African languages. To him I repeated the phrases. The sound "Kin-tay," he said, was a Mandinka tribe surname. And "Kamby Bolongo" was probably the Gambia River in Mandinka dialect. Three days later, I was in Africa.   /8

In Banjul, the Capital of Gambia, I met with a group of Gambians. They told me how for centuries the history of Africa has been preserved. In the older villages of the back country there are old men, called *griots*, who are in effect living archives. Such men know and, on special occasions, tell the cumulative histories of clans, or families, or villages, as those histories have long been told. Since my forefather had said his name was Kin-tay (properly spelled Kinte), and since the Kinte clan was known in Gambia, they would see what they could do to help me.   /9

I was back in New York when a registered letter came from Gambia. Word had been passed in the back country, and a *griot* of the Kinte clan had, indeed, been found. His name, the letter said, was Kebba Kanga Fofana. I returned to Gambia and organized a safari to locate him.   /10

There is an expression called "the peak experience," a moment which, emotionally, can never again be equaled in your life. I had mine, that first day in the village of Juffure, in the back country in black West Africa.   /11

When our 14-man safari arrived within sight of the village, the people came flocking out of their circular mud huts. From a distance I could see a small, old man with a pillbox hat, an off-white robe and an aura of "somebodiness" about him. The people quickly gathered around me in a kind of horseshoe pattern. The old man looked piercingly into my eyes, and he spoke in Mandinka. Translation came from the interpreters I had brought with me.   /12

"Yes, we have been told by the forefathers that there are many of us from this place who are in exile in that place called America."   /13

Then the old man, who was 73 rains of age — the Gambian way of saying 73 years old, based upon the one rainy season per year — began to tell me the lengthy ancestral history of the Kinte clan. It was clearly a formal occasion for the villagers. They had grown mouse-quiet, and stood rigidly.   /**14**

Out of the *griot's* head came spilling lineage details incredible to hear. He recited who married whom, two or even three centuries back. I was struck not only by the profusion of details, but also by the Biblical pattern of the way he was speaking. It was something like, "— and so-and-so took as a wife so-and-so, and begat so-and-so. . . ."   /**15**

The *griot* had talked for some hours, and had got to about 1750 in our calendar. Now he said, through an interpreter, "About the time the king's soldiers came, the eldest of Omoro's four sons, Kunta, went away from this village to chop wood — and he was never seen again. . . ."   /**16**

Goose pimples came out on me the size of marbles. He just had no way in the world of knowing that what he told me meshed with what I'd heard from the old ladies on the front porch in Henning, Tenn. I got out my notebook, which had in it what Grandma had said about the African. One of the interpreters showed it to the others, and they went to the *griot*, and they all got agitated. Then the *griot* went to the people, and *they* all got agitated.   /**17**

I don't remember anyone giving an order, but those 70-odd people formed a ring around me, moving counterclockwise, chanting, their bodies close together. I can't begin to describe how I felt. A woman broke from the circle, a scowl on her jet-black face, and came charging toward me. She took her baby and almost roughly thrust it out at me. The gesture meant "Take it!" and I did, clasping the baby to me. Whereupon the woman all but snatched the baby away. Another woman did the same with her baby, then another, and another.   /**18**

A year later, a famous professor at Harvard would tell me: "You were participating in one of the oldest ceremonies of humankind, called 'the laying on of hands.' In their way, these tribespeople were saying to you, 'Through this flesh, which is us, we are you and you are us.'"   /**19**

Later, as we drove out over the back-country road, I heard the staccato sound of drums. When we approached the next village, people were packed alongside the dusty road, waving, and the din from them welled louder as we came closer. As I stood up in the Land Rover, I finally realized what it was they were all shouting: "Meester Kinte! Meester Kinte!" In their eyes I was the symbol of all black people in the United States whose forefathers had been torn out of Africa while theirs remained.   /**20**

Hands before my face, I began crying — crying as I have never cried in my life. Right at that time, crying was all I could do.   /**21**

I went then to London. I searched and searched, and finally in the British Parliamentary records I found that the "king's soldiers" mentioned by the *griot* referred to a group called "Colonel O'Hare's forces," which had been sent up the Gambia River in 1767 to guard the then British-operated James Fort, a slave fort.   /**22**

I next went to Lloyds of London, where doors were opened for me to research among all kinds of old maritime records. I pored through the records of slave ships that had sailed from Africa. Volumes upon volumes of these records exist. One afternoon about 2:30, during the seventh week of searching, I was going through my 1023rd set of ship records. I picked up a sheet that had on it the reported movements of 30 slave ships, my eyes stopped at No. 18, and my glance swept across the column entries. This vessel had sailed directly from the Gambia River to America in 1767; her name was the *Lord Ligonier;* and she had arrived in Annapolis (Naplis) the morning of September 29, 1767.   /23

Exactly 200 years later, on September 29, 1967, there was nowhere in the world for me to be except standing on a pier at Annapolis, staring sea-ward across those waters over which my great-great-great-great-grandfather had been brought. And there in Annapolis I inspected the microfilmed records of the *Maryland Gazette.* In the issue of October 1, 1767, on page 3, I found an advertisement informing readers that the *Lord Ligonier* had just arrived from the River Gambia, with "a cargo of choice, healthy SLAVES" to be sold at auction the following Wednesday.   /24

In the years since, I have done extensive research in 50 or so libraries, archives and repositories on three continents. I spent a year combing through countless documents to learn about the culture of Gambia's villages in the 18th and 19th centuries. Desiring to sail over the same waters navigated by the *Lord Ligonier,* I flew to Africa and boarded the freighter *African Star.* I forced myself to spend the ten nights of the crossing in the cold, dark cargo hold, stripped to my underwear, lying on my back on a rough, bare plank. But this was sheer luxury compared to the inhuman ordeal suffered by those millions who, chained and shackled, lay in terror and in their own filth in the stinking darkness through voyages averaging 60 to 70 days.   /25

Review Questions

1. What is Haley's general subject?
2. What is the specific process he is describing?
3. What are the steps of this process?
4. What is the tone of the essay?
5. How does Haley maintain reader interest?
6. Does Haley make a point? If so, what is it?
7. To which audience has he addressed this essay?

The Search for Life on Mars

Norman H. Horowitz

Norman H. Horowitz (1915-   ) is a biologist who was born in Pittsburgh and educated at the University of Pittsburgh and Cal Tech. His scientific interests include the biochemical nature of inheritance, enzymes, evolutionary bio-chemistry, and the search for extra-terrestrial life. The following selection is part of an article that appeared in *Scientific American* concerning the Viking mission to Mars.

Is there life on Mars? The question is an interesting and legitimate scientific one, quite unrelated to the fact that generations of science-fiction writers have populated Mars with creatures of their imagination. Of all the extraterrestrial bodies in the solar system Mars is the one most like the earth, and it is by far the most plausible habitat for extraterrestrial life in the solar system. For that reason a major objective of the Viking mission to Mars was to search for evidences of life. /1

The two Viking spacecraft were launched from Cape Canaveral in the summer of 1975. Each spacecraft consisted of an orbiter and an attached lander. When the spacecraft arrived at Mars in July and August of 1976, each was put in a predetermined orbit around the planet, and the search for a landing place began. Cameras aboard the orbiters were the principal source of information on which the choice of the landing sites was based; important data also came from infrared sensors on the orbiters and from radar observatories on the earth. The sole consideration in the final selection of the sites was the safety of the spacecraft. It would be a mistake to suppose, however, that the sites were therefore without biological interest. Biological criteria dominated the initial decisions as to the latitude at which each spacecraft would land. Once the latitudes had been chosen there was relatively little difference between sites at different longitudes. /2

On command from the earth each lander separated from its orbiter. With the help of its retroengines and parachute it dropped to the surface of Mars. Both orbiters continued to circle the planet, operating their own scientific instruments and relaying to the earth data transmitted from the landers. Both landings were in the northern hemisphere of Mars, and the Martian season was summer. (Mars has seasons like those on the earth, but each season lasts approximately twice as long. The Martian year is 687 Martian days; each Martian day, named a sol by the Viking team to distinguish it from a terrestrial day, is 24 hours 39 minutes long.) On July 20, 1976, the *Viking 1* lander came to rest in the Chryse Planitia region of Mars, some 23 degrees north of the equator. Six weeks later the *Viking 2* lander settled down in the Utopia Planitia region, some 48 degrees north of the equator. In longitude the two landers are separated by almost exactly 180 degrees, thus placing them on opposite sides of the planet. Since the instrumentation of the two landers is identical, the difference in their landing sites is the only distinction between them. /3

The first biologically significant task carried out by each lander was the analysis of the Martian atmosphere. Life is based on the chemistry of light elements, notably carbon, hydrogen, oxygen and nitrogen. To be suitable as an abode of life a planet must have those elements in its atmosphere. Spectroscopic observations from the earth and from spacecraft that had flown past Mars in previous years had already shown that carbon dioxide was the principal component of the Martian atmosphere. Small quantities of carbon monoxide, oxygen and water vapor had also been detected. Nitrogen had not been detected in any form, however, and atmospheric theory suggested that Mars had lost most of its nitrogen in the past.   /4

Each Viking lander analyzed the atmosphere by means of two mass spectrometers. One spectrometer, operating during the descent to the surface, sampled and analyzed the atmospheric gases every five seconds. The second spectrometer operated on the ground. The results showed that the atmosphere near the ground was approximately 95 percent carbon dioxide, 2.5 percent nitrogen and 1.5 percent argon, and that it also held traces of oxygen, carbon monoxide, neon, krypton and xenon. At both landing sites the atmospheric pressure was 7.5 millibars. (The atmospheric pressure at sea level on the earth is 1,013 millibars.)   /5

Since the Viking spacecraft revealed that nitrogen is indeed present in the Martian atmosphere, we can say that the elements necessary for life are available on Mars. Missing from the list of gases, however, is one critically important compound: water vapor. Although earlier measurements had shown that traces of water vapor are present in the Martian atmosphere, the quantity varies with season and place. The Viking orbiters carried out a survey of water vapor over the entire planet with infrared spectrometers. The results showed that the highest concentration of atmospheric water vapor was at the edge of the north polar cap (the summertime hemisphere), and that the concentration fell off toward the south (the opposite of what is found on the earth). In the polar region the amount of water vapor in the atmosphere would form a film only a tenth of a millimeter thick if all of it were to be condensed on the planet's surface. At the landing sites the concentration of water vapor ranged between 10 and 30 percent of the concentration at the pole.   /6

These numbers put into quantitative terms a long-known fact about Mars: It is a very dry place. Mars has ice at its poles, but nowhere on its surface are there oceans or lakes or any other bodies of liquid water. The absence of liquid water is related to the dryness of the atmosphere through a fundamental law of physical chemistry: the phase rule. The phase rule states that for liquid water to exist on the surface of a planet the pressure of the water vapor in the atmosphere must at some times and in some places be at least 6.1 millibars. The Viking measurements imply that the vapor pressure of water at the surface of Mars in the northern hemisphere is at most .05 millibar, even if all the water vapor is concentrated in the lower atmosphere. At that low pressure liquid water cannot remain in the liquid phase; depending on the temperature, it must either freeze or evaporate. By the same token raindrops cannot form in the Martian atmosphere and ice cannot melt on the Martian surface.   /7

The extreme dryness presents a difficult problem for any Martian biology. Liquid water is essential for life on the earth. All terrestrial species have high and apparently irreducible requirements for water; none could live on Mars. If there is life on Mars, it must operate on a different principle as far as water is concerned. If Mars had a more favorable environment in the past, however, and if the planet did not dry up too fast, species may have had time to evolve and adapt to present conditions. Pictures made by the *Mariner 9* spacecraft, which went into orbit around Mars in 1971, suggested that Mars may indeed have had running water on its surface in the past. The pictures from the Viking orbiters have confirmed that impression. The evidence consists of channels in the Martian desert that resemble dry riverbeds. There seems to be little doubt that the channels were carved by rapidly flowing liquid, and there is widespread argreement that the most probable liquid is water.   /8

If liquid water once existed on Mars, could life have arisen on the planet? If the life evolved to meet changing conditions, could it exist there still? There is no way to settle these questions by deductive reasoning or even by experimentation in laboratories on the earth. They can be answered only by the direct exploration of Mars, and that is what the Viking spacecraft did.   /9

Five different types of instrument on each Viking lander were involved in the search for evidences of life: two cameras for photographing the landscape, a combined gas chromatograph and mass spectrometer for analyzing the surface for organic material and three instruments designed to detect the metabolic activities of any microorganisms that might be present in the soil. In this brief account I shall not be able to mention the names of the many scientists, engineers and managers whose joint efforts made all the Viking projects possible. They work in universities, industrial laboratories and the National Aeronautics and Space Administration and its field centers. Their names are recorded in the growing technical literature dealing with this historic mission.   /**10**

Each of the Viking landers carried two cameras of the facsimile type, which built up a picture of the scene by scanning it in a series of narrow strips. Such cameras make pictures slowly, but they are rugged and versatile. Their resolution was moderately high: a few millimeters at a distance of 1.5 meters. They produced pictures in black and white, in color and in stereo. The two cameras on each lander could between them survey the entire horizon around the spacecraft.   /**11**

As life-seeking tools cameras have inherent advantages and disadvantages. Their chief advantage lies in the fact that a picture contains a large amount of information. In principle it would be possible to prove unequivocally the existence of life on Mars with a single photograph. For example, if a line of trees were visible on the horizon or if footprints appeared on the ground in front of the spacecraft one morning, there would be no room for doubt that there is life on Mars. Another advantage lies in the fact that pictorial evidence is independent of all assumptions about the chemistry and physiology of Martian organisms. The organisms need not respond in certain ways to certain substances or treatments in order to be recognized. The cameras could identify, say, a mushroom made of titanium as a form of life if one were to sprout up from under a rock in the course of the mission. Of course, reliance on pictorial evidence rests on its own set of assumptions about the morphology of living things. The most obvious disadvantage of the camera as a life-seeking instrument is the fact that an entire world of life can exist below the camera's limit of resolution.   /**12**

Of all the results of the Viking mission the wonderful photographs of the

Martian desert at the two landing sites are the most impressive. The photographs have been eagerly scanned by alert and hopeful eyes, but no investigator has yet seen anything suggesting a living form.   /13

The next step was to analyze the soil for any organic constituents. Among the elements carbon is unique in the number, variety and complexity of the compounds it can form. The special properties of carbon that enable it to form large and complex molecules arise from the basic structure of the carbon atom. That structure enables the carbon atom to form four strong bonds with other atoms, including other carbon atoms. The molecules thus formed are very stable at ordinary temperatures, so stable, in fact, that there seems to be no limit to the size they can attain. The connection between life and organic chemistry (that is, the chemistry of carbon) rests on the fact that the attributes by which we identify living things — their capacity to replicate themselves, to repair themselves, to evolve and to adapt — originate in properties that are unique to large organic molecules. It is the highly complex information-rich proteins and nucleic acids that endow all the living things we know, even "simple" ones such as bacteria and viruses, with their essential nature. No other element, including that favorite of science-fiction writers, silicon, has the capacity carbon has to form large and complex structures that are so stable. It is no accident that even though silicon is far more abundant than carbon on the earth, it has only minor and nonessential roles in biochemistry. Biochemistry is largely a chemistry of carbon.   /14

Such fundamental facts lead to the conclusion that wherever life arises in the universe it will most likely be based on carbon chemistry. That view has been strengthened by the discovery of organic compounds of biological interest in meteorites and in clouds of dust in interstellar space. Although these compounds are nonbiological in origin, they are closely related to the amino acids and the nucleotides that are the respective building blocks of proteins and of nucleic acids. The fact that they are formed in settings remote from the earth implies that carbon chemistry gives rise to familiar organic compounds throughout the universe. This fact in turn suggests that life elsewhere in the universe will be based on an organic chemistry similar to our own, although not necessarily identical with it.   /15

Such considerations led to the decision to include an organic-analysis experiment aboard the Viking landers. The instrument used in the experiment was the mass spectrometer that had analyzed the atmosphere combined with a gas chromatograph and a pyrolysis furnace. A sample of the Martian soil was first heated in the furnace through a series of steps up to a temperature of 500 degrees Celsius. Any volatile materials released were passed through the gas chromatograph. Since each of the different compounds has a different molecular weight, composition and polarity, among other properties, it passed through the columns of the gas chromatograph at a unique rate, and so the compounds were separated from one another. As each compound emerged from the chromatographic column it was directed into the mass spectrometer for identification. Since essentially all organic matter is cracked, or decomposed, into smaller fragments at 500 degrees C., the method is capable of detecting organic compounds that have a wide range of molecular weights.   /16

Two soil samples were analyzed at each landing site. The only organic compounds detected were traces of cleaning solvents known to have been present in the apparatus. The fact that the solvents were detected shows the instruments were functioning properly. The heated samples gave off carbon dioxide and a small amount of water vapor; nothing else was found.   /**17**

This result is surprising and weighs heavily against the existence of biological processes on Mars. The combined gas chromatograph and mass spectrometer aboard each Viking lander is a sensitive instrument, capable of detecting organic compounds at a concentration of a few parts per billion, a level that is between 100 and 1,000 times below their concentration in desert soils on the earth. Even if there is no life on Mars, it has been supposed the fall of meteorites onto the Martian surface would have brought enough organic matter to the planet to have been detected. Because Mars is near the asteroid belt, from which meteorites originate, it is believed to receive a much larger number of meteorite impacts than either the earth or the moon. Indeed, a question that was frequently discussed before the Viking spacecraft were launched was whether or not it would be possible to distinguish biological organic matter on Mars from the meteoritic organic matter that was expected to be present. The absence of organic matter at the parts-per-billion level, however, suggests that on Mars organic compounds are actively destroyed, probably by the strong ultraviolet radiation from the sun.   /**18**

The other experiments aboard the Viking landers searched not just for organic matter in the soil but for living organisms. On the earth microorganisms such as bacteria, yeasts and molds are the hardiest of all species. There are few places on the earth where microbial forms do not live; they are the last survivors in environments of extreme temperature and aridity. The reasons for their hardiness are interesting but need not detain us here. Suffice it to say that if there is life on Mars, the chance of detecting it would be maximized by searching for microorganisms in the Martian soil.   /**19**

Review Questions

1. What is the primary question Horowitz is considering in this essay?
2. How does Horowitz's process analysis begin to provide an answer to the question he is considering?
3. Is Horowitz's explanation of the process he is describing sufficiently clear to be comprehensible to a nonscientific audience?
4. Does some of his terminology suggest that his audience might be a technically and scientifically sophisticated one?
5. What position does Horowitz ultimately take with regard to his initial question?

23

Cause and Effect Essays

Goodbye, San Francisco

Martin Koughan

Martin Koughan is a free-lance writer who has published articles in the *Washington Post* and the *Boston Globe*. He lives in the San Francisco Bay area and many of his articles concern that location. "Goodbye, San Francisco" is taken from a longer essay describing the probable causes and effects of a major earthquake in the Bay Area.

It is a beautiful spring day in San Francisco, a welcome relief from the incessant winter rains. Crowds stroll aimlessly around Union Square, inspecting the craftwork of sidewalk peddlers. Department stores are jammed with shoppers in search of seasonal bargains. Restaurant workers gird themselves for the dinnertime crush. In the subway, BART commuters stand shoulder to shoulder, cursing the laggard Fremont trains. The freeways are hopelessly clogged with weekenders eager to get away as early as possible on this lovely Friday afternoon. The time is 4:32 P.M.   /1

It comes with no warning. An earsplitting crack, inconceivably loud and terrific, brings all activity to an abrupt halt. In a fraction of a second, more than a million people realize that the moment has come at last. The Bay Area sits atop a system of active earthquake faults 300 miles long. There is nothing to do but pray. The rumbling and heavy grinding noises multiply with ominous intensity. Soon the ground rolls like a choppy sea; high-rise buildings sway like reed grass in a strong wind.   /2

On the Embarcadero Freeway, cars roll off the elevated structure as it slithers and jerks; sections of the upper level have already fallen. At the marina, the ground settles dramatically, allowing the bay's frigid waters to rush down residential streets. The Golden Gate Bridge shakes furiously; the southern approaches have collapsed. Explosions wrack the Bank of America building, the Wells Fargo tower. Office windows shatter, disgorging desks and files and human bodies.   /3

Across the bay in Richmond, oil-storage tanks rupture, gushing thousands of barrels of raw crude into the bay. San Quentin's walls are reduced to rubble; guards and prisoners huddle together as ceilings crumble around them. South of the city, the hills around the Crystal Springs Reservoirs tumble into the water, which then overflows the nineteenth-century dam. In less than a minute, the dam disintegrates, shooting a thirty-foot wall of water down the creek beds toward the city of San Mateo and the elegant mansions of Hillsborough. At the International Airport, the control tower has fallen, the runways are twisted, and a 747 jumbo jet overturns, bursting into flames.   /4

What seems like an eternity has actually been ninety seconds. At first there is only silence, thick black smoke, and the sickening smell of gas. Survivors stand transfixed. Some laugh uncontrollably; some cry. Screams from the injured begin to emerge from the rubble.   /5

In the central city, power ceases, raw sewage pollutes drinking water, natural gas seeps everywhere, all telephones are dead. Most radio transmissions towers remain standing, but the equipment at every radio station is badly damaged. There is no one to instruct the panicked populace.   /6

Spectacular blazes roar unimpeded through scores of shattered highrises. More than a quarter of the firefighting units have been lost; the only source of water is emergency cisterns. Some fires must be allowed to burn, some injured must be denied medical attention. These are excruciating decisions that no one wants to make. Relief stations spring up haphazardly; there is not enough of anything.   /7

Response from Sacramento is immediate, but all rescue efforts are stymied. One earthquake epicenter, just south of San Francisco in Daly City, measured 8.3 on the Richter scale. Another, on the Hayward fault in the East Bay, was recorded at 8.1. This is an enormous complication: the radius of the affected area is more than 300 miles. Communities that were relied upon for disaster assistance have suffered more damage than they can handle. No hospital within 100 miles of San Francisco has survived the quake unaffected; field hospitals will have to be flown in from all over the state, but all Bay Area airports are out of service, and there is no place to land the C-130s laden with men and supplies.   /8

San Francisco is now an island. Everything south of Candlestick Park on Route 101 is under water. All bay bridges are impassable. Interstate 280 and the Coastal Highway are blocked by landslides and earth movements that exceed fifteen feet in some places. The only way to reach the city is by boat or helicopter;

the Coast Guard has already dispatched every craft at its disposal, but their contribution is pitifully inadequate. It will take more than ten hours for major relief forces to reach the stricken city.   /9

The earthquake victims remain in the streets, afraid to return to the battered buildings. Transistor radios provide the only contact with the outside world. News reports blunt some hysterical rumors, but the news is bad. San Mateo is inundated, Berkeley and Oakland devastated. Warnings against looting are disregarded; people fight for scarce medical supplies, blankets, and food. Hours pass but no relief arrives; the situation is increasingly hopeless.   /10

Darkness comes earlier than usual this night: thick black smoke shrouds the city. The wind picks up, fueling the fires that rage unabated. It begins to rain, but no one heads for shelter. The streets appear safer. In the pouring rain people huddle together, soaked and shivering, many of them dying from exposure, unable to receive the most basic attention for their wounds.   /11

At 8:15 P.M., the first destructive aftershock hits, leveling buildings that survived the initial tremor. More aftershocks will continue for two days. Evacuation is slow and arduous; no attempt is made to dig for survivors in the rubble — there is neither time nor manpower.   /12

The plight of San Francisco receives worldwide attention; promises of support and expressions of sympathy pour in from all over the globe. Rescue and cleanup operations will consume the better part of two months. The Great San Francisco Earthquake leaves in its wake an estimated $25 billion worth of damage, 500,000 injured persons, and more than 100,000 dead.   /13

Unfortunately, the preceding fiction is all too close to probable fact. There is no question that an earthquake of this magnitude awaits its day in San Francisco's future. Widespread attempts to suppress these fears do nothing to postpone the inevitable, or make it any less terrible. With every passing day, San Francisco moves one step closer to a cataclysmic confrontation with the forces of nature.   /14

About 200 million years ago, the continents were connected in a single, colossal land mass. At some time and for some as yet unknown reason, this mass fragmented, setting the individual pieces in motion. But the theory of continental drift is not the whole story. According to the theory of plate tectonics, the continents are only the visible portions of much larger slabs; the earth's crust is actually divided into ten major plates, or blocks, that move in relation to one another. North America, for example, represents less than half of the North American plate, which extends from California to the Mid-Atlantic Range. Global systems of faults, chains of volcanoes and mountains, rifts in the ocean floor, and deep oceanic trenches are the constantly changing boundaries between these huge shifting plates. The glacial motion of these vast pieces of the planet creates inevitable collisions of unimaginable magnitude and power.   /15

About 30 million years ago, the North American plate encountered the North Pacific plate, which extends to Japan. This collision was so violent that it was responsible, over thousands of intervening centuries, for California's dramatic topography — the rugged coastal mountain ranges, the broad valleys, and even the majestic Sierra Nevada. One-third of California, including the entire coast up to San Francisco, remains geologically part of the ocean floor, with the San Andreas Fault system marking the division between it and the continent. The North Pacific plate is now creeping in fits and starts north and west of the North American plate at the rate of a half-inch per year, slowed only in those areas where the two plates become locked. It is in these areas of blockage that strain builds up to a point where it eventually overwhelms the obstacle. The result is an earthquake whose severity depends on the latent energy in the strain and the length of the area that breaks all at once. There has been virtually no seismic activity in San Francisco for sixty years; how much longer it can withstand these irrepressible tectonic forces is conjectural.   /**16**

Given the seriousness of the danger, the wonder is that so little has been done to prepare for it. The reason can be summed up in a single word: economics. California is the Golden West, the Great American Frontier where fortunes are made and life starts anew. Talk about earthquakes is bad for business. San Francisco was destroyed by earthquakes in 1906; 521 city blocks were devastated by a fire that raged uncontrolled for three days because the earth tremors had ruptured underground water mains. Yet the Eastern financial interests who rebuilt the Bay Area dubbed the disaster "The Great San Francisco Fire," completely ignoring the cause of the conflagration; and this fantastic self-deception endured for decades. Consequently, no realistic earthquake-bracing laws were instituted until 1947, and the bulk of the city and its services has been rebuilt as heedlessly as before. The city of San Francisco is as vulnerable today as it was at the turn of the century. And the 1906 earthquake, which all but removed the city from the map, had an epicenter more than fifty miles north of the city. The destructive potential of an equally intense tremor closer to the city is almost immeasurable.   /**17**

Review Questions

1. What does Koughan say are the probable causes of this hypothetical earthquake?
2. What are the effects?
3. Why does Koughan first discuss the effects, then the causes?
4. What is the point Koughan is trying to make in this essay? Does he do so effectively?

Confessions of a Female Chauvinist Sow

Anne Roiphe

Anne Roiphe (1935-   ) was born in New York City and educated at Sarah Lawrence College. Her articles have appeared in various publications, including the *New York Times Magazine.* Her books include *Diggin' Out* (1967), *Up the Sandbox* (1970), and *Long Division* (1972). Most of her writing is personal, with a strong feminist bent.

I once married a man I thought was totally unlike my father and I imagined a whole new world of freedom emerging. Five years later it was clear even to me — floating face down in a wash of despair — that I had simply chosen a replica of my handsome daddy-true. The updated version spoke English like an angel but — good God! — underneath he was my father exactly: wonderful, but not the right man for me.   /1

Most people I know have at one time or another been fouled up by their childhood experiences. Patterns tend to sink into the unconscious only to reappear, disguised, unseen, like marionette strings, pulling us this way or that. Whatever ails people — keeps them up at night, tossing and turning — also ails movements no matter how historically huge or politically important. The women's movement cannot remake consciousness, or reshape the future, without acknowledging and shedding all the unnecessary and ugly baggage of the past. It's easy enough now to see where men have kept us out of clubs, baseball games, graduate schools; it's easy enough to recognize the hidden directions that limit Sis to cake-baking and Junior to bridge-building; it's now possible for even Miss America herself to identify what *they* have done to us, and, of course, *they* have and *they* did and *they* are. . . . But along the way we also developed our own hidden prejudices, class assumptions and an anti-male humor and collection of expectations that gave us, like all oppressed groups, a secret sense of superiority (co-existing with a poor self-image — it's not news that people can believe two contradictory things at once).   /2

Listen to any group that suffers materially and socially. They have a lexicon with which they tease the enemy: ofay, goy, honky, gringo. "Poor pale devils," said Malcolm X loud enough for us to hear, although blacks had joked about that to each other for years. Behind some of the women's liberation thinking lurk the rumors, the prejudices, the defense systems of generations of oppressed women whispering in the kitchen together, presenting one face to their menfolk and another to their card clubs, their mothers and sisters. All this is natural enough but potentially dangerous in a revolutionary situation in which you hope to create a future that does not mirror the past. The hidden anti-male feelings, a result of the old system, will foul us up if they are allowed to persist.   /3

During my teen years I never left the house on my Saturday night dates without my mother slipping me a few extra dollars — mad money, it was called. I'll explain what it was for the benefit of the new generation in which people just sleep with each other: the fellow was supposed to bring me home, lead me safely through the asphalt jungle, protect me from slithering snakes, rapists and the like. But my mother and I knew young men were apt to drink too much, to slosh down so many rye-and-gingers that some hero might well lead me in front of an oncoming bus, smash his daddy's car into Tiffany's window or, less gallantly, throw up on my new dress. Mad money was for getting home on your own, no matter what form of insanity your date happened to evidence. Mad money was also a wallflower's rope ladder; if the guy you came with suddenly fancied someone else, well, you didn't have to stay there and suffer, you could go home. Boys were fickle and likely to be unkind; my mother and I knew that, as surely as we knew they tried to make you do things in the dark they wouldn't respect you for afterwards and in fact would spread the word and spoil your rep. Boys liked to be flattered; if you made them feel important they would eat out of your hand. So talk to them about their interests, don't alarm them with displays of intelligence — we all knew that, we groups of girls talking into the wee hours of the night in a kind of easy companionship we thought impossible with boys. Boys were prone to have a good time, get you pregnant, and then pretend they didn't know your name when you came knocking on their door for finances or comfort. In short, we believed boys were less moral than we were. They appeared to be hypocritical, self-seeking, exploitative, untrustworthy and very likely to be showing off their precious masculinity. I never had a girl friend I thought would be unkind or embarrass me in public. I never expected a girl to lie to me about her marks or sports skill or how good she was in bed. Altogether — without anyone's directly coming out and saying so — I gathered that men were sexy, powerful, very interesting, but not very nice, not very moral, humane and tender, like us. Girls played fairly while men, unfortunately, reserved their honor for the battlefield.   /4

Why are there laws insisting on alimony and child support? Well, everyone knows that men don't have an instinct to protect their young and, given half a chance, with the moon in the right phase, they will run off and disappear. Everyone assumes a mother will not let her child starve, yet it is necessary to legislate that a father must not do so. We are taught to accept the idea that men are less than decent; their charms may be manifold but their characters are riddled with faults. To this day I never blink if I hear that a man has gone to find his fortune in South America, having left his pregnant wife, his blind mother and taken the family car. I still gasp in horror when I hear of a woman leaving her asthmatic infant for a rock group in Taos because I can't seem to avoid the assumption that men are naturally heels and women the ordained carriers of what little is moral in our dubious civilization.   /5

My mother never gave me mad money thinking I would ditch a fellow for some other guy or that I would pass out drunk on the floor. She knew I would be considerate of my companion because, after all, I was more mature than the boys that gathered about. Why was I more mature? Women just are people-oriented; they learn to be empathetic at an early age. Most English students (students interested in humanity, not artifacts) are women. Men and boys — so the myth goes — conceal their feelings and lose interest in anybody else's. Everyone knows that even little boys can tell the difference between one kind of a car and another — proof that their souls are mechanical, their attention directed to the non-human.   /6

I remember shivering in the cold vestibule of a famous men's athletic club. Women and girls are not permitted inside the club's door. What are they doing in there, I asked? They're naked, said my mother, they're sweating, jumping up and down a lot, telling each other dirty jokes and bragging about their stock market exploits. Why can't we go in? I asked. Well, my mother told me, they're afraid we'd laugh at them.   /7

The prejudices of childhood are hard to outgrow. I confess that every time my business takes me past that club, I shudder. Images of large bellies resting on massage tables and flaccid penises rising and falling with the Dow Jones average flash through my head. There it is, chauvinism waving its cancerous tentacles from the depths of my psyche.   /8

Minorities automatically feel superior to the oppressor because, after all, they are not hurting anybody. In fact, they feel they are morally better. The old canard that women need love, men need sex — believed for too long by both sexes — attributes moral and spiritual superiority to women and makes of men beasts whose urges send them prowling into the night. This false division of good and bad, placing deforming pressures on everyone, doesn't have to contaminate the future. We know that the assumptions we make about each other become a part of the cultural air we breathe and, in fact, become social truths. Women who want equality must be prepared to give it and to believe in it, and in order to do that it is not enough to state that you are as good as any man, but also it must be stated that he is as good as you and both will be humans together. If we want men to share in the care of the family in a new way, we must assume them as capable of consistent loving tenderness as we.   /9

I rummage about and find in my thinking all kinds of anti-male prejudices. Some are just jokes and others I will have a hard time abandoning. First, I share an emotional conviction with many sisters that women given power would not create wars. Intellectually I know that's ridiculous; great queens have waged war before; the likes of Lurleen Wallace, Pat Nixon and Mrs. General Lavelle can be depended upon in the future to guiltlessly condemn to death other people's children in the name of some ideal of their own. Little girls, of course, don't take toy guns out of their hip pockets and say "Pow, pow" to all their neighbors and friends like the average well-adjusted little boy. However, if we gave little girls the six-shooters, we would soon have double the pretend body count.   /10

Aggression is not, as I secretly think, a male-sex-linked characteristic: brutality is masculine only by virtue of opportunity. True, there are 1,000 Jack the Rippers for every Lizzie Borden, but that surely is the result of social forms. Women as a group are indeed more masochistic than men. The practical result of this division is that women seem nicer and kinder, but when the world changes, women will have a fuller opportunity to be just as rotten as men and there will be fewer claims of female moral superiority.   /11

Now that I am entering early middle age, I hear many women complaining of husbands and ex-husbands who are attracted to younger females. This strikes the older woman as unfair, of course. But I remember a time when I thought all boys around my age and grade were creeps and bores. I wanted to go out with an older man: a senior or, miraculously, a college man. I had a certain contempt for my coevals, not realizing that the freshman in college I thought so desirable, was some older girl's creep. Some women never lose that contempt for men of their own age. That isn't fair either and may be one reason why some sensible men of middle years find solace in young women.   /**12**

I remember coming home from school one day to find my mother's card game dissolved in hysterical laughter. The cards were floating in black rivers of running mascara. What was so funny? A woman named Helen was lying on a couch pretending to be her husband with a cold. She was issuing demands for orange juice, aspirin, suggesting a call to a specialist, complaining of neglect, of fate's cruel finger, of heat, of cold, of sharp pains on the bridge of the nose that might indicate brain involvement. What was so funny? The ladies explained to me that all men behave just like that with colds, they are reduced to temper tantrums by simple nasal congestion, men cannot stand any little physical discomfort — on and on the laughter went.   /**13**

The point of this vignette is the nature of the laughter — us laughing at them, us feeling superior to them, us ridiculing them behind their backs. If they were doing it to us we'd call it male chauvinist pigness; if we do it to them, it is inescapably female chauvinist sowness and, whatever its roots, it leads to the same isolation. Boys are messy, boys are mean, boys are rough, boys are stupid and have sloppy handwriting. A cacophony of childhood memories rushes through my head, balanced, of course, by all the well-documented feelings of inferiority and envy. But the important thing, the hard thing, is to wipe the slate clean, to start again without the meanness of the past. That's why it's so important that the women's movement not become anti-male and allow its most prejudiced spokesmen total leadership. The much-chewed-over abortion issue illustrates this. The women's-liberation position, insisting on a woman's right to determine her own body's destiny, leads in fanatical extreme to a kind of emotional immaculate conception in which the father is not judged even half-responsible — he has no rights, and no consideration is to be given to his concern for either the woman or the fetus.   /**14**

Woman, who once was abandoned and disgraced by an unwanted pregnancy, has recently arrived at a new pride of ownership or disposal. She has traveled in a straight line that still excludes her sexual partner from an equal share in the wanted or unwanted pregnancy. A better style of life may develop from an assumption that men are as human as we. Why not ask the child's father if he would like to bring up the child? Why not share decisions, when possible, with the male? If we cut them out, assuming an old-style indifference on their part, we perpetuate the ugly divisiveness that has characterized relations between the sexes so far.   /**15**

Hard as it is for many of us to believe, women are not really superior to men in intelligence or humanity — they are only equal.   /**16**

Review Questions

1. What is the cause and effect relationship Roiphe is establishing here?
2. What is the point Roiphe is making in this essay?

3. Does the tone of the piece add to or detract from Roiphe's point?
4. What is the significance of Roiphe's title?
5. Are you sympathetic to Roiphe's position?

Who Cares for America's Children?

Urie Bronfenbrenner

Urie Bronfenbrenner (1906-   ) is a professor of psychology, child development, and family studies at Cornell University, College of Human Ecology. He is the editor of *Influences on Human Development* (1972), and the author of *Two Worlds of Childhood: U.S. and U.S.S.R.* His social writing is directed to the improvement of public policy.

I shall be short, but not very sweet. America's families and their children are in trouble. Trouble so deep and pervasive as to threaten the future of our nation. The source of the trouble is nothing less than a national neglect of children, and of those primarily engaged in their care: America's parents.   /1

We like to think of America as a child-centered society, but our actions belie our words. A hard look at our institutions and ways of life reveals that our national priorities lie elsewhere. The pursuit of affluence, the worship of material things, the hard sell and the soft, the willingness to accept technology as a substitute for human relationships, the imposition of responsibility upon families without support, and the readiness to blame the victims of evil for the evil itself have brought us to the point where a broken television set or a broken computer provokes more indignation and more action than a broken family or a broken child.   /2

America, the richest and most powerful country in the world, stands thirteenth among the nations in combating infant mortality; even East Germany does better. Moreover, our ranking has dropped steadily in recent decades. A similar situation obtains with respect to maternal and child health, day care, children's allowances, and other basic services to children and families.   /3

But the figures for the nation as a whole, dismaying as they are, mask even greater inequities. For example, infant mortality for nonwhites in the United States is almost twice that for whites, and there are a number of Southern states, and Northern metropolitan areas, in which the ratios are considerably higher.   /4

Ironically, of even greater cost to the society than infants who die are the many more who sustain injury but survive with disability. Many of these suffer impaired intellectual function and behavioral disturbance including hyperactivity, distractability, and low attention span, all factors contributing to school retardation and problem behavior. Again, the destructive impact is greatest on the poorest segments of the population, especially nonwhites. It is all the more tragic that this massive damage and its subsequent cost in reduced productivity, lower income, unemployability, welfare payments, and institutionalization are avoidable if adequate nutrition, prenatal care, and other family and child services are provided, as they are in a number of countries less prosperous than ours.   /5

But it is not only children from disadvantaged families who show signs of progressive neglect. For example, an analysis I carried out a few years ago of data on child-rearing practices in the United States over a twenty-five-year period reveals a decrease, especially in recent years, in all spheres of interaction between parents and children. A similar conclusion is indicated by results of cross-cultural studies comparing American parents with those from Western and Eastern Europe. As parents and other adults move out of the lives of children, the vacuum is filled by the age-segregated peer group.   /6

Recently my colleagues and I completed a study showing that, at every age and grade level, children today show a greater dependence on their peers than they did a decade ago. Our evidence indicates that susceptibility to group influence is higher among children from homes in which one or both parents are frequently absent. In addition, "peer-oriented" youngsters describe their parents as less affectionate and less firm in discipline. Attachment to age mates appears to be influenced more by a lack of attention and concern at home than by any positive attraction of the peer group itself. In fact, these children have a rather negative view of their friends, and of themselves as well. They are pessimistic about the future, rate lower in responsibility and leadership, and are more likely to engage in such behavior as lying, teasing other children, "playing hooky" or "doing something illegal."   /7

Our national rhetoric notwithstanding, the actual patterns of life in America are such that children and families come last. Our society expects its citizens first of all to meet the demands of their jobs, and then to fulfill civic and social obligations. Responsibilities to children are to be met, of course, but this is something one is expected to do in his spare time.   /8

But when, where and how? In today's world, parents find themselves at the mercy of a society which imposes pressures and priorities that allow neither time nor place for meaningful activities and relations between children and adults, which downgrade the role of parent and the functions of parenthood, and which prevent the parent from doing the things he wants to do as a guide, friend and companion to his children.   /9

The frustrations are greatest for the family of poverty, where the capacity for human response is crippled by hunger, cold, filth, sickness and despair. No parent who spends his days in search of menial work and his nights in keeping rats away from the crib can be expected to find the time, let alone the heart, to engage in constructive activities with his children or serve as a stable source of love and discipline. The fact that some families in poverty do manage to do this is a tribute to them, but not to the society or community in which they live.   /10

For families who can get along, the rats are gone but the rat race remains. The demands of a job, or often two jobs, which claim mealtimes, evenings and weekends as well as days; the trips and moves one must make to get ahead or simply hold one's own; the ever-increasing time spent in commuting; the parties, the evenings out, the social and community obligations — all of the things one has to do if he is to meet his primary responsibilities — produce a situation in which a child often spends more time with a passive babysitter than with a participating parent or adult.   /11

Even when the parent is at home, a compelling force cuts off communication and response among family members. Although television could, if used creatively, enrich the activities of children and families, it now only undermines them. Like the sorcerer of old, the television set casts its magic spell, freezing speech and action, turning the living into silent statues so long as the enchantment lasts. The primary danger of the television screen lies not so much in the behavior it produces — although there is danger there — as in the behavior it prevents: the talks, the games, the family festivities and arguments through which much of the child's learning takes place and through which his character is formed. Turning on the television set can turn off the process that transforms children into people.   /12

In our modern way of life it is not only parents of whom children are deprived, it is people in general. A host of factors conspire to isolate children from the rest of society: the fragmentation of the extended family, the separation of residential and business areas, the disappearance of neighborhoods, the elimination of small stores in favor of supermarkets, zoning ordinances, occupational mobility, child-labor laws, the abolishment of the apprentice system, consolidated schools, television, telephones, the substitution of the automobile for public transportation or just plain walking, separate patterns of social life for different age groups, the working mother, the delegation of child care to specialists; all these manifestations of progress operate to decrease opportunity and incentive for meaningful contact between children and persons older or younger than themselves.   /13

And here we confront a fundamental and disturbing fact: *Children need people in order to become human.* The fact is fundamental because it is firmly grounded both in scientific research and in human experience. It is disturbing because the isolation of children from adults threatens simultaneously the growth of the individual and the survival of the society. The young cannot pull themselves up by their own bootstraps. It is primarily through observing, playing and working with others older and younger than himself that a child discovers both what he can do and who he can become, that he develops both his ability and his identity. It is primarily through exposure and interaction with adults and children of different ages that a child acquires new interests and skills, and learns the meaning of tolerance, cooperation and compassion.   /14

Hence, to relegate children to a world of their own is to deprive them of their humanity and to deprive ourselves of humanity as well. Yet this is what is happening in America today. We are experiencing a breakdown in the process of making human beings human. By isolating our children from the rest of society, we abandon them to a world devoid of adults and ruled by the destructive impulses and compelling pressure, both of the age-segregated peer group and of the aggressive and exploitive television screen. By setting our priorities elsewhere and by putting children and families last, by claiming one set of values while pursuing another, we leave our children bereft of standards and support, and our own lives impoverished and corrupted.   /15

This reversal of priorities, which amounts to a betrayal of our children, underlies the growing disillusionment and alienation among young people in all segments of American society. Those who grew up in settings where children, families, neighborhoods and communities still counted are able to act out their frustration in positive ways through constructive protest, through participation and through public service. Those who come from circumstances in which the family, the neighborhood and the community could not function — be it in slum or suburb — can only strike out against an environment they have experienced as indifferent, callous, cruel, and unresponsive.   /16

The failure to reorder our priorities, the insistence on business as usual, and the continued reliance on rhetoric as a substitute for radical reforms can have only one result: the far more rapid and pervasive growth of alienation, apathy, drugs, delinquency and violence among the young and among the not so young in all segments of our national life. We face the prospect of a society which resents its own children and fears its youth.   /17

Review Questions

1. What is the cause and effect relationship Bronfenbrenner details?
2. What is the point he is trying to make?
3. How does Bronfenbrenner incorporate the results of his research into a suggestion for changing social patterns?
4. What is the meaning of the pun in the title of this essay?
5. Have you been convinced to accept Bronfenbrenner's point of view?

Politics and the English Language

George Orwell

George Orwell (1903-1950), a British essayist and novelist whose real name was Eric Blair, was born in India. For a time he was a member of the Indian Imperial Police in Burma, and he also spent some time in Paris, London, and Spain, where he fought on the Republican side in the Spanish Civil War. *Burmese Days* (1934) recounts some of his experiences in Burma, and *Down and Out in Paris and London* (1933) depicts the poverty he endured in these cities as a young writer.

In addition to his personal experiences, Orwell's themes include language, the sociopolitical conditions of his time, and most of all, human freedom. He is best known for his novels, *Animal Farm* (1946) and *Nineteen Eighty-Four* (1949). The essay reprinted below was collected in *Shooting an Elephant and Other Essays* (1950). It is a cause and effect essay detailing the relationship between language and politics.

Most people who bother with the matter at all would admit that the English language is in a bad way, but it is generally assumed that we cannot by conscious action do anything about it. Our civilization is decadent and our language — so the argument runs — must inevitably share in the general collapse. It follows that any struggle against the abuse of language is a sentimental archaism, like preferring candles to electric light or hansom cabs to aeroplanes. Underneath this lies the half-conscious belief that language is a natural growth and not an instrument which we shape for our own purposes.   /1

Now, it is clear that the decline of a language must ultimately have political and economic causes: it is not due simply to the bad influence of this or that individual writer. But an effect can become a cause, reinforcing the original cause and producing the same effect in an intensified form, and so on indefinitely. A man may take to drink because he feels himself to be a failure, and then fail all the more completely because he drinks. It is rather the same thing that is happening to the English language. It becomes ugly and inaccurate because our thoughts are foolish, but the slovenliness of our language makes it easier for us to have foolish thoughts. The point is that the process is reversible. Modern English, especially written English, is full of bad habits which spread by imitation and which can be avoided if one is willing to take the necessary trouble. If one gets rid of these habits one can think more clearly, and to think clearly is a necessary first step towards political regeneration: so that the fight against bad English is not frivolous and is not the exclusive concern of professional writers. I will come back to this presently, and I hope that by that time the meaning of what I have said here will have become clearer. Meanwhile, here are five specimens of the English language as it is now habitually written.   /2

These five passages have not been picked out because they are especially bad — I could have quoted far worse if I had chosen — but because they illustrate various of the mental vices from which we now suffer. They are a little below the average, but are fairly representative samples. I number them so that I can refer back to them when necessary:

(1) I am not, indeed, sure whether it is not true to say that the Milton who once seemed not unlike a seventeenth-century Shelley had not become, out of an experience ever more bitter in each year, more alien [*sic*] to the founder of that Jesuit sect which nothing could induce him to tolerate.

Professor Harold Laski
(Essay in *Freedom of Expression*)   /3

(2) Above all, we cannot play ducks and drakes with a native battery of idioms which prescribes such egregious collocations of vocables as the Basic *put up with* for *tolerate* or *put at a loss* for *bewilder.*

Professor Lancelot Hogben *(Interglossa)*   /4

(3) On the one side we have the free personality: by definition it is not neurotic, for it has neither conflict nor dream. Its desires, such as they are, are transparent, for they are just what institutional approval keeps in the forefront of consciousness; another institutional pattern would alter their number and intensity; there is little in them that is natural, irreducible, or culturally dangerous. But *on the other side,* the social bond itself is nothing but the mutual reflection of these self-secure integrities. Recall the definition of love. Is not this the very picture of a small academic? Where is there a place in this hall of mirrors for either personality or fraternity?

Essay on psychology in *Politics* (New York)   /5

(4) All the "best people" from the gentlemen's clubs, and all the frantic fascist captains, united in common hatred of Socialism and bestial horror of the rising tide of the mass revolutionary movement, have turned to acts of provocation, to foul incendiarism, to medieval legends of poisoned wells, to legalize their own destruction of proletarian organizations, and rouse the agitated petty-bourgeoisie to chauvinistic fervor on behalf of the fight against the revolutionary way out of the crisis.

Communist pamphlet   /6

(5) If a new spirit is to be infused into this old country, there is one thorny and contentious reform which must be tackled, and that is the humanization and galvanization of the B.B.C. Timidity here will bespeak canker and atrophy of the soul. The heart of Britain may be sound and of strong beat, for instance, but the British lion's roar at present is like that of Bottom in Shakespeare's *Midsummer Night's Dream* — as gentle as any sucking dove. A virile new Britain cannot continue indefinitely to be traduced in the eyes, or rather ears, of the world by the effete languors of Langham Place, brazenly masquerading as "standard English." When the Voice of Britain is heard at nine o'clock, better far and infinitely less ludicrous to hear aitches honestly dropped than the present priggish, inflated, inhibited school-ma'amish arch braying of blameless bashful mewing maidens!

Letter in *Tribune*   /7

Each of these passages has faults of its own, but, quite apart from avoidable ugliness, two qualities are common to all of them. The first is staleness of imagery; the other is lack of precision. The writer either has a meaning and cannot express it, or he inadvertently says something else, or he is almost indifferent as to whether his words mean anything or not. This mixture of vagueness and sheer incompetence is the most marked characteristic of modern English prose, and especially of any kind of political writing. As soon as certain topics are raised, the concrete melts into the abstract and no one seems able to think of turns of speech that are not hackneyed: prose consists less and less of *words* chosen for the sake of their meaning, and more and more of *phrases* tacked together like the sections of a prefabricated hen-house. I list below, with notes and examples, various of the tricks by means of which the work of prose-construction is habitually dodged:

Dying metaphors. A newly invented metaphor assists thought by evoking a visual image, while on the other hand a metaphor which is technically "dead" (e.g. *iron resolution*) has in effect reverted to being an ordinary word and can generally be used without loss of vividness. But in between these two classes there is a huge dump of worn-out metaphors which have lost all evocative power and are merely used because they save people the trouble of inventing phrases for themselves. Examples are: *Ring the changes on, take up the cudgels for, toe the line, ride roughshod over, stand shoulder to shoulder with, play into the hands of, no axe to grind, grist to the mill, fishing in troubled waters, on the order of the day, Achilles' heel, swan song, hotbed.* Many of these are used without knowledge of their meaning (what is a "rift," for instance?), and incompatible metaphors are frequently mixed, a sure sign that the writer is not interested in what he is saying. Some metaphors now current have been twisted out of their original meaning without those who use them even being aware of the fact. For example, *toe the line* is sometimes written *tow the line.* Another example is *the hammer and the anvil,* now always used with the implication that the anvil gets the worst of it. In real life it is always the anvil that breaks the hammer, never the other way about: a writer who stopped to think what he was saying would be aware of this, and would avoid perverting the original phrase.   /8

Operators or verbal false limbs. These save the trouble of picking out appropriate verbs and nouns, and at the same time pad each sentence with extra syllables which give it an appearance of symmetry. Characteristic phrases are *render inoperative, militate against, make contact with, be subjected to, give rise to, give grounds for, have the effect of, play a leading part (role) in, make itself felt, take effect, exhibit a tendency to, serve the purpose of, etc., etc.* The keynote is the elimination of simple verbs. Instead of being a single word, such as *break, stop, spoil, mend, kill,* a verb becomes a *phrase,* made up of a noun or adjective tacked on to some general-purposes verb such as *prove, serve, form, play, render.* In addition, the passive voice is wherever possible used in preference to the active, and noun constructions are used instead of gerunds *(by examination of* instead of *by examining).* The range of verbs is further cut down by means of the *-ize* and *de-* formations, and the banal statements are given an appearance of profundity by means of the *not un-* formation. Simple conjunctions and prepositions are replaced by such phrases as *with respect to, having regard to, the fact that, by dint of, in view of, in the interests of, on the hypothesis that;* and the ends of sentences are saved by anticlimax by such resounding common-places as *greatly to be desired, cannot be left out of account, a development to be expected in the near future, deserving of serious consideration, brought to a satisfactory conclusion,* and so on and so forth.   /9

Pretentious diction. Words like *phenomenon, element, individual* (as noun), *objective, categorical, effective, virtual, basic, primary, promote, constitute, exhibit, exploit, utilize, eliminate, liquidate,* are used to dress up simple statements and give an air of scientific impartiality to biased judgments. Adjectives like *epoch-making, epic, historic, unforgettable, triumphant, age-old, inevitable, inexorable, veritable,* are used to dignify the sordid processes of international politics, while writing that aims at glorifying war usually takes on an archaic color, its characteristic words being: *realm, throne, chariot, mailed fist, trident, sword, shield, buckler, banner, jackboot, clarion.* Foreign words and expressions such as *cul de sac, ancien régime, deus ex machina, mutatis mutandis, status quo, gleichschaltung, weltanschauung,* are used to give an air of culture and elegance. Except for the useful abbreviations *i.e., e.g.,* and *etc.,* there is no real need for any of the hundreds of foreign phrases now current in English. Bad writers, and especially scientific, political and sociological writers, are nearly always haunted by the notion that Latin or Greek words are grander than Saxon ones, and unnecessary words like *expedite, ameliorate, predict, extraneous, deracinated, clandestine, subaqueous* and hundreds of others constantly gain ground from their Anglo-Saxon opposite numbers.[1] The jargon peculiar to Marxist writing (*hyena, hangman, cannibal, petty bourgeois, these gentry, lacquey, flunkey, mad dog, White Guard,* etc.) consists largely of words and phrases translated from Russian, German or French; but the normal way of coining a new word is to use a Latin or Greek root with the appropriate affix and, where necessary, the size formation. It is often easier to make up words of this kind (*deregionalize, impermissible, extramarital, nonfragmentary* and so forth) than to think up the English words that will cover one's meaning. The result, in general, is an increase in slovenliness and vagueness.   /**10**

Meaningless words. In certain kinds of writing, particularly in art criticism and literary criticism, it is normal to come across long passages which are almost completely lacking in meaning.[2] Words like *romantic, plastic, values, human, dead, sentimental, natural vitality,* as used in art criticism, are strictly meaningless, in the sense that they not only do not point to any discoverable object, but are hardly ever expected to do so by the reader. When one critic writes, "The outstanding feature of Mr. X's work is its living quality," while another writes, "The immediately striking thing about Mr. X's work is its peculiar deadness," the reader accepts this as a simple difference of opinion. If words like *black* and *white* were involved, instead of the jargon words *dead* and *living,* he would see at once that language was being used in an improper way. Many political words are similarly abused. The word *Fascism* has now no meaning except in so far as it signifies "something not desirable." The words *democracy, socialism, freedom, patriotic, realistic, justice,* have each of them several different meanings which cannot be reconciled with one another. In the case of a word like *democracy,* not only is there no agreed definition, but the attempt to make one is resisted from all sides. It is almost universally felt that when we call a country democratic we are praising it: consequently the defenders of every kind of régime claim that it is a democracy, and fear that they might have to stop using the word if it were tied down to any one meaning. Words of this kind are often used in a consciously dishonest way. That is, the person who uses them has his own private definition, but allows his hearer to think he means something quite different. Statements like *Marshal Pétain was a true patriot, The Soviet Press is the freest in the world, The Catholic Church is opposed to persecution*, are almost always made with intent to deceive. Other words used in variable meanings, in most cases more or less dishonestly, are: *class, totalitarian, science, progressive, reactionary, bourgeois, equality.*   /11

Now that I have made this catalogue of swindles and perversions, let me give another example of the kind of writing that they lead to. This time it must of its nature be an imaginary one. I am going to translate a passage of good English into modern English of the worst sort. Here is a well-known verse from *Ecclesiastes:*

"I returned and saw under the sun, that the race is not to the swift, nor the battle to the strong, neither yet bread to the wise, nor yet riches to men of understanding, nor yet favour to men of skill; but time and chance happeneth to them all."   /12

Here it is in modern English:

"Objective consideration of contemporary phenomena compels the conclusion that success or failure in competitive activities exhibits no tendency to be commensurate with innate capacity, but that a considerable element of the unpredictable must invariably be taken into account."   /13

This is a parody, but not a very gross one. Exhibit (3), above, for instance, contains several patches of the same kind of English. It will be seen that I have not made a full translation. The beginning and ending of the sentence follow the original meaning fairly closely, but in the middle the concrete illustrations — race, battle, bread — dissolve into the vague phrase "success or failure in competitive activities." This had to be so, because no modern writer of the kind I am discussing — no one capable of using phrases like "objective consideration of contemporary phenomena" — would ever tabulate his thoughts in that precise and detailed way. The whole tendency of modern prose is away from concreteness. Now analyse these two sentences a little more closely. The first contains forty-nine words but only sixty syllables, and all its words are those of everyday life. The second contains thirty-eight words of ninety syllables: eighteen of its words are from Latin roots, and one from Greek. The first sentence contains six vivid images, and only one phrase ("time and chance") that could be called vague. The second contains not a single fresh, arresting phrase, and in spite of its ninety syllables it gives only a shortened version of the meaning contained in the first. Yet without a doubt it is the second kind of sentence that is gaining ground in modern English. I do not want to exaggerate. This kind of writing is not yet universal, and outcrops of simplicity will occur here and there in the worst-written page. Still, if you or I were told to write a few lines on the uncertainty of human fortunes, we should probably come much nearer to my imaginary sentence than to the one from *Ecclesiastes.*   /14

As I have tried to show, modern writing at its worst does not consist in picking out words for the sake of their meaning and inventing images in order to make the meaning clearer. It consists in gumming together long strips of words which have already been set in order by someone else, and making the results presentable by sheer humbug. The attraction of this way of writing is that it is easy. It is easier — even quicker, once you have the habit — to say *In my opinion it is not an unjustifiable assumption that* than to say *I think*. If you use ready-made phrases, you not only don't have to hunt about for words; you also don't have to bother with the rhythms of your sentences, since these phrases are generally so arranged as to be more or less euphonious. When you are composing in a hurry — when you are dictating to a stenographer, for instance, or making a public speech — it is natural to fall into a pretentious, Latinized style. Tags like *a consideration which we should do well to bear in mind* or *a conclusion to which all of us would readily assent* will save many a sentence from coming down with a bump. By using stale metaphors, similes, and idioms, you save much mental effort, at the cost of leaving your meaning vague, not only for your reader but for yourself. This is the significance of mixed metaphors. The sole aim of a metaphor is to call up a visual image. When these images clash — as in *The Fascist octopus has sung its swan song, the jackboot is thrown into the melting pot* — it can be taken as certain that the writer is not seeing a mental image of the objects he is naming; in other words he is not really thinking. Look again at the examples I gave at the beginning of this essay. Professor Laski (1) uses five negatives in fifty-three words. One of these is superfluous, making nonsense of the whole passage, and in addition there is the slip *alien* for akin, making further nonsense, and several avoidable pieces of clumsiness which increase the general vagueness. Professor Hogben (2) plays ducks and drakes with a battery which is able to write prescriptions, and, while disapproving of the everyday phrase *put up with,* is unwilling to look *egregious* up in the dictionary and see what it means; (3), if one takes an uncharitable attitude towards it, is simply meaningless: probably one could work out its intended meaning by reading the whole of the article in which it occurs. In (4), the writer knows more or less what he wants to say, but an accumulation of stale phrases chokes him like tea leaves blocking a sink. In (5), words and meaning have almost parted company. People who write in this manner usually have a general emotional meaning — they dislike one thing and want to express solidarity with another — but they are not interested in the detail of what they are saying. A scrupulous writer, in every sentence that he writes, will ask himself at least four questions, thus: What am I trying to say? What words will express it? What image or idiom will make it clearer? Is this image fresh enough to have an effect? And he will probably ask himself two more: Could I put it more shortly? Have I said anything that is avoidably ugly? But you are not obliged to go to all this trouble. You can shirk it by simply throwing your mind open and letting the ready-made phrases come crowding in. They will construct your sentences for you — even think your thoughts for you, to a certain extent — and at need they will perform the important service of partially concealing your meaning even from yourself. It is at this point that the special connection between politics and the debasement of language becomes clear.   /15

   In our time it is broadly true that political writing is bad writing. Where it is not true, it will generally be found that the writer is some kind of rebel, expressing his private opinions and not a "party line." Orthodoxy, of whatever color, seems to demand a lifeless, imitative style. The political dialects to be found in pamphlets, leading articles, manifestos, White Papers and the speeches of undersecretaries do, of course, vary from party to party, but they are all alike in that one almost never finds in them a fresh, vivid, homemade turn of speech. When one watches some tired hack on the platform mechanically repeating the familiar phrases — *bestial atrocities, iron heel, bloodstained tyranny, free peoples of the world, stand shoulder to shoulder* — one often has a curious feeling that one is not watching a live human being but some kind of dummy: a feeling which suddenly becomes stronger at moments when the light catches the speaker's spectacles and turns them into blank discs which seem to have no eyes behind them. And this is not altogether fanciful. A speaker who uses that kind of phraseology has gone some distance towards turning himself into a machine. The appropriate noises are coming out of his larynx, but his brain is not involved as it would be if he were choosing his words for himself. If the speech he is making is one that he is accustomed to make over and over again, he may be almost unconscious of what he is saying, as one is when one utters the responses in church. And this reduced state of consciousness, if not indispensable, is at any rate favorable to political conformity.   /16

In our time, political speech and writing are largely the defence of the indefensible. Things like the continuance of British rule in India, the Rusian purges and deportations, the dropping of the atom bombs on Japan, can indeed be defended, but only by arguments which are too brutal for most people to face, and which do not square with the professed aims of political parties. Thus political language has to consist largely of euphemism, question-begging and sheer cloudy vagueness. Defenceless villages are bombarded from the air, the inhabitants driven out into the countryside, the cattle machine-gunned, the huts set on fire with incendiary bullets: this is called *pacification*. Millions of peasants are robbed of their farms and sent trudging along the roads with no more than they can carry: this is called *transfer of population* or rectification of frontiers. People are imprisoned for years without trial, or shot in the back of the neck or sent to die of scurvy in Arctic lumber camps: this is called *elimination of unreliable elements*. Such phraseology is needed if one wants to name things without calling up mental pictures of them. Consider for instance some uncomfortable English professor defending Russian totalitarianism. He cannot say outright, "I believe in killing off your opponents when you can get good results by doing so." Probably, therefore, he will say something like this:

"While freely conceding that the Soviet régime exhibits certain features which the humanitarian may be inclined to deplore, we must, I think, agree that a certain curtailment of the right to political opposition is an unavoidable concomitant of transitional periods, and that the rigors which the Russian people have been called upon to undergo have been amply justified in the sphere of concrete achievement."   /17

The inflated style is itself a kind of euphemism. A mass of Latin words falls upon the facts like soft snow, blurring the outlines and covering up all the details.

The great enemy of clear language is insincerity. When there is a gap between one's real and one's declared aims, one turns as it were instinctively to long words and exhausted idioms, like a cuttlefish squirting out ink. In our age there is no such thing as "keeping out of politics." All issues are political issues, and politics itself is a mass of lies, evasions, folly, hatred and schizophrenia. When the general atmosphere is bad, language must suffer. I should expect to find — this is a guess which I have not sufficient knowledge to verify — that the German, Russian, and Italian languages have all deteriorated in the last ten or fifteen years, as a result of dictatorship.   /**18**

But if thought corrupts language, language can also corrupt thought. A bad usage can spread by tradition and imitation, even among people who should and do know better. The debased language that I have been discussing is in some ways very convenient. Phrases like *a not unjustifiable assumption, leaves much to be desired, would serve no good purpose, a consideration which we should do well to bear in mind,* are a continuous temptation, a packet of aspirins always at one's elbow. Look back through this essay, and for certain you will find that I have again and again committed the very faults I am protesting against. By this morning's post I have received a pamphlet dealing with conditions in Germany. The author tells me that he "felt impelled" to write it. I open it at random, and here is almost the first sentence that I see: "[The Allies] have an opportunity not only of achieving a radical transformation of Germany's social and political structure in such a way as to avoid a nationalistic reaction in Germany itself, but at the same time of laying the foundations of a co-operative and unified Europe." You see, he "feels impelled" to write — feels, presumably, that he has something new to say — and yet his words, like cavalry horses answering the bugle, group themselves automatically into the familiar dreary pattern. This invasion of one's mind by ready-made phrases *(lay the foundations, achieve a radical transformation)* can only be prevented if one is constantly on guard against them, and every such phrase anaesthetizes a portion of one's brain.   /**19**

I said earlier that the decadence of our language is probably curable. Those who deny this would argue, if they produced an argument at all, that language merely reflects existing social conditions, and that we cannot influence its development by any direct tinkering with words and constructions. So far as the general tone or spirit of a language goes, this may be true, but it is not true in detail. Silly words and expressions have often disappeared, not through any evolutionary process but owing to the conscious action of a minority. Two recent examples were *explore every avenue* and *leave no stone unturned,* which were killed by the jeers of a few journalists. There is a long list of flyblown metaphors which could similarly be got rid of if enough people would interest themselves in the job; and it should also be possible to laugh the *not un-* formation out of existence,[3] to reduce the amount of Latin and Greek in the average sentence, to drive out foreign phrases and strayed scientific words, and, in general, to make pretentiousness unfashionable. But all these are minor points. The defence of the English language implies more than this, and perhaps it is best to start by saying what it does *not* imply.   /**20**

To begin with it has nothing to do with archaism, with the salvaging of obsolete words and turns of speech, or with the setting up of a "standard English" which must never be departed from. On the contrary, it is especially concerned with the scrapping of every word or idiom which has outworn its usefulness. It has nothing to do with correct grammar and syntax, which are of no importance so long as one makes one's meaning clear, or with the avoidance of Americanisms, or with having what is called a "good prose style." On the other hand it is not concerned with fake simplicity and the attempt to make written English colloquial. Nor does it even imply in every case preferring the Saxon word to the Latin one, though it does imply using the fewest and shortest words that will cover one's meaning. What is above all needed is to let the meaning choose the word, and not the other way about. In prose, the worst thing one can do with words is to surrender to them. When you think of a concrete object, you think wordlessly, and then, if you want to describe the thing you have been visualizing you probably hunt about till you find the exact words that seem to fit it. When you think of something abstract you are more inclined to use words from the start, and unless you make a conscious effort to prevent it, the existing dialect will come rushing in and do the job for you, at the expense of blurring or even changing your meaning. Probably it is better to put off using words as long as possible and get one's meaning as clear as one can through pictures or sensations. Afterwards one can choose — not simply *accept* — the phrases that will best cover the meaning, and then switch round and decide what impression one's words are likely to make on another person. This last effort of the mind cuts out all stale or mixed images, all prefabricated phrases, needless repetitions, and humbug and vagueness generally. But one can often be in doubt about the effect of a word or a phrase, and one needs rules that one can rely on when instinct fails. I think the following rules will cover most cases:

(i)   Never use a metaphor, simile or other figure of speech which you are used to seeing in print.
(ii) Never use a long word where a short one will do.
(iii) If it is possible to cut a word out, always cut it out.
(iv) Never use the passive where you can use the active.
(v)   Never use a foreign phrase, a scientific word or a jargon word if you can think of an everyday English equivalent.
(vi) Break any of these rules sooner than say anything outright barbarous.
      /21

These rules sound elementary, and so they are, but they demand a deep change of attitude in anyone who has grown used to writing in the style now fashionable. One could keep all of them and still write bad English, but one could not write the kind of stuff that I quoted in those five specimens at the beginning of this article. /22

I have not here been considering the literary use of language, but merely language as an instrument for expressing and not for concealing or preventing thought. Stuart Chase and others have come near to claiming that all abstract words are meaningless, and have used this as a pretext for advocating a kind of political quietism. Since you don't know what Fascism is, how can you struggle against Fascism? One need not swallow such absurdities as this, but one ought to recognize that the present political chaos is connected with the decay of language, and that one can probably bring about some improvement by starting at the verbal end. If you simplify your English, you are freed from the worst follies of orthodoxy. You cannot speak any of the necessary dialects, and when you make a stupid remark its stupidity will be obvious, even to yourself. Political language — and with variations this is true of all political parties, from Conservatives to Anarchists — is designed to make lies sound truthful and murder respectable, and to give an appearance of solidity to pure wind. One cannot change this all in a moment, but one can at least change one's own habits, and from time to time one can even, if one jeers loudly enough, send some worn-out and useless phrase — some *jackboot, Achilles' heel, hotbed, melting pot, acid test, veritable inferno* or other lump of verbal refuse — into the dustbin where it belongs.   /23

Review Questions

1. What is Orwell's thesis in this essay?
2. How does the cause and effect pattern work in this essay?
3. How does Orwell use cause and effect to illustrate his point?
4. Who is Orwell's intended audience?
5. Does Orwell's essay conclude with thoughts about the same topic it addressed initially?

Notes

[1] An interesting illustration of this is the way in which the English flower names which were in use till very recently are being ousted by Greek ones, *snapdragon* becoming *antirrhinum, forget-me-not* becoming *myosotis*, etc. It is hard to see any practical reason for this change of fashion: it is probably due to an instinctive turning-away from the more homely word and a vague feeling that the Greek word is scientific.

[2] Example: "Comfort's catholicity of perception and image, strangely Whitmanesque in range, almost the exact opposite in aesthetic compulsion, continues to evoke that trembling atmospheric accumulative hinting at a cruel, an inexorably serene timelessness.... Wrey Gardiner scores by aiming at simple bull's-eyes with precision. Only they are not so simple, and through this contented sadness runs more than the surface bitter-sweet of resignation." (Poetry Quarterly)

[3] One can cure oneself of the *not un-* formation by memorizing this sentence: *A not unblack dog was chasing a not unsmall rabbit across a not ungreen field.*

24

Persuasion Essays

The Obligation to Endure

Rachel Carson

Rachel Carson (1907-1964) was born in Springfield, Pennsylvania, and educated at Pennsylvania College for Women and Johns Hopkins University. She spent many years at the Marine Biological Laboratories in Woods Hole, Massachusetts, as an aquatic biologist, ornithologist, and conservationist.

Carson was also a winner of a National Book Award. Her writings include *The Sea Around Us* (1951), *The Edge of the Sea* (1955), *Silent Spring* (1962), *The Sense of Wonder* (1965), and *The Rocky Coast* (posthumously published in 1971). All are devoted to ecological issues. The selection following is taken from *Silent Spring.*

The history of life on earth has been a history of interaction between living things and their surroundings. To a large extent, the physical form and the habits of the earth's vegetation and its animal life have been molded by the environment. Considering the whole span of earthly time, the opposite effect, in which life actually modifies its surroundings, has been relatively slight. Only within the moment of time represented by the present century has one species — man — acquired significant power to alter the nature of his world.   /1

During the past quarter century this power has not only increased to one of disturbing magnitude but it has changed in character. The most alarming of all man's assaults upon the environment is the contamination of air, earth, rivers, and sea with dangerous and even lethal materials. This pollution is for the most part irrecoverable; the chain of evil it initiates not only in the world that must support life but in living tissues is for the most part irreversible. In this now universal contamination of the environment, chemicals are the sinister and little-recognized partners of radiation in changing the very nature of the world — the very nature of its life. Strontium 90, released through nuclear explosions into the air, comes to earth in rain or drifts down as fallout, lodges in soil, enters into the grass or corn or wheat grown there, and in time takes up its abode in the bones of a human being, there to remain until his death. Similarly, chemicals sprayed on croplands or forests or gardens lie long in soil, entering into living organisms, passing from one to another in a chain of poisoning and death. Or they pass mysteriously by underground streams until they emerge and, through the alchemy of air and sunlight, combine into new forms that kill vegetation, sicken cattle, and work unknown harm on those who drink from once-pure wells. As Albert Schweitzer has said, "Man can hardly even recognize the devils of his own creation."   /2

It took hundreds of millions of years to produce the life that now inhabits the earth — eons of time in which that developing and evolving and diversifying life reached a state of adjustment and balance with its surroundings. The environment, rigorously shaping and directing the life it supported, contained elements that were hostile as well as supporting. Certain rocks gave out dangerous radiation; even within the light of the sun, from which all life draws its energy, there were short-wave radiations with power to injure. Given time — time not in years but in millennia — life adjusts, and a balance has been reached. For time is the essential ingredient; but in the modern world there is no time.   /3

The rapidity of change and the speed with which new situations are created follow the impetuous and heedless pace of man rather than the deliberate pace of nature. Radiation is no longer merely the background radiation of rocks, the bombardment of cosmic rays, the ultraviolet of the sun that have existed before there was any life on earth; radiation is now the unnatural creation of man's tampering with the atom. The chemicals to which life is asked to make its adjustment are no longer merely the calcium and silica and copper and all the rest of the minerals washed out of the rocks and carried in rivers to the sea; they are the synthetic creations of man's inventive mind, brewed in his laboratories, and having no counterparts in nature.   /4

To adjust to these chemicals would require time on the scale that is nature's; it would require not merely the years of a man's life but the life of generations. And even this, were it by some miracle possible, would be futile, for the new chemicals come from our laboratories in an endless stream; almost five hundred annually find their way into actual use in the United States alone. The figure is staggering and its implications are not easily grasped — 500 new chemicals to which the bodies of men and animals are required somehow to adapt each year, chemicals totally outside the limits of biologic experience.   /5

Among them are many that are used in man's war against nature. Since the mid-1940's over 200 basic chemicals have been created for use in killing insects, weeds, rodents, and other organisms described in the modern vernacular as "pests"; and they are sold under several thousand different brand names.   /6

These sprays, dusts, and aerosols are now applied almost universally to farms, gardens, forests, and homes — nonselective chemicals that have the power to kill every insect, the "good" and the "bad," to still the song of birds and the leaping of fish in the streams, to coat the leaves with a deadly film, and to linger on in soil — all this though the intended target may be only a few weeds or insects. Can anyone believe it is possible to lay down such a barrage of poisons on the surface of the earth without making it unfit for all life? They should not be called "insecticides," but "biocides."   /7

The whole process of spraying seems caught up in an endless spiral. Since DDT was released for civilian use, a process of escalation has been going on in which ever more toxic materials must be found. This has happened because insects, in a triumphant vindication of Darwin's principle of the survival of the fittest, have evolved super races immune to the particular insecticide used, hence a deadlier one has always to be developed — and then a deadlier one than that. It has happened also because, for reasons to be described later, destructive insects often undergo a "flareback," or resurgence, after spraying, in numbers greater than before. Thus the chemical war is never won, and all life is caught in its violent crossfire.   /8

Along with the possibility of the extinction of mankind by nuclear war, the central problem of our age has therefore become the contamination of man's total environment with such substances of incredible potential for harm — substances that accumulate in the tissues of plants and animals and even penetrate the germ cells to shatter or alter the very material of heredity upon which the shape of the future depends.   /9

Some would-be architects of our future look toward a time when it will be possible to alter the human germ plasm by design. But we may easily be doing so now by inadvertence, for many chemicals, like radiation, bring about gene mutations. It is ironic to think that man might determine his own future by something so seemingly trivial as the choice of an insect spray.   /10

All this had been risked — for what? Future historians may well be amazed by our distorted sense of proportion. How could intelligent beings seek to control a few unwanted species by a method that contaminated the entire environment and brought the threat of disease and death even to their own kind? Yet this is precisely what we have done. We have done it, moreover, for reasons that collapse the moment we examine them. We are told that the enormous and expanding use of pesticides is necessary to maintain farm production. Yet is our real problem not one of *overproduction?* Our farms, despite measures to remove acreages from production and to pay farmers *not* to produce, have yielded such a staggering excess of crops that the American taxpayer in 1962 is paying out more than one billion dollars a year as the total carrying cost of the surplus-food storage program. And is the situation helped when one branch of the Agriculture Department tries to reduce production while another states, as it did in 1958, "It is believed generally that reduction of crop acreages under provisions of the Soil

Bank will stimulate interest in use of chemicals to obtain maximum production on the land retained in crops." /11

All this is not to say there is no insect problem and no need of control. I am saying, rather, that control must be geared to realities, not to mythical situations, and that the methods employed must be such that they do not destroy us along with the insects. /12

The problem whose attempted solution has brought such a train of disaster in its wake is an accompaniment of our modern way of life. Long before the age of man, insects inhabited the earth — a group of extraordinarily varied and adaptable beings. Over the course of time since man's advent, a small percentage of the more than half a million species of insects have come into conflict with human welfare in two principal ways: as competitors for the food supply and as carriers of human disease. /13

Disease-carrying insects become important where human beings are crowded together, especially under conditions where sanitation is poor, as in time of natural disaster or war or in situations of extreme poverty and deprivation. Then control of some sort becomes necessary. It is a sobering fact, however, as we shall presently see, that the method of massive chemical control has had only limited success, and also threatens to worsen the very conditions it is intended to curb. /14

Under primitive agricultural conditions the farmer had few insect problems. These arose with the intensification of agriculture — the devotion of immense acreages to a single crop. Such a system set the stage for explosive increases in specific insect populations. Single-crop farming does not take advantage of the principles by which nature works; it is agriculture as an engineer might conceive it to be. Nature has introduced great variety into the landscape, but man has displayed a passion for simplifying it. Thus he undoes the built-in checks and balances by which nature holds the species within bounds. One important natural check is a limit on the amount of suitable habitat for each species. Obviously then, an insect that lives on wheat can build up its population to much higher levels on a farm devoted to wheat than on one in which wheat is intermingled with other crops to which the insect is not adapted. /15

The same thing happens in other situations. A generation or more ago, the towns of large areas of the United States lined their streets with the noble elm tree. Now the beauty they hopefully created is threatened with complete destruction as disease sweeps through the elms, carried by a bettle that would have only limited chance to build up large populations and to spread from tree to tree if the elms were only occasional trees in a richly diversified planting. /16

Another factor in the modern insect problem is one that must be viewed against a background of geologic and human history: the spreading of thousands of different kinds of organisms from their native homes to invade new territories. This worldwide migration has been studied and graphically described by the British ecologist Charles Elton in his recent book *The Ecology of Invasions*. During the Cretaceous Period, some hundred million years ago, flooding seas cut many land bridges between continents and living things found themselves confined in what Elton calls "colossal separate nature reserves." There, isolated from others of their kind, they developed many new species. When some of the land masses were joined again, about 15 million years ago, these species began to move out into new territories — a movement that is not only still in progress but is now receiving considerable assistance from man. /17

The importation of plants is the primary agent in the modern spread of species, for animals have almost invariably gone along with the plants, quarantine being a comparatively recent and not completely effective innovation. The United States Office of Plant Introduction alone has introduced almost 200,000 species and varieties of plants from all over the world. Nearly half of the 180 or so major insect enemies of plants in the United States are accidental imports from abroad, and most of them have come as hitchhikers on plants. /18

In new territory, out of reach of the restraining hand of the natural enemies that kept down its numbers in its native land, an invading plant or animal is able to become enormously abundant. Thus it is no accident that our most troublesome insects are introduced species. /19

These invasions, both the naturally occurring and those dependent on human assistance, are likely to continue indefinitely. Quarantine and massive chemical campaigns are only extremely expensive ways of buying time. We are faced, according to Dr. Elton, "with a life-and-death need not just to find new technological means of suppressing this plant or that animal"; instead we need the basic knowledge of animal populations and their relations to their surroundings that will "promote an even balance and damp down the explosive power of outbreaks and new invasions." /20

Much of the necessary knowledge is now available but we do not use it. We train ecologists in our universities and even employ them in our governmental agencies but we seldom take their advice. We allow the chemical death rain to fall as though there were no alternative, whereas in fact there are many, and our ingenuity could soon discover many more if given opportunity. /21

Have we fallen into a mesmerized state that makes us accept as inevitable that which is inferior or detrimental, as though having lost the will or the vision to demand that which is good? Such thinking, in the words of the ecologist Paul Shepard, "idealizes life with only its head out of water, inches above the limits of toleration of the corruption of its own environment . . . Why should we tolerate a diet of weak poisons, a home in insipid surroundings, a circle of acquaintances who are not quite our enemies, the noise of motors with just enough relief to prevent insanity? Who would want to live in a world which is just not quite fatal?" /22

Yet such a world is pressed upon us. The crusade to create a chemically sterile, insect-free world seems to have engendered a fanatic zeal on the part of many specialists and most of the so-called control agencies. On every hand there is evidence that those engaged in spraying operations exercise a ruthless power. "The regulatory entomologists . . . function as prosecutor, judge and jury, tax assessor and collector and sheriff to enforce their own orders," said Connecticut entomologist Neely Turner. The most flagrant abuses go unchecked in both state and federal agencies. /23

It is not my contention that chemical insecticides must never be used. I do contend that we have put poisonous and biologically potent chemicals indiscriminately into the hands of persons largely or wholly ignorant of their potentials for harm. We have subjected enormous numbers of people to contact with these poisons, without their consent and often without their knowledge. If the Bill of Rights contains no guarantee that a citizen shall be secure against lethal poisons distributed either by private individuals or by public officials, it is surely only because our forefathers, despite their considerable wisdom and foresight, could conceive of no such problem.   /**24**

I contend, furthermore, that we have allowed these chemicals to be used with little or no advance investigation of their effect on soil, water, wildlife, and man himself. Future generations are unlikely to condone our lack of prudent concern for the integrity of the natural world that supports all life.   /**25**

There is still very limited awareness of the nature of the threat. This is an era of specialists, each of whom sees his own problem and is unaware of or intolerant of the larger frame into which it fits. It is also an era dominated by industry, in which the right to make a dollar at whatever cost is seldom challenged. When the public protests, confronted with some obvious evidence of damaging results of pesticide applications, it is fed little tranquilizing pills of half truth. We urgently need an end to these false assurances, to the sugar coating of unpalatable facts. It is the public that is being asked to assume the risks that the insect controllers calculate. The public must decide whether it wishes to continue on the present road, and it can do so only when in full possession of the facts. In the words of Jean Rostand, "The obligation to endure gives us the right to know."   /**26**

Review Questions

1. What point is Carson arguing?
2. What evidence does she present in support of her point?
3. Does she demonstrate knowledge of her subject matter?
4. Is she arguing inductively or deductively?
5. Are her persuasions convincing?

The Yeti

Edward W. Cronin, Jr.

Edward W. Cronin, Jr., a zoologist, worked in the Himalayas as the leader of an expedition of scientists in the Arun Valley in Nepal. He also headed the Arun Valley Wildlife Expedition, a multidisciplinary ecological survey of the valley. The following selection, taken from a longer article on the yeti, is an example of inductive logic. The author presents evidence, draws conclusions, and suggests the ramifications of his argument.

In December, 1972, Dr. Howard Emery, expedition physician, and I decided to make a research trip to the high altitude areas around Kongmaa La mountain. The objective was to make our first reconnaissance of this remote, alpine area, and to investigate the winter conditions of the ecosystem.   /1

We left base camp in the Kasuwa Khola side-valley on December 14. The first days were a slow trek through an upper-temperate forest where a deciduous canopy of winter-bare branches cast twisted shapes against a gray sky. As we climbed we encountered heavier snows, which made traveling difficult; our porters turned back because of the cold. On the seventeenth, accompanied by two Sherpa assistants, we emerged on a high alpine ridge connecting to Kongmaa La. The weather was beautiful, with a clear sky and warm sun. The icy summit of Makalu dominated the horizon to the northwest. In the late afternoon, we discovered a depression in the ridge at about 12,000 feet, offering a flat place with firm snow that was suitable for camp. The area was small, less than half an acre, a completely clear snowfield unmarked by animal prints.   /2

The slopes on the side of the ridge were precipitous, falling several thousand feet to the Barun River on the north and the Kasuwa River on the south. We made camp, pitching two light tents, had dinner around an open fire, and retired just after dark. The evening was calm.   /3

Shortly before dawn the next morning, Dr. Emery climbed out of our tent. He called excitedly. There, beside the trail we had made to our tents, was a new set of footprints. While we were sleeping, a creature had approached our camp and walked directly between our tents. The Sherpas identified the tracks without question as yeti footprints.   /4

We immediately made a full photographic record of the prints before the sun touched them. Like the conditions Shipton had encountered, the surface consisted of crystalline snow, excellent for displaying the prints. These conditions were localized to our camp area, and were the result of the effects produced on the depression by the sun and the winds of the earlier days. The prints were clearest in the middle of the depression, directly beside our trail, where some ten to fifteen prints, both left and right feet, revealed the details of the toes and the general morphology of the creature's foot. Some of the right footprints were actually on our previous trail, making them difficult to interpret; other prints of the right foot were distinct.   /5

The prints measured approximately nine inches long by four and three quarters inches wide. The stride, or distance between individual prints, was surprisingly short, often less than one foot, and it appeared that the creature had used a slow, cautious walk along this section. The prints showed a short, broad, opposable hallux, an asymmetrical arrangement of the four remaining toes, and a wide, rounded heel. These features were present in all the prints made on firm snow, and we were impressed with their close resemblance to Shipton's prints.   /6

We then proceeded to explore the rest of the trail left by the creature. By the direction of the toes on the clear footprints, I determined that the creature had come up the north slope. I investigated these prints first, following the trail back down the slope. Because the north slope received less sun, it was covered with very deep snow, and the tracks consisted of large punch holes in the snow, revealing little detail. I descended several hundred yards, but the heavy snow made walking impossible, and I was forced to cling to the slope with my hands; the creature must have been exceptionally strong to ascend this slope in these conditions. From a vantage point, I could look down the trail, which continued toward the bottom of the valley in a direction generally perpendicular to the slope, but there seemed little advantage in climbing farther down, and I returned to the top of the ridge.   /7

From our camp, the tracks continued out onto the south slope, but here the increased exposure to the sun had melted most of the snow, and there were bare patches of rock and alpine scrub which made following the trail difficult. We walked farther up the ridge toward Kongmaa La to get a view of the trail from above, and discovered what appeared to be the prints of the same creature coming back onto the top of the ridge. They crossed back and forth several times. Here the ridge was covered with low bushes which enabled deeper snow to accumulate, and the prints were again confused punch holes. The trail then went back down onto the south slope, and we attempted to follow, but lost the prints on the bare rock and scrub. The slope was extremely steep, and searching for the prints was arduous and dangerous. We realized that whatever creature had made them was far stronger than any of us.   /8

We considered the possibility of a hoax perpetrated by our Sherpas, but discounted it, realizing that the Sherpas were not capable of making the full trail of prints we could see from the top of the ridge. They would not have had the time. We also doubted their ability to make prints which were so consistent with each other and which so closely matched the yeti footprints that we were familiar with from photographs.   /9

We sent word with one of the Sherpas down to the other members of the expedition. Jeffrey McNeely, expedition mammalogist, came up to the ridge later and made plaster casts of the prints.   /10

During the following three days, we kept a careful watch for the possible reappearance of the creature. We made a new camp farther up the ridge, and spent the days examining other snowfields. At night, taking advantage of a bright moon that clearly illuminated the surrounding slopes, we watched from the front of our tent for possible nocturnal activity. There were no further signs.   /11

Upon reflection, there are several aspects of this incident which constitute valuable additional information about the yeti: /12

1. The circumstances eliminate the hypothesis that all yeti prints are the function of melting by the sun or wind erosion. We know that the prints were made during the night of the seventeenth, or very early on the morning of the eighteenth. We photographed them before sunrise. We knew wind had not affected them, since a comparison of our own footprints made on the morning of the eighteenth with our footprints made on the seventeenth showed little, if any, distortion.   /13

2. The prints are not referrable to a local animal. During the expedition, we

devoted special efforts to examining all large mammal prints made in snow; we noted possible variations produced by different snow conditions, terrain, and activities of the animal (i.e., running, walking, etc.); a photographic record was made. As professional biologists with extensive experience in the Himalayas, we feel we can eliminate any possibility that the prints were made by any known, normal mammal.   /14

3. The prints support the hypothesis that the various yeti reports refer to one species. The prints are similar to those photographed by Shipton, differing only in being smaller, with a shorter hallux, and perhaps indicating an immature or female yeti. (Sexual dimorphism, that is, difference in size between the sexes, is known from *Gigantopithecus* and many other primates.)   /15

4. The prints support the hypothesis that the yeti is an ape. Like Shipton's photograph, our prints show a foot morphology typical of Pongidae.   /16

5. The arrangement of the prints supports the hypothesis that the yeti uses bipedal progression. The prints demonstrated a left-right-left-right pattern; there was no overlapping; there was no indication that more than two appendages were used in making a lengthy series of prints.   /17

6. The weight of the creature that made the prints is less than or equal to the weight of an average man. My footprints (I weighed approximately 185 pounds, including winter clothes and boots) were slightly deeper, suggesting that the creature weighed about 165 pounds.   /18

7. The circumstances support the hypothesis that the yeti is nocturnal.   /19

8. The creature displayed some inquisitiveness, since it made a detour along the ridge in order to enter our camp and pass between the tents. It is possibly significant that the creature appeared to be immature.   /20

9. The track of the creature supports the hypothesis that the yeti inhabits the forested regions. The tracks came from the heavily forested valley of the Barun, and rather than going in the direction of the higher snowfields, crossed the ridge and appeared to be continuing back down toward the forests of the Kasuwa.   /21

10. The circumstances suggest tht the yeti is very strong and well adapted to traveling across the Himalayan topography.   /22

11. The prints lend credibility to the general theory of the yeti. Their resemblance to the numerous footprints previously reported, such as Shipton's, which were made twenty-one years before and a long distance from Kongmaa La, suggest a uniformity of data strongly indicating the existence of an unknown creature in the Himalayas.   /23

Based on this experience, I believe that there is a creature alive today in the Himalayas which is creating a valid zoological mystery. It is possibly a known species in a deformed or abnormal condition, although the evidence points to a new form of bipedal primate. Or perhaps an old form — a form that man once knew and competed with, and then forced to seek refuge in the seclusion of the Himalayas.   /24

Even though I am intrigued with the yeti, both for its scientific importance and for what it says about our own interests and biases, I would be deeply saddened to have it discovered. If it were to be found and captured, studied and confined, we might well slay our nightmares. But the mystery and imagination it evokes would also be slain. If the yeti is an old form that we have driven into the mountains, now we would be driving it into the zoos. We would gain another possession, another ragged exhibit in the concrete world of the zoological park, another Latin name to enter on our scientific ledgers. But what about the wild creature that now roams free of man in the forests of the Himalayas? Every time man asserts his mastery over nature, he gains something in knowledge, but loses something in spirit.   /**25**

Review Questions

1. What is the point of Cronin's argument?
2. How does he use his data as a basis for making this point?
3. How does Cronin refute the counterarguments to his position?
4. What ramifications of his conclusions are presented in this essay?
5. Are you convinced by Cronin's argument?

A Modest Proposal

Jonathan Swift

Jonathan Swift was born in Dublin in 1667 and educated at Trinity College, Dublin, and at Oxford. He was ordained an Anglican minister and eventually became Dean of St. Patrick's Cathedral in Dublin. Swift was a political activist and lobbied for rights for Ireland and against subjugation of the Irish by England, despite his avowed scorn for Ireland. Among his best-known writings are *A Tale of a Tub, Battle of the Books,* and *Travels into Several Remote Nations of the World . . . by Captain Lemuel Gulliver.* He died in 1745.

"A Modest Proposal," published in 1729, is a bitter denunciation of English oppression of the Irish. It was widely read, although few of Swift's readers took it literally.

It is a melancholy object to those who walk through this great town or travel in the country, when they see the streets, the roads, and cabin doors, crowded with beggars of the female sex, followed by three, four, or six children, all in rags and importuning every passenger for an alms. These mothers, instead of being able to work for their honest livelihood, are forced to employ all their time in strolling to beg sustenance for their helpless infants, who, as they grow up, either turn thieves for want of work, or leave their dear native country to fight for the Pretender in Spain, or sell themselves to the Barbadoes.   /**1**

I think it is agreed by all parties that this prodigious number of children in the arms, or on the backs, or at the heels of their mothers, and frequently of their fathers, is in the present deplorable state of the kingdom a very great additional grievance; and therefore whoever could find out a fair, cheap, and easy method of making these children sound, useful members of the commonwealth would deserve so well of the public as to have his statue set up for a preserver of the nation.   /2

But my intention is very far from being confined to provide only for the children of professed beggars; it is of a much greater extent, and shall take in the whole number of infants at a certain age who are born of parents in effect as little able to support them as those who demand our charity in the streets.   /3

As to my own part, having turned my thoughts for many years upon this important subject, and maturely weighed the several schemes of other projectors, I have always found them grossly mistaken in their computation. It is true, a child just dropped from its dam may be supported by her milk for a solar year, with little other nourishment; at most not above the value of two shillings, which the mother may certainly get, or the value in scraps, by her lawful occupation of begging; and it is exactly at one year old that I propose to provide for them in such a manner as instead of being a charge upon their parents or the parish, or wanting food and raiment for the rest of their lives, they shall on the contrary contribute to the feeding, and partly to the clothing, of many thousands.   /4

There is likewise another great advantage in my scheme, that it will prevent those voluntary abortions, and that horrid practice of women murdering their bastard children, alas, too frequent among us, sacrificing the poor innocent babes, I doubt, more to avoid the expense than the shame, which would move tears and pity in the most savage and inhuman breast.   /5

The number of souls in this kingdom being usually reckoned one million and a half, of these I calculate there may be about two hundred thousand couples whose wives are breeders; from which number I subtract thirty thousand couples who are able to maintain their own children, although I apprehend there cannot be so many under the present distress of the kingdom; but this being granted, there will remain an hundred and seventy thousand breeders. I again subtract fifty thousand for those women who miscarry, or whose children die by accident or disease within the year. There only remain an hundred and twenty thousand children of poor parents annually born. The question therefore is, how this number shall be reared and provided for, which, as I have already said, under the present situation of affairs, is utterly impossible by all the methods hitherto proposed. For we can neither employ them in handicraft or agriculture; we neither build houses (I mean in the country) nor cultivate land. They can very seldom pick up a livelihood by stealing till they arrive at six years old, except where they are of towardly parts; although I confess they learn the rudiments much earlier, during which time they can however be looked upon only as probationers, as I have been informed by a principal gentleman in the country of Cavan, who protested to me that he never knew above one or two instances under the age of six, even in a part of the kingdom so renowned for the quickest proficiency in that art.   /6

I am assured by our merchants that a boy or a girl before twelve years old is no salable commodity; and even when they come to this age they will not yield above three pounds, or three pounds and half a crown at most on the Exchange; which cannot turn to account either to the parents or the kingdom, the charge of nutriment and rags having been at least four times that value.　/7

I shall now therefore humbly propose my own thoughts, which I hope will not be liable to the last objection.　/8

I have been assured by a very knowing American of my acquaintance in London, that a young healthy child well nursed is at a year old a most delicious, nourishing, and wholesome food, whether stewed, roasted, baked, or boiled; and I make no doubt that it will equally serve in a fricassee or a ragout.　/9

I do therefore humbly offer it to public consideration that of the hundred and twenty thousand children, already computed, twenty thousand may be reserved for breed, whereof only one fourth part to be males, which is more than we allow to sheep, black cattle, or swine; and my reason is that these children are seldom the fruits of marriage, a circumstance not much regarded by our savages, therefore one male will be sufficient to serve four females. That the remaining hundred thousand may at a year old be offered in sale to the persons of quality and fortune through the kingdom, always advising the mother to let them suck plentifully in the last month, so as to render them plump and fat for a good table. A child will make two dishes at an entertainment for friends; and when the family dines alone, the fore or hind quarter will make a reasonable dish, and seasoned with a little pepper or salt will be very good boiled on the fourth day, especially in winter.　/10

I have reckoned upon a medium that a child just born will weigh twelve pounds, and in a solar year if tolerably nursed increaseth to twenty-eight pounds.　/11

I grant this food will be somewhat dear, and therefore very proper for landlords, who, as they have already devoured most of the parents, seem to have the best title to the children.　/12

Infant's flesh will be in season throughout the year, but more plentiful in March, and a little before and after. For we are told by a grave author, an eminent French physician, that fish being a prolific diet, there are more children born in Roman Catholic countries about nine months after Lent than at any other season; therefore, reckoning a year after Lent, the markets will be more glutted than usual, because the number of popish infants is at least three to one in this kingdom; and therefore it will have one other collateral advantage, by lessening the number of Papists among us.　/13

I have already computed the charge of nursing a beggar's child (in which list I reckon all cottagers, laborers, and four fifths of the farmers) to be about two shillings per annum, rags included; and I believe no gentleman would repine to give ten shillings for the carcass of a good fat child, which, as I have said, will make four dishes of excellent nutritive meat, when he hath only some particular friend or his own family to dine with him. Thus the squire will learn to be a good landlord, and grow popular among the tenants; the mother will have eight shillings net profit, and be fit for work till she produces another child.　/14

Those who are more thrifty (as I must confess the times require) may flay the carcass; the skin of which artifically dressed will make admirable gloves for ladies, and summer boots for fine gentlemen.   /15

As to our city of Dublin, shambles may be appointed for this purpose in the most convenient parts of it, and butchers we may be assured will not be wanting; although I rather recommend buying the children alive, and dressing them hot from the knife as we do roasting pigs.   /16

A very worthy person, a true lover of his country, and whose virtues I highly esteem, was lately pleased in discoursing on this matter to offer a refinement upon my scheme. He said that many gentlemen of his kingdom, having of late destroyed their deer, he conceived that the want of venison might be well supplied by the bodies of young lads and maidens, not exceeding fourteen years of age nor under twelve, so great a number of both sexes in every county being now ready to starve for want of work and service; and these to be disposed of by their parents, if alive, or otherwise by their nearest relations. But with due deference to so excellent a friend and so deserving a patriot, I cannot be altogether in his sentiments; for as to the males, my American acquaintance assured me from frequent experience that their flesh was generally tough and lean, like that of our schoolboys, by continual exercise, and their taste disagreeable; and to fatten them would not answer the charge. Then as to the females, it would, I think with humble submission, be a loss to the public, because they soon would become breeders themselves; and besides, it is not improbable that some scrupulous people might be apt to censure such a practice (although indeed very unjustly) as a little bordering upon cruelty; which, I confess, hath always been with me the strongest objection against any project, how well soever intended.   /17

But in order to justify my friend, he confessed that this expedient was put into his head by the famous Psalmanazar, a native of the island Formosa, who came from thence to London above twenty years ago, and in conversation told my friend that in his country when any young person happened to be put to death, the executioner sold the carcass to the persons of quality as a prime dainty; and that in his time the body of a plump girl of fifteen, who was crucified for an attempt to poison the emperor, was sold to his Imperial Majesty's prime minister of state, and other great mandarins of the court, in joints from the gibbet, at four hundred crowns. Neither indeed can I deny that if the same use were made of several plump young girls in this town, who without one single groat to their fortunes cannot stir abroad with a chair, and appear at the playhouse and assemblies in foreign fineries which they never will pay for, the kingdom would not be the worse.   /18

. Some persons of a desponding spirit are in great concern about that vast number of poor people who are aged, diseased, or maimed, and I have been desired to employ my thoughts what course may be taken to ease the nation of so grievous an encumbrance. But I am not in the least pain upon that matter, because it is very well known that they are every day dying and rotting by cold and famine, and filth and vermin, as fast as can be reasonably expected. And as to the younger laborers, they are now in almost as hopeful a condition. They cannot get work, and consequently pine away for want of nourishment to a degree that if any time they are accidentally hired to common labor, they have not strength to perform it; and thus the country and themselves are happily delivered from the evils to come.   /**19**

I have too long digressed, and therefore shall return to my subject. I think the advantages by the proposal which I have made are obvious and many, as well as of the highest importance.   /**20**

For first, as I have already observed, it would greatly lessen the number of Papists, with whom we are yearly overrun, being the principal breeders of the nation as well as our most dangerous enemies; and who stay at home on purpose to deliver the kingdom to the Pretender, hoping to take their advantage by the absence of so many good Protestants, who have chosen rather to leave their country than to stay at home and pay tithes against their conscience to an Episcopal curate.   /**21**

Secondly, the poorer tenants will have something valuable of their own, which by law may be made liable to distress, and help to pay their landlord's rent, their corn and cattle being already seized and money a thing unknown.   /**22**

Thirdly, whereas the maintenance of an hundred thousand children, from two years old and upwards, cannot be computed at less than ten shillings a piece per annum, the nation's stock will be thereby increased fifty thousand pounds per annum, besides the profit of a new dish introduced to the tables of all gentlemen of fortune in the kingdom who have any refinement in taste. And the money will circulate among ourselves, the goods being entirely of our own growth and manufacture.   /**23**

Fourthly, the constant breeders, besides the gain of eight shillings sterling per annum by the sale of their children, will be rid of the charge of maintaining them after the first year.   /**24**

Fifthly, this food would likewise bring great custom to taverns, where the vintners will certainly be so prudent as to procure the best receipts for dressing it to perfection, and consequently have their houses frequented by all the fine gentlemen, who justly value themselves upon their knowledge in good eating; and a skillful cook, who understands how to oblige his guests, will contrive to make it as expensive as they please.   /**25**

Sixthly, this would be a great inducement to marriage, which all wise nations have either encouraged by rewards or enforced by laws and penalties. It would increase the care and tenderness of mothers toward their children, when they were sure of a settlement for life to the poor babes, provided in some sort by the public, to their annual profit instead of expense. We should see an honest emulation among the married women, which of them could bring the fattest child to the market. Men would become as fond of their wives during the time of their pregnancy as they are now of their mares in foal, their cows in calf, or sows when they are ready to farrow; nor offer to beat or kick them (as is too frequent a practice) for fear of a miscarriage.   /**26**

Many other advantages might be enumerated. For instance, the addition of some thousand carcasses in our exportation of barreled beef, the propagation of swine's flesh, and improvements in the art of making good bacon, so much wanted among us by the great destruction of pigs, too frequent at our tables, which are no way comparable in taste or magnificence to a well-grown, fat, yearling child, which roasted whole will make a considerable figure at a lord mayor's feast or any other public entertainment. But this and many others I omit, being studious of brevity. /27

Supposing that one thousand families in this city would be constant customers for infants' flesh, besides others who might have it at merry meetings, particularly weddings and christenings, I compute that Dublin would take off annually about twenty thousand carcasses, and the rest of the kingdom (where probably they will be sold somewhat cheaper) the remaining eighty thousand. /28

I can think of no one objection that will possibly be raised against this proposal, unless it should be urged that the number of people will be thereby much lessened in the kingdom. This I freely own, and it was indeed one principal design in offering it to the world. I desire the reader will observe, that I calculate my remedy for this one individual kingdom of Ireland and for no other that ever was, is, or I think ever can be upon earth. Therefore let no man talk to me of other expedients: of taxing our absentees at five shillings a pound: of using neither clothes nor household furniture except what is of our own growth and manufacture: of utterly rejecting the materials and instruments that promote foreign luxury: of curing the expensiveness of pride, vanity, idleness, and gaming in our women: of introducing a vein of parsimony, prudence, and temperance: of learning to love our country, in the want of which we differ even from Laplanders and the inhabitants of Topinamboo: of quitting our animosities and factions, nor acting any longer like the Jews, who were murdering one another at the very moment their city was taken: of being a little cautious not to sell our country and conscience for nothing: of teaching landlords to have at least one degree of mercy toward their tenants: lastly, of putting a spirit of honesty, industry, and skill into our shopkeepers; who, if a resolution could now be taken to buy only our native goods, would immediately unite to cheat and exact upon us in the price, the measure, and the goodness, nor could ever yet be brought to make one fair proposal of just dealing, though often and earnestly invited to it. /29

Therefore I repeat, let no man talk to me of these and the like expedients, till he hath at least some glimpse of hope that there will ever be some hearty and sincere attempt to put them in practice. /30

But as to myself, having been wearied out for many years with offering vain, idle, visionary thoughts, and at length utterly despairing of success, I fortunately fell upon this proposal, which, as it is wholly new, so it hath something solid and real, of no expense and little trouble, full in our own power, and whereby we can incur no danger in disobliging England. For this kind of commodity will not bear exportation, the flesh being of too tender a consistence to admit a long continuance in salt, although perhaps I could name a country which would be glad to eat up our whole nation without it. /31

After all, I am not so violently bent upon my own opinion as to reject any offer proposed by wise men, which shall be found equally innocent, cheap, easy, and effectual. But before something of that kind shall be advanced in contradiction to my scheme, and offering a better, I desire the author or authors will be pleased maturely to consider two points. First, as things now stand, how they will be able to find food and raiment for an hundred thousand useless mouths and backs. And secondly, there being a round million of creatures in human figure throughout this kingdom, whose sole subsistence put into a common stock would leave them in debt two millions of pounds sterling, adding those who are beggars by profession to the bulk of farmers, cottagers, and laborers, with their wives and children who are beggars in effect; I desire those politicians who dislike my overture, and may perhaps be so bold to attempt an answer, that they will first ask the parents of these mortals whether they would not at this day think it a great happiness to have been sold for food at a year old in this manner I prescribe, and thereby have avoided such a perpetual scene of misfortunes as they have since gone through by the oppression of landlords, the impossibility of paying rent without money or trade, the want of common sustenance, with neither house nor clothes to cover them from the inclemencies of the weather, and the most inevitable prospect of entailing the like or greater miseries upon their breed forever. /**32**

I profess, in the sincerity of my heart, that I have not the least personal interest in endeavoring to promote this necessary work, having no other motive than the public good of my country, by advancing our trade, providing for infants, relieving the poor, and giving some pleasure to the rich. I have no children by which I can propose to get a single penny; the youngest being nine years old, and my wife past childbearing. /**33**

Review Questions

1. What are the steps Swift uses to put forth his argument?
2. Are there any lapses in Swift's logic?
3. What are the real solutions Swift is proposing?
4. Who is Swift's audience?
5. How do you know this piece is satire?

Mere Survival Is Not Enough for Man

René Dubos

René Dubos (1901-   ) was born in France and educated both in France and the United States. He became a U.S. citizen in 1924. A microbiologist and pathologist,

Dr. Dubos is the discoverer of various antibiotics. His work in science has been honored by the Lasker Award and membership in the National Academy of Sciences. He is currently on the faculty of The Rockefeller University in New York.

In addition to his scientific work, Dr. Dubos is also the author of more than twenty books, including *The Unseen World* (1962), *Man Adapting* (1965), *So Human an Animal* (1969), for which he won a Pulitzer Prize, and *The Professor, The Institute, and DNA* (1976) about Dr. Oswald Avery's discovery of DNA at the Rockefeller Institute in 1944. A main theme in Professor Dubos' writing is the physiological, chemical, biological, and social effects of the environment on all aspects of life. In the essay to follow, Dubos argues that it is not enough for humanity to merely survive; we must maintain the quality of human life as well.

I am tired of hearing that man is on his way to extinction, along with most other forms of life. Like many others, I am alarmed by the destructive effects of our power-intoxicated technology and of our ungoverned population growth; I know that scientists have even worked a specific timetable for the extinction of mankind. But my own view of man as a biological animal suggests that something worse than extinction is in store for us.   /1

Man will survive as a species for one reason: He can adapt to almost anything. I am sure we can adapt to the dirt, pollution and noise of a New York or Tokyo. But that is the real tragedy — we can adapt to it. It is not man the ecological crisis threatens to destroy but the quality of human life, the attributes that make human life different from animal life.   /2

Wild animals can survive and even multiply in city zoos, but at the cost of losing the physical and behavioral splendor they possess in their natural habitat. Similarly, human beings can almost certainly survive and multiply in the polluted cage of technological civilization, but we may sacrifice much of our humanness in adapting to such conditions.   /3

The dangers inherent in adaptability were dramatically shown by the illustrious French bacteriologist Louis Pasteur in a lecture to students of the Ecole des Beaux Arts in Paris, in 1864. Pasteur pointed out that most human beings crowded in a poorly ventilated room usually fail to notice that the quality of the air they breathe deteriorates progressively; they are unaware of this deterioration because the change takes place by imperceptible steps.   /4

Then, to illustrate the danger of such adaptation to an objectionable environment, Pasteur placed a bird in a closed container and allowed it to remain in the confined atmosphere for several hours. The bird became rather inactive but survived. In contrast, when a new bird of the same species was introduced into the same cage where the first bird remained alive, it immediately died.   /5

The precise interpretation of this experiment is complex, but the lesson is clear. Like animals, men tend to make some form of adjustment to dangerous conditions, when these develop slowly without giving clear signs of the deleterious effects. Paradoxically, most of the threatening situations we face today have their origins in the immense adaptability of mankind.   /6

The worse effects of environmental pollution are probably yet to come since it is only during recent decades that certain chemical pollutants have reached high levels almost everywhere and that children have been exposed to these pollutants almost constantly from the time of birth.   /7

But the quality of the environment cannot be measured only in terms of gross defects such as air, water, or food pollution. Environmental conditions experienced early in life (including the formative months before birth) cause the most profound and lasting changes in man. But human beings continue to be shaped by their environment throughout their lives. What we call humanness is the expression of the interplay between man's nature and the environment, an interplay which is as old as life itself and which is the mechanism for creation on earth.   /8

Rational and blasé as we may be, and scornful of any thought that there is a "ghost in the machine," we still believe deeply that life is governed by forces that have their roots in the sky, soil and water around us. And there is, in fact, a profound biological basis for this belief. Many basic biological rhythms in man, such as body temperature, hormone secretion, blood pressure, vary with the seasons or other cosmic forces. Some of man's deepest biological traits are governed by the movement of the earth around the sun, others are connected with the movement of the moon around the earth and still others result from the daily rotation of the earth on its axis. All of these fluctuations in biological characteristics probably derive from the fact that the human species evolved under the influence of cosmic forces that have not changed. These mechanisms became inscribed in the genetic code and persist today even when they are no longer needed under the conditions of modern life.   /9

We have retained so many behavioral traits inherited from our Stone Age ancestors that, according to Dr. David Hamburg, professor of psychiatry at Stanford University, the best relic we have of early man is modern man.   /10

The survival of the distant past in human nature manifests itself at almost every moment of our daily life. We build wood fires in steam-heated city apartments; we keep plants and animals around us as if to maintain direct contact with our own origins; we travel long and far on weekends to recapture some aspect of the wilderness from which our ancestors emerged centuries ago. When we can afford it, we go back to hunting, first using guns, then bows and arrows; very soon, I am sure, we shall use spears armed with points that we shall fashion from stones with our own hands — not out of necessity, but as a symbol of return to the Stone Age.   /11

Our genetic makeup and therefore our most basic needs are still essentially the same as those of the Paleolithic hunters from whom we originated. Those early hunters moved freely among trees and grass, streams and rocks, tame and wild animals. They engaged in occupations which were at times dangerous and which always sharpened their wits. They had to make decisions on their own, rather than being entirely programmed for a limited social role. The maintenance of biological and mental health requires that technological societies provide in some form the biological freedom enjoyed by our Paleolithic ancestors.   /12

The primordial habitat in which the human race evolved still shapes man's most basic responses in adapting to conditions of modern life. Our reaction to crowding and to strangers, our sense of social order, even our forms of conflict, are conditioned by deep imprints from the biological past. A human environment must allow ways for man to express his aboriginal nature, to satisfy those needs that are rooted in the Stone Age, however great the outward changes brought by urbanization and technology.   /13

Ecologists and medical scientists have been chiefly concerned with the undesirable effects of the physical environment of man. But the creative aspects are more interesting and more important in the long run. The problem of the environment involves the salvation and enhancement of those positive values which man uses to develop his humanness. It involves, ultimately, a social organization in which each person has much freedom in selecting the stage on which to act his life: a peaceful village green, the banks of a river, the exciting plaza in a great city. Survival is not enough. Seeing the Milky Way, experiencing the fragrance of spring and observing other forms of life continue to play an immense role in the development of humanness. Man can use many different aspects of reality to make his life, not by imposing himself as a conqueror on nature, but by participating in the continuous act of creation in which all living things are engaged. Otherwise, man may be doomed to survive as something less than human.   /14

Review Questions

1. What point is Dubos arguing?
2. What structure does his argument take: inductive reasoning or deductive reasoning? Explain.
3. What evidence does Dubos present to support his contentions?
4. Are Dubos' arguments convincing?
5. To what audience do you think this article is addressed?

Part Four

Handbook

Useful Tools

This handbook section is intended as a quick guide to basic writing skills. Use it, along with the checklists at the end, to refresh your memory of grammatical and punctuational rules while writing your essay, and to correct any mechanical errors your instructor might have found in grading your paper.

Most of the essays you prepare in college will be written in formal English — a style of writing that differs from informal English (such as that you would use in a letter to a friend) and from spoken English. Your command of formal English is therefore an important prerequisite to any assigned paper.

The following references, used in combination with this handbook, contain the information you will need in developing a formal writing style: a dictionary, a thesaurus, and a style sheet.

The Dictionary

One of the most useful and essential references is the dictionary. Its alphabetical listings include accurate information on spelling, syllabication, pronunciation, word origin, definition, usage, synonyms, and antonyms. The introduction to each dictionary will provide you with information on the abbreviations and symbols used throughout the dictionary entries. Although there are many editions of dictionaries on the market, there are three types with which college students should be familiar.

The College Dictionary • This moderate size dictionary (put out by many different publishers) is a desk reference containing most of the words you will need for reading or writing with a focus on modern usage. Every college student should own a recently published copy. The best college dictionaries on the market are *American Heritage Dictionary of the English Language* (Houghton), *Funk and Wagnalls Standard College Dictionary* (Funk), *Random House College Dictionary* (Random), *Webster's New Collegiate Dictionary* (Merriam), and *Webster's New World Dictionary* (Collins and World).

The Unabridged Dictionary • Again, there are several versions of this dictionary on the market. The unabridged dictionary contains every current word in the English language. It is the place to find uncommon or esoteric words — namely, those words that do not appear in college dictionaries. It is not necessary to own an unabridged dictionary, but you should have access to one (in the library or elsewhere). The best unabridged dictionaries are *The Funk and Wagnalls New*

Standard Dictionary of the English Language (Funk), *The Unabridged Random House Dictionary of the English Language* (Random), and *Webster's Third New International Dictionary of the English Language* (Merriam).

The Oxford English Dictionary   •   If you need to find the precise origin of a word (not only its roots, but where and when it first appeared in written English, how it was used, and how its meaning changed or evolved), the *O.E.D.* is the place to look. This book is impractical to have at home since it consists of twelve volumes plus a supplement and is extremely expensive, but most libraries own a set.

The Thesaurus

If you are searching for synonyms (or antonyms), and the information in the dictionary is not sufficient, you should use the thesaurus, a reference that provides synonyms and antonyms for each alphabetically listed word. *Roget's Thesaurus* is the best-known book of this type.

You should be careful when using a thesaurus, however, to select synonyms for the *exact* connotation of the word you are considering. Many a gaff has been made by writers who chose a synonym for an unsuitable connotation of a word.

The Style Sheet

Many composition instructors want their students to follow certain technical rules (about typing, essay format, and so on). These rules are listed in various style sheets prepared for this purpose. Your instructor should tell you if you are to purchase such a style sheet. Some colleges publish their own; some adhere to the rules listed in *The Modern Language Association Handbook Style Sheet* or the style sheet of the American Psychological Association.

If you are preparing a research paper, or you intend to use footnotes or a bibliography in an essay, it will be necessary to adjust the format of your footnote and bibliography entries to the technical rules set forth in the style sheet of your choice.

Words

Traditionally, words have been placed into classes called *parts of speech* according to their forms and meanings within sentences. The characteristic features of these various classes are detailed in the following sections.

Nouns

A noun is a word used to name something — a person, a place, an object, an idea. Following are the categories into which nouns can be divided.

1. **Abstract nouns** refer to ideas or qualities (desire, jealousy, existentialism, love), whereas **concrete nouns** refer to physical things that can be perceived by the senses (chair, milk, odor, sunset, siren).
2. **Common nouns** refer to a general class of persons, places, things, actions, ideas (boy, yard, house, conversation, democracy), whereas **proper nouns** refer to specific, formally named persons, places, or things, and are always capitalized (Tom Miller, Missouri, Empire State Building).
3. **Collective nouns** refer to a group (class, audience, orchestra). If the group is being considered as a whole, it takes a singular verb. (Example: The *audience* rose to its feet.) If the group is considered in terms of its individual members, it takes a plural verb. (Example: The *orchestra* are tuning their instruments.)

Nouns can function in the following ways:

1. **As subjects**
- of sentences or independent clauses (Example: The *boy* stuffed his pocket with string, but his *mother* didn't mind.)
- of dependent or subordinate clauses (Example: Although the *boy* stuffed his pocket with string, his mother didn't mind.)
2. **As objects**
- of verbs (Example of direct object: The boy stuffed *string* in his pocket. Example of indirect object: The boy gave his *mother* the string.)
- of verbals (Example: The boy wanted to put the *string* in his pocket.)
- of prepositions (Example: The boy put the string in his *pocket.*)
3. **As predicate nominatives,** also known as predicate nouns, predicate complements, or subjective complements (Example: He is a *student. Student* means the same thing as *he.*)

4. **As predicate objects,** also known as objective complements, which complete the meaning of the object of the verb (Example: The mother called the boy a *pack rat.* [*Pack rat* complements or completes the word *boy,* which is the object of the verb *called.*])

5. **As appositives** (Example: The boy, a *pack rat,* stuffed his pocket with string.)

6. **As nouns of address** (Example: *Tommy,* you are a pack rat!)

Self-Quiz

1. Write a proper noun equivalent for each common noun listed below:
   a. a building
   b. a car
   c. a person
   d. a hospital
   e. a college

2. Write an appropriate appositive for the italicized word or words in each of the following sentences:
   a. The *man* knelt down, ready to begin the race.
   b. The gun fired once and the *victim* slumped to the ground.
   c. Do *Bonnie and Jeanne* want to go?
   d. The *University President* decided to step down.

3. In the following sentences, underline each predicate nominative once and each predicate objective twice:
   a. She is a hard worker.
   b. She called the student a liar.
   c. The sophomore was a fraternity pledge.
   d. He labeled the experiment a failure.
   e. The moon is green cheese.

4. Change each italicized noun in the following sentences to make it more specific:
   a. That *thing* isn't very attractive.
   b. The *boy* is on the telephone.
   c. This *item* has several cracks in it.
   d. The *person* sat in the corner.

Pronouns

A pronoun is a word that replaces a noun. There are several different types of pronouns, some of which are detailed here.

1. **Personal pronouns** (I, you, he, they, him, it, us) are used as subjects of sentences or independent clauses (Example: *He* ate like a glutton.); as subjects of dependent or subordinate clauses (Example: Although *he* eats like a glutton, his

mother continues to overfeed him.); as direct objects of verbs (Example: The glutton ate *it* quickly.); as indirect objects of verbs (Example: The glutton served *himself* another slice of pie.); as objects of verbals (Example: The glutton wanted to eat *it* all.); and as objects of prepositions. (Example: He served it to *her*.) Personal pronouns are also used as predicate complements (Example: It was *she*.) and as appositives. (Examples: He allowed two people, *him and me*, to leave. Two people, *he and I*, left quickly.)

2. **Interrogative pronouns** (what, which, whose, who) are used in questions. (Example: *Who* is it?)

3. **Relative pronouns** (that, which, who, what) are used in relative clauses. (Examples: Give it to the woman *who* is sitting near the door. I don't like *what* you did. I want the one *that* didn't fall on the floor.)

4. **Demonstrative pronouns** (this, that, these, those) are used to show or point out something. (Example: Did you see *that?*)

5. **Indefinite pronouns** (each, any, few, one, none, either) are used to refer to nonspecific persons, places, or things. (Example: I don't want *anyone* to move.)

Common Errors Involving Pronouns

Lack of Pronoun Agreement • A singular antecedent must take a singular pronoun; a plural antecedent must take a plural pronoun.

> Everyone must do *his* (not *their*) homework.
> One of the girls received *her* (not *their*) book.
> Will everyone go to *his* (not *their*) seat!
> Each of them is responsible for *her* (not *their*) own behavior.

Vague Use of *This* or *That* • Sometimes writers use *this* or *that* to refer to an entire idea contained in a previous sentence or paragraph, a practice which generally results in vagueness. If you cannot think of the specific noun to which *this* or *that* refers, do not use these pronouns.

> Vague: Today's bad weather has caused me to change my plans. *This* is not what I had expected.
> Clearer: Today's bad weather, which I had not expected, has caused me to change my plans.

Case Form Errors • These errors can occur in various forms, as indicated in the following examples.

1. Using the subjective case of a pronoun when its position calls for it to be in the objective case:

> Incorrect: The man gave the cake to her and *I*.
> Correct: The man gave the cake to her and *me*.

2. Mistaking the case form of a pronoun in a clause: a pronoun used as the subject of a clause is *always* in the subjective case.

Incorrect: He fed *whomever* was hungry.
Correct: He fed *whoever* was hungry.

3. Mistaking the case form of a pronoun placed before a parenthetical expression such as *I know, I think, I said,* and so on:

Incorrect: She is a student *whom* I think will do well in calculus.
Correct: She is a student *who* I think will do well in calculus.

(In this example, *I think* is parenthetical and *who* is the subject of *will do well.*)

4. Using the pronoun *who* for *whom* after a preposition:

Incorrect: Her companion, with *who* she had traveled throughout Europe, returned home alone.
Correct: Her companion, with *whom* she had traveled throughout Europe, returned home alone.

Self-Quiz

Underline the correct pronoun in each sentence. Be able to explain your choice.
   1. (We, Us) freshmen are gaining experience quickly.
   2. My roommate and (I, me) will not be at dinner.
   3. She gave the message to (her and me, her and I, she and I).
   4. I speak to (whoever, whomever) I want.
   5. I spoke to (whoever, whomever) wanted to listen.
   6. That is a person (who, whom) I know will flunk out.
   7. That is a person (who, whom) I would like to know.
   8. To (whom, who) did you give my notebook?
   9. (His, Him) practicing makes an intolerable noise in the dorm.
   10. It's (I, me).
   11. Each member of the class received (her, their) assignment.

Verbs

A verb is a word that *expresses action or state of being.* It says something about what a noun *does* (action) or what it *is* (being). There are two kinds of verbs: *transitive verbs,* which express action and have an object. (Example: I *gave* him a banana.) and *intransitive verbs,* which express a state of being and do not take an object, but link a subject with a predicate nominative or a predicate adjective. (Example: I *am* happy.)

Principal Parts   •   Each verb has three *principal parts* — the infinitive, the past tense, and the past participle — on which all verb forms are based. *Regular* verbs add *d* or *ed* to the infinitive to form the other principal parts (bake, baked, baked); *irregular* verbs change their stem to form the last two principal parts (see, saw, seen; be, was, been).

Tense   •   The form of verbs — that is, the *tense* — changes according to the time expressed — *when* the action is taking place or *when* the state of being is in force.

- The *present tense* indicates present action (I look) or state of being (I am).
- The *past tense* indicates past action (I looked) or state of being (I was).
- The *future tense* indicates future action (I shall look) or state of being (I shall be).
- The *present perfect tense* indicates past action (I have looked) or state of being (I have been) which is still going on in the present.
- The *past perfect tense* indicates past action (I had looked) or state of being (I had been) which was completed in the past.
- The *future perfect tense* indicates action (I shall have looked) or state of being (I shall have been) which will be completed before some future action or state of being.

Number   •   Verbs can take a singular form (I *sing*, she *sings*) or a plural form (we *sing*, they *sing*) depending on the subject of the sentence.

Mood   •   Verbs have a feature called *mood,* to indicate the manner in which they are used. The *indicative mood* is used for statements of fact (Example: I *gave* at the office.); the *imperative mood* is used for issuing commands or giving directions (Example: *Give* it back!); and the *subjunctive mood* is used for statements contrary to fact or those in the area of potential or possibility (Examples: I wish I *were* king. I demand that he *see* a copy. If this *be* true, then I will go.).

Voice   •   Verbs also have a property called *voice,* which indicates whether the subject of the verb performs the action or undergoes it. The verb is in the *active voice* when the subject performs the action (Example: The boy *ate* the apple.); it is in the *passive voice* when the subject is being acted upon or is receiving the action (Example: The apple *was eaten* by the boy.).

Common Errors Involving Verbs

Inconsistency of Tense   •   It is necessary to proofread your essays very carefully to avoid this common error, which, if committed within a sentence, a series of sentences, or even a series of paragraphs, will confuse your reader.

Inconsistent: In the afternoon, he *takes* a cab to the downtown area. Then he *went* shopping at the mall, where he *meets* a friend from the old neighborhood.

Consistent: In the afternoon, he took a cab to the downtown area. Then he *went* shopping at the mall, where he *met* a friend from the old neighborhood.

Lack of Subject-Verb Agreement   •   The verb must agree in *number* with the subject — an easy rule of thumb to apply except where compound subjects and tricky prepositional phrases are involved.

Incorrect: My brother and my sister *thinks* well of me.
Correct: My brother and my sister *think* well of me.

Incorrect: The herd of cows *are* in the field.
Correct: The herd of cows *is* in the field.

Split Infinitives   •   Avoid the awkward placement of words between the *to-*part of an infinitive and the verb part.

Awkward: The general hoped to quickly advance.
Smoother: The general hoped to advance quickly.

Excessive or Awkward Use of the Passive Voice   •   Although writers occasionally use the passive voice as an alternative to the active voice for emphasis (Example: That apple, not the other one, was eaten by the boy.) and for stylistic variety, the overuse of passive voice constructions can result in extra words and awkward phrasing — dull, flat prose with no action or life. Smoothness can be achieved by using the active voice predominantly.

Awkward: The bike was left outside by the boy in the rain.
Smoother: The boy left the bike outside in the rain.

Self-Quiz

1. Underline the correct tense within each set of parentheses in the following sentences:

It was midnight. The lights were out. Everything was dark. Suddenly a man (jumps, jumped) out from behind a curtain.

"Your money or your life!" he (shouts, shouted).

I (had seen, saw) this intruder before. When I was a small boy, he (had worked, worked) for us as a farmhand.

"Matt," I shouted. "Don't you remember me?"

"Barney!" he (cries, cried), dropping his weapon. "I didn't know you (lived, live) here. I (will go, will have gone) straight if you (will help, help) me settle my problem. I (have not been, am not) a crook for long. I (have never done, never did) this before. Please, listen to me!"

"Every one of the crooks who (breaks, break) in here (have, has) the same story," I said, trying not to let my sympathies show. "Not one of you (have, has) any respect for privacy."

2. Correct or improve the following sentences:

a. "I hope to shortly show you how to behave yourself," I said.

b. "If I was down-and-out, I certainly wouldn't hide behind window curtains sporting a weapon," I added.

c. "If I have a problem, I would go to the proper place to get help."

d. "I would want to always try all legal avenues first, before I broke the law."

e. "Moreover, I would never have stolen from someone I knew."

f. I provided all these reasons for Matt to immediately stop his criminal pursuits.

g. It seemed to me that each of the reasons I suggested were valid.

h. At least one of the reasons were going to hit home.

i. My speech was listened to by a very repentant criminal, in order that he gain my assistance in solving his problems.

j. I had felt pretty pleased with myself, having rehabilitated a criminal.

k. After Matt had left through the window, however, as silently as he had come, I had noticed, to my chagrin, that my TV set was gone.

Modifiers

Modifiers are words which explain, qualify, or describe other words. There are five basic types of modifiers:

1. **Adjectives,** which describe nouns and pronouns (Examples: I painted the house *blue.* I painted *it* blue.)

2. **Adverbs,** which modify verbs, adjectives, and other adverbs, showing where, when, how, and to what degree (Example: I *slowly* painted the house. I painted the house *light* blue. I painted the house *very* light blue.)

3. **Participles,** which act as adjectives (Example of present participle: The *perspiring* painter stopped for a drink. Example of past participle: This is a *painted* object.)

4. **Infinitives,** which can act as adjectives or adverbs (Examples: I have promises *to keep.* She spoke up *to enter* her name on the list.)

5. **Verbals,** which are nouns that function as adverbs (Examples: I am going *home.* He sleeps *nights.*)

Modifiers can be inflected — that is, changed in form. Intensity can be shown by inflecting modifiers (good, better, best; low, lower, lowest), as can quantity (this, these; that, those).

Common Errors Involving Modifiers

Dangling or Misplaced Modifiers • The most common error concerning modifiers is the dangling or misplaced modifier. A modifier should appear near the word it modifies, and there should be no confusion about which word it modifies.

Dangling participle:	*Lying* on my back, the stars shone brightly.
Revised:	*Lying* on my back, I could see the stars shining brightly.

Lying does not modify *stars;* it modifies *I.*

Dangling adverb:	*Slowly,* we saw the hands of the clock move.
Revised:	We saw the hands of the clock move *slowly.*

Slowly refers to the movement of the clock, not to *we.*

Dangling infinitive:	*To race,* the entry book had to be signed by the runner.
Revised:	*To race,* the runner had to sign the entry book.

To race does not refer to *entry book,* but to *runner.*

Misplaced adjective:	*Dirty,* we had to repaint the sign.
Better:	*Dirty,* the sign had to be repainted.
Best:	The *dirty* sign had to be repainted.

Incomplete Comparisons • When using inflected (comparative or superlative) forms of adjectives or adverbs *(slower, slowest; more slowly, most slowly),* it is necessary to complete the comparisons being made.

Incorrect:	She is traveling *more slowly.*
Correct:	She is traveling *more slowly than* her brother.

Incorrect:	The basement is the *lowest.*
Correct:	The basement is the *lowest of the three levels* in the house.

Use of the -*wise* Construction • A common error is the addition of the suffix -*wise* to a word to indicate a general subject area; -*wise* is only correct in words such as *clockwise.*

Incorrect:	*Educationwise,* this country is quite advanced.
Correct:	This country is quite advanced in the area of education.

Self-Quiz

Some of the following sentences are correct in their use of modifiers and some are incorrect. Rewrite those sentences which contain errors.

1. The peach tree is the most beautiful tree in the garden.

2. The second quarter of the game was worse.
3. Singing in the shower, the steam hid me completely.
4. To eat, the table had to be set.
5. To eat, we had to sit down.
6. Likewise, he will read three chapters.
7. Dreaming, the boy was happy.
8. I like the green one the most.
9. The better of the two students was excused.
10. Wrongly, the weatherman predicted rain.
11. Healthwise, I am feeling fine.

Sentences

A sentence is an expression of one or more complete thoughts or ideas. It consists of a *subject* (a noun) and a *predicate* (a verb plus its objects, complements, and modifiers). These sentence parts can be single words, as in the following examples:

She (subject) **is nice** (predicate).
He (noun) **ate** (verb) **a** (article) **red** (adjective) **apple** (object).

Phrases

A sentence may also be comprised of *phrases*. A phrase is a group of words, having neither a subject nor a predicate, which serves a specific grammatical function within a sentence. The various functions served by phrases are as follows:

1. **Verb phrases** consisting of multiple parts of the verb, which serve the function of a verb in a sentence (Example: This *has been going* on for a long time.)
2. **Prepositional phrases**, which contain a preposition and an object of the preposition, and which serve as adjectives or adverbs (Examples: The day *of the snowstorm* was October 31. It grew cold *at the beach*.)
3. **Gerund phrases** consisting of the "ing" form of a verb, plus modifiers, and functioning as nouns (Example: *Night swimming* is tiring.)
4. **Participial phrases** consisting of the "ing" form of a verb, plus modifiers, and functioning as adjectives (Example: He turned off the lamp *lighting up the alcove*.)

5. **Infinitive phrases** consisting of the "to" form of a verb, plus modifiers, and functioning as nouns (Example: *To see clearly* is important.)

Clauses

Sentences are also made up of *clauses*. Clauses consist of a subject and a verb. There are two basic types of clauses:

1. **Independent clauses,** which can function alone as complete sentences (Example: [It was two A.M.] and [the room was still.])
2. **Dependent clauses,** which contain a subject and verb, but which cannot stand alone as complete sentences. Dependent clauses can function as nouns, adjectives, or adverbs.

That the sun will shine on Sunday is not certain. (noun clause)
When I go out, it almost always rains. (abverb clause)
She is a woman *who can be trusted.* (adjective clause)

Sentence Types

Clauses can be arranged to form sentences in the following ways:

1. A **simple sentence** consists of one independent clause. (Example: He went to sleep.)
2. A **compound sentence** consists of two or more independent clauses. A co-ordinate conjunction (such as *and* or *but*) connects clauses of equal rank. (Example: He went to sleep, *and* he dreamed about his home.)
3. A **complex sentence** consists of one independent clause and one or more dependent clauses. A subordinate conjunction (such as *although, whenever,* or *since*) is used at the beginning of the subordinate clause. The dependent clause can be placed before or after the independent clause. (Examples: *Since* she went to sleep early, she was assured of being well-rested in the morning. He requested roast chicken, *although* he did not usually like poultry.)
4. A **compound-complex sentence** consists of two or more independent clauses, and one or more dependent clauses. Both coordinate and subordinate conjunctions may be used in this case. (Example: *Since* he didn't like flowers, he rarely bought them; *but* he purchased a bouquet for his sister, nonetheless.)

Common Errors in Sentences

The following errors in sentence structure generally result in awkwardness:

Overuse of the Passive Voice • The passive voice often results in extra wording or awkward phrasing.

Awkward: It was known by him that three students had been selected.
Smoother: He knew that three students had been selected.

Lack of Conciseness • The use of several words to express what one word or a short phrase would convey contributes to awkwardness. Try to be concise in your writing.

Awkward: Because the weather tends to be cold at night in the winter, the fact that he has an extra-heavy sleeping bag to go camping with appeals to his sense of practicality.
Smoother: His extra-heavy sleeping bag is useful for camping in cold winter weather.

Fragments • Another frequent cause of awkwardness is the incomplete sentence, or fragment. Even a long group of words can be a fragment if it does not have both a subject and a predicate, or if it isn't a complete independent clause.

Fragment: The boy wearing the tan beret. (no verb)
Complete: The boy wearing the tan beret was running home.

Fragment: Although he didn't like spinach. (not an independent clause: the use of the subordinate conjunction "although" indicates that the clause is subordinate, or dependent, and therefore cannot stand alone.)
Complete: He ate his vegetable, although he didn't like spinach.

Run-on Sentences • Sentences which extend beyond the confines of one of the sentence patterns referred to earlier (simple, complex, compound, compound-complex) are called run-on sentences, and constitute poor writing. Often, a run-on will have the elements of more than one independent clause, but will not be punctuated correctly.

Run-on: I wonder why every time it rains the ground gets muddy I get my feet wet.
Revised: I wonder why every time it rains and the ground gets muddy, I get my feet wet.

Parallel Constructions • Similar ideas in the same sentence should be expressed in similar clause patterns. If you use the active voice for one clause in a compound sentence, you should use the active voice for the second as well.

Not parallel: She ran down the street, and a fence was hurdled.
Parallel: She ran down the street, and she hurdled a fence.

If you use a series in one pattern in the first clause, use a similar pattern in the second.

Not parallel:	Ted bought his history, English, and math texts; Mary purchased an algebra book, then a French book, and a speech book was also on her list.
Parallel:	Ted bought his history, English, and math texts; Mary purchased her algebra, French, and speech books.

Self-Quiz

1. In each of the following sentences, identify the error or the reason for awkwardness; then rewrite the sentence so that it is correct — and smooth.

    a. It was understood by the coach that seven of the players were off their diet.

    b. Instead of being something that nobody wanted to do much about in the way of cleaning up, it was on the agenda of the social service club.

    c. Because no one is willing to go.

    d. Nonetheless, we never said you could join us we do not wish you to do so!

    e. It was midnight; we could see the moon and the stars were visible too.

    f. The way the river flows isn't understood by us.

2. Write a paragraph incorporating at least one simple sentence, one compound sentence, one complex sentence, and one compound-complex sentence.

3. Write a paragraph in which you purposely include as many errors as you can think of. Exchange your paper with that of a classmate and correct each other's errors.

Punctuation

Words, phrases, clauses, and sentences make sense only when they are correctly punctuated. Punctuation marks tell the reader how and when to pause, inflect the voice, stop, and continue.

Periods

A period (.) is placed at the end of every declarative sentence and signifies a stop. Periods are also used

- after abbreviations (P.M.; *et al.;* Mrs. Kline; U.S.). Periods are not generally used, however, after each letter of an acronym — an abbreviation which spells a word

— or in abbreviations of more than four letters (UNICEF, NOW, USSR, ASPCA).

- in monetary designations ($1.95).
- to separate chapter and verse (Luke 1.24; *Hamlet* I.ii.8).
- before decimals (.01%).
- to designate omissions. Three periods (. . .) are used to indicate an omission within a sentence; four periods (. . . .) are used to show an omission at the end of a sentence.

Common Errors Involving Periods

1. Placing a period outside a quotation mark:

   Incorrect: His only response was, "I give up".
   Correct: His only response was, "I give up."

2. Neglecting to end a sentence with a period when it is complete, thus making it a run-on:

   Incorrect: The cranberry sauce was served the turkey came last of all.
   Correct: The cranberry sauce was served. The turkey came last of all.

3. Placing a period after a phrase or dependent clause, thus creating a fragment:

   Incorrect: Although it was sunny.
   Correct: Although it was sunny, she carried an umbrella.

Self-Quiz

The following sentences are correct except that they do not have any periods. Insert all necessary periods in their correct places.

1. The narrator said, "Whoever does not intend to stay through the final curtain call should leave now"
2. The USSR is an economic rival of the US
3. The actor spoke just one word: "No"
4. Henry Brice, Jr, played an important role in UN affairs
5. She read from *Othello* II iii 12
6. "No," she yelled, "I will not join you"

Commas

Commas are used to separate sentence elements. The following rules governing comma use are aimed at ensuring that the flow of thought in your writing is presented with clarity.

1. Use a comma to separate introductory elements from the rest of the sentence. (Example: After a while, it began to rain.) *Note:* The comma can be omitted if the introductory element is short and if the absence of a comma does not cause a lack of clarity. (Example: Earlier she had announced her plans.)

2. Use a comma to separate a dependent clause or phrase from the rest of the sentence. (Example: He liked the ice cream, although it tasted sour.)

3. Use commas to set off nonrestrictive phrases and clauses. (Example: The man, entering the garden, sat down. ["Entering the garden" describes the subject, but does not limit it or restrict it.])

4. Use commas to set off parenthetical elements, such as internal commentary like *he thought, she said, they wondered* and conjunctive adverbs like *therefore, consequently, however.* (Examples: He spoke, I thought, without reason. The book, moreover, was too long.)

5. Use commas to set off exclamations. (Example: Oh, I wish I could go!)

6. Use commas to separate parts of a sentence that are coordinate, or equal in value or structure. (Example: The moon was high, and the stars were bright.) The comma may be omitted, however, between short independent clauses connected with *and.* (Example: We laughed and we cried.)

7. Use commas to separate parts of a series. (Examples: The train huffed, puffed, and chugged up the hill. There were three reasons: the time, the effort, and the cost. He ate pickles, potato chips, and sandwiches. He came, he saw, he conquered.) *Note:* The final comma before the conjunction is optional.

8. Use commas to clarify words and phrases that would otherwise confuse the reader. (Example: Whatever I am, I am not a liar.)

9. Use commas to separate the elements of a date. (Example: On July 4, 1976, the United States celebrated its 200th birthday.)

10. Use commas to separate the elements in an address. (Example: Until last year, she lived at 1726 Brandon, Pine Bluff, Arkansas.)

11. Use a comma to separate quoted material from the rest of the sentence. (Example: He asked, "What is going on here?") *Note:* When a comma is used at the end of a quotation, it always precedes the final quotation mark, regardless of the sense of the sentence. (Example: "Whatever the outcome," he said, "I'll go.") When a quoted passage fits into the context of the sentence, however, no commas are needed. (Example: The author wrote "I told you so" in the margin of her manuscript.)

Common Errors Involving Commas

Comma Splice • A sentence consisting of two coordinate independent clauses, separated by a comma but without a coordinate conjunction (such as *but* or *and*), is called a comma splice, or comma fault. (Example: The water in the pond was warm, we went for a swim at noon.) The sentence is corrected by the insertion of a coordinate conjunction (Example: The water in the pond was warm, and we went for a swim at noon.) or by the substitution of a semicolon for the comma (Example: The water in the pond was warm; we went for a swim at noon.).

Confusion Over Restrictive and Nonrestrictive Clauses • A restrictive clause restricts, limits, or defines, the noun or pronoun it modifies. It is *not* set off by commas because it is essential to the understanding of the sentence. (Example: The girl who was sitting on the park bench was reading. [Here, *who was sitting on the park bench* restricts, or defines, *which* girl is being indicated: it is the girl who is sitting on the bench, *not* another girl who may be doing something else.])

A nonrestrictive clause describes, but does not limit or define, the noun or pronoun it modifies. It is not essential to the reader's understanding of the sentence, and it *is*, therefore, set off by commas. (Example: The girl, who was sitting on the park bench, was reading. [Here, the girl is the focus of attention; the fact that she was sitting on the park bench is incidental to the main idea in the sentence.]) Thus the same sentence can have two different implications, depending on whether commas are used.

Unnecessary Commas Between Subject and Verb • This problem often occurs when the subject element is long. (Example: Pollution from many combined sources, has turned the river into a fire hazard. [The sentence can be corrected simply by removing the comma.])

Self-Quiz

Insert commas wherever necessary in the following sentences. Be prepared to explain each comma.

1. Though no one was there I entered the school.
2. No one answered not even the owner.
3. The child licking her fingers asked for more.
4. In my home town Akron no one ever does that.
5. I accepted the job although I had a lot of other work to do.
6. The zoo was jammed with visitors and the reptile house was impossible to see.
7. The zoo was crowded but the botanical gardens weren't.

8. The long colorful band marched in unison.
9. The weak but attractive voice belongs to the new choir member.
10. He gave the biscuit to the dog and the cat looked on.
11. If he goes go too.
12. I think therefore I am.
13. I had eaten apples peaches and plums the day I got a stomach ache.
14. I didn't want to do that again ever.
15. He asked for a whistle.
16. He asked whether a whistle was part of the uniform.
17. My brother was born on August 7 1957.
18. On December 24 it snowed.
19. Carol lives at 81 East Hudson Street Villanova Pennsylvania.
20. The dog a beagle was overweight.
21. Please tell me Marion if you will read this book tonight.
22. The article was written by Peggy Solan M.A.
23. There were 148003 people at the rally.
24. Joan had four notebooks Marie only three.
25. I misspelled "editor" didn't I?

Semicolons

The semicolon (;) is a mark of internal punctuation that is equivalent to a period in its power to bring an independent clause to an end. Specific uses of semicolons are as follows:

- to join closely related independent clauses not connected by a coordinate conjunction (Example: The rosebush was in full bloom; the garden smelled of roses.)
- to join independent clauses connected by coordinate conjunctions, but which are very long or contain internal commas (Example: The rabbit, which had been hiding all the while, came out at the sound of the horn; and the hounds, scenting her, took up the chase.)
- to join independent clauses connected by conjunctive adverbs (Example: I don't like hunting; however, I found Saturday's chase very exciting.)
- to join units in a series when the units contain internal commas (Example: I read *Gulliver's Travels*, by Swift; *Tom Jones*, by Fielding; and *Pride and Prejudice*, by Austen.)

Note: Semicolons, when used in conjunction with quotation marks or parentheses, are always placed *outside* of the final quotation mark or parenthesis. (Example: The professor said, "It is 9 o'clock"; then she dismissed the class.)

Common Errors Involving Semicolons

Most semicolon errors involve confusion of the semicolon with the comma. Remember: the "strength" of the semicolon is comparable to that of the period at the end of a complete sentence, whereas the comma generally signals a mere pause within the sentence.

Self-Quiz

Insert a semicolon where needed in the following sentences. If you think a comma, not a semicolon, is called for, write it in accordingly.

1. It was Thanksgiving the turkey smelled delicious.

2. Years ago I used to visit Wildwood Crest, a suburb of Wildwood, New Jersey but if I remember correctly, I have not been there for fourteen years.

3. I gave up on the physics exam, moreover, I dropped the course.

4. There were three things I wanted to do: visit my grandmother, who was always very glad to see me, call my uncle, with whom I hadn't spoken in six months and write a note to my cousin in Europe.

5. No one heard the prowler (not even my mother) but the dog knew.

6. My father is a great cook, he always provides the food at family reunions.

7. I love to run there is no better exercise.

8. She had to be in Colorado by the 11th, therefore she decided to leave Chicago on the 7th.

Colons

The colon is a mark of internal punctuation that signals something to follow. Indeed, it often follows the words *as follows* in a sentence. Here is a list of rules governing colon usage.

1. Use a colon to introduce a series of examples explained in the main clause. (Example: The flavors of ice cream I like are as follows: vanilla, coffee, and strawberry. *Or* I like three flavors of ice cream: vanilla, coffee, and strawberry. [A comma following *ice cream* in either case would be confusing, since the items in the series are separated by commas.])

Note: Do not use a colon after a verb or preposition in a sentence to introduce a series, as in this example: The flavors of ice cream I like are: vanilla, coffee, and strawberry.

2. Use a colon to indicate that a statement is to follow. (Example: This is what distinguishes an insect from a spider: it has six legs rather than eight.)

3. Use a colon to introduce long or formal direct quotations. (Example: Irony can be illustrated in Shakespeare's 94th sonnet: "For sweetest things turn sourest by their deeds./Lilies that fester smell far worse than weeds.")

4. Use a colon to restate (and thus amplify or illustrate) the idea contained in a preceding clause. (Example: The movie version of *Moby Dick* is not as effective as the book: to fully experience the story, one must read the original.)

5. Use a colon for purposes of mechanical separation:
- after the salutation in a business letter (Example: Dear Sir:)
- in expressions of time (Example: It is now 11:25)
- in biblical references (Example: Genesis I:24)

Common Errors Involving Colons

Mistaking a Colon for a Semicolon   •   Although the terms are similar, the semicolon and colon have very different uses and are not interchangeable.

Incorrect: The following students have been selected; Mary, Chris, and Philip.
Correct: The following students have been selected: Mary, Chris, and Philip.

Overuse of the Colon   •   As previously noted, the colon should not appear after a verb or preposition introducing a series.

Incorrect: This summer I am planning to: learn how to type, study French, and jog every day.
Correct: This summer I am planning to learn how to type, study French, and jog every day.

Self-Quiz

Are the following sentences punctuated correctly or incorrectly? Explain.
1. I like: vanilla ice cream.
2. I studied three languages: French, in high school; Spanish, in college; and Italian, on my own.
3. The following are red; apples, roses, and cherries.
4. Let me explain: I thought the meal was paid for.
5. I wanted it for Ginger: my dog.

Apostrophes

The apostrophe is a mark used to indicate contractions, possessives, and certain special plurals.

Contractions • The rule for contracting two words into one is to use an apostrophe in place of the missing letter or letters. (Examples: are not = aren't, let us = let's, cannot = can't)

Possessives • Possession, or ownership, can be expressed in two ways:

1. The *fur of the cat* is grey.
2. The *cat's fur* is grey.

The apostrophe serves the same purpose as the *of the* construction — namely, to indicate the possessive relationship between *cat* and *fur*.
    The rules governing the use of apostrophes are as follows:

- Singular nouns and plural nouns not ending in s form the possessive by adding 's. (Examples: the lamb's tail, the men's car)
- Plural nouns ending in s form the possessive by adding the apostrophe only. (Example: the horses' tails)
- Indefinite adjectives form the possessive by adding 's. (Example: anyone's guess)

Special Plurals • The apostrophe can also be used to form the plurals of certain symbols and of words referred to as words. (Examples: How many 2's are in the formula? She had trouble distinguishing her *that's* from her *which's*.)

Common Errors Involving Apostrophes

The most common error in this category is the confusion of *its* (possessive) with *it's* (the contraction of *it* and *is*). As a rule of thumb, just remember that none of the possessive personal pronouns — *its, hers, his, yours, theirs, ours* — take apostrophes.

Quotation Marks

Quotation marks are used in the following ways:

- in dialogue (Example: He said, "Please shut the door." "No," I replied.)
- in short quoted passages (Example: Emerson said, "Trust thyself: every heart vibrates to that iron string.")

Note: Long passages are single-spaced, indented, and not set off by quotation marks. Quotations which are not indented, but which are comprised of more than one paragraph, take quotation marks at the beginning of each paragraph and at the end of the last paragraph.

- to indicate foreign words, italicized words, or words used in an unusual or sarcastic way or otherwise deserving special attention (Examples: The seminar was attended by "cordon bleu chefs." She thought it was a "chic" thing to do.) Do not overdo this use of quotation marks, however, as it may cause your writing to seem artificial and unsophisticated.
- to indicate an article, a chapter, a short story, a short play, and essay or a poem (Example: Poe's "The Raven" is his favorite poem.)

Note: Longer works (novels, full-length plays, books, epic poems, newspapers, and so on) are underlined.

The rules governing the use of quotation marks are as follows:
1. Expressions such as *he said* are usually separated from quotations by a comma. (Example: He said, "Why?")

Note: An exception can be made when the quoted part is integral to the sense of the sentence such that it would seem artificial to insert the comma. (Example: He said "no.")

2. Periods and commas are *always* placed within quotation marks, regardless of the sense of the sentence. (Examples: He said, "Don't do that." He said, "I didn't go," didn't he?)

3. Colons and semicolons always belong outside the quotation marks. (Example: He said, "People who live in glass houses should have window shades"; no one laughed.)

Common Errors Involving Quotation Marks

1. Mistakenly placing a comma or a period outside quotation marks

   Incorrect: He read "The Raven".
   Correct: He read "The Raven."

2. Overuse of quotation marks to show unusual words

Self-Quiz

Add quotation marks wherever necessary in the following sentences:
1. He said, Will you join me?
2. He read Whitman's poem, Crossing Brooklyn Ferry.
3. Did he say Please?
4. The French word is monsieur.
5. He said that he liked my book.

Revision Checklists

After the first draft of your essay is written, you must allow ample time to proofread it. Using the four checklists that follow, read through your paper and correct all organizational, rhetorical, stylistic, and mechanical errors. As an additional check, you might have a friend read your paper while keeping in mind the questions posed in the checklists.

Also allow some time to check your final draft for typos, omissions, and errors made in the process of copying.

Structure and Organization

- Does your essay fulfill the assignment or purpose for which it was written?
- Is your purpose clear?
- Have you effectively narrowed your subject?
- Have you arrived at a thesis? Is it clearly stated? Well-developed? Well-illustrated and supported?
- Do you prove your point (or answer your question) at the end?
- Have you identified your audience? Is the essay suitable to that audience?
- Are you consistent in your use of narrative voice?
- Are your sentences clear and comprehensible?
- Are your paragraphs well-structured and logically arranged? Are your transitions clear? Does each paragraph further your thesis? Does each paragraph have a topic sentence?
- Does your essay have a beginning, a middle, and an end?

Rhetorical Technique

- Have you used the appropriate rhetorical mode (method of development)?
- Have you used inductive reasoning (making accurate observations and drawing conclusions) or deductive reasoning (presenting premises as evidence, drawing conclusions from these premises) to prove your point? Is your reasoning sound? Have you left out any steps?
- Have you defined your terms to avoid ambiguity?

Style

- Is the style of your essay appropriate to the subject and audience?
- Is the tone appropriate?
- Have you used figurative language?
- Have you checked for denotation and connotation?
- Are your words vague?

Grammar and Punctuation: Have you corrected . . .

- sentence fragments?
- run-on sentences?
- errors in the use of commas (especially comma splices), colons, semicolons, apostrophes, and quotation marks?
- dangling or misplaced modifiers?
- vague wording?
- the use of *this* or *that* as a pronoun when either does not refer to specific noun?
- footnoting inaccuracies (if your instructor has requested that you use them)?
- lack of verb tense consistency?
- lack of subject-verb agreement?
- split infinitives that result in awkwardness?
- misuse of the subjunctive mood?
- confusion of *its* and *it's?*
- awkward phrasing, especially when it results from inverted sentences or passive constructions?
- lack of conciseness?
- lack of parallel constructions?
- spelling errors?

Index

Trouble-Shooting Index